DIALECTICS AND DECADENCE

DIALECTICS AND DECADENCE

Echoes of Antiquity in Marx and Nietzsche

George E. McCarthy

ROWMAN & LITTLEFIELD PUBLISHERS, INC.

ROWMAN & LITTLEFIELD PUBLISHERS, INC.

Published in the United States of America
by Rowman & Littlefield Publishers, Inc.
4720 Boston Way, Lanham, Maryland 20706

3 Henrietta Street
London WC2E 8LU, England

British Cataloging-in-Publication Information Available

Library of Congress Cataloging-in-Publication Data
McCarthy, George E.
Dialectics and decadence : echoes of antiquity in Marx and
Nietzsche / George E. McCarthy.
p. cm.
Includes bibliographical references and index.
1. Marx, Karl, 1818–1883. 2. Nietzsche, Friedrich Wilhelm,
1844–1900. 3. Civilization, Ancient. I. Title.
B3305.M74M27 1994 193—dc20 93-49607 CIP

ISBN 0-8476-7920-9 (cloth: alk. paper)
ISBN 0-8476-7921-7 (pbk.: alk. paper)

Printed in the United States of America

⊗ TM The paper used in this publication meets the minimum requirements of
American National Standard for Information Sciences—Permanence of
Paper for Printed Library Materials, ANSI Z39.48—1984.

To my son and daughter
Devin Scott and Alexa Danielle

That someday—

Where I stand in darkness, you will bathe in light
Where I am lost, you will know
Where I know, you will imagine
Where I hope, you will experience
Where I dream, we will always be together.

With all my love and affection

Contents

Acknowledgments

I would like to thank the National Endowment for the Humanities for its generous support of three events that have been very helpful in the development of my understanding of ancient Greece: the 1991 NEH Summer Seminar "Archaeology and Ancient History: Approaches and Sources" held at the Isthmia excavations and Ancient Corinth; the 1992 NEH summer institute "Athenian Democracy" at the University of California, Santa Cruz; and the NEH and American School of Classical Studies at Athens conference "Democracy Ancient and Modern" held at Georgetown University and the National Archives in Washington, D.C. It was at these three events that I was fortunate to meet prominent classicists, ancient historians, and classical political theorists who helped me clarify my thoughts on many issues. There are many people to whom I am indebted, but I would like to mention a few who were kind and helpful to an egregious interloper—Professors Charles Hedricks and Peter Euben of the University of California, Santa Cruz; Tim Gregory of Ohio State University; and Nick Kardulias of Kenyon College.

Mention should be made of the tireless efforts of the library staff at Kenyon College who never questioned any of my, at times, outrageous and unusual requests for help: Cindy Wallace, Nadine George, Carol Marshall, Andrea Peakovic, Joan Pomajevich, Jennifer Ross, and Jami Peelle. Members of the Kenyon community have also aided me in working through new areas of research including Professors William McCulloh, Harrianne Mills, Eugene Dwyer, Roy Rhodes, Frank Lane, and Thomas Kessler. Finally, I am grateful to the Kenyon College students who helped proofread sections of this book: Sarah Butzen, Stacey Smiar, Alfred Snyder, Jennifer Usher, Kate Usher, and Elisa Niemack.

Introduction

This work examines and compares the epistemologies and ethics of two of the most prominent and radically diverse German social theorists of the nineteenth century: Karl Marx (1818–1883) and Friedrich Nietzsche (1844–1900). At first glance, two more completely different philosophers cannot be found. One defended socialism and the other aristocratic elitism, one was a student of Hegel and the other a student of Kant, and one believed in moral truth and the other nihilism. Max Weber said that the political and methodological diversity of these two individuals provided the foundations for the development of modern social theory. The central aim of this work is to trace the source of the imagination and inspiration for their ideas back to classical antiquity. We will see that the full range of their ethics and epistemologies is better understood within the context of their understanding of classical Greece. There is a clear continuity that runs between ancient Greece and nineteenth-century German social thought.

Marx and Nietzsche were students of Greek antiquity. Nietzsche, a trained classical philologist whose doctoral thesis examined the intellectual sources of Diogenes Laertius, said, "Greek antiquity provides the classical set of examples for the interpretation of our entire culture and its development." To some extent this has already been recognized, but the emphasis here will be on Nietzsche's interpretation of Greek metaphysics, ethics, and tragedy. This will be examined in his research and lectures on pre-Platonic Greek philosophy from Thales to Anaxagoras, his theory of Greek tragedy, his rejection of Socratic and scientific rationalism, and his critique of Christianity in the development of his epistemology and ethics. Marx was also a trained classical philologist and philosopher who wrote his doctoral dissertation on the post-Aristotelian philosophy of nature of Democritus and Epicurus. He intended to teach Greek philosophy and history at the University of Bonn.

Of specific interest is the question, why did Marx return to the post-Platonic philosophers, whereas Nietzsche was concerned with the pre-Platonic writings? What were the different questions and issues that fired their imaginations, stirred their souls, and influenced their choices of classical philosophers to investigate?

The first part of this book, *Romance with Antiquity: Dreaming of Democracy in a Moral Economy*, begins with an examination of the influence of Greek philosophy and literature on the work of Marx. During the eighteenth and nineteenth centuries, Winckelmann, Goethe, Schiller, Hölderlin, and Hegel, in their poetry, literature, and aesthetics, turned to the Greeks for ideas and inspiration. Their art and writings reflected a pursuit of simplicity, beauty, nobility, and serenity. In the midnineteenth century, the soft breeze blowing off the Acropolis toward the University of Berlin reached Marx. His doctoral dissertation, *The Difference between the Democritean and Epicurean Philosophy of Nature* (1841), examined the theory of physics and astronomy of Democritus and Epicurus and offered his first insights into the primacy of individual freedom and his rejection of the methods of the natural sciences. Aristotle's *Nicomachean Ethics* and *Politics* provided the philosophical foundations for his early and later ideas on democracy, social organization, distinctions between human needs and individual rights, and relationships between individual freedom and the community. These Greek works even provided the formal structure within which to understand the relationship between historical and dialectical science, on the one hand, and ethics in the *Grundrisse* and *Capital*, on the other. His labor theory of value and economic crisis theory must be interpreted through this spreading "Greek fire."

Seven times throughout the first volume of *Capital*, Aristotle is either directly quoted in Greek or centrally mentioned. Marx places his economic crisis theory within the heart of Aristotle's theory of social justice (distributive, rectificatory, and reciprocal justice), household management, and the political community. At every turn in the development of his major ideas about market commerce or capitalist production from the initial stages of his labor theory of value to his analysis of surplus value, abstract labor, and the social organization of production, Marx turns to Aristotle for insight and guidance.

Reexamining Marx through the eyes of Aristotle's ethics and politics opens up new horizons of interpretation. In this first volume of *Capital*,

Marx's theory of value is directly paralleled with Aristotle's theory of market equality and commensurability; Marx's theory of the changing historical and social foundations of capitalism with Aristotle's natural law of slavery and the economy (critique of historical fetishism); his theory of appearances and commodity exchange with Aristotle's distinction between use value and exchange value; his analysis of simple circulation of commodities (C-M-C) and his critique of commerce and profit making (M-C-M), that is, the satisfaction of human needs and the satisfaction of profit acquisition, alongside Aristotle's theory of the *Oeconomic* and *Chrematistic*; his notion of the contradictions of capital (profits of merchants' capital and usury of moneylenders' capital) with Aristotle's theory of *chrematistike*; his theory of species being and the social form and organization of production with Aristotle's theory of the political nature of man; and, finally, Marx's view of the revolutionary and emancipatory potential of modern technology and industry with Aristotle's dreams about the Greek inventions of Daedalus and Hephaestos.

With Aristotle's rejection of *chrematistike* (unnatural wealth acquisition and money making) and a market economy constantly in view, Marx moved from a critique of political economy toward a theory of moral economy. The conflicts and struggles produced by modern society are translated and interpreted through the political and aesthetic language of the polis. This perspective opens up a whole new avenue of social critique and evaluation of *Capital*. The apparent contradictory aspects of Marx's philosophy and economics, his early and later works, as well as his different methodologies all begin to take on a different hue. His economic theory becomes infused into an all-encompassing theory of ethics and social justice.

Chapter 2 undertakes an analysis of the institutions and values of fifth-century Athenian polity and Aristotle's views on democracy in the *Politics*. Focus on the Athenian Assembly, *Boule*, and jury courts helps clarify the central features of the Athenian democratic system, as well as Aristotle's own insightful comments on its organization, structure, and principles. The debate over Aristotle's ideal polity and the traditionally conservative interpretations of his defense of aristocracy or monarchy are closely examined and rejected. The argument will be made that Marx's view of the future and participatory democracy had their origins in Greek thought, thus providing a broader, more comprehensive, and more profound understanding of democracy than is found in all forms of liberal thought. It is over the nature of democracy in Marx that the clash between the ancients and moderns reaches its peak. Both the historical and philosophical dimensions of the ancients are then juxtaposed with Marx's analysis of the democratic imagination and reality found in the Paris Commune of 1871.

The second half of this chapter makes the transition from politics to epistemology in order to show how Marx's politics and theory of democracy are intimately connected to his attempt to resolve the epistemological dilemmas of nineteenth-century philosophy. From his political theory to his theory of knowledge and methodology, practical discourse and public discussion within a democratic polity respond to the many questions concerning the nature of truth, knowledge, and science. Like Aristotle, he will reject both science (*episteme*) and art (*techne*) as making legitimate claims to political truths (*phronesis*). One way to approach these questions is by examining the relationships between method and temporality in Marx's later writings. His methods are closely connected to the different temporal dimensions—present, past, and future: the dialectical method of *Capital* (1867–94) revealed the present inherent contradictions of capitalism based on the split between use value and exchange value, production for the satisfaction of human needs and production for the realization of private profit; the historical method of the *Grundrisse* (1857–58) examined the underlying past structural and economic foundations of capitalism in the development of modern industrial society; and the political method of democratic consensus found in the *Civil War in France* (1871) emerged as he studied the social revolution of the Paris Commune and its radical economic and political decentralization of power.

Herein lay the secrets to Marx's vision of a democratic future. One could even say that these three distinct methods reflected the specific methodological influences of Hegel, Kant, and Aristotle, respectively. Hegel's dialectical method and theory of contradictions influenced Marx's view of the contradictions of capitalism; the application of Kant's transcendental logic influenced the study of history in an attempt to uncover the universal and necessary structures of capitalist society; and Aristotle's view of justice and democracy, epistemology and politics influenced Marx's ideas about needs, democracy, and "theory and practice."

Chapter 3 solidifies Marx's relationship with antiquity and develops his ethical theory beyond the Greeks by providing an investigation into the influence of ancient Israel and the prophetic tradition on his moral philosophy, his rejection of moral and methodological abstractionism, and his critique of fetishism. Being steeped in the political writings and scriptural interpretations of Benedict de Spinoza and having studied the Hebrew prophets and Old Testament with Bruno Bauer during his last years at the University of Berlin, Marx was aware of the prophets' ethical prescriptions against inequality, wealth accumulation, class differences, and the degradation of poverty. He was also aware of the relevance of the ethical covenant, critique of idolatry and false gods, and the jubilee and sabbatical years for the continuous renewal of the Hebraic moral community. These ideas become incorporated into his critique of economic alienation, commodity fetishism, and market liberties, his rejection of the methods and ideals of political economy and positivism, his defense of aesthetic creativity, human emancipation, and radical freedom, and his search for the ethical standards for a just society free from the anarchy of modern capitalist production. The Hebrew tradition also counteracts the dominance of property and class found in Attica, while calling for a moral and egalitarian society.

The second part of this volume, *Antiquity by Moonlight: Tragic Imagination in an Age of Nihilism*, examines the relation between Nietzsche and classical Greece and its effects on his critique of pure and practical reason: epistemology and moral philosophy. Nietzsche's doctoral thesis examined the origins of the ideas of Diogenes Laertius. Though never submitted, it was later published as a *Gratulationsschrift* at the University of Basel—*Beiträge zur Quellenkunde und Kritik des Laertius Diogenes*. Throughout his writings, Greek philosophy and art played a pivotal role in his vision of humanity, from his earliest works on Theognis, Democritus, and Diogenes Laertius down to *The Birth of Tragedy* (1872), *Philosophy during the Tragic Age of the Greeks* (1873), *Early Greek Philosophy* (1871–73), *The Philosopher: Reflections on the Struggle between Art and Knowledge* (1872), *The Struggle between Science and Wisdom* (1875), and finally to *Twilight of the Idols* (1888). What is especially fascinating about Nietzsche is that he appropriates the Greek experience in his early writings through the perspective of Immanuel Kant, Arthur Schopenhauer, and Friedrich Lange. Nietzsche's analysis of pre-Socratic metaphysics and science, the development of a theory of drama on the basis of his readings of Aeschylus and Sophocles, his reliance on Winckelmann, Goethe, Schiller, and Schopenhauer for his aesthetic insights, his integration of Schiller's theory of optimism and tragic reconciliation and Schopenhauer's theory of pessimism and tragic resignation, his understanding of history in terms of Aristotle's notion of *phronesis*, and the later development of his ideas on the *Übermensch* and nihilism are all filtered through his primary Greek vision—the centrality of aesthetic creativity and the development of individual character in a meaningless and painful universe. Burdened by the terrors and horrors of existence reflected in death, suffering, and an unforgiving fate, the Greeks created a world of beauty, harmony, and purpose. In place of wars, political and economic unrest, and human mortality, they created a mythology of anthropomorphic gods, divine retribution, eternal peace, and social justice.

Nietzsche saw his major contribution to the development of a theory of tragedy as integrating the artistic drives of the dynamic, creative, and destructive Dionysian impulse with that of the mythmaking, form-giving, and meaning-creating Apollonian impulse. This was also another way of integrating Schiller and Schopenhauer. Nietzsche's analysis of Greek philosophy, including the works of Thales, Anaximander, Heraclitus, Parmenides, and Anaxagoras, is important in that it parallels the development of his ideas from *The Birth of Tragedy*. His central focus is on their ideas of being and becoming, wisdom and suffering, Apollo and Dionysus. From these early Greek philosophers, he learns that physics is a "science" that projects anthropomorphic metaphors onto the world. Whether he is discussing Greek drama or Greek philosophy, he views the world as a human creation in which language, illusions, conventions, and metaphors construct meaning from an abyss of absurdity. There is ultimately no reality, no meaning, no values, and no teleology. In these early writings, there is a clear connection between his theories of tragedy, epistemology, and metaphysics.

Marx and Nietzsche reacted strongly to the Enlightenment view of knowledge and truth, while respecting the primacy of the individual. But rather than viewing the individual as a bundle of sense impressions or a receptacle of natural rights, they saw the person in terms of the natural law tradition of classical Greece. They also admired the formation of the subject and its rebellion against the recalcitrant social system of the polis and the reified philosophical systems of Plato and Aristotle. Marx returned to the post-Aristotelian philosophy of Epicurus, and Nietzsche returned to the pre-Platonic thought of the Sophists in search of the courage and wisdom to escape the alienation and decadence of Western rationality.

The methodologies of Marx and Nietzsche had one major ingredient in common. Both were infused with the spirit of the dialectic, without being weighed down by its mechanics or metaphysics. Skepticism, unlike its use in the Cartesian tradition, was not simply a convenient starting point. Once the idea of an absolute end to the search for knowledge in religion, art, and philosophy was rejected, their thoughts became infused with the dilemma raised by Hume in his *Enquiry Concerning Human Understanding.* The relationships between thought and reality, concepts and experience became a source of continuous concern for them. The spiritual heart of both their philosophies rested in a regaining of "power" and control over their lives, which had previously been surrendered to Christian morality and modern science, and to the philosophies, values, and institutions of liberal politics and classical political economy.

Reason had been debased by its reduction to a predictive science whose purpose was domination and rule over people. Reason had been turned into a force against individuals, imprisoning and eclipsing their bodies and imaginations, dictating correct moral behavior or proper economic and political action, imposing categorical imperatives or economic natural laws, and restricting the possibilities of history and social development and the potentialities of self-enlightenment and liberation. Human experience and sensuality had become a form of alienated objectivity that dictated the correct moral action or proper course of social activity. Laws of economic and moral development became direct expressions of nature and universality. Objectivity was draped with the mantle of neutrality and truth, while subjectivity was perceived as deviant, personal, and particularistic. Under these historical and cultural conditions, religion, morality, and political economy were criticized as undercutting the very possibility for the expression of human rationality and freedom. The individual had been sacrificed on the fetishized altar of idolatry; the forms of idolatrous illusions were a matter of historical perspective.

In Chapter 5, Nietzsche's epistemology is closely considered. In his works *On Truth and Falsity in their Ultramoral Sense* (1873), *The Use and Abuse of History* (1874), and the *Nachlass* (1883–88), some of which appeared in translated form as *The Will to Power*, he developed his theory of perspectivism in which he argued that facts are always filtered through a preexisting theory. Objective experience is always preformed and prestructured by the decadence of Western civilization in religion, philosophy, and science with their claims to universal truth. Belief in objectivity is a form of distorted understanding in which the process of becoming is replaced by a reified substance. Illusions of transcendent truth and universal reality and illusions of objectivity and self replace the more transient perspectives of the moment. In the process, a morality is created that threatens to reduce rationality and moral values to a very narrow range of thought. The

result, according to Nietzsche, is a "suicide of reason." Both Marx
and Nietzsche viewed this process of alienation and decadence as
reaching its peak with the development of modernity and liberalism.

  Nietzsche viewed the development of Kantian practical reason as
the modern apex of moral rationality originally developed by Socrates
and Plato. But while rejecting Kant's moral philosophy, he continued,
like Marx, to view the world in terms of ethical categories. Throughout
his major works on morality from *Thus Spoke Zarathustra* (1883–85)
to *Beyond Good and Evil* (1886), *The Genealogy of Morals* (1887), and
Twilight of the Idols (1888), he presents the ultimate ideal of humankind to live morally and freely, but in a society characterized by the
"transvaluation of values." By this he means a complete critical
rethinking of the nature of morality, objectivity, and rationality. This
represented as much a continuation of the Kantian imperative as it did
its rejection. As the ideas implicit in the latter's constitution theory of
truth lead to their transcendence in Nietzsche's theory of perspectivism, so too the categorical imperative was transcended by "overcoming" traditional morality. As in the case of Marx's writings, this should
not be interpreted as a rejection of morality, only its critical rethinking
and transformation.

  Nietzsche's ethical philosophy is encapsulated in his theory of
decadence, the will to power, eternal return, *Übermensch*, moral
nihilism, the psychology of slave morality, and his critique of Christian
and Kantian morality. This is the focus of Chapter 6. Regarding his
critique of Kantian moral philosophy and Christianity, there is some
overlap between his ideas and Hegel's "The Spirit of Christianity and
its Fate" found in the latter's early theological writings. From the way
Nietzsche approaches nihilism, it is clear that the concept does not
represent his approach to ethics, but rather, it provides him with a
sociological and psychological method by which to uncover the historical foundations of religion and moral philosophy. Nihilism results from
an undermining of religion and morality with the development of
science and positivism. It is also a reflection of the former's inner
nature. Traditional morality, by accepting a notion of a static and
transcendent value system, destroys true rationality and morality in
the process, since, for Nietzsche, it destroys the dynamic impulse to
create moral values. It distorts the very possibility of subjectivity.
Creativity and self-realization are the chief characteristics and goals
of the *Übermensch*, the striving individual who overcomes moral
decadence (loss of the subjective and creative element in the individual) and regains control over the original constitutive act of creating

and implementing the categorical imperative. The insights gained from his earlier interests in classical aesthetics and drama are now joined to his ethical writings. Dionysian wisdom has come full circle.

The final part of this book, *Unbinding Prometheus: Classical Imagination and Vision in Nineteenth-Century Germany*, briefly outlines the mostly opposite paths that Marx and Nietzsche took with their insights. Marx moved toward socialism and radical democracy, whereas Nietzsche moved toward the cultivation of virtue and individual character. Nietzsche was very critical of socialism and rejected what he saw as its egalitarian and leveling impulses. But this is not dissimilar to Marx's own criticisms of both crude communism and vulgar Marxism in the *Paris Manuscripts*. In this comparison of their works, we must distinguish between their philosophical positions and their reactions to historical circumstances. What we will see is that Marx borrowed heavily from Aristotle's *Nicomachean Ethics* (books 1, 5, 6, 8, and 9) on the nature of the good of man, justice, intellectual virtues (practical wisdom, technical reason, and philosophical wisdom), and friendship within the polis, whereas Nietzsche borrowed from books 2, 3, 4, 5, and 10 on moral virtues, philosophical contemplation, and happiness. Marx developed the Aristotelian moment, which emphasized the political and ethical community, as he moved in the direction of a democratic society built on the principle of the satisfaction of human needs. Nietzsche, in his isolation and loneliness, in his personal pain and suffering, moved in the direction of an aristocracy of virtue and artistic creativity.

The last chapter of this work argues briefly for a new and admittedly controversial thesis: the integration of Marx's critique of political economy and Nietzsche's theory of aesthetics and ethics. The argument begins by showing that political and economic democracy provides part of the necessary structural conditions for the full development of individual potentialities leading to self-realization. But the moral development of the individual is also crucial. Cultural aristocracy is not incompatible with social democracy, since the purpose of an egalitarian society is to encourage and promote intellectual and spiritual differences, diversity, and individual development. The danger to democracy comes not from cultural differences, individual achievement, or even an aristocracy of virtue and character. The real danger lies in an aristocracy of concentrated wealth and institutionalized class power. Economic and political equality (Marx) is absolutely necessary for intellectual and spiritual inequality (Nietzsche). The development of character and self-determination cannot be accomplished in a class society based on market exchange as Aristotle had already recognized. Marx was also aware that it would be in a true and radical democracy that individual autonomy and moral freedom could be realized. From this perspective, both thinkers represent two distinct moments of Aristotelian ethics as they are worked out in modernity. Alasdair MacIntyre, when dealing with the important issue of which ethical philosophy to follow in his work *After Virtue*, asked the question, "Nietzsche or Aristotle?"[1] The answer lies not in a choice between them, but in the modern integration of the two Aristotelian themes of practical reason found in Marx and Nietzsche: social ethics and moral imagination.

Part I

Romance with Antiquity: Dreaming of Democracy in a Moral Economy

Chapter One

Marx and Classical Antiquity: Aristotle's Politics and Theory of Moral Economy

Introduction

There have been a number of new works published recently tracing the influence of Greek philosophy, art, and literature on the development of the ideas of Karl Marx.[1] The relation between the fifth- and fourth-century B.C. Athenians and nineteenth-century German political economy is a story gradually unfolding today. As a student in the *Gymnasium* in Trier, at the University of Bonn, and later as an advanced doctoral student at the University of Berlin, Marx was steeped in the cultural and philosophical traditions of ancient Greece. At the university, he belonged to Greek poetry and reading clubs, adored the works of German Hellenism including Winckelmann, Goethe, Hölderlin, and Heine, and voraciously read everything he could about the Greeks. At the University of Bonn, he attended courses in the winter semester of 1835–36 on the history of Roman law with Professor Walter, on mythology of the Greeks and Romans with Professor Welcker, and on questions about Homer with Professor von Schlegel. In the summer term of 1836, he participated in courses on the elegiacs of Propertius with Professor von Schlegel and on the theories of natural right with Professor Puggé. Between the winter terms of 1836–37 and 1838–39, he was taking courses at the University of Berlin with a concentration in law: criminal law, ecclesiastical law, common German civil procedure, Prussian civil procedure, criminal legal procedure, Prussian law, and inheritance law. During the summer term of 1839, he attended Bruno Bauer's lectures on Isaiah and the prophetic tradition, and, finally, during the winter term of 1840–41, he took Euripides and Greek tragedy with Herr Doktor Geppert.[2]

Marx, in his doctoral dissertation, *The Difference between the Democritean and Epicurean Philosophy of Nature*, written between 1840 and 1841, examined the relationships between Democritean and Epicurean physics and philosophy of nature. This work provided him with the opportunity to develop many of his philosophical starting points, especially his ideas about morality and natural science, self-consciousness and freedom, appearance and reality, theory and *praxis* as critique, truth and happiness (*ataraxia*), and materialism and the critique of theology and religion.[3] By closely examining Epicurus's theory of atomic declination and repulsion, qualities and properties of atoms (existence and essence), theory of meteors and heavenly bodies, and theories of causality and happiness, Marx clarified his own philosophical positions that would stay with him throughout his life. In his early preparations and initial notes for this work, he drew heavily upon the writings and inspiration of Diogenes Laertius, Plutarch, Lucretius, Seneca, Eusebius, Cicero, Stobaeus, Sextus Empiricus, and, of course, Aristotle. In his preparatory notebooks he writes, "The Greeks will forever remain our teachers by virtue of this magnificent objective naîveté, which makes everything shine, as it were, naked, in the pure lights of its nature, however dim that light may be."[4] Panajotis Kondylis, in his work *Marx und die Griechische Antike*, maintains that the classical ideal of the Greeks afforded Marx the opportunity of combating the transcendental expectations of traditional Christianity with a philosophy that rejoiced in the sensuous and real, the moral and rational, and the individual and free. It is the philosophy of the modern Prometheus: "The classical Greek ideal represents life here in its sensuous roots, in its pulsating energy and power, in its striving force of will—at the same time, it shows a harmony in its elements, in the gracefulness of the reconciliation of its oppositions and in the quiet security, which rises from its existential fullness."[5] Kondylis argues that the two major classical ideals that inspired Marx were the ethos of earthly and sensuous existence and the values and attitudes of the free and autonomous individual.

Marx briefly continued his examination of Epicurus and Democritus in *The German Ideology* (1845–46) where he rejected the idealism, "speculative distortions," and philosophy of history of the Left Hegelian Max Stirner. He rejected Stirner's history of Greek philosophy with its exclusive emphasis on philosophical abstractions and muddled thinking, as well as historical indifference and worldly contempt. He also rejected Stirner's escape from the real world of the sensuous and empirical into the world of reason, spirit, and consciousness. The latter ignored Aristotle's empiricism by jumping from Socrates and the Sophists to the Neoplatonism of Skepticism, Stoicism, and Epicureanism. Marx sees himself as saving Epicurus from Stirner's false interpretations of Greek philosophy. As in the case of the dissertation, Epicurus is mentioned as the truly radical representative of classical enlightenment because of his rejection of religion and gods. Marx began to see Greek philosophy as a form of consciousness within a broader context of his evolving theory of historical materialism as he called into question the traditional philosophical categories of realism and idealism, and idealism and materialism.[6] Philosophy had to be pictured within an understanding of the fall of the Greek polis, the Hellenistic world, the rise and fall of the Roman Empire, and the birth of Christianity. In order to understand the transformation of Greek philosophy, it was necessary to appreciate the historical transformation of ancient Greek and Roman society.

About ten years later in the rough draft of the *Grundrisse*, Marx undertook an initial outline of the precapitalist economic and social formations of the classical commune, the nature of ancient and communal property relations, and the contradictions between political freedoms and economic inequalities in the polis.[7] Here he examined the major forms of social contradictions within the ancient mode of production: the first is the conflict between the economy and state, that is, between the communal foundations of landownership in both free citizenship and political equality and the differentiation and inequality of private ownership of property, and the second, the conflict between the requirements of political order and population growth, on the one hand, and expansionistic warfare and colonization, on the other. Economic production of the individual proprietor undermined the political requirements of the polis for shared communal values, egalitarianism, and unity; but it was the political realm that provided the objective foundations for economic activity. These social divisions and tensions led to internal class antagonisms and exploitation, economic and territorial expansion, slavery, and imperialism.

Finally, at the end of his life between 1880 and 1882, he undertook a more comprehensive examination of precapitalist societies in his *Ethnological Notebooks*, which contain extensive excerpts from Lewis Morgan's *Ancient Society* (1877), as well as extracts from the works of John Budd Phear, Henry Summer Maine, and John Lubbock.[8] It also included passages taken from a wide range of ancient writers including Homer, Herodotus, Thucydides, Aeschylus, Sophocles, Aristotle, Dionysius of Halicarnassus, Tacitus, Julius Caesar, Cicero, Seneca,

Livy, and Plutarch. One of the main concerns of Marx at this time was uncovering the social and political transformations that affected Greece from Homeric times, to the legal reforms of Solon and the constitution of Kleisthenes (509 B.C.), and to the reforms of Pericles and Ephialtes in the late fifth century. After Marx's death, Engels would pull together much of the material gathered by him on nineteenth-century classical anthropology and historiography of Greece and Rome, including the writings of Morgan, Grote, Schömann, Böckh, Hermann, Niebuhr, and Mommsen for his work *Origins of the Family, Private Property and the State* (1884). In it he examined the origins of the Greek gens, phratries, tribes, and city-states, and the rise of the Athenian constitution and state in relation to other precapitalist societies, especially the Iroquois Indians.[9]

When he completed his dissertation, Marx was prepared to teach Greek philology, philosophy, and history. Through the intercession of his mentor and friend Bruno Bauer, he hoped to obtain a position at the University of Bonn teaching these subjects. But as a result of both Bauer's own political problems with the German educational system, which were caused in part by his recalcitrant atheism and criticisms of Christianity, and Marx's own interests in liberal causes of freedom of the press and human rights, he never did receive an academic appointment. And the rest, so to speak, is history. But these earliest and deepest experiences and love affair (*Griechensehnsucht*) with the ancients stayed with Marx until his death. They influenced every aspect of his theories and writings. Possibly one of the most important lessons he learned while studying in Berlin was taken from Hegel's *Phenomenology of Spirit* and *Philosophy of Right*. Hegel recognized that human freedom required the historical and institutional realization of the Objective Spirit. That meant that in order for moral and political values to be made real and relevant, philosophy and critical thought must be made concrete and objective. Moral philosophy cannot remain expressive of abstract thought if its ideals are to come alive and be made real. For this to occur, there can be no separation between moral philosophy and history, ethics and political economy, theory and practice. The Kantian antinomies must be transcended and the model for this lay in Aristotle's writings.

The comparisons of Marx and Aristotle began a few years ago with a recognition of the philosophical similarities of their positions. For example, one of these early statements was by Richard Miller, who, in his essay "Marx and Aristotle: A Kind of Consequentialism," compared the basic features of Aristotle's theory of happiness and the good life found in *Nicomachean Ethics* and Marx's *Economic and Philosophic Manuscripts of 1844*. Miller noted that Aristotle's major tenets for the good life included a minimum of basic material goods within the economic system, the exercise of human capacities, the development of intelligence, the exercise of rational deliberation and choice, expression of character through virtuous action, a society grounded in friendship and mutual caring, pleasure as the unhindered exercise of human capabilities, and the recognition of the unnaturalness of monetary ends. This Miller compared to eight features of Marx's theory of alienated labor: capitalism degrades human capabilities by not providing an economic minimum for human life; work does not express human needs; work produces alienated labor and personal stultification; alien forces of the market determine life, and not rational choice; labor power becomes a means to life and not its expression; people become commodities and means in the process of commodity exchange; the economic system produces the pain of alienation and lost possibilities of self-expression and social development; and money is pursued for its own sake as something natural. Marx's theory of the good life, species being, and alienation is seen as a reflection of Aristotle's theory of happiness, or *eudaimonia*.

There are more secondary sources that favorably compare Marx's and Aristotle's theory of social justice with their rejection of utilitarian and natural rights theory, their stress on the ultimate ethical and political values of friendship, mutual caring, rationality, and human dignity, their theories of human needs and self-realization, their underlying metaphysics and teleology of activity and potentiality, and their epistemological assumptions about subjectivity and objectivity. For both men, it is in the perfectibility of mankind that the potentiality of the democratic imagination lies. In *Marx and the Ancients*, I outlined the impact of Aristotle's theory of justice in the *Nicomachean Ethics* on Marx with special reference to the *Grundrisse*. Now it is time to trace the relationship between Aristotle's theory of *chrematistike* (the art of unnatural wealth acquisition and money making) and *oikonomia* (a moral economy based on friendship and civic virtue) in the *Politics* and Marx's economic crisis theory in *Capital*. In the latter work, the connections between the ancients and moderns is made more clear as Marx builds his own theory of *chrematistike*, or chrematistics, within a moral critique of political economy.

For Aristotle, justice was a much broader and more comprehensive concept than it has become in modern liberal philosophy with its almost exclusive attention to distributive justice. Rather, the Greek concept referred not only to distributive justice but also to corrective and reciprocal justice, as well as to economic exchange, civic friendship, classical democracy, *phronesis* (practical wisdom), public deliberation, and political judgment. Also stressed in *Marx and the Ancients* was the relation between Aristotle's ethics and political theory, ethics and metaethics, and Marx's ethical philosophy and structural analysis of liberal capitalism. Marx had logically formed his critique of political economy in much the same way that Aristotle had examined the nature of the virtuous citizen and political constitutions. They both asked about the relationship between moral values and individual self-realization, on the one hand, and the economic and political structures that would protect and nurture those values, on the other. From another perspective, Marx wedded together both Kant's critique of practical reason and Aristotle's ethical concern for political and economic theory. He integrated the former's concern for human dignity, personal autonomy, and individual self-consciousness with a study of the moral economy that would give human freedom life.

The formal similarities between Marx and Aristotle were a valuable tool in discerning the issue of Marx's theory of ethics and social justice. Now, however, the focus of this work has shifted to the volumes of *Capital* and Marx's mature theory of economic crises. Because *Marx and the Ancients* emphasized the formal and logical relationships between the ancients and the moderns, this chapter will closely examine the textual references in *Capital* to Aristotle and the direct substantive influence of Aristotle's political writings on the final stages of Marx's economic theory. This requires a critical hermeneutics and depth exegesis of both *Politics* and *Capital*.

Moral Economy from the Heights of the Ancients

Marx mentions Aristotle thirty times in the extant portions of his doctoral dissertation, *The Difference between the Democritean and Epicurean Philosophy of Nature* (1840–41), twenty times in *Notebooks on Epicurean Philosophy* (1839), and eight times in *The German Ideology* (1846). There are scattered references to Aristotle throughout his early and later writings, but it is in his later economic theory that the Greeks become more important. Marx's economic crisis theory develops in the *Grundrisse, A Contribution to the Critique of Political Economy, Capital*, and *Theories of Surplus Value*. He mentions Aristotle four times in the *Grundrisse*. In the introduction to the *Grundrisse*

(1857–58), he criticizes the one-sided individualism of eighteenth-century Robinsonades's theory of human nature and civil society by referring back to Aristotle's view in the *Politics* that man is by nature political. He also connects his theory of production and consumption in the *Grundrisse* to Aristotle's theory of potentiality and actuality in the *Metaphysics*; in "Chapter on Money" a connection is made by Marx to Aristotle's view of the potentiality of money as the form for the equivalence and convertibility of commodities and also as the medium and basis for surety of exchange. Finally, there is an indirect reference to Aristotle's theory of four causes when he examines the labor process in terms of the three moments of materials, instruments, and labor.[10] Marx refers to Aristotle's *Nicomachean Ethics* or *Politics* eight times throughout *A Contribution to the Critique of Political Economy*, part I (1859).[11] The eight references to Aristotle include two references to the *Nicomachean Ethics* and six to the *Politics*. On the very first page of chapter 1, "The Commodity," Marx draws upon the distinction between use value and exchange value found in book I, chapter 9 of the Bekker edition of the *Politics*; a few pages later he makes further mention of this same distinction. Again in chapter 1, he examines Aristotle's statement about the relation between the primitive family and growth of trade. At the beginning of chapter 2, "Money or Simple Circulation," he reflects on the notion of the commensurability of all commodities in money form as found in Aristotle's *Nicomachean Ethics*, book V, chapter 8. Later in this same chapter, he studies the nature of money as a conventional and legal means of circulation from book V, chapter 8 of the *Nicomachean Ethics*, as well as its historical origins found in book I, chapter 9 of the *Politics*. Marx considers two forms of circulation: economics (C-M-C) and chrematistics (M-C-M) from Aristotle's *Politics*, book I, chapter 9. Finally, still in chapter 2, he refers to Aristotle's comments on gold and silver as expressions of money. The eight references to Aristotle in *The German Ideology* are, for the most part, passing scholarly references rather than the bases for substantive analyses.

In the first volume of *Capital* (1867), Marx acknowledges Aristotle as the "greatest thinker of antiquity" and crucial to the development of his labor theory of value. In his dissertation, he frequently drew upon Aristotle's *On the Soul*, *Metaphysics*, *On the Generation of Animals*, *Physics*, *On Becoming and Decaying*, and *On the Heavens*, whereas in his later economic writings, he drew mainly from the *Nicomachean Ethics* and *Politics*. In a letter written to Arnold Ruge from Köln in 1843 and published in the *Deutsch-Französische Jahr-*

bücher, Marx speaks about the imagination and vision inspired by the Greeks, but lost to the moderns, "The self-confidence of the human being, freedom, has first of all to be aroused again in the hearts of these people. Only this feeling, which vanished from the world with the Greeks, and under Christianity disappeared into the blue mist of the heavens, can again transform society into a community of human beings united for their highest aims, into a democratic state."[12]

In volume 1 of *Capital*, Marx refers to Aristotle seven crucial times.[13] Reference is made to him four times within the first five chapters in which the nature of the commodity as use value and exchange value, the circulation of money, and market exchange are examined.[14] These particular references form an integral part of Marx's overall theme of integrating the polity and *praxis* of classical antiquity with a critique of liberalism and modern political economy. Both men are building a moral economy based on substantive ethical values of the community, friendship, and critique of profit making. George Wilson once remarked, "No one, not even Aristotle's staunchest admirers among the economics fraternity, believes that it makes any difference whatsoever to an understanding of contemporary economics what Aristotle or Aquinas had to say—nor did economic analysis derive much, if any, benefit from Book I of the *Politics* or Book V of the *Nicomachean Ethics* or *Summa Theologica*."[15] On the other hand, it does seem to have made an important difference to Marx.

The next few sections of this book will examine in detail the relationships between Aristotle's *Politics* and Marx's *Capital*. The former's theory of value and critique of chrematistics will be studied in light of their influence on the evolution of the latter's theory of commodity and capital production, exchange, and surplus value. As Marx traces modern society as it moves from its initial foundations in commodity exchange and money circulation to surplus extraction and capital production, he introduces each new topic with a reference to Aristotle. As he moves from exchange and circulation to industrial production, from commerce and trade to industrial capitalism and the social foundations of production, from exchange value and abstract value to surplus value and profits, Marx looks at modernity through the eyes of classical antiquity. The historical, philosophical, and aesthetic distance between these times seem to disappear even as his analysis gets historically and sociologically richer and deeper. He refers to Aristotle in chapters 1, 2, 4, 5, 13, and 15 and these specific references will be closely examined. He does not mention Aristotle's name directly in the second volume of *Capital*, "The Process of Circulation of Capital," and only once in the third volume, "The Process of Capitalist Production as a Whole." In what is sometimes referred to as the fourth volume of *Capital*—the three volumes of the *Theories of Surplus Value*—Aristotle is mentioned three times: in volume 1, Marx refers to Aristotle and "unproductive labor"; and in volume 3 of this series, Marx refers to the unnaturalness of interest and usury in Aristotle's *Politics*.[16]

Marx's critique of political economy also rests on Aristotle's vision of the democratic polity. This issue will be examined in detail in Chapter 2. We will trace the influences of the first volume of *Capital* on his later writings. In the first chapter of *Capital*, Marx's theories of abstract social labor and value rely on Aristotle's theory of value and equivalency from the *Nicomachean Ethics*; in section four of the first chapter, Marx's theories of the historical context of production, fetishism, false objectivity, and the social relations of production are clarified by reference to the social forms of production among the ancients. The second chapter, dealing with Marx's theory of value and commodity exchange, and his critique of bourgeois and socialist theories of justice, begins by mentioning Aristotle's distinction between use value and exchange value from the *Politics*. Chapter 4 places Marx's discussion about commerce and the two forms of simple circulation of commodities (C-M-C and M-C-M) within Aristotle's theory of wealth acquisition and his distinction between economics (household management) and chrematistics (trade and commerce for profit), that is, exchange for use and need satisfaction and exchange for money and profit accumulation. In chapter 5, Marx examines the sphere of circulation, profits, and the contradictions of capital by returning to Aristotle's theory of merchants' capital and moneylenders' capital. In the key chapter on cooperation (chapter 13) in which he studies the social nature and organization of labor and people's species being and in which he introduces the whole discussion on the social and historical conditions for capitalist production, Marx relies on Aristotle's theory of man as a political animal. Finally, in chapter 15, Marx equates the slavery of modernity in the factory—intensified labor, distorted division of labor and self-development, and economic exploitation—with ancient forms of slavery and the technological potential of modern industry to reach beyond it.

Out of Aristotle's critique of unlimited and unnatural wealth acquisition flows Marx's whole rejection of bourgeois economics and commodity exchange. Aristotle is very helpful to Marx in the development of his theory of circulation and commerce. However, Marx must reach past the limits of Aristotle's understanding of the ancient economy when he moves beyond circulation of commodities and money into the areas of the creation of surplus value, profit accumulation, and the social modes of capitalist production.

At the beginning of each of the following subsections comparing Marx and Aristotle, the specific reference to Aristotle's ideas in Marx's work will be given in full. Clarification of the quotation will begin with an examination of the original idea as it was developed in the *Nicomachean Ethics* or *Politics*. This will then be followed immediately by a deeper analysis of its role in aiding an appreciation of Marx's position in each chapter. By attempting to clarify the social foundations of commodity exchange and private property, the distinctions between production for immediate use and consumption or market exchange, and production for the satisfaction of basic human needs or profit realization, Marx develops his theory of value. To accomplish this, he turns to Aristotle. In the initial chapters of *Capital*, at every key point that defines and frames his later arguments, Marx returns to classical Greece and Aristotle's critique of unnatural and distorted forms of economics. Whether it is his theory of human needs, species being, distinction between use value and exchange value, irrationality of the market, undermining of human possibilities, value and commodity exchange, or economic crisis (theories of underconsumption, disproportionality, and rising organic composition of capital), Marx is indebted to Aristotle's view of society. That is, Marx's whole critique of political economy as reflected in the values of liberalism and structures of capitalism are ultimately based on his reading of Aristotle's critique of false acquisition and money making. What Marx has done is to rewrite and update Aristotle's works on ethics and political theory for the modern audience. The new theory is a neo-Aristotelianism informed by German idealism, nineteenth-century political economy, and French socialism.

Influence of Aristotle's *Politics* on Marx's *Capital*

Chapter 1 of *Capital*: Theory of Value and Commodity Exchange

The text from chapter 1 reads as follows:

The two latter peculiarities of the equivalent form will become more intelligible if we go back to the great thinker who was the first to analyze so many forms, whether of thought, society, or Nature, and amongst them also the form of value. I mean Aristotle. In the first place, he clearly enunciates that the money-form of commodities is only the further development of the simple form of value—*i.e.*, of the expression of the value of one commodity in some other commodity taken at random; for he says—5 beds = 1 house (κλίναι πέντε ἀντὶ οἰκίας) is not distinguished from 5 beds = so much money (κλίναι πέντε ἀντὶ . . . ὅσου αἱ πέντε κλίναι). He further sees that the value-relation which gives rise to this expression makes it necessary that the house should qualitatively be made the equal of the bed, and that, without such an equalization, these two clearly different things could not be compared with each other as commensurable quantities. "Exchange," he says, "cannot take place without equality, and equality not without commensurability" (οὔτ' ἰσότης μὴ οὔσης συμμετρίας). Here, however, he comes to a stop and gives up the further analysis of the form of value. "It is, however, in reality, impossible (τῇ μὲν οὖν ἀληθείᾳ ἀδύνατον), that such unlike things can be commensurable"—*i.e.*, qualitatively equal. Such an equalisation can only be something foreign to their real nature, consequently only "a makeshift for practical purposes."

Aristotle therefore, himself, tells us, what barred the way to his further analysis; it was the absence of any concept of value. What is that equal something, that common substance, which admits of the value of the beds being expressed by a house? Such a thing, in truth, cannot exist, says Aristotle. And why not? Compared with the beds, the house does represent something equal to them, in so far as it represents what is really equal, both in the beds and the house. And that is—human labour.

There was, however, an important fact which prevented Aristotle from seeing that, to attribute value to commodities, is merely a mode of expressing all labour as equal human labour, and consequently as labour of equal quality. Greek society was founded upon slavery, and had, therefore, for its natural base, the inequality of men and their labour-powers. The secret of the expression of value, namely, that all kinds of labour are equal and equivalent, because, and so far as they are human labour in general, cannot be deciphered, until the notion of human equality has already acquired the fixity of a popular prejudice. This, however, is possible only in a society in which the great mass of the produce of labour takes the form of commodities, in which, consequently, the dominant relation between man and man, is that of owners of commodities. The brilliancy of Aristotle's genius is shown by this alone, that he discovered, in the expression of the value of commodities, a relation of equality. The peculiar conditions of the society in which he lived, alone prevented him from discovering what, "in truth," was at the bottom of this equality.[17]

Drawing upon Aristotle's *Nicomachean Ethics*, book V, chapter 5, in the first chapter of *Capital*, Marx develops Aristotle's theory of value, the equality of exchange, and the commensurability of commercial goods. These ideas provide Marx with the beginning of his sociological theory of abstract value and commodity exchange. Aristotle's analysis of economics is found in two places in his writings, book V of the *Nicomachean Ethics* and book I of the *Politics*.[18] In the former, he undertakes a characterization of the nature of commodity exchange within the framework of the different forms of social, legal, and economic justice. In the latter, he is concerned with the nature of barter and exchange between households in the polis. In the *Nicomachean Ethics*, he breaks the concept of justice into two main divisions: universal justice and particular justice. Universal justice involves acting according to the imperatives of moral virtue for the good and happiness of the individual and political community. It is virtue toward others expressed in activities and the creation of law.

Particular justice is concerned with three distinct forms of justice: distributive (*dianemetikos*), rectificatory or corrective (*diorthotikos*), and reciprocal (*antipeponthos*). Distributive justice deals with the just distribution of the social awards of honor, status, or money according to the standards of merit measured by either political citizenship, economic wealth, noble birth, or aristocratic excellence. Equality, proportionality, and fairness are the abstract principles that are exhibited in all forms of political constitutions: democracy, oligarchy, and aristocracy. Each form of political community supplies the content to the formal principles of measurement. Thus, democracy will measure merit and fairness in terms of political citizenship, an oligarchy will utilize the standard of nobility, and an aristocracy will use the principles of virtue and moral excellence. In every case, justice involves the equality of those members defined by the nature of the political constitution. Injustice consists of an individual having too much or too little as defined by its standards of measurement.

Rectificatory justice is found in civil proceedings. It refers to a judicial rectification and reestablishment of social proportionality and harmony (equalization and correction) following the action of unjust behavior. Whether the result of voluntary or involuntary action, whether the result of an economic theft, fraud, or an unjust exchange, a judge in a civil court must reestablish the social balance that existed before the unjust action occurred. This is generally accomplished by means of awarding damages to the injured party. There is no recognition here by Aristotle of a need for punitive damages as exists in the modern legal system. He is only concerned with reestablishing arithmetical proportion in the moral and constitutional order of the polity. Justice (*dikaion*) is a bisection (*dichastes*) or division into equal parts (*dicha*) by a judge (*dicastes*).

After distributive and rectificatory justice, the third form of justice, for Aristotle, is reciprocal or economic justice. Reciprocal justice entails the structural foundations of the polity and the manner in which economic activity is normatively regulated by the broader political values of the community. In a complex society such as a Greek city-state, economic exchange is necessary for the survival of the whole community. Economic exchange (*sunallagmata*) holds the community together and, in turn, must be based on just economic relations.

The central question, for Aristotle, is, how is proportionate equality in exchange or a just economy maintained? Even more importantly, what are the standards of measurement for a just exchange of goods? When a home builder and shoemaker engage in an exchange of goods, how many shoes equal one house? For exchange or reciprocal action to be possible, there must be some standard of measurement that permits shoes and houses to be compared and exchanged. A just exchange occurs when the two distinct goods are made proportionately equal, that is, when one house equals ten pairs of shoes. Aristotle makes his opinion very clear. Even though individuals, the quality of their work, and the final products are all different, it is social custom expressed in monetary relations that makes goods commensurable. When there is no equality of exchange, there is no just or valid exchange. Another dimension to the difficulty is that the skill of the maker and the quality of the goods may be vastly different. The market also attempts to draw a proportionality between radically different skills and occupations. How do these elements affect the exchange relation; how are prices determined; and how are products made commensurable in the exchange process?

Aristotle argues that the convention of money circulation was created to solve these problems as an abstract measure of all things. Money was also intended to deal with the expansion of the households and the formation of the political community. It should be noted here that Nietzsche will pick up on this very point. If, as the Sophists contend, humans are the measure of all things, it seems that the idea is grounded in a basic economic fact and principle. Money is the standard of measurement and the medium of exchange. As long as it is used for the purposes of completing the self-sufficiency of the household (replenishing the material deficiencies and needs of the household) and not for financial gain, Aristotle views it as a natural extension of barter. But what reduces all different kinds and qualities of goods to a common denominator? For Aristotle, it is need (*chreia*) that reduces all particularities to proportional similarities. But it is not simply a case in which the economic world is made commensurate and equal by the demand for particular goods. Money is not simply the concrete and physical manifestation of a psychological need. Money (*nomisma*) is a convention of agreement and law (*nomos*) created for the purpose of facilitating economic measurement and exchange. "That demand (*chreia*) holds things together as a single unit is shown by the fact that when men do not need one another, i.e. when neither needs the other or one does not need the other, they do not exchange."[19]

Rather, Aristotle places his theory of household needs within a broader configuration and discussion of his theory of natural acquisition and property, household exchange, self-sufficiency, material surplus and economic deficiency, civic friendship and political community, moral virtue, rational discourse, and development of human capacities, and, finally, the natural purpose of individual and community life. The first book of the *Politics* represents a continuation of the *Nicomachean Ethics* and must be seen as a continuation of the themes of friendship and the good life from the latter work. Without the exchange of surplus goods for economic necessities, there would be no political associations, since the latter are too large to be internally self-sufficient. In turn, however, without a commensurability of goods (exchange), without proportional equality in exchange (fairness), and without a monetary economy (measurement and medium of circulation), no exchange would be possible. The foundation of distributive justice lies in proportional equality (not arithmetical equality) between individuals so that at the end of an exchange, everyone is given a fair share or proportion (*metadosis*).[20]

But the question remains: fair share in relation to what criteria? Aristotle doesn't go into this kind of fine detail, but does indicate that the determination of fairness in exchange is related to the nature of property and the purpose of exchange. Exchange takes place not simply because there is a need, but because this need expresses an economic deficiency within a household that could impair its responsibility in preparing the individual for the life of the polis. Thomas Lewis views the category "economic deficiency" as a normative concept containing the moral content of natural exchange.[21] The other households in the community, acting out of civic friendship and mutual concern, supply the missing economic goods in order to permit their fellow citizens to participate politically in the decision-making process. The sharing of economic surplus is also necessary in order that citizens may devote their time to the development of their moral and intellectual virtues rather than misusing their time in the pursuit of financial gain and economic security. The moral development of the individual and political community defines the natural limits to acquisition and rights to property. Though property should be privately owned, according to Aristotle, there is a prior responsibility and obligation for the communal use of that property.[22] As Karl Polanyi has stated, "The just price, then, derives from the demands of *philia* as expressed in the reciprocity which is the essence of all human community."[23]

The community has legitimate claims, based on friendship and concern for the household's well-being, to the surplus produced by each household because the purpose of property acquisition lies in ethics and not in economics. This is the basis for Aristotle's theory of natural acquisition and critique of market economy, since the latter destroys the moral foundations of the polis and virtuous life.[24] The criterion or standard of measurement (*axia*) for one's fair share (geometric proportionality or equality) is the dignity, worth, or merit of an individual, which is different with each form of the best constitution: freedom in a democracy, virtue in an aristocracy, and wealth in an oligarchy. The nature of equality differs in each of these constitutions as does the nature of proportional equality. Castoriadis connects these standards of worth in distributive justice with Aristotle's discussion of reciprocity. The sharing of scarce goods in a natural exchange also will be decided by whether a constitution bases itself on freedom for all citizens, on virtue, noble birth, or on the wealth of the few.[25]

Toward the end of chapter 5, Aristotle moves beyond the issue of proportional equality maintained by monetary calculation. He states that economic justice is a mean between acting unjustly and being unjustly treated; it is a mean between moral extremes and insures that one individual will not have too much of what is desirable and another too little. In an exchange relation characterized by the household values of "fairness, mutuality, and common purpose," the buyer or seller cannot make a gain on the exchange.[26] Profit making is not an acceptable characteristic of this type of economic activity. In the same way, when borrowing money from a close family member, the request for interest payment or profit would seriously jeopardize the affection of the parties involved. Family affection (*philia*) does not admit of economic gain. Its purpose is to solidify and reinforce the communal social values of the household, as well as the friendship within the broader community. Justice is a mean in accordance with moderation and proportionality, whereas injustice is excess and extreme as manifested in profit accumulation. The value of economic activity rested with the maintenance of the community. It is for this reason that equivalency in exchange was to be determined by need and mutual concern and not bargaining or market rationality. Prices are to be set and maintained by the principles of justice and the political authority of the state as defined by the local community or law.[27]

At times it appears that Aristotle is looking for the mechanism that holds the exchange process together and makes various forms of economic activity commensurable. This is the much debated issue about Aristotle's theory of commodity exchange and the just price. How is the social convention of money able to act as the measurement between the builder and shoemaker, between house building and shoemaking, between houses and shoes? Does money measure the status of the producers, the type of activity involved, or the different products made? Or does money as social convention measure the proportionate needs of individuals within the community? There is no clear answer to these questions and to that extent Aristotle leaves us in confusion as he begins with money and moves to need as the basis for commensurability of exchange.[28] This is the issue that Marx will pick up on with the development of his theory of value. "The brilliancy of Aristotle's genius is shown by this alone, that he discovered, in the expression of the value of commodities, a relation of equality."[29] However, there is a more important aspect to this question that ties commensurability of products with the expectations and needs of the community. Goods are commensurable not because they are reducible to monetary formulation, but because they are a material reflection of basic human needs. Money is an intermediary not between people's wants and market choices, but between neighbor's needs. What distinguishes the true value of a product is the complex tradition of ethical customs and social expectations of what is appropriate and what is not. Reciprocity of needs, communal sharing, and neighborly concern provide the context for the determination of the costs.[30] Proportionate equality defines a fair exchange, not the products themselves or their prices or the amount of labor contained in them. It is not an autonomously working market based on supply and demand, or the private ownership and disposition of property regulated through economic exchange. Rather prices were determined by a tradition whose goal was to maintain and strengthen the bonds of the household and the polis (theory of the just price).[31]

Reciprocity as *philia* (good will and friendship) is maintained through barter and exchange. Polanyi associates this with Malinowski's analysis of status, redistribution, and gift exchange among the Trobriand Islanders.[32] But the basis for exchange is never resolved by Aristotle. Does it lie in the worth or status of the exchanger (thus based on inequality), membership in the polis (based on citizenship and equality), the quality or skill of the laborer, or the actual labor time in the commodities? I would come down on the side of those who say that the answer lies in need and reciprocal justice as interpreted through the social customs and communal values of the political community. Just as goods are to be shared within the family for the benefit of the household, so too are goods to be shared within the community for the benefit of the polis. Social justice becomes the arbiter between people's material needs. Justice in exchange is established when the physical needs of one member are fairly balanced by the physical and social needs (friendship) of another. The exchange process was instituted to deal with the growing economic complexity of Greek society, while at the same time to maintain the social organization of the household. It is grace and need that are to regulate economic exchange "within the framework of the community" and not material gain or commercial success. "We should serve in return one who has shown grace to us, and should another time take the initiative in showing it."[33] One gives freely with the expectation that when in need, the generosity and grace will be returned in kind.

Money is simply an abstract tool used to measure differences. Money doesn't make all things equal and commensurate. This results from society's moral standards of rational behavior and view of equality of citizens. If an exchange within or between households leaves one party of the exchange with less, it is an injustice to the moral standards of the family and neighborhood (*nomos*). "But in associations for exchange, this sort of justice does hold men together— reciprocity (*antipeponthos*) in accordance with a proportion and not on the basis of precisely equal return. For it is by proportionate requital that the city holds together."[34] Lewis has argued that whereas the limits to interhousehold exchange lie in the moral foundations of the community—friendships, respect for human dignity, and mutual concern of others—the limits to wealth acquisition in commodity exchange between the builder and shoemaker must rest with a just price determined by law and tradition."[35] This is important for Lewis because "the market is so inherently hostile to the proper use of property."[36]

There has been much written about Aristotle's meaning and intention in these sections.[37] Whichever side of the debate one accepts, Aristotle is arguing that the standard of reciprocal justice does not lie in economics itself, but in some moral standard set by the political community. Economics is always viewed as embedded in moral relationships and responsibilities. Market success and profit accumulation are defective extremes because they distort proportionality established by the community. Aristotle has not created a price theory of the market, but rather a political theory of moral economics in which individual and community needs, mutual sharing of family members and neighbors, love, and friendship ultimately determine the justice of economic exchange. This is what defines something as too much or too little.

The final form of justice discussed is universal or political justice, which entails the rational organization of society around a set of political principles. It represents the rule of law as opposed to the tyranny of the rule of man. It helps construct a society in which political deliberation and rational discourse decide the fate of man based on the principles of equity and prudence. The forms of distributive, legal, economic, and political justice in book V of the *Nicomachean Ethics* are preceded by a discussion of moral virtues and followed by an analysis of intellectual virtues (scientific knowledge, philosophical contemplation, political wisdom, and technical knowledge). Economic theory and the critique of unnatural and unlimited acquisition were important parts of Aristotle's discussion of the nature of justice, since economic reciprocity and mutual sharing of common stores formed the material foundations for friendship, community, and the polis.

In chapter 1 of *Capital*, Marx picks up where Aristotle left off. In one sense, he continues Aristotle's critique of chrematistics, but from another perspective, he ventures into areas that Aristotle did not consider. Marx's analysis of capitalism is framed by his theory of value, which attempted to explain the commensurability of products in a market society. This was not the goal of Aristotle's analysis. Marx borrows heavily from Aristotle's critique of market exchange, profit accumulation, misuse of private property, commercial trading, distinction between *oikonomia* and *chrematistike*, and finally, his overall critique of political economy. He is also indebted to many of Aristotle's insights into the nature of equality, democracy, justice, fairness and needs, equivalent and proportional exchange, just price, natural acquisition, reciprocity and redistribution, mutuality and friendship, and moral embeddedness of the economy. As with Aristotle, he will integrate a theory of social ethics and justice into his economic theory of property and capitalist development. He starts by reducing capitalism to its most simple form of commodity and exchange. Every commodity is a thing with quantitative and qualitative properties that must be capable of satisfying some human need. The different qualities and properties of a product express different possibilities and uses to which it may be put. Quantitative characteristics express its relations to other commodities and establish the possibility for exchange based on satisfying human needs. It is the latter relationship that interests Marx. Not in its utility, but in its exchangeability lies the question that since Aristotle has been at the heart of capitalist exchange. What is exchange value and what is the common substance that establishes the conditions for the possibility of exchange itself?

As with Aristotle, Marx attempts to unravel the mystery of commodity exchange. How is it possible that in the market twenty yards of linen could be exchanged for one coat? He asks the same question, but the analysis of market exchange represents only the beginning of his examination of capitalism. Though he starts with the exchange of particular commodities in a free market, Marx quickly moves to a higher level of economic abstraction to investigate the nature of money, prices, and profits in the market. From here he continues to become more abstract in order to penetrate deeper into the nature of capitalism with an analysis of the exchange of labor and labor power. From the circulation of labor power, he moves to an analysis of the social relationships and organization of production and the creation of abstract labor, surplus value, and profits in capitalist firms. The first volume of *Capital* moves from simple commodity exchange in the market to complex organizations of production around class relationships, private property, and economic exploitation. Marx develops his theory of liberalism as he examines the structures and values of chrematistic exchange and chrematistic production. "Thus Marx's theory of alienation may be seen as a full elaboration of Aristotle's distinction between *oikonomia*, economic activity geared to communal needs and the production of use values, and *chrematistike*, money-making in a society governed by *pleonexia* and oriented to the production of exchange values."[38]

The secret to understanding the riddle of the market lies in the dualism of the commodity and the fact that underlying the possibility of exchange is value. Marx credits Aristotle with first discovering the value form of commodity exchange and the relationship between simple commodity form and money form. Aristotle also recognized that underlying the value relation is a qualitative commensurability and equality of commodities in exchange. He failed to pursue the analysis of the value form, because it was something unnatural and artificial to economic products. Though Aristotle recognized the value of commodities, he failed to understand the common element that made them qualitatively commensurable and equal. Marx attributed this to the existence of a mode of production grounded in slavery and not characterized by private property, the market, and commodity exchange. For products to be made equal, the market must pervade the general life of the community and provide the model for all economic activity and human interrelationships in general. A slave society was an impediment to this universalization of commodity exchange and hindered Aristotle from seeing it as a central foundation for a new social form of production and exchange.[39]

Marx's major point is that Aristotle never developed an analysis of the form of value. This is also his critique of classical political economy of Smith and Ricardo. They never pursued this line of thinking because of their interest in the quantitative magnitude of value as expressed in price theory and their failure to examine value form as an historical product not defined by nature. Thus, they did not see the historical and logical implications of value form manifested as commodity form, money form, and capital form, that is, as different forms of social production.

The first chapter of volume 1 of *Capital* deals with just this question of the qualitative form of value. Beginning with the distinction between use value (utility) and exchange value (market worth expressed as a relation of value) of a commodity, Marx critically examines the notion of "common substance" of commodity exchange. Rejecting the possibility that this substance is an objective and quantitative property of the commodity itself, he argues that it must be the result of an abstraction from all utility. After abstracting from use value, the qualitative aspects of useful labor, and the quantitative elements of exchange, the common remaining substance is homogeneous and congealed human labor. This abstract labor—what Marx calls value— immediately pulls him away from nature, necessity, money, or commerce as explanations for exchange. The whole foundation of Marx's critique of political economy rests upon this theory of value that places our understanding of the commodity, as the primitive kernel and seminal principle of capitalist production, in labor and its social conditions. It is the foundation for our understanding of simple exchange of two commodities, the circulation of money, commercial capitalism, and ultimately, industrial capitalism itself. The important insight at this stage of his study is that "exchange value is the only form in which the value of commodities can manifest itself or be expressed."[40]

The discussion about commodities moves from simple commodity exchange to simple commodity production. The particular magnitude of commodities is determined on the basis of the labor time socially necessary for their production. Equality of value is defined as an exchange relationship in which each commodity contains an equal amount of socially necessary labor required for production. "Commodities, therefore, in which equal quantities of labour are embodied, or which can be produced in the same time, have the same value."[41] Marx's method also abstracts from consideration of technological, social, and natural influences in the productivity of labor. The value of commodities would be affected by the economic technology, social organization of production, means of production, and skill of the worker. That is, both the social and natural ecology determines the quantity of value. For purposes of focus, Marx does not take these aspects of production into consideration during the early stage of his analysis. Central attention is on the commodity and abstract labor temporarily removed from the social relations of production.

Just as the commodity is divided into use value and exchange value, labor may be distinguished by its utility in the creation of use values (useful labor) and transformation of material nature (value form of labor as abstract labor). Within a complex division of labor, the qualitative differences between different forms of labor such as tailoring and weaving produce different use values. The magnitude of abstract labor in each product produces the value of each commodity. Even now in this chapter on commodities, Marx is anticipating his economic crisis theory formulated in volume 3. The distinctions between the qualitative and quantitative components of labor, between useful labor and productivity, which produce utilizable products, and abstract labor, which produces value, and between use value and exchange value, lie at the heart of his economic crisis theory. Marx only hints at the problem here, but there is a possible disjunction and break between tailoring and weaving whose activities produce both "homogeneous congelations of undifferentiated labor" and a certain amount of useful commodities. Value and commodity production are not always in full synchronization and an unintegrated economic system may cause serious disturbances in the system. "Nevertheless, an increased quantity of material wealth may correspond to a simultaneous fall in the magnitude of its value. This antagonistic movement has its origin in the two-fold character of labour. . . . The same change in productive power, which increases the fruitfulness of labour, and, in consequence, the quantity of use values produced by that labour, will diminish the total value of this increased quantity of use values, provided such change shorten the total labour-time necessary for their production; and *vice versa*."[42] This means that under conditions of greater productivity brought about by advances in technology, new social forms of organization, and so forth, more products could be produced with less expenditures of labor power. Greater technical productivity and creation of more commodities for mass consumption do not affect the total amount of abstract labor produced at any one time. One development is the result of technical efficiency and the other the amount of abstract labor expended in production. More commodities and less value produced in commodity production is the fissure that could cause serious problems in a fully developed industrial society. Marx is laying the foundations for his theory of the tendencies of the rise in the organic composition of capital and the falling rate of profit in this potential split between the economic and technological base of production and the social formation at the heart of commodity exchange. More on this in Chapter 2.

Aristotle, according to Marx, failed to pursue his analysis in book V of the *Nicomachean Ethics* into the nature and form of value of commodities.[43] This value form will provide Marx with the basis for his arguments and will also connect commodity production with money circulation and capital. Marx distinguishes between the bodily form and value form of commodities in order to further expand his analysis of the nature of value itself.

> If, however, we bear in mind that the value of commodities has a purely social reality, and that they acquire this reality only in so far as they are expressions or embodiments of one identical social substance, viz., human labour, it follows as a matter of course, that value can only manifest itself in the social relation of commodity to commodity. In fact we started from exchange value, or the exchange relation of commodities, in order to get at the value that lies hidden behind it.[44]

Because this argument is so important, he spends much of his time in the chapter on commodities examining the nature of value forms.

The simplest and most elementary form of value is always expressed in terms of one other commodity. The value of one product is expressed by the use value of another. Twenty yards of linen equals one coat. The value form of linen is manifested not by its bodily form or use value, but instead by its relation to the coat.

As a simple equivalent, commodity exchange has two parts to its value form: relative form and equivalent form. Its relative form exists when the value of linen is expressed as a relation to the coat. This is made possible because they were commonly formed by social relations of abstract labor. The use value of the coat becomes the equivalent form of linen. The physical form and utility of the coat become the form of the value of linen. The coat helps concretely to express and materialize the common substance—social relations and abstract labor—hidden within the linen. The two commodities are equivalent and directly exchangeable. Marx says that classical political economy failed to understand these forms of value and, in turn, attributed the commensurability of commodities to the exchange process and money itself. They mystify the social foundations of commodity exchange. They do not realize that "the most simple expression of value, such as 20 yds. of linen = 1 coat, already propounds the riddle of the equivalent form for our solution."[45]

The expenditure of all forms of human labor produces use value. However, for Marx, it is only in certain types of societies that the creation of products turns into the making of commodities. In the most elementary form of value, only one commodity may correspond to the value of another. When the value form is expanded to include a series of other commodities such that twenty yards of linen equals one coat, ten pounds of tea, forty pounds of coffee, and so forth, Marx develops the general form of value in its relation to particular commodities. This expanded form is simply the sum of all elementary value forms. Finally, after a particular commodity represents the general form of value, it is in time replaced by a single substance or universal commodity that, as money, becomes the measure of all other commodities. Gold has traditionally been seen as the universal equivalent of all these relations because what is ultimately being compared is the abstract human labor. The relationships between commodities are what give "objective existence" to the value included in each commodity. Instead of a fragmented relation between one particular commodity standing as the measure of others in a serial fashion, there is one substance that acts as the universal equivalent of all commodities. This universal equivalent is money or the general form of value. All different commodities are now capable of being measured by one universally accepted standard. Marx has moved from an analysis of the single form of value (two commodities) to the particular form of value (series of commodities) to the general form of value (money). "The simple commodity form is therefore the germ of the money form."[46]

To the modern reader, this analysis of the different forms of value smacks of Hegelian metaphysics and irrelevant philosophical meanderings. To this charge it is clear that Marx's method of presentation is framed within nineteenth-century theory of value and dialectics of German Idealism. The flow of the argument from simple to complex forms of relations and equivalency, the evolution from singular to particular to universal forms of value reminds one of Hegel's *Science of Logic*. But the underlying content of the argument still rings true today. Marx is arguing that political economists cannot treat economic relations as objectified products of natural processes existing in nature or in commercial exchange. Value is ultimately the product of historical and social forms of production and abstract labor.[47] It was this insight that Aristotle could not reach and that has been forgotten today with the split between economics and sociology. The contrast between one discipline's concern for commerce, exchange, and distribution of social wealth and the other's concern for the social relations and organization of production hinders the insight that underlying economic relations are political and social powers to control events. For Marx, it is sociology that ultimately explains economics, but without the unfolding of the dynamics of economics, sociology studies nothing of importance. The two have to be reintegrated in a new social and moral economy.

What Marx is attempting to do is provide the foundations for his argument that simple commodity exchange between two commodities is the hidden secret to an understanding of advanced forms of capitalist enterprise in commerce and industry. What Marx is doing, in fact, is tracing the genesis of the money form of value. When commodities, money, profits, and capital are finally seen for what they are—reified and objectified social and historical relationships—then Marx has made an enormous methodological advance against those classical political economists who viewed society as a natural, static, and fetishized event.

There it is a definite social relation between men, that assumes, in their eyes, the fantastic form of a relation between things. In order, therefore, to find an analogy, we must have recourse to the mist-enveloped regions of the religious world. In that world the productions of the human brain appear as independent beings endowed with life, and entering into relation both with one another and the human race. So it is in the world of commodities with the products of men's hands. This I call the Fetishism, which attaches itself to the products of labour, so soon as they are produced as commodities, and which is therefore inseparable from the production of commodities.[48]

This naturally leads to a discussion of the nature of fetishism in the last section of the first chapter of *Capital*. This section provides the methodological clarification of Marx's own critique of the reified categories of political economy. Economics has mistaken commodities, exchange, circulation, and money for independent realities that must be explained using naturalistic and mechanistic terminology. It creates its own objectified world inhabited not by the ancient gods of Greek mythology or the modern one of Christianity, but by the elaborate natural and mathematical laws of supply and demand, production and consumption. What are lost are the social and historical foundations of these economic categories. It undermines the creative process (*praxis*) in which the world is constituted through an aesthetic activity by substituting for it a world of reified categories and unarticulated perceptions of external natural laws of political economy.

Chapter 1 of *Capital*: Slavery, Production, and Fetishism of Value

At the very end of the first chapter of *Capital* on the analysis of commodities, Aristotle's *Politics*, book I, chapters 3–7, is mentioned in what appears to be a one-line throwaway in a footnote.

Truly comical is M. Bastiat, who imagines that the ancient Greeks and Romans lived by plunder alone. But when people plunder for centuries, there must always be something at hand for them to seize, the objects of plunder must be continually reproduced. It would thus appear that even Greeks and Romans had some process of production, consequently, an economy, which just as much constituted the material basis of their world, as bourgeois economy constitutes that of our modern world. Or perhaps Bastiat means, that a mode of production based on slavery is based on a system of plunder. In that case he treads on dangerous ground. If a giant thinker like Aristotle erred in his appreciation of slave labour, why should a dwarf economist like Bastiat be right in his appreciation of wage-labour?[49]

It is not at all clear what Marx is referring to in this reference. However, the context of the note may help explain it. It occurs in the section entitled "The Fetishism of Commodities and the Secret Thereof." This section helps clarify the methodological implications of Marx's theory of value and its underlying theory of objectivity. He had examined the "metaphysical subtleties and theological niceties" of commodities and concluded that the categories and theories of classical bourgeois political economy reflect the institutions and structures of a particular historical mode of production. Alternative forms of production would have alternative theories. He outlines four alternative modes of production: the individualism of the Robinson Crusoe economy, the feudal system of the European Middle Ages, a family economy, and a communitarian economy. Marx's critique of political economy rests on its inability to get beneath the surface of exchange and the natural necessity of production in order to question its own historical foundations and social forms of production. Since it cannot raise these issues, it cannot solve the riddle of the underlying common substance and commensurability of commodities. It cannot develop a theory of value to explain commodity exchange and production. Aristotle, too, was incapable of solving the problem or of investigating slavery as a necessary part of the production process. As we will see in Marx's further reference to Aristotle's view of slavery in chapter 15 of *Capital*, Aristotle was interested in the issue of slavery as it affected the natural order and the life and possibilities of the masters.

The value of each product exchanged as a commodity, as the most universal and simple form of capitalist production, is determined by the social form of production, abstract labor, and the socially necessary labor time for commodity production. Value is not determined by either nature or the exchange process. Value lies hidden within the deeper structures of the social form of production. Marx's critique of fetishism is thus a critique of positivism to the extent that it treats political economy only in terms of what is immediately evident and phenomenally present to experience. This crude empiricism or fetishism reduces the deep structures of history and society to a false objectivity of relations between things rather than between human beings. Thus, this reference to Aristotle is a methodological rebuke for his failure to delve beneath the surface to substructures of the economy. The real question is, is the rebuke justified?

Chapter 2 of *Capital*: Economics of Use Value and Exchange Value

In the second chapter of *Capital*, Marx takes up the themes found in the *Politics*, book I, chapter 9, where Aristotle starts to outline his theory of unnatural acquisition of property.

For two-fold is the use of every object. . . . The one is peculiar to the object as such, the other is not, as a sandal which may be worn, and is also exchangeable. Both are uses of the sandal, for even he who exchanges the sandal for the money or food he is in want of, makes use of the sandal as a sandal. But not in its natural way. For it has not been made for the sake of being exchanged (Aristotle, *Politics*, I, 9).[50]

Marx uses this as he begins to develop his own theory of the contradictions between use value and exchange value. After first examining the natural methods for acquiring goods, property, and wealth (*oikonomia*), Aristotle investigates the unnatural methods (chrematistike), which are detrimental to the nature of the polity. He understands that the distinction between the natural and unnatural modes of economic activity is not recognized by many people. This is due to the fact that both use the same techniques of exchange and money for circulation of goods. The distinction revolves around the central issues of the natural form of economics, the teleology of society, the relation between means and ends, techniques and skills of acquisition, and the goals of economic activity. In this section, Aristotle makes the distinction between the use of a commodity for the satisfaction of a human need and the exchange of goods for either money or another product. He states very clearly that only the former use is the proper one. Aristotle uses the example of a shoe and contends that its primary and proper use is in immediate consumption or need satisfaction. This is the natural purpose for which it was made. Exchange is not unnatural, but its justification is to be found not in the piece of property itself, but in the broader needs of Greek society. The social need for the readjustment of inequalities of distribution of nature's goods is necessitated by the growth of large communities. According to Aristotle, exchange and barter were not necessary in the earliest households, but as households united to form larger communities and finally the polis, exchange was made necessary in order to reestablish the balance, harmony, and self-sufficiency of the earliest forms of household associations.

When exchange moves beyond the natural limits of harmony and self-sufficiency to become commercial or retail trade (*kapelike*), then economic activity becomes unnatural.[51] "Mutual need of the different goods made it essential to contribute one's share for the common good (*metadosis*), and it is on this basis that many of the non-Greek peoples still proceed, i.e., by exchange: they exchange one class of useful goods for another."[52] Goods that are readily available in one community are exchanged for unavailable goods in another. When the trading partner lies at a distance or not within a common political boundary, coined money becomes the necessary medium of exchange. A commonly available commodity becomes the accepted medium of exchange, such as iron, silver, and so forth. For Aristotle, exchange of basic commodities was necessitated by the size, complexity, and division of labor of the political community. Exchange of goods was still viewed as a natural extension of hunting, fishing, and agriculture. It played a crucial role in the maintenance of the polity. However, when human needs and mutual sharing are replaced by the desire for money making and profits, then *oikonomia* is subverted to *chrematistike*.[53] Commerce and trade developed out of the initial exchange of necessities, as imports and exports of surplus goods took on a life of their own. No longer grounded in its natural purpose "to reestablish nature's own equilibrium of self-sufficiency,"[54] trade became independent of its original purpose and limits.

The new definition of wealth, the medium of commercial trade, and the structures of commercial activity are all conventions that distort the natural meaning of wealth and exchange of necessities. The techniques of acquiring goods are the same, but the meanings and goals of certain social activities have shifted. Commercial profit distorts and subverts the traditional values and institutions of the political community. Productive exchange for a healthy polity is traded for a profitable economy within an unhealthy society. Aristotle notices that money is both the measurement of value of commodities, as well as the limit to exchange. Not having limits on trading or the profits derived therefrom results in a class society characterized by deep divisions of wealth and poverty. The issues of economic inequality and social division have to be understood within the context of Aristotle's theories about friendship, moral and intellectual virtue, and truth as political wisdom and deliberation. For Aristotle, economics, as a form of metaethics, is a subbranch of ethics and enhances or restricts the realization of the natural goals of society through the form of exchange it undertakes. Chapter 9 of *Politics* continues with an analysis of the distinction between household management and the perverted form of the acquisition of property. It is this part of the chapter that becomes the basis for Marx's reference in chapter 4 of *Capital*.

The exchange process is built around the circulation of commodities measured in terms of money. The value of money still lies in the abstract labor contained in it. However, in exchange this particular commodity has had its own value form transformed into money, as the phenomenal form or appearance of the universal equivalent of all commodities. This whole sequence of analysis of exchange and money is important to Marx because it reveals the true essence of money and commercial circulation as expanded forms (transformed value forms) of simple commodity exchange.

As in the case of commodity exchange, the hidden secret of exchange lies in the expanded social foundations of simple production itself. Commodities and money are different forms in which historical social relations manifest themselves in economic events and categories. Thus money is not an artificial symbol or conventional fiction that mediates exchange relations. Rather, it is a transformed commodity that historically began at the edges of traditional societies where contact was made with other societies attempting to supplement or maintain their economic self-sufficiency. "Hence the magic of money. In the form of society now under consideration, the behavior of men in the social process of production is purely atomic. Hence their relations to each other in production assume a material character independent of their control and conscious individual action."[55] The value and magnitude of value of commodities in circulation is not determined by nature or convention, but by the social form of production. Money acts as the medium of exchange, the universal measure of value and standard of price, and, in its final form, it appears as capital itself.

Because money is a commodity and a form of private property, it establishes an economy that produces class, inequality, and conflict. It results in a political economy rather than a moral economy. Marx says that "the ancients therefore denounced money as subversive of the economic and moral order of things."[56] Money is capable of buying and selling anything and of satisfying all wants, except those needs that are precluded by the nature of the political and economic system created by an exchange economy. In turn, markets develop abilities, talents, and potential for self-realization compatible with the logic and needs of profits. There is an important difference between an economic theory of wants and an ethical theory of needs. The need for community and ethics, a just political constitution, democratic public discourse and deliberation, and even social and political friendship are excluded in a market economy that levels everything to the common denominator of acquisition and money. Everything is made equal in simple market exchange. But this process of abstraction and commensurability of commodities creates not only the foundations for a commercial market, but also the basis for the reduction of all moral and

intellectual virtues to saleable commodities themselves. Marx reminds
the reader that even the Delphic temples, as monuments to gods
and prophetic wisdom, were used as gold depositories. Money can
transform the moral values of society into their opposites, as well as
turn injustice, cowardice, and baseness into enviable virtues. It becomes the principle of life and the standard measurement of achievement and virtue. To make this point even more poignant, Marx quotes
the lines of Creon from Sophocles's *Antigone*:

> Money! Nothing worse
> in our lives, so current, rampant, so corrupting.
> Money—you demolish cities, root men from their homes,
> you train and twist good minds and set them on
> to the most atrocious schemes. No limit,
> you make them adept at every kind of outrage,
> every godless crime—money.[57]

A chrematistic mode of acquisition levels and equalizes all commodities in the market so that there is a common measure of their individual
worth. With this form of economics, there is also another and more
insidious kind of leveling: a moral leveling. At this point in his analysis,
Marx makes an extremely important and powerful point that cannot
be overstressed, especially when we consider Nietzsche's moral philosophy in Chapter 6 of this volume. A market economy based on
exchange value and profit accumulation undermines the very possibility of moral and intellectual excellence because everything is reduced
to the common denominator of money, profit, and success.[58] Those
values conducive to economic efficiency and productivity become the
real moral and intellectual virtues of society. Even heaven or Aristotle's virtues can be purchased by money. Marx's argument moves from
economic theory and an examination of exchange value and the market
to the abstracting and leveling of moral virtues, that is, from industrial
crisis to ethical pathology. To favor a society grounded in personal and
civic virtue (moral economy) is to oppose a chrematistic political
economy.

Chapter 4 of *Capital*: Economics, Chrematistics, and the Critique of Political Economy

In chapter 4 Marx turns to book I, chapter 9 of the *Politics* to develop
Aristotle's theory of value, unnatural acquisition, chrematistics, and
critique of market exchange.

Aristotle opposes Oeconomic to Chrematistic. He starts from the former. So far as it is the art of gaining a livelihood, it is limited to procuring those articles that are necessary to existence, and useful either to a household or the state. "True wealth (ὁ ἀληθινὸς πλοῦτος) consists of such values in use; for the quantity of possessions of this kind, capable of making life pleasant, is not unlimited. There is, however, a second mode of acquiring things to which we may by preference and with correctness give the name of Chrematistic, and in this case there appear to be no limits to riches and possessions. Trade (ἡ καπηλικὴ is literally retail trade, and Aristotle takes this kind because in it values in use predominate) does not in its nature belong to Chrematistic, for here the exchange has reference only to what is necessary to themselves (the buyer and seller)." Therefore, as he goes on to show, the original form of trade was barter, but with the extension of the latter, there arose the necessity for money. On the discovery of money, barter of necessity developed into καπηλική, into trading in commodities, and this again, in opposition to its original tendency, grew into Chrematistic, into the art of making money. Now Chrematistic is distinguished from Oeconomic in this way, that, "in the case of Chrematistic circulation is the source of riches (ποιητικὴ χρημάτων . . . διὰ χρημάτων διαβολῆς). And it appears to revolve about money, for money is the beginning and end of this kind of exchange (τὸ γάρ νόμισμα στοιχεῖον καὶ πέρας τῆς ἀλλαγῆς ἐστίν). Therefore also riches, such as Chrematistic strives for, are unlimited. Just as every art that is not a means to an end, but an end in itself, has no limit to its aims, because it seeks constantly to approach nearer and nearer to that end, while those arts that pursue means to an end, are not boundless, since the goal itself imposes a limit upon them, so with Chrematistic, there are no bounds to its aims, these aims being absolute wealth. Oeconomic not Chrematistic has a limit . . . the object of the former is something different from money, of the latter the augmentation of money. . . . By confounding these two forms, which overlap each other, some people have been led to look upon the preservation and increase of money ad infinitum as the end and aim of Oeconomic" (Aristotle, *Politics*, ed. Bekker, I, 8, 9, passim).[59]

The initial contradiction between use value and exchange value is expanded to include the broader economic contradictions between economics and chrematistics. It is upon these contradictions that Marx's dialectical interpretation and critique of liberalism are based. His critique of the classical political economy of Smith, Malthus, Franklin, and Ricardo ultimately rests upon Aristotle's critique of trade, commercial profit, and interest making in classical Greece. Aristotle begins the *Politics* with an analysis of domestic and political economy in the polis.

In the first book, there are four chapters (8, 9, 10, and 11) that examine the nature of economics of the household in ancient Greece. Aristotle is concerned with distinguishing between the natural and unnatural forms of the acquisition of goods and property, which he characterizes as household-management (*oikos*) and chrematistics. The former term refers to the economics of the family and the exchange necessary for the material well-being of the household (*metabletike* or *allage*), whereas the latter refers to various forms of acquisition, money making, and wealth creation, such as commerce or retail market trade (*kapelike*) and interest accumulation (*tokos*). Certainly Aristotle's theory of the household economy, money, and unnatural acquisition in the *Politics* is connected to his theory of needs and friendship in the *Nicomachean Ethics*. Chapter 8 of the first book studies the natural method of acquisition of goods; chapter 9 compares the natural and the unnatural processes, social and political economy; chapter 10 further details the forms and significance of chrematistics or money-making methods of acquisition; and chapter 11 examines various practical arts and techniques for acquiring wealth.

Aristotle's critique of political economy (chrematistics) rests on his whole ethical and political philosophy: his notions about sharing (*metadosis*) and friendship (*philia*), human needs, the limited market, the boundaries of nature, the ends of the *oikos* and polis, realization of personal and community happiness and the good life, and the practice of moral virtues. Within this context his critique of unlimited wealth acquisition makes more sense.

In book I, chapter 9 of the *Politics*, Aristotle outlines seven reasons why chrematistics is detrimental to the polis. For him, chrematistics represents a critique of unlimited property acquisition that (1) undermines the ethical values of the political community; (2) distorts human needs into market wants; (3) turns economics into a technique for the unlimited acquisition of material goods, money making, and profits; (4) transforms household and community economics into an unnatural activity; (5) confuses the ends of the *oikos* and polis with the economic means of unlimited acquisition; (6) mistakes the perpetuation of life for the good life and a concern for scarcity with a fear of death; and (7) results in the inversion of moral and intellectual virtues into means for the acquisition of property.[60] Chrematistics turns sharing and reciprocity into exploitation of strangers, human needs into market wants, limited exchanges into profitable trade, natural balance into unnatural acquisition, health of the household into the poison of the market, happiness and the good life into pleasure and fear of death, and, finally, virtue into market skills. Exchange becomes unnatural when it makes us a slave to our bodies and the physical world and when its goal is that of eternal life rather than the good life, and physical pleasure rather than the pleasure arising from the realization of our rational and moral capabilities.[61]

Though economic exchange has its origins in nature—the growth of the community and the expanding needs of the family—its original purpose has been perverted by the rise of the market. The earliest household communities rested on economic reciprocity and sharing of goods in order to sustain the life of the family. Households interacted as if the different families were part of one larger household. Thus material goods were not sold for profit and personal gain, but were intended to help each other. This was a small community built on family, friendship, and mutual sharing of scarce resources for the benefit of the whole community.[62] Community contributions were essential if this form of economic activity was to succeed. The surpluses of one farm were to be exchanged for the surpluses of another.

Aristotle maintains strongly one point: this is not a *market economy* based on money, utility, market prices, and production for exchange. Rather the surpluses of households are bartered for the excess of other families. It is a *moral economy* in which economic production for immediate use is subordinate to the moral values of the wider political community. Polanyi calls this "an embedded economy" in which "the lives of men are embedded in a tissue of common experience."[63] Agricultural production is based on the ethical priorities of friendship and family love. With the development of a chrematistic economy, household sharing and reciprocity are replaced by market forces and exchange value in which exchange takes place between strangers. In commercial trade with foreigners, the social underpinnings of sharing and friendship are loosened and in the process so too are the spiritual foundations of the community.

Aristotle is very insistent that exchange is not unnatural. It satisfies the needs of the family and local community and reestablishes the natural equilibrium between man and nature and man and man. The purpose of exchange is not the satisfaction of ever-expanding and artificially created wants in the market, but the satisfaction of social needs for material self-sufficiency and maintenance of the community. The community is reinforced since the bond that holds its members together is not convenience or utility of a social contract, but the mutual respect for their shared responsibilities and values as economic providers and public citizens. Even the introduction of money is not

necessarily unnatural if its purpose is to reinforce the ethical imperatives of the households.

The next criticism of chrematistics is a critique of the expanded
market. What was at first a necessary, simple, and informal exchange
of surplus use values in order to ensure the safety and well-being of the
household and community became a market trade for the acquisition of
profits. Now the purpose of exchange has shifted to the learning
of economic techniques and calculations, market exchanges, profit
orientation, and a formal, money economy. This changed orientation
has resulted in an unnatural material activity. Money in this new
system has become both the basis of circulation and the unit of
measurement; it has abstracted exchange from the ethical needs of
friendship and mutual sharing to become an end in itself.

The ends of the *oikos* and polis have been replaced by the unlimited
search for money and profits. What formerly had been a means to the
ethical life of the community has turned into an end itself. For Aristotle, friendship, sharing, reciprocity, and needs are all lost in a market
economy geared to the management of society for profit. To clarify his
main point of the reversal of means-ends relations, he gives the
example of the physician's art of healing. It too has an end and
technical means at its service. But the use of medical technology is
limited by the goal of reaching health. When that is secured there is no
longer any reason to continue applying the art of healing. In contrast,
chrematistic acquisition of property has no limit—neither moral nor
physical health of the community or the individual. The unlimited
acquisition of wealth distorts the proper balance and place of property
and wealth acquisition in the community, which is to serve higher
social and political purposes. When the health of the political community is replaced by profit making, there are no longer internal rational
and moral barriers to economic activity and acquisition.

Aristotle argues that perverted acquisition results from a confusion
between the quantitative and qualitative sides of life. People confuse
being well with being, the good life with life itself. Again there is a
misunderstanding of the relationship between means necessary to
accomplish certain ends and the ends themselves. When life and the
fear of death become abstracted from the moral community, they
become reified and take on an existence of their own. The purpose of
unnatural trade is a happiness of physical pleasure. The purposes of
economic activity, being removed from broader social concerns, take
on their own meaning and value. The possibilities of the good life being
forgotten and lost in this process of abstraction, individuals search for

that which merely continues life and pleasure. The fear of death and material scarcity become the driving forces of chrematistics.

Finally, in a life oriented to business success and physical pleasure, all moral and intellectual virtues become perverted and distorted. This moral inversion occurs when virtues are transformed into economic skills—when moderation becomes economic cautiousness, reason becomes calculation and technique, courage becomes confidence and entrepreneurial risk taking, and steadfastness becomes hard work and persistence. In this unnatural moral inversion, virtues are transformed into means for the acquisition of wealth and power.

At the start of *Politics*, there is a discussion about the nature of economic acquisition, commerce, interest making, and so forth. Economics provided the material foundations for Greek culture and political life. While economics did not provide the categories describing the inner worth, the creative impulse, the end of human potentialities, or the goal of self-realization, it did provide the material substratum and basic necessities for these higher goals. Without economics there is no polity. Human nature and potential are not to be measured by the standards of economic choices and possibilities. However, the distinction between a natural and unnatural method of acquisition is important to the extent that an unnatural method of accumulation would have serious and detrimental consequences for the development of a healthy political constitution. To that extent economics is a crucial foundation stone to freedom and equality. But before individuals can be free, the polity must be emancipated from economic necessity.

Aristotle begins chapter 8 by raising the question of the relation between the acquisition of goods and the household economy. He asks further whether the acquisition of goods in general (also referred to by Aristotle as chrematistics) is part of household management. The term "chrematistics" is used with a variety of meanings in these chapters. Though it does refer to the method of the acquisition of goods, it is used more frequently to describe the perverted and unnatural form of economic activity. Aristotle answers his own question when he examines the different forms of economic life: nomadic, hunting, and agricultural. These three are the main natural forms because nature provides mankind from its own bounty and because these forms or their combinations result in a self-sufficiency that does not depend on external trade or exchange. Nature itself has as its end the provision of material for human survival. Within the framework of Aristotelian teleology, nature's place is to provide the material environment for man's being, while the natural purpose of the political community is to provide for his well-being or good life. Property acquisition is just the economic foundation for the polity. But there must be a balance between the purpose of nature and the purpose of man. They must be integrated into a harmonious whole. And thus the acquisition of property (art) is subordinate to the wider purpose of nature. The techniques and social arrangements surrounding property must be compatible with the ultimate goal of society, which is *eudaimonia*, or happiness.

Household management provides everything that is useful for the survival of the family. Economic acquisition is therefore only a means to more important ends, which are: creating the conditions for utility for the household or state, limiting accumulation of wealth and property, establishing the conditions for economic self-sufficiency, satisfying human needs, and forming the foundations for the good life. This is the natural form of property accumulation, since it sets limits to its means (tools) and is subordinate to ethical and political values. Economics is the means to a life of moral virtue of courage, moderation, and truthfulness, of intellectual virtue of practical and philosophical wisdom, of social virtue of public participation, political discourse, and political wisdom, and, finally, of social justice of distributive, corrective, and reciprocal justice. These are the values associated with happiness: that is, social justice, political community, civic friendship, and social equity necessitate a natural mode of economic life that does not interfere with this teleology, but rather enhances and encourages it.

In chapter 9 beginning at line 1257b25, Aristotle turns to the distinction between household management and the false method of acquisition of wealth. It is the contradictory values, goals, and institutions of these two forms of economic activity that give Aristotle and later Marx the foundation for critiques of political economy. The issue of natural ends is raised once more with the example of the *telos* and *techne* of the art of medical healing. The natural teleology of medicine and economics helps explain their distinctive and secondary roles in the polity. Do medicine and economics have limits? While medicine has the goal of unlimited health, its means are limited. On the other hand, the household economy does not have as its function the unlimited acquisition of wealth. Though both household management and chrematistics use techniques for acquiring wealth and their modes of acquisition are similar, their purposes are quite dissimilar. In the latter case, the end is accumulation itself, whereas in the former, the end is the establishment of a healthy domestic economy and household. Just as the unnatural application of medical techniques should be restrained by a concern for physical health and well-being, the unnatural acquisition of property must be limited by the values of social justice, happiness, and the good life.

Aristotle again contends that the two modes of acquisition are confused with each other and chrematistics is taken to be the only natural form of economic activity. But the problem lies in the confusion over the natural ends of humankind and the technical methods used to achieve those ends. By not distinguishing between the unlimited desire for life and the limits to material acquisition, money making becomes the end of chrematistics, as well as its means. The desire for unlimited expansion of economic activity also leads to unlimited application of the means. The means and ends become indistinguishable. Every technical skill has at its goal the accomplishing of tasks without limit. Limits are placed on the application of a method or skill, not by the skill itself, but by the end of the activity. Where in household management, economic activity is subordinate to the natural goals of the family and polity, the turning of means (acquisition of goods) into ends for the household and state subverts the natural law and purpose of human association. When both the ends and means are the same—acquisition of property—that is, when the end does not set limits but is transformed into a means, then economic activity is subverted to chrematistics. "So, while it seems that there must be a limit to every form of wealth, in practice we find that the opposite occurs; all those engaged in acquiring goods go on increasing their coin without limit, because the two modes of acquisition of goods are so similar."[64]

The whole political process of the polity: public discourse, deliberation, rational argumentation, compromise, and the experience of practical wisdom is transformed into a political method of technical calculation and economic success. *Phronesis* (practical wisdom) has been replaced by *techne* (technique); *praxis* (political activity and doing) has been replaced by *poiesis* (political fabrication and making); and political practice, experience, and wisdom replaced by political rationalism and formal reason. Art has replaced nature. The confusion between economics and chrematistics also distorts the relation between life and its physical maintenance and the good life and the activity appropriate to its realization. The inability to distinguish between the two, then, results in activity appropriate for one being inappropriately applied to the other. For example, in the unlimited search for profits in trade or moneylending, moral virtues are seduced to market virtues, and a moral economy is undermined by the incipient market economy, domestic economy by political economy. Aristotle argues that courage, military leadership, and medical healing have been distorted by replacing their natural teleology with the unnatural desire for profits and material acquisition. Moral virtues are transformed into technical means for the appropriation of material wealth. "But these people turn all skills into skills of acquiring goods, as though that were the end and everything had to serve that end."[65] Anticipating Kant's theory of the kingdom of ends and his criticisms of defining and measuring human activity in terms of the price mechanism in the *Critique of Practical Reason*, Aristotle rejects unrestrained money making and wealth acquisition for having reversed the relationship between means and ends. This antinomy between life and the good life, means and ends, chrematistics and household management will be continued later in the twentieth century with the distinctions between formal rationality and substantive rationality (Weber), subjective reason and objective reason (Horkheimer), work and action (Arendt), one-dimensional people and multidimensional humankind (Marcuse), and communicative rationality and instrumental rationality (Habermas).

Marx begins part II of the first volume of *Capital* with a reference to the *Politics*. In particular, he mentions Aristotle's distinction between the two modes of acquiring goods: economics and chrematistics. Marx interprets the first as referring to economic exchange such as barter and trade for the purposes of satisfying particular needs (use value), whereas the second form developed into the trading of commodities and exchange value. Chrematistics is here a form of commerce in which the unlimited acquisition of commodities and property is the final goal. There is always some overlap between the two forms of activity, but the danger is in confusing the two entirely. Modern political economy, in failing to appreciate Aristotle's distinctions, has also failed to recognize the purpose for economic activity and its role in society as a whole. In the early *Economic and Philosophic Manuscripts of 1844*, Marx presented the reader with an introduction to his theory of *praxis*, aesthetic creativity, and species being through his analysis of alienation. Instead of being an expression of an individual's self-realization and creative possibilities, work became a means for the maintenance of pure existence. Even at this stage there was the implicit recognition of Aristotle's distinction between life and the good life.

However, by the time of his later economic writings, he again turns to Aristotle to frame the crucial distinction between appropriate and distorted forms of material acquisition. Reference to Aristotle also occurs at the very point when Marx is moving from his examination of commodities and money to capital and production. The critique of capitalist production rests on Aristotle's rejection of chrematistic activities in the polis. This form of acquisition takes economic activity that was meant for the maintenance of the household and the state into a means for private acquisition. This distorts the very purpose and meaning of economics, which is to serve the higher goals of human development in the form of rational discourse and public participation in the polis. Money, exchange, and trade were to provide the material basis for citizenship and social justice. With commerce and material gain, social justice is surrendered to the needs of economic expansion and profit making. For Marx, chrematistic surplus value and capital undermine species being, the community, the possibilities of democracy, and the self-expression of humanity's essence. There is also a fundamental alteration in the definition of humankind from a being that creates itself in its social forms into an economic animal.

This discussion of Aristotle's distinction between the household economy and chrematistics is crucial for an understanding of Marx's analysis of capital and the historical and logical transformation of simple commodity exchange into capitalist commodity exchange, money into capital, money circulation into material production. The reference to this distinction occurs in chapter 4 of *Capital*, "The General Formula for Capital." If the commodity was the starting point for an understanding of money, exchange, and circulation, then, as Marx states in the first line of chapter 4, commerce and commodity circulation are the starting point for an analysis of capital. It is a more developed and complex value form of simple commodity exchange.

Money as the form of circulation is expressed by the formula C-M-C, but, in the form of capital, money is the end of circulation not simply its means, or M-C-M. The initial stage of development of capital is in money form. There is an antithetical dualism between the first phase of the purchase of money, M-C, and the second phase consisting of the sale of the commodity to produce surplus money. This is the usual form of merchants' capital, whereas the form taken by a banker is more direct and eliminates the need for an intermediate commodity. M-M' is the form of interest-bearing capital of the banker. The purpose of trade is no longer to exchange one product for another, to satisfy human needs and use value (consumption) C-M-C, where money is used as simply the medium of exchange and the standard of prices.

Rather, exchange value and a money surplus are the goals of commercial trading using commodities as means to further the exchange of money. Acquisition and increase in wealth are the purposes of capital exchange. For Marx, this economic exchange is "purposeless and absurd." In more simple forms of trade, economics had a specific and higher purpose of providing the material foundations for society in order that higher values and goals might be pursued. When economics is reduced to acquisition of surplus value, then chrematistics becomes the goal of a society that has lost its traditions, values, and mores; society has lost its vision and purpose. Not only has exchange become a tautology where money is exchanged for money, but also human life has become meaningless and absurd. At this point it is no longer possible to deal with the issue of social justice. "This boundless greed after riches, this passionate chase after exchange-value, is common to the capitalist and the miser; but while the miser is merely a capitalist gone mad, the capitalist is a rational miser."[66] Perhaps Marx was one of the first to see the existential dilemma created by chrematistics and Nietzsche may be read as developing and transforming its implications.

Simple commodity exchange has been inverted and transformed into the circulation of money. When money is transformed from a means of exchange to the goal of exchange, when buying becomes a means to selling dearer, then money has become capital. The circulation of capital becomes an end in itself for the purpose of the unlimited expansion of value (surplus value).

Chapter 5 of *Capital*: Chrematistics, Contradictions, and Moral Economy

In chapter 10 of the first book of *Politics*, Aristotle details more fully the nature of chrematistic trade and moneylending, and it is just this distinction that is important for Marx's development of his theory of relative surplus value and economic exploitation.

What we have said with reference to merchants' capital applies still more to money-lenders' capital. In merchants' capital, the two extremes, the money that is thrown upon the market, and the augmented money that is withdrawn from the market, are at least connected by a purchase and a sale, in other words by the movement of the circulation. In moneylenders' capital the form M-C-M' is reduced to the two extremes without a mean, M-M', money exchanged for more money, a form that is incompatible with the nature of money, and therefore remains inexplicable from the standpoint of the circulation of commodities. Hence Aristotle: "since chrematistic is a double science, one part belonging to commerce, the other to economic, the latter being necessary and praiseworthy, the former based on circulation and with justice disapproved (for it is not based on Nature, but on mutual cheating), therefore the user is most rightly hated, because money itself is the source of his gain and is not used for the purposes for which it was invented. For it originated for the exchange of commodities, but interest makes out of money, more money. Hence its name (το'κος interest and offspring). For the begotten are like those who beget them. But interest is money of money, so that of all modes of making a living, this is the most contrary to Nature" (Aristotle, *Politics*, I, 10).[67]

Aristotle asks whether the acquisition of goods is to be part of the household economy. He makes an interesting observation that nature provides the material goods for a household. The household manager's function is to properly distribute the goods available at any particular time. He says that just as the statesman does not make citizens, but uses them; just as the weaver does not make the wool, but uses the product of nature; so too the manager of the household does not make the goods acquired, but nature provides the food, shelter, and clothing. Aristotle understands the workings of the household economy more as a distribution mechanism for the health of the family than as a social organization for production or commercial center. "For it is a function of nature to provide food for whatever is brought to birth, since that from which it is born has a surplus which provides food in every case."[68] Is it possible that the acquisition of goods is not dealt with because the family members are not part of the production process itself? Animal husbandry and agriculture provide the material foundations for Greek society. Since the production process is organized around the social relations of slavery and the latter is "natural" to this social system, then the production process is part of nature and not the social system. This is the natural purpose for which slavery was created. It will be Marx who raises this type of question in the future regarding the social and class relations surrounding the production system. That which will be the heart of his analysis and critique of political economy is not examined by Aristotle. It is explained away by the nature and teleology of slavery.

Aristotle concludes this chapter by stating that the acquisition of goods from trade "is justly regarded with disapproval, since it arises not from nature but from men's gaining from each other."[69] The charging of interest is also rejected along with commercial activity. But it is condemned as the most serious infraction of the natural order.

The former is rejected because a means (currency) is turned into an end in itself, whereas the latter is rejected because trading requires the exploitation of man. Profits are accrued at the expense of others and the community. In both cases, the natural interests of the whole and the natural technique of economic exchange are perverted. The original purposes for which trade was created are inverted, with the end of society becoming the accumulation of property and wealth. The creation of economic wealth is not the purpose for which humans live. In the next chapter, Aristotle does begin to examine the techniques and knowledge of acquiring wealth in agriculture and trade. He mentions stock raising, tillage, beekeeping, commerce, moneylending, and wage labor. His comments on physical labor are interesting. "Those occupations which require most skill are those in which there is the smallest element of chance, the most mechanical are those which cause most deteriorization to the bodies of the workers, the most slavish those in which most use is made of the body, and the most ignoble those in which there is least need to exercise virtue too."[70]

His most useful recommendation for those who wish to engage in profit-making enterprises is to corner the market and create a monopoly. This is very perceptive of Aristotle, since he recognizes in the fourth century B.C. that profit is made not by minding the laws of market competition, but by negating them. The same technical advice is made to the statesman who wishes to acquire political wealth or power. This form of political monopoly, however, is a perversion of the rational process of public deliberation.

Marx mentions Aristotle again in chapter 5 of *Capital*, "The General Formula for Capital," in order to develop the relations and implications he sees between merchants' capital and interest-bearing capital. He is also interested in exploring the underlying dualisms and contradictions within capital itself: use value versus exchange value, consumption versus production, purchase versus sale, exchange versus accumulation, economics versus chrematistics, and need satisfaction versus satisfaction of the needs of capital. These very contradictions in capital will by the end of Marx's analysis in volume 3 rock the very theoretical foundations of capitalism itself.

The quotation above from chapter 5 again mentions Aristotle's distinction between economics and chrematistics, trade and commerce. With moneylenders' capital, the exchange between money and more money, value and surplus value, perverts the purpose for which money was invented. Marx raises the question as to the origin of surplus value. Does it lie in the exchange process or elsewhere? The difficulty posed by the question lies in the confusion by orthodox economists over the relation between value, exchange value, and surplus value. In a commercial exchange, there is a transformation of the value form of goods from commodities to money. The commodity has changed its form, but its value (homogeneous social labor) has not been altered. This means, according to Marx, that value has not been added during the exchange process. Surplus value must be explained by looking elsewhere. The law of commodity exchange maintains that in the circulation of commodities only equivalents are exchanged. Use values are exchanged, as well as exchange values, but no surplus value is added in the process.

Marx quotes a long passage from Condillac who contends that surplus is created in commercial circulation because the goods satisfy our needs differently and to a different degree. But Marx adds that this only confuses the issue since use value and exchange value are themselves confused. The value of commodities are determined by abstract labor and the magnitude of these values is determined by the socially necessary labor time required to produce them. Value is not created or determined by individual or social needs. Market demands do not hierarchically organize prices according to individual priorities and wants. Value is defined in terms of production not circulation and the secret to surplus value lies in the nature of capital not in the nature of simple commodity exchange or circulation. In circulation only equivalents are exchanged. Theft or overcharging are not legitimate explanations. There is no mechanism for the creation of a surplus here. He rejects the hypothesis that nominal price rises could account for increasing value. Since this may affect a particular transaction it would have no influence on the general economy. The profits that accrue to merchants' capital or interest-bearing capital also cannot be explained by means of commodity circulation. "Twist and turn then as we may, the fact remains unaltered. If equivalents are exchanged, no surplus value results, and if non-equivalents are exchanged, still no surplus value. Circulation, or the exchange of commodities, begets no value."[71]

The secret to capital and surplus value is finally revealed in the social organization and private means of production, that is, in the social form of production and the creation of abstract value and in the distinction between labor and labor power. Marx has reached the limits of Aristotle's distinction between economics and chrematistics. Their contradiction will not explain capitalist production because there is no developed theory of value within it. Nor will modern natural rights theory or utilitarianism penetrate beyond the circulation process into the deeper structures of capitalist production and the sale of labor power. Aristotle, John Locke, and Jeremy Bentham are locked into commodity exchange and commercial circulation. The critique of political economy demands that the secret to commodities lies within the production of capital itself. The limits of Aristotle's categories are at the same time the limits of the categories of liberal political theory with its thesis of innate natural rights. The justification of capitalist exchange based on the principles of freedom, equality, property, and individual utility (Bentham's principles of utilitarianism), whatever their limitations for explaining the actual process of capitalist exchange and profit accumulation, are more a mirror of simple commodity circulation. They do not reflect the complexity of capitalist production or its class relationships and, when taken as a justification for the entire social formation, only mystify and blur the real economic and sociological conditions of surplus acquisition, profit accumulation, and legitimation of private property.

Marx contends that liberal values only rationalize the simple market exchange of commodities. He argues that the political theory of liberalism is a form of free trade sophistry reminiscent of Protagoras's and the Eleatics' ability to twist and compromise any argument for their own purposes.[72] This historical mode of production, from Marx's perspective, is best expressed in its values of the self-interested search for utility and pleasure, the free will to engage in market exchange, the equality of market participants and their goods, and the free disposition and alienation of property. The rights to life, liberty, and property, according to Marx, are the values of simple commodity exchange. An analysis of the process of production and surplus value uncovers a different set of values underlying a more advanced form of economic liberalism.

Chapter 13 of *Capital*: Humanity's Communal Nature in Polity and Civil Society

Reference to Aristotle's definition of man as a political animal from *Politics*, book I, chapter 2 comes just at a point in chapter 13 when Marx raises the issue of social cooperation in the production process.

Apart from the new power that arises from the fusion of many forces into one single force, mere social contact begets in most industries an emulation and a stimulation of the animal spirits that heighten the efficiency of each individual workman. Hence it is that a dozen persons working together will, in their collective working-day of 144 hours, produce far more than twelve isolated men each working 12 hours, or than one man who works twelve days in succession. The reason of this is that man is, if not as Aristotle contends, a political, at all events a social animal.[73]

The norms, ideals, organization, and potential of modern industrial social relations of production lie hidden deep within the social and economic nature of the production process itself. In book I, chapter 2 of the *Politics* and in book IX, chapter 8 of the *Nicomachean Ethics*, Aristotle claims that man is a political animal. The state is a natural formation and only barbarians "mad on war" and gods can live outside it. It is the highest form of social organization built around the polity whose purpose is human perfection and happiness. According to Aristotle, what differentiates bees, other animals, and man is rational speech (*logos*). Though bees are by nature social animals in the manner they perform economic activity, they do not possess rational speech that makes possible critical self-reflection and political participation in the polis. The comparison raises questions about the nature of humankind and social justice. "For the real difference between man and other animals is that humans alone have perception of good and evil, just and unjust, etc. It is the sharing of a common view in *these* matters that makes a household and a state."[74]

The state is made of component parts, as we have already seen. Just as in the case of an amputated arm or leg, the amputee remains a person, but the severed limb is no longer an arm or leg. It has lost its function and definition and retains an identity in name only. The same is true of the state. The state has priority over its constituent elements and it is the organic unity of the parts that defines it as a natural political association. Only within the polity does the individual define himself as human and rational, because it is only within the public sphere of the political community that rational deliberation and self-reflection occur. The fullest evolution of humanity is possible only with the fullest development of human rationality and political participation. This, in turn, requires the fullest development of the virtuous citizen and its embodiment in law and social justice. This is what defines the rational function and capabilities of humanity; this is what defines humans as distinctively human. Political culture, traditions, and laws become the basis for the definition of individual capabilities and functions that manifest man as a whole being. Because man is political by nature, the true state is concerned with the education of the moral virtues of the citizen, the development of the good life, rationality, and justice. It is in the state that the potentialities of nature (teleology) can be developed as it provides the concrete form for individual freedom and civic participation. Man is defined in terms of language, discourse, and participation in the public sphere; the polis expresses the objective conditions and limits of human speech. In the *Nicomachean Ethics*, Aristotle develops these themes through his ideas on friendship and happiness.

Toward the beginning of part IV of the first volume of *Capital*, Marx refers to the social nature of people. While he does make reference to Aristotle's definition in the *Politics* that man is a political animal, he adjusts the definition to fit his social and economic concerns in *Capital*. It represents a broadening of Aristotle's definition since Marx dealt with the political nature of human beings in his writings from his early *Critique of Hegel's Philosophy of Right* and *Economic and Philosophic Manuscripts of 1844* to his later *Critique of the Gotha Program*. The concept of species being not only has anthropological and philosophical importance in defining the parameters of human possibilities; in *Capital* the concept also has relevance when considering issues of productivity, efficiency, and labor power. The collective force of social production is another dimension of the organization of labor that must be considered when examining the nature of capital and the social means of production. Capitalist production is characterized by a mode of production in which large amounts of labor are brought together under the guidance of the capitalist for the purpose of producing surplus value.

Marx divides modern capitalism into two periods. The first he calls the manufacturing period, which lasted from the middle of the sixteenth to the end of the eighteenth century. The second period, from the eighteenth to the nineteenth century, is that of modern industry and the factory system. Following Adam Smith, he argues that during the manufacturing period the revolutionary development of industrial capitalism lay in the changes in the social form of production and not in modern machinery and technology. The collective combination of fragmented and isolated workers into a complex social organization controlled by capital produced an unheard-of economic growth and productivity. This revolutionary social reorganization of production was based on collective labor, cooperation, the division and specialization of labor, decomposition of production and fragmentation of labor, the coordination of isolated and detailed functions, and class hierarchy. This occurs within a competitive market economy formed around a new economic order of unparalleled integration, productivity, and expansion.

Social labor represented a major advance in industrial technology and social engineering based as it was on the "collective power of the masses." The means of production were revolutionized because the social foundations of production were too. "If, therefore, on the one hand, it presents itself historically as a progress and as a necessary phase in the economic development of society, on the other hand, it is a refined and civilized method of exploitation."[75] A paradox parallels this new social form since with the greater coordination, cooperation, and integration of the components of production, there is also a concomitantly greater fragmentation, division, and lack of integration among the workers who are turned into "crippled monstrosities." After examining this new form of production, Marx borrows a comment from Adam Ferguson's *History of Civil Society*: "We make a nation of Helots, and have no free citizens."[76] With the increased rationalization of production, the social relations have been reduced to slavery. The difference is that the overlords have changed from the Spartiates to the bourgeoisie. Marx does recognize the relationship between classical political economy and classical Greek philosophy— Smith and Aristotle. Aristotle becomes impossible with Smith, since the decomposition and specialization of labor under the control of capital within this new social formation reinforces the loss of the public sphere where economics was subservient to politics.

Marx juxtaposes the views of political economy with those of classical antiquity. Where the former praised the social division of labor as facilitating the productivity and growth of capital, the accumulation of exchange value, and the production of more and cheaper commodities, the ancients stressed the development of human talents and potential, the quantity of use value produced and the quality of its products. Referring to Plato's *Republic*, Homer's *Odyssey*, Archilochus, Sextus Empiricus, Isocrates' *Busiris*, Pericles, Thucydides' *The Peloponnesian Wars*, and Xenophon's *Cyropaedia*, Marx shows the Greek view of society's benefit from a division of labor.

Hence both product and producer are improved by the division of labour. If the growth of the quantity produced is occasionally mentioned, this is only done with reference to the greater abundance of use values. There is not a word alluding to exchange value or to the cheapening of commodities. This aspect, from the standpoint of use value alone, is taken as well by Plato, who treats division of labour as the foundation on which the division of society into classes is based, as by Xenophon, who with characteristic bourgeois instinct, approaches more nearly to division of labour within the workshop. Plato's *Republic*, in so far as division of labour is treated in it, as the formative principle of the State, is merely the Athenian idealisation of the Egyptian system of castes, Egypt having served as the model of an industrial country to many of his contemporaries also, amongst others to Isocrates, and it continued to have this importance to the Greeks of the Roman Empire.[77]

Just as in an army, the fire power of a combined regiment is greater than the sum of an equal number of isolated soldiers, so too in industry the combined labor of an enterprise is more efficient, productive, and faster than the unconnected work of independent workers. Collective labor uses the means of production more economically over a wider geographical area, coordinates a large mass of labor, and raises the animal spirit and intensity of work. This social form of the labor process is the beginning of a capitalist mode of production. Cooperation becomes part of the very fabric of capitalist production. "The combined working-day produces, relatively to an equal sum of isolated working-days, a greater quantity of use values and consequently, diminishes the labour-time necessary for the production of a given useful effect."[78] Here too there is a contradiction built into this positive element of capitalism. The productive power of social labor also results in the need for supervising, coordinating, and controlling a recalcitrant work force, which is resistant to new technical means for exploiting larger amounts of surplus value. Subordination and control of the work force must wait for the development of the factory and mechanized production. Marx mentions with a mixture of irony and humor that the despotism of capitalist cooperation and subjection of labor to capital in the workplace are ideologically held separate from the anarchy and liberty of the market. The idolatry of natural rights and individual freedoms hides the oppression of collective and homogeneous labor. The anarchy of the market dulls the senses to the despotism of manufacturing.

Chapter 15 of *Capital*: Slave Antiquity, Modern Technology, and the Industrial Revolution

Aristotle's theory of slavery and its role in the natural order of the political community from *Politics*, book I, chapter 4, is mentioned by Marx for an unusual purpose as he explores the emancipatory potential of new techniques of production.

"If," dreamed Aristotle, the greatest thinker of antiquity, "if every tool, when summoned, or even of its own accord, could do the work that befits it, just as the creations of Daedalus moved of themselves, or the tripods of Hephaestos went of their own accord to their sacred work, if the weavers' shuttles were to weave of themselves, then there would be no need either of apprentices of the master workers, or of slaves for the lords." And Antipatros, a Greek poet of the time of Cicero, hailed the invention of the water-wheel for grinding corn, an invention that is the elementary form of all machinery, as the giver of freedom to female slaves, and the bringer back of the golden age. Oh! those heathens! They understand, as the learned Bastiat, and before him the still wiser MacCulloch have discovered, nothing of Political Economy and Christianity. They did not, for example, comprehend that machinery is the surest means of lengthening the working day. They perhaps excused the slavery of one on the ground that it was a means to the full development of another. But to preach slavery of the masses, in order that a few crude and half-educated parvenus, might become "eminent spinners," "extensive sausage-makers," and "influential shoe-black dealers," to do this, they lack the bump of Christianity.[79]

In chapters 3 to 7 of the first book of the *Politics*, Aristotle outlines his ideas about ancient slavery, and in chapters 6 and 7 the main arguments in favor of the naturalness of slavery are stated. *Politics* begins with a statement about Aristotle's analytic method and the breakdown of the complexity of the Greek city-state into its simplest component parts. To this end, the book begins with an overview of the natural parts of the state: husband and wife, household, village, and state. In turn, household management is divided into three parts: master and slave, husband and wife, and father and children with a fourth part concerned with the acquisition of goods and property. Nature has defined each association as having different functions and goals with each requiring different techniques of rule whether it is the master's rule over the slave, the monarchical rule of the household, or the rule by the statesman in the polis. Marriage seeks the preservation of the species; the household the satisfaction of material needs; the village the expansion of the household and exchange for economic security; and the state, as the combination of several villages, seeks the protection of life and the good life in a self-sufficient political community. The state's goal is the creation of the perfection of reason and the beauty of the soul. What interested Aristotle, in particular, were the functions and types of governance displayed in each relationship, as well as the forms of knowledge and behavior appropriate to each pair. In all cases, he used observation and opinions to establish the empirical beginnings for his arguments, but then followed the functions of each part to the whole to determine the normative goal of each component. This play between the "is" and the "ought" runs throughout his work.

In the first sentence of chapter 4, book I of the *Politics*, Aristotle makes the point that "neither life itself nor the good life is possible without a certain minimum supply of the necessities."[80] Slavery is just an economic tool used to accomplish certain necessary physical tasks. The slave is both a piece of property and part of the household. But the difficult and elusive question that Aristotle seems to raise in this confusing chapter is whether slavery is natural to the political order or just necessary for its economic survival. Is slavery natural or just part of the necessary order of society due to the limitations of certain available skills and techniques of economic activity? Aristotle ponders, if "shuttles in a loom could fly to and from . . . then master-craftsmen would have no need of servants nor masters of slaves."[81] It is tempting to exercise a possible flight of fancy and inquire if Aristotle was, for a brief moment, asking the question about whether slavery was more a product of the nature of the economy than of the nature of man. In a different type of society with more advanced technology and machinery that would have the characteristics of Daedalus's self-moving statue or Hephaestos's moving tripods, would slavery itself be unnecessary and even unnatural? The thought does not remain long and Aristotle is off on another issue. This time in a one hundred and eighty degree shift in attention, he examines the purpose of slavery and its relation to the teleology of action and life. The possible implications of Aristotle's imaginative reflections on this theme have left him as he moves from the issue of production to that of action. But the powerful implications of Aristotle's statement is not lost, as Marx recognizes its implications for modern wage slavery.

The purpose of slavery is not production per se, but the creation of the social foundations for the good life of *praxis*. Aristotle juxtaposes production and action and, in so doing, states that the slave is to serve action and life, and not production. Is Aristotle making a distinction between productive labor and nonproductive labor or ministering to the needs of the household directly? Or is the argument a transcendental one? That is, slavery as a tool of production is not of interest to Aristotle, only its metaethical function of providing the economic conditions for a virtuous life of citizenship.

Aristotle philosophizes that slavery can be both a characteristic of the individual and part of his or her general function. The essence of slavery lies in its nature of being a nonautonomous part or tool of the household economy; the slave is owned by someone else as a piece of property and used for purposes outside the direction of the slave. Aristotle makes the distinction between a legal slave defeated in battle and captured in war and a natural state of slavery. The former is a slave by conquest and convention and the latter is a slave by individual disposition and the expediency of the polity. Just as it is necessary and expedient for the soul to rule the body, the mind to rule the emotions, husband to rule the wife, and father to rule the children, it is natural that slaves, being a living part of the master, be ruled by him. When slaves are ill-fitted to develop their minds and must work with their bodies, when their function determines that they must exercise only their physical attributes, then they are slaves by nature. But there are many noble persons who by the quirk of fate have fallen into slavery. They are slaves by historical exigencies, military force, and legal conventions.

In this last reference to Aristotle in the first volume of *Capital* in the chapter entitled "Machinery and Modern Industry," Marx pays Aristotle the highest compliment possible by extolling him as the greatest thinker of antiquity. Aristotle dreamt of a political community in which technological development had achieved such heights of mechanization and automation that there would no longer be any need of slavery. According to Marx, that level of development has been achieved with the advent of capitalism. The problem is that the advancement of scientific and technological revolutions has been restrained and undermined by the social form of class production. Marx quotes from a poem by Antipatros:

> Spare the hand that grinds the corn, Oh, miller girls, and softly sleep.
> Let Chanticleer announce the morn in vain!
> Deo has commanded the work of the girls to be done by the Nymphs,
> And now they skip lightly over the wheels,
> So that the shaken axles revolve with their spokes
> And pull round the load of the revolving stones.
> Let us live the life of our fathers, and let us rest from work
> And enjoy the gifts that the Goddess sends us.[82]

The ancient philosophers and poets understood the hopes that technological development and control over nature bring good fortune and prosperity. Both Aristotle and Antipatros had a vision of a different type of political and social relations grounded in the achievements of science and technology. The freeing of humankind from the burdens of labor and the necessities of their physical existence would permit more leisure, and enjoyment of life, and undermine the class structure. Marx reading these earliest writings anticipated a transformation that would turn labor into creative work, self-centered egoism into self-realization of species being, the fight for subsistence and survival into an expression of beauty and harmony, and, finally, the realm of necessity into a realm of freedom. But the ancients could not anticipate either the dramatic changes produced by a modern industrial society or the religious revolution of Christianity that would turn real human possibilities into unrealizable utopian visions, freedom into necessity, and earthly hopes into announcements of the *Parousia*. In the capitalist system, the potentially liberating aspects of Western technology were turned into means of intensifying labor, lengthening the workday, fragmenting the labor process, turning humans into automatons, exploiting human labor, and increasing surplus labor. The technology and social organization of the factory took the place of the shackles of ancient slavery. The immediate bonds of master and slave were replaced by the indirect despotism of wage labor, social contract, and private property. Increasing mechanization of production, rising productivity, cheapening the costs for commodities, augmenting of human labor by machinery, and shortening the time required to produce the basics for human life (necessary labor) are all turned into opportunities to increase surplus value and the rate of economic exploitation. The benefits of the scientific and technological revolutions were applied to the maintenance of capitalist social relations of production. As Marx says:

> The shortening of the working-day is, therefore, by no means what is aimed at, in capitalist production, when labour is economised by increasing its productiveness. It is only the shortening of the labour-time, necessary for the production of a definite quantity of commodities, that is aimed at. The fact that the workman, when the productiveness of his labour has been increased . . . [finishes the job sooner] by no means prevents him from continuing to work 12 hours as before, nor from producing in those 12 hours 1,200 articles instead of 120.[83]

The previous reference to Aristotle occurred in chapter 13, "Cooperation." Marx used the reference to make his point about the revolutionary transformation of handicrafts and manufacturing during the early stages of capitalist development. There the revolution was one of the social mode of production. In chapter 15, Marx deals with the

Industrial Revolution and the technological advances caused by the advent of modern machinery, the instruments of labor, and the factory system. "The starting-point of Modern Industry is, as we have shown, the revolution in the instruments of labour, and this revolution attains its most highly developed form in the organized system of machinery in a factory."[84] By reducing the technical skills required by the handicrafts, modern machinery made possible the purchase of the labor power of the whole family. Women and children could work in the factories and supervise or run the machinery. The Industrial Revolution universalized the slavery of wage labor since now the husband "sells his wife and child. He becomes a slave dealer."[85] The details of child abuse, malnourishment, child labor, deprivation, and extreme poverty during this period are well documented by Marx in the historical sections of this chapter.

Machinery aids in the production of relative surplus value by lowering costs of labor power and commodities, prolonging the workday, intensifying productivity, and increasing efficiency. It also has the added benefit of creating a systematic control over labor by introducing women and men into the labor market. But again there is a contradiction attached to these positive developments for the capitalist. According to Marx,

> the application of machinery to the production of surplus value implies a contradiction which is immanent in it, since of the two factors of the surplus value created by a given amount of capital, one, the rate of surplus value, cannot be increased, except by diminishing the other, the number of workmen. This contradiction comes to light, as soon as by the general employment of machinery in a given industry, the value of the machinery-produced commodity regulates the value of all commodities of the same sort; and it is this contradiction, that in its turn, drives the capitalist, without his being conscious of the fact, to excessive lengthening of the working-day, in order that he may compensate the decrease in the relative number of labourers exploited, by an increase not only of the relative, but of the absolute surplus-labour.[86]

The great technological and social advances have produced a social system in which the shortening of the workday for purposes of the intellectual and moral self-development of the individual is replaced by the search for increasing profits and wealth. Surplus value, the foundation for capitalist profit, can only be produced through the exploitation of the worker. With a reduction of the number of workers due to the introduction of systematic and integrated machinery in the factory, a contradiction develops. This idea will be developed further in Chapter 2 of this volume in the discussion about Marx's theories of contradiction and economic crises. For the purposes of our present analysis, he is making the argument that there is an immanent defect in the very structures of capitalism that may lead to a serious crisis or worse. The mechanization of the workplace has important micro and macro implications.

The whole production system reminds Marx of the absurdity and meaninglessness of the labors of Sisyphus. The theory of alienation developed in his early writings returns in this chapter on machinery and modern industry. The mechanization and specialization of labor by capital distorts the true relationship between intellectual and manual labor, subordinates the worker to the logic and demands of capital, turns political and social freedoms into ossified ideologies, and intensifies the economic exploitation of humankind. The community is transformed into factory cooperation and "barrack discipline" that deprive labor of its creative and aesthetic aspects. Machinery perverts its own possibilities. Reality as the ideal and potential that lies within the actual is unable to be expressed or realize itself due to the perversion of human tools and machinery for the purposes of capital accumulation and profit maximization.

This is a complete inversion of the labor process in which the worker is forced to conform to the technical and economic factors of production. Economics is no longer subservient to higher moral and intellectual values, but reduces human capacities and capabilities to the demands of machinery and markets. This inversion of reality is extended to the tight discipline and autocratic subordination of workers to the organizational needs of the factory. Marx describes this process as a "Herculean enterprise" accomplished by means of capitalists' monopoly over the means of production, the power of machinery over creative labor, the separation of manual labor from intellectual labor, and the victory of dead labor (capital) over living labor. Marx, in an interesting and ironic juxtaposing of ideas and historical periods, connects the concept of Hercules' labors with the invention of Arkwright and the legal reforms of the Spartan constitution by Lycurgus with the social regulations of the factory. Greek mythology and the reestablishment of the moral order of the cosmos, as well as the constitution and restructuring of a just society, are reduced to simply the invention of new machinery and disciplinary codes of behavior in the workplace, respectively.

The labors of Hercules were undertaken at the command of Zeus after he refused a command of the gods. Their purpose was to reestablish the good standing of Hercules with Zeus. Thus labor had a moral purpose for reestablishing the ethical order of the universe. Marx mentions the "Herculean enterprise" but refers to the difficulties of imposing labor discipline and order in the factory. These were the accomplishments of the technician and inventor Richard Arkwright. The constitution-building capabilities of the Greeks, by which the institutions and freedoms of the polis were created, were perverted to the point where Lycurgus, the founder of the Spartan constitution, is viewed as creating the legal regulations of factory work. Politics and ethics are reduced to political *techne*. Marx's reference to both Hercules and Lycurgus was mentioned to emphasize the distance between a society built around the logic of the factory and one in which labor had a moral and constitution-building content. Work extends beyond labor and physical exertions, but it also transcends simple creations of material artifacts. Work also implies a moral and political dimension that modern technology and political economy do not consider. The result of these historical developments leads to the conclusion "that machinery, after the horrors of the period of introduction and development have subsided, instead of diminishing, in the long run increase the number of slaves of labour."[87] With this critique of the abuses of modern science and technology, we have reached the limits of the application of Aristotle's theory of chrematistics to modernity.

Ethical and political ideals become mere cogs in the tragic machinery of modernity. Marx is the modern Oedipus, uncovering the hidden secrets (mysterious nature and metaphysical subtleties of the fetishism of the commodity), the many riddles (economic and social contradictions), and, ultimately, the tragedy of modernity. The answer to these riddles and contradictions is Marx's belief that industrial society looks beyond the present crippled individual to "the fully developed individual, fit for a variety of labours, ready to face any change of production, and to whom the different social functions he performs, are but so many modes of giving free scope to his own natural and acquired powers."[88]

The last reference to Aristotle in *Capital* occurs in volume 3, part V, "Division of Profit into Interest and Profit of Enterprise: Interest Bearing Capital." After discussing the natural law and economic crises of capitalist production—the tendency of the rate of profit to fall and the immanent contradictions of social production—Marx returns to the themes of chrematistic exchange from chapter 5 of the first volume of *Capital*: commercial capital, merchant's capital, and interest-bearing capital. Aristotle's theory of moral economy and critique of political economy has come full circle. Here Marx details the decomposition of modern capital in the form of the ownership of capital and the work of management and supervision. The labor of supervision and management is always necessary in societies based on class contradictions between capital and labor and the antagonisms of class ownership of property from the ancients to the moderns.

Aristotle: " Ὁ γὰρ δεσπότης οὐκ ἐν τῷ κτᾶσθαι τοὺς δούλους, ἀλλ' ἐν τῷ χρῆσθαι δούλους. . . ." ("For the master"—the capitalist—"proves himself such not by obtaining slaves"—ownership of capital which gives him power to buy labour-power—"but in employing slaves"—using labourers, nowadays wage-labourers, in the production process.) " Ἐστὶ δὲ αὐτὴ ἡ ἐπιστήμη οὐδὲν μέγα ἔχουσα οὐδὲ σεμνόν" ("But there is nothing great or sublime about this science.") "ἅ γὰρ τὸν δοῦλον ἐπίστασθαι δεῖ ποιεῖν, ἐκεῖνον δεῖ ταῦτα ἐπίστασθαι ἐπιτάττειν." ("But whatever the slave must be able to perform, the master must be able to order.") "Διὸ ὅσοις ἐξουσία μὴ αὐτοὺς κακοπαθεῖν, ἐπίτροπος λαμβάνει ταυτὴν τὴν τιμήν, αὐτοὶ δὲ πολιτεύονται ἢ φιλοσοφοῦσιν." ("Whenever the masters are not compelled to plague themselves with supervision, the manager assumes *this honour*, while the masters attend to affairs of state or study philosophy.") (Aristotle, *Politics*, Bekker ed., Book I, Chapter 7.)

Aristotle says in just so many words that supremacy in the political and economic fields imposes the functions of government upon the ruling powers, and hence that they must, in the economic field, know the art of consuming labour-power. And he adds that this supervisory work is not a matter of great moment, and that for this reason the master leaves the "honour" of this drudgery to an overseer as soon as he can afford it.[89]

Marx criticizes all attempts to mystify and then justify these relationships by turning exploitation and servitude of labor into expressions of social justice, by subverting moral economy into political economy. It is here that the apologists for both slavery and wage labor maintain the naturalness and universality of the social system, the justice of protecting individual rights of workers or the natural course of the market, and the "just compensation" of the wage contract. Profits and compensation for management and supervision are viewed as further forms of just compensation resulting from the economic expenses of the owners and personal benefits that accrue to the workers.

Now it is time to move beyond the categories of Aristotle and classical nineteenth-century political economy to the analysis of Marx's developed theory of value and surplus value.

Beyond Aristotle: Surplus Value, Abstract Labor, and Chrematistic Production

Aristotle's theory of economics and chrematistics provided Marx with a representation of the outer limits of simple commodity exchange and simple circulation of money and capital. Aristotle also provided Marx with an examination of the structural limits of the Greek economy. The limits of Greece are the limits of liberalism and commercial capitalism. Ending with his neo-Aristotelian analysis of economic liberalism, natural rights theory (life, equality, and property), and utilitarianism (Bentham and "Free-trader Vulgaris"), Marx undertakes an examination of capitalist production and expansion of his theory of value beginning with part III of volume 1 of *Capital*. "This sphere that we are deserting, within whose boundaries the sale and purchase of labour-power goes on, is in fact a very Eden of the innate rights of man."[90] The central focus now is on the social division of labor, and the process of production and the creation of absolute and relative surplus value. Where Aristotle pursued the conflicts between two contradictory forms of economic behavior—*oikonomia* and *chrematistike*, Marx shows the contradictions between the rights and liberties of market exchange and the despotism and slavery of capitalist production. Marx moves beyond chrematistic commerce and commodity exchange to chrematistic production and exploitation of surplus value. This necessitates that we move from commercial exchange to the social relations and organization of production. After one hundred and seventy-five pages of *Capital*, Marx is prepared to move beyond Aristotle and detail the process of capitalist production.

The theory of value is now expanded beyond the antinomies of exchange value and use value to include the phenomenon of self-expanding value derived from abstract labor and the structures of production. Since it is labor that gives value to commodities, the expansion of a theory of value lies in a more detailed understanding of the nature of social production. The making of products contains both a subjective component in the living labor of the worker and an objective component in the congealed, dead labor contained in the machinery and means of production. For Marx, the secret to surplus value lies in the relation between use value and exchange value. The capitalist purchases the exchange value of labor power, but because of the nature of the social relations of production has full control over the use value of labor (unpaid labor). This distinction between labor, as the total energy and work an individual is capable of producing in any given unit of time, and labor power, whose value is determined by the labor time socially necessary for its reproduction and renewal, contains the secret to Marx's theory of value. The value of labor power is measured by the wages necessary to purchase the basic means of subsistence. Capital purchases the labor power of the worker in the form of subsistence wages, but, in fact, gains access to the full labor of the individual. The time spent working in the factory by the laborer for his or her physical survival and basic subsistence is called necessary labor time, whereas the excess time spent in work over this amount is called surplus labor time. The worker sells the exchange value of labor power and the capitalist purchases the total use value of labor. The difference between exchange and use values, between labor power and labor, is the surplus produced by the worker in a particular social mode of production. An unusual condition is produced in this exchange.

Based on the principles of simple commodity exchange, equal value is exchanged for equal value. Labor has been transformed into a commodity for sale through the social division of labor and the capitalist obtains the labor power of each individual for its full worth defined as wages necessary for purchasing the basic necessities of life (means of subsistence). However, in purchasing the labor power, the capitalist controls the full labor abilities of the worker. This developed form of commodity exchange, commercial market, and production based on private property and free labor that are all legally protected by the innate rights of nature and positive law of the state form the foundation for capital. This social formation marks the transition from money to capital as self-expanding value. The transition from simple commodity exchange and money to capital is also marked by the transition to wage slavery and economic exploitation of wage labor.

In capitalist production, labor has the power to create value, as well as to transfer value. These two properties of labor act as the basis for Marx's distinction between variable and constant labor. Through the expenditure of labor, value is produced in the creation of commodities. But in this process, value is also transferred from the machinery and instruments of labor, which themselves are products of previous labor and have past labor contained in them. As we have seen already, only labor is capable of creating value. During production, part of this past, abstract labor is transferred to and preserved in the new commodity being produced as part of its wear and tear. Marx calls this the metempsychosis of value. Use value is created by the destruction of the exchange value of technology and machinery. Together with the living labor, this past, dead labor constitutes the total value of the product. Variable capital, as labor power, and constant capital, as the means and factors of production, are the two forms of value that capital has assumed and the only two causes of value creation. The historical unfolding of these dualisms, dichotomies, and contradictions in the workplace are contained in chapter 10, "The Working Day." The discussion of equality, fairness, and justice in market exchange in parts I and II of *Capital* are transformed into the study of exploitation, slavery, and degradation of labor in the later sections of this volume on the class relations of production. It is no longer a free and fair exchange, but one characterized by a situation in which the worker "is compelled by social conditions, to sell the whole of his active life, his very capacity for work, for the prices of the necessities of life, his birthright for a mess of pottage."[91]

The social system is so constructed that the goal of capitalist production is to produce increasing amounts of surplus value of which there are two kinds: absolute surplus value and relative surplus value. This is the real foundation of a modern chrematistic economy. If surplus value is obtained by reducing the necessary labor time (wages) and increasing surplus labor time (profits), then absolute surplus value achieves this by prolonging the hours of the workday. Relative surplus value accomplishes the same end by reducing necessary labor time. Both seek the same results by causing a fall in the value of labor power and thus a fall in its overall cost by increasing labor productivity, and lowering the costs of production and constant capital. The explanation for lowering the exchange value of commodities lies in the law of value and the law of capitalist competition. To increase surplus value, it is necessary for the capitalist to gain a larger control over the market. This explains the drive to cheapen costs through increased productivity of labor. Thus technology and the means of production are transformed and perverted by the goal of profit maximization. In turn, the goals of reducing the work load, increasing the satisfaction and inner productivity of labor, and fulfilling the modern potential for a moral economy are sacrificed.

Classical Antiquity and the Critique of Liberalism

One can argue that Marx's method is very complex and subtle. The prevailing form of economic analysis in *Capital* comes from a combination of Kant's critique of pure and practical reason, the dialectical development of the categories and structures of political economy from Hegel's phenomenology and logic, and the general framework of the argument comes from Aristotle's metaphysics and physics. By breaking down the analysis of the capitalist mode of production into matter or substance (commodity) and form (social relations of production), the structure of Aristotle's metaphysics is being used to frame Marx's critique of liberalism. This, of course, is united to the epistemological arguments of Hegel that the object (commodity) and its properties (quality and quantity, essence and appearance, mediate and immediate, and logic and being) are, in fact, reflections of the subject and self-consciousness (class relations of production). This is subtly integrated into the "critique" of the theories of classical British political economy.

However, at every corner and turn of Marx's economic theory, Aristotle stands as a signpost. When Marx defines the nature of commodity, exchange, money, capital, and surplus value, he turns to Aristotle for guidance, inspiration, and vision. Marx begins *Capital* by stating that the simplest component of wealth and exchange in a capitalist economy is the commodity and in part IV, when shifting his examination to the production of relative surplus value, he states that the fundamental form of the capitalist mode of production is social cooperation. He refers to Aristotle when he inquires into the nature of the commensurability and equality of exchange, the transcendental and historical foundations of commodity exchange and money circulation, the nature of capital and profits, the contradictions of capital production and surplus value, the social nature of species being and the social form of production, and the potentialities of industrial production and technological advancement.

At every important stage in his analysis of exchange, circulation, and production, a reference to Aristotle appears to give weight to his argument, providing it with a broader historical context and deeper philosophical tradition. There are three references to Aristotle in part I of the first volume of *Capital* on money and commodities when he touches upon Aristotle's ideas on the common substance and commensurability of exchange, ancient slavery, and the dualism between use value and exchange value. There are two references to Aristotle in part II on the transformation of money into capital in which he distinguishes between a moral economy (*oikonomia*) and a political economy (*chrematistike*) and between the profits of merchants' capital and the usury of interest-bearing capital. Finally, there are two references in part IV on the production of relative surplus value in which Marx refers to the social and political nature of mankind and the utopian potential of technology and emancipation from slavery. No mention is made of Aristotle in part II on the production of absolute surplus value or the other sections of the work. But by this point, Marx had moved beyond simple commodity exchange and commercial circulation into the method and structure of modern capitalist production.

Marx's critique of liberalism and its form of political economy represents an expansion of Aristotle's critique of chrematistics and profit accumulation. As Marx moves in his analysis of capitalism from commodities, exchange, money, and capital to surplus value; as he moves from his initial theory of value and exchange value, his theory of price and money circulation to his theory of surplus value; as he moves from simple commodity exchange of products to the exchange of labor power; and as he moves from simple production of commodities to production of profits, he supports his argument, he grounds his justification, and anchors his criticism in Aristotle's defense of a moral economy and rejection of political economy.

In the material discussed above, there has been an attempt to read *Capital* by first following the specific references to Aristotle and then proceeding to unpack Marx's own analysis. From this depth exegesis of *Capital*, we have seen how Marx borrows heavily from Aristotle's *Nicomachean Ethics* and the *Politics* to supply both the matter and form of his critique of modern political economy. Those elements of Aristotle's theory that come out in the eight references to him include: Aristotle's theory of value and the commensurability and equality of the market; the distinction between use value and exchange value; a critique of a market economy, chrematistics, and defense of a moral economy (*oikonomia*); the emancipatory potential of technology; the relations between a moral economy and political community; a theory of public discourse, practical ethics, and democracy; the notion of self-realization of human potential and the rational nature of humanity (species being); and, finally, by implication, a discussion of the good life and happiness (*eudaimonia*) in the political community, on the one hand, and friendship and citizenship, on the other. Below the surface throughout *Capital*, Marx is subtly juxtaposing the modern political theories of chrematistics (natural rights theory and utilitarian theory) with Aristotle's classical statement on moral economy. Using both an immanent and an ethical critique, he moves from a negation and rejection of political economy, market rationality, and the modern norms of rights, individualism, and pleasure to a consideration of a moral economy grounded in justice, discursive rationality, and values of virtue, community, species being, and democracy. Instead of performing a philosophical critique of modernity as he had done in his earliest criticisms of Hegel's theory of the state and alienated labor, he constructs a criticism of liberalism based on ethical and metaethical (structures of political economy) considerations.[92]

As in the case of the *Paris Manuscripts*, however, the development of the positive content of the argument is undertaken indirectly through the critique of the structures and values of political economy. In his immanent critique, he shows the incompatibility between the values of liberalism (life, liberty, property, pleasure, and self-interest) and the structures of wage slavery in the factory. But at a more profound level, with his references to Aristotle, he reveals a new level to his critique. It is Aristotle's theory of moral economy that supplies the ethical principles that are incorporated into his analysis and transcendence of capitalism. The structures of capital undermine the possibilities for human emancipation with wage labor and exploitation; democratic interaction and public participation with a slavery of surplus value and capital production; a moral community grounded in friendship and civic virtue with a morality of self-interest, competition and profits; individual freedom and self-development with a leveling of moral and intellectual virtues in a morality of the market; and, finally, practical wisdom (*phronesis*) and *praxis* of the ancients with the priorities of Enlightenment science and technology. Marx's "critique of political economy" relies on two important traditions: a radicalization of the critical method in Kant's critiques of pure and practical reason, which includes his theory of the categorical imperative, the notion of a kingdom of ends and its rejection of a utilitarian morality of means, and the acceptance of Aristotle's critique of chrematistics and defense of moral economy.

Marx's critical theory of economics in *Capital* represents a defense of moral economy, an ethical condemnation of capitalism, and a theory of social justice. Aristotle's theory of moral economy provides Marx with the ethical foundations for this critique of capitalist production. Using Aristotle, he has shown the limits of the structures, values, and categories of nineteenth-century liberalism.[93] His critique of political economy is filtered through his appreciation of Athenian justice based on political democracy, civic friendship, mutual sharing, and economic moderation. Like the Greeks, he integrates democracy, freedom, and equality as the basis for a just society whose goal is the maturation of noble virtue and the good life. In effect, what Marx has done is to supply the missing ingredient to Aristotle's *Politics*. By developing a comprehensive theory of class, inequality, exploitation, and economic crisis, he has made a substantive contribution to democracy begun 2,500 years ago by Kleisthenes. To civic virtue and political participation, he has joined *economic* freedom, equality, and democracy. In Chapter 2 of this volume Marx's theory of justice is expanded with the development of his neo-Aristotelian theory of participatory democracy.

From Marx's dissertation on Epicurus's physics, his integration of ethics and science, happiness (*ataraxia*) and theory of meteors and heavenly bodies to Marx's appreciation of Aristotle's theory of moral economy and the political community, there is a closing of the philosophical circle begun in his earliest writings. From religion to economics, from Epicurus's critique of universality and natural law in physics to Marx's historical materialism, critique of reification and alienation, and critique of natural law in economics, Marx returns to his original insights into the nature of reality and the relations between concepts and existence, theory and history (*The Difference between the Democritean and Epicurean Philosophy of Nature*, p. 72). In the end, he completes his initial ideas with his defense of the freedom of self-consciousness against all forms of religiosity and adherence to alien products of the economic mind whether from utilitarianism or classical political economy. In the end the truth is the same as in the beginning. Quoting from Aeschylus's *Prometheus Bound*, Marx began his dissertation in the same way he concluded his major work *Capital*:

The confession of Prometheus: "In simple words, I hate the pack of gods," is its own confession, its own aphorism against all heavenly and earthly gods who do not acknowledge human self-consciousness as the highest divinity. It will have none other beside . . .

"Be sure of this, I would not change my state
Of evil fortune for your servitude
Better to be the servant of this rock
Than to be faithful boy to Father Zeus."[94]

[Or as he will say in his later writings:
"Better to be the servant of this rock
Than to be faithful boy to Father Capital."]

Chapter Two

Ancient and Modern Democracy: Politics and Epistemology in Marx's Later Writings

Introduction

Having completed our discussion of Marx's and Aristotle's economic theories and critiques of market exchange, we will now turn to their theories of political community and democracy. The latter are fascinating concepts in Marx's political theory for it contains his political and social ideals, his response to the crises of capitalist society, the concrete, moral content of his critique of practical reason, and his solutions to the epistemological questions raised in eighteenth- and nineteenth-century German debates about the nature of knowledge and truth. Political *praxis*, practical discourse, and democratic activity represent solutions to the nature of the just society (political theory), the nature of the free and creative workplace (political economy), and the problems and dangers surrounding political science and political *techne* as forms of knowledge: politics as a science and as an art (epistemology). Insights into the direction and diversity of Marx's political theory require that we begin with an examination of fifth- and fourth-century B.C. Athenian democracy and Aristotle's conception of the democratic polity.

As we saw in the last chapter, Marx was steeped in the political, economic, and aesthetic perspectives of the ancients. In particular, through his readings of Herodotus's *The History*, Thucydides' *The Peloponnesian Wars*, and Aristotle's *Nicomachean Ethics* and *Politics*, as well as nineteenth-century British, French, and German historians of classical Greece such as George Grote, Theodor Mommsen, Georg Schömann, Carl Hermann, A. Böckh, Fustel de Coulanges, and De la

Malle, Marx was aware of the developing new and positive evaluation of Athenian democracy, which had moved beyond the negative and aristocratic appellations of mob role, irrationality, and anarchy of Athens in the fifth and fourth centuries.[1] Some of this material appeared in the eight-page section of the *Grundrisse* that dealt with the classical world. There was little that has been added to the present-day knowledge of Athens that was not available during Marx's lifetime, except for the discovery of one of Aristotle's student's notes *The Constitution of Athens* and later archaeological materials unearthed since his death.[2] However, the basic structures of Athenian democracy as presented in the scholarship from England and the Continent were very similar to what we know today about the Greek polis. After Marx's references to Aristotle in *Capital*, there is almost no reference to him in his later writings. But by this time Marx's whole economic and political theory was standing on the ruins of the past.

Alan Gilbert in his book *Democratic Equality* has argued that Marx's view of the Paris Commune of 1871 represented the institutional design that made his Aristotelian perspective real and alive. Gilbert sees the Commune as the expression of Marx's vision of Greek ideals and ethical vision.[3] Though there is no direct statement by Marx connecting the two events, there are enough normative and institutional similarities that would make a comparison helpful for understanding his theory of the state. This argument has been made elsewhere, but the connections have generally been made by showing the continuity of thought between Marx's early philosophical writings and the later political ones. To this connection we must add the volumes of material he was reading by German and English historians on the subject of ancient Greece.[4]

Over two thousand years separate the political and economic experiments in Athens and the Paris Commune. The democratic imagination of Athens and Paris were similar in values, purpose, and structures. Both emphasized direct democracy, popular sovereignty of the general will, accountability and supervision of magistrates and officials by the public (recall and *euthynai*), pay for public service, and a critique of bureaucracy and professionalism. Questions arise over the nature of the classical and modern views of democracy, equality, and freedom. How much is the latter an expression of the former in Marx's eyes? And did the Athenian polis offer him a vantage point from which to interpret the French Civil War and the formation of the Commune in defiance of both the Prussian and French armies? Did the Greeks sensitize him to the type of institutions necessary to have popular control and self-determination? And finally, did Marx see the Paris Commune as expanding beyond the limits of fifth-century Athens to break new grounds in political and economic democracy? Did it offer a solution to the Aristotelian dilemma of natural and unnatural slavery? I believe the Greeks provided Marx with a concrete ideal that was just emerging in the nineteenth century after many years of enforced hibernation.

Historical Overview of Classical Athenian Democracy

We must begin with the questions, what is democracy and how did the Greeks themselves understand what they had accomplished in history? The first extant reference to democracy (*demokratia*, or power of the *demos*) is found in Herodotus's writings on the Persian Wars in the second half of the fifth century. Herodotus speaking through the Persian Otanes said, "The rule of the many, on the other hand, has, in the first place, the fairest of names, to wit, *isonomy*; and further it is free from all those outrages which a king is wont to commit. There, places are given by lot, the magistrate is answerable for what he does, and measures rest with the commonality. I vote, therefore, that we do away with monarchy, and raise the people to power. For the people are all in all."[5]

Herodotus's definition of democracy emphasized the political and legal equality of all citizens. The Athenians (adult male Athenians) were equal before the law, as well as equal in their rights and free to participate in their creation, execution, and perpetuation in the Assembly, public offices, and jury courts. The fundamental principles here are *isonomia* (political equality) and *isegoria* (freedom and equal right of speech). These two principles of free speech and political equality were manifested in three key Athenian institutions: selection of officials by lot, accountability of all public officials, and decision making by popular sovereignty in the Assembly. The use of selection by means of a lottery limited the growth of animosities and factions, aristocracy and privilege, officials and bureaucracy. This political apparatus restricted the development of independent organs within the state capable of interfering with the workings and sovereignty of the *demos* (people). Pericles, in his famous Funeral Oration made during the winter of 431–30 B.C. and honoring the first Athenian war casualties of the Peloponnesian War with Sparta and its allies, praises the democratic spirit of Athens. In particular, he emphasizes the equality of all citizens under the law; public life as open to all; tolerant attitudes within the political community; and the principle of the rule of law.

> Our constitution is called a democracy (demokratia) because power is in the hands not of a minority but of the whole people. When it is a question of settling private disputes, everyone is equal before the law; when it is a question of putting one person before another in positions of public responsibility, what counts is not membership of a particular class, but the actual ability which the man possess. No one, so long as he has it in him to be of service to the state, is kept in political obscurity because of poverty. And, just as our political life is free and open, so is our day-to-day life in our relations with each other. . . . We are free and tolerant in our private lives; but in public affairs we keep to the law. This is because it commands our deepest respect.[6]

By the fifth century B.C. the institutional form and guiding principles of Athenian democracy began to take shape through the reforms of Solon, Kleisthenes, Ephialtes, and Pericles. Solon introduced popular elections in the Assembly and opened up the *demos* to the nonaristocracy; Kleisthenes transferred all power to the Assembly; and Ephialtes broadened the powers of the Assembly, *Boule*, and jury courts.[7] It was during the midcentury that the fundamental mosaic of popular institutions was created in which popular participation, equality, and individual freedom were institutionalized in the political sphere of Attica. During this period, the three central institutions that gave voice to popular sovereignty were formed: the Assembly (*Ekklesia*), the Council of 500 (*Boule*), and the jury courts (*Dikasteria*). They expressed the general will and consciousness of the whole *demos* and in the process produced a model of democracy whose principles and values would last for over two thousand years. It was just this experience with democracy that was incorporated into the political vision of Marx with the formation of the Paris Commune. The Athenian political system, which evolved over a period of two centuries, was in the end not vanquished by internal social anarchy or civil disruptions, mob rule, or the irrationality of the populace, but by the victorious armies of the invading Macedonians under Philip on the field of Chaeronea (338 B.C.).

Solon (638–558 B.C.), responding to the ravages of domestic class conflict, introduced radical social and political reform in Athens. He forgave debts, brought legal protection to the peasants, and began to integrate the peasants into the privileges of the aristocracy. Four propertied classes were created that would remake the Athenian landscape: *pentakosiomedimnoi* (aristocracy), *hippeis* (cavalrymen), *zeugitai* (hoplite warriors), and *thetes* (laborers). These new groupings gave access to graduated rights to public office. Solon was involved in a delicate balancing of economic power and political office. Only the two upper classes could hold the most important political and military positions in society. But the poorest citizens (*thetes*) were entitled to vote in the Assembly and law courts. At this time, the most important political organ was the Council of the Areopagus composed of former high aristocratic officials known as archons. But Solon introduced limited checks on the aristocracy by moving the appeals on the judicial decisions of the Areopagus to the Assembly acting as the *heliaia* and by the initiation of public prosecution for wrongdoing by any citizen regardless of social class. The power of the aristocracy was beginning to be questioned and constitutionally limited.

With Kleisthenes, about 508–7 B.C., the democratic reforms took a qualitative leap forward. He, too, began to circumscribe the powers of the aristocracy who continued to hold the highest offices in the polis. A new criterion for citizenship was created with the formation of ten new tribes based on geography (Athens, countryside, and coastal areas), rather than on kinship or family relations. Now all decisions were submitted to the Assembly and not the Areopagus. Whereas Solon had instituted a more popular government through judicial reform, Kleisthenes created a new legislative system stressing the popular sovereignty of the Assembly. The political rights and powers of Athenian citizenship were greatly expanded in proportion to the loss of power of the old aristocracy.

Ephialtes (462 B.C.) directly confronted and attacked the powers and privileges of the members of the Areopagus by bringing them to trial for their misconduct while in public office. He stripped the Areopagus of its acquired powers as the guardian of the constitution and divided these powers among the Assembly, *Boule,* and jury courts. The all-important judicial oversight over all public officials through review and public accountability while in office was removed from the Areopagus to the *Boule* and jury system. As the Assembly emerged out of these reforms, it gave to the people nominal and formal rights of self-government and self-determination. This democratic system survived the thirty years' war with Sparta and two attempts at oligarchic overthrow of the constitution. It was a remarkable and resilient democratic achievement.

Aristotle (384–22 B.C.), in book VI, chapter 2 of the *Politics,* outlines in more detail the institutional features of democracy.[8] Its defining structural features are stated most clearly and succinctly in the long summary he provides. They include (1) the eligibility and election of all citizens to office by lot; (2) all citizens to participate as both ruler and ruled in turn; (3) no property qualifications for office; (4) short-term limits and rotation of government positions; (5) offices to be open to as many citizens as possible; (6) the judicial function to be exercised by all citizens through lot; (7) all important cases affecting the polis, especially treason, questions of citizenship, and cases of public scrutiny of officials (*eisangelia*) to be handled by the *demos* in the jury system; (8) the popular Assembly was to be sovereign in all matters; and finally, (9) payment for participation in the Assembly, council, and the law courts. This system is arranged so as to prevent the accumulation and aggregation of political power around a particular individual or office of the state. It opens the whole apparatus of the legislative, judicial, and executive functions of government to popular participation, control, and supervision. "For if, as is held by some, freedom (*eleutheria*) is especially to be found in democracy, and also equality (*isotes*), this condition is most fully realized when all alike share most fully in the constitution. But since the people are a majority, and the decision of the majority is sovereign, this must be a democracy (*demokratia*)."[9]

The Assembly (*Ekklesia*) was the general meeting of the full citizen body of Athens about forty times a year to discuss, deliberate, and ultimately decide upon all the major issues that affected the polis: war and peace, alliances and treaties, access to grain and sea lanes, citizenship, impeachment and ostracism, taxation and revenues, social and fiscal policy, revenues and public building construction, festivals and religious events, and elected military and finance officials.[10] The meetings were held on the Pnyx about three hundred yards from the Acropolis, southwest of the Agora. For the most important issues of ostracism and granting of citizenship, a quorum of six thousand citizens was necessary. This is also the probable limit of those who could fit into the assembly area on the Pnyx in the late fifth century. Once the discussion started, any citizen could participate and discussions were decided on the basis of a majority hand count. Ballots were used only in the most serious cases. The agenda (*probouleumata*) for these meetings was set by the *prytaneis*, as the standing committee of the *Boule*. The prytany was composed of fifty members of a tribe (out of the *Boule's* five hundred members) who took responsibility monthly for the day-to-day operations of the state. It was to this small group that foreign ambassadors would first come when arriving in Athens and from this group that the chairman, to preside over the *Boule* and Assembly, was chosen daily by lot. Once selected, the Athenian citizen could never occupy this office again.

The *Boule*, or Council of 500, which was created by Kleisthenes, not only prepared the agenda for every Assembly, but was responsible for overseeing the decrees and laws of the general will; drafted proposals for consideration by the Assembly; was the agent of the Assembly for diplomatic and financial issues; and had scrutiny and oversight over the implementation of Assembly decisions, internal revenues and expenditures, treasuries of religious funds, leases of mines, lands, taxes, and import duties, collection of tribute and allied war funds, and over the army, navy, and ports, especially the building of triremes, and so forth.[11] The *Boule* met over two hundred days a year, which means it met every day except on days of religious festivals. It also drafted some legislation and had oversight over the implementation of its own decisions, especially in the areas of internal revenues and public expenditures. This political organ was thus the representative and executive of the Assembly. Through its powers of financial audits and examinations (*euthynai*), it had control over public officials. Trials for misconduct and misappropriation of funds would be conducted by the courts.

According to David Stockton, "only the Boule—and those who kept in close touch with it—had a comprehensive grasp of the overall state of the public finances. In brief, it was the body to which all the multifarious agents of the Athenian *demos* were, in the first instance at least, answerable and accountable."[12] Ultimate authority always rested in the hands of the people, but the *Boule* was the working committee that ran the daily operations of the government. Members of the council came from all over Attica and were chosen by lot, thereby reflecting the composition of the Assembly itself. Participation was for one year and each citizen was limited to two non-consecutive terms. The *Boule* was also charged with running public buildings and festivals, and could enforce its own decisions through limited fines and imprisonment.

By the second half of the fifth century, the judicial system was in the hands of the *Dikasteria*, or jury courts. Six thousand Athenians chosen by lot were to participate in this system each year. Pericles introduced pay for jury service and this opened the judicial system up to the broadest range of the demos—the poor. The pay of two obols a day represented about half the daily wages of an average laborer at the time. Payment for attendance at the Assembly, which was introduced in the 390s, was two to three times that of the jury pay. About one-seventh to one-fifth of the total citizen population of Athens would participate in the judicial system each year. Having no professional lawyers, prosecutors, or public defenders, the administration of justice was performed by the average citizen at both the local level (judges in the *deme*) and the state level. The juries themselves could number from 201 to several thousand jurists for the most important cases. Socrates' trial had 501 jurists or *dicasts*.

What did these institutions mean for popular sovereignty, direct democracy, and self-determination? First, they meant that substantial portions of the *demos* could participate in the legislative, executive, and judicial decisions that affected every citizen. A political culture that incorporated art and tragedy, religion and worship, education and philosophy developed that suffused every citizen, encouraged their broad political participation, enticed their interests, piqued their curiosity, and occupied a good part of their leisure time. From deliberating in the local demes in their villages and small communities to their activities in the jury courts, *Boule*, and Assembly, many citizens participated in the broad fabric of political life. To this must be added all those involved as military leaders, financial officers of the state, public officials, ambassadors, and a whole host of other public servants of the *demos*. And all these were accountable through the *euthynai* and *eisangelia* to the constant review and protective eyes of the citizen bodies. It is difficult to convey to those who have lived under the modern variations of democracy, the depth and range, the culture and practice of these democratic institutions established by the Greeks. As opposed to the modern overemphasis on individual liberties, natural rights, passive voting, and protection of property, the Greeks saw the expression of human nature and freedom in terms of political participation at every level.[13] This has been very nicely summarized by Stockton who says that the Athenians differed from all others

> in their attitude to life, the very air of individuality, open-mindedness, and independence which they breathe, the excitement and novelty (and, implicitly, the fragility) of this great experiment in participation and equality. . . . In its eloquent advocacy of the virtues of "government of the people, by the people, and for the people" it was the earliest, and for many readers remains the finest, statement of what a democracy should aspire to be.[14]

It is from the philosophy of Aristotle and the Greek *praxis* of democracy that Marx derived aspects of his vision of modern participatory democracy. Throughout his life he was critical of the limits of the one-sidedness of liberalism. Where it sought to protect individual rights, he saw a defense of property, self-interest, and market liberties; where it sought political emancipation, he saw an emancipation of narrow egoism; where it defended market and economic liberties, he saw inequality, class abuses, and exploitation. Political rights and legal freedom without the appropriate economic and social structures to support them lead to political oppression and economic exploitation, liberty without freedom, individual rights without community and species being. In this situation, the very institutions of liberalism undermined its own stated values. Liberalism is a stage toward socialism because only socialism can defend, incorporate, and expand upon the former's fundamental principles. Individual rights and differences can only be protected in a society without gross inequalities of power and wealth. The latter makes a mockery of the principles of liberalism. The protection of individual rights, freedom of self-determination and self-realization, as well as personal choices of happiness require a prior social emancipation. Marx's critique of liberalism implies a transcendence of its emancipatory potential and contradictory value system. It also entails a rejection of its restrictive principles, such as the absolute protection of property, market rationality, and class privileges.

From this perspective, Marx's discourse on democracy is a continuous attempt to expand the rationality and emancipatory potential within liberalism, while leaving behind many of its anthropological assumptions about the nature of men and women and its market (chrematistic) connotations. Capitalist liberty undermines social freedom, market choices distort options for the general good, self-interest foils attempts at self-realization, the private sphere weakens public responsibilities and obligations, and individual utility eclipses the possibilities of political happiness. In other words, liberalism is an incoherent political philosophy that transforms a moral economy into a political economy. The very possibility of realizing our potential as rational human beings, of defining our sense of self in terms of the community and others, and of developing a personal identity, fairness, social justice, and virtuous character in terms of friendship toward others is lost. Liberalism emphasizes an artificially created sense of self defined in terms of unlimited consumer wants, individual taste, and private, market choices that can only be maintained by repressing those very characteristics that make us human and life worth living: shared values of the community, happiness, rational discourse, democratic self-determination, and a sense of both the joy and mystery of life. In *On the Jewish Question*, Marx's juxtaposing of political and human emancipation, market liberties and political freedoms, natural rights and species development, and liberalism and democracy forms the basis for his radical critique of capitalism and the theoretical foundations for his view of true democracy.

Nearly thirty years lie between his discourse on rights and emancipation in his early writings and his analysis of the Paris Commune of 1871, but the continuity is clear. There seems to be interesting similarities between the institutions of the Commune and those of fifth-century classical Athens. A more fully developed examination of the Paris Commune has been undertaken elsewhere.[15] However, the most important structural components of this experiment rested in those aspects of democracy that fifth-century Athens and nineteenth-century Paris shared: the desire for popular sovereignty, self-determination, social responsibility, public scrutiny and accountability of its officials (*euthynai* and *eisangelia*, on the one hand, and recall, on the other), small-scale political communities, and political equality and freedom. Where the Paris Commune differs from classical Athens is in its direct democracy. Athens had nearly two centuries to develop and perfect its political institutions, whereas the Commune had only about two and a half months. Marx did not have the time to develop the full implications of a theory of public space for communication and deliberation. Most of his life was spent criticizing and rejecting the class foundations of the bourgeois state.

Aristotle on Political Democracy

As has already been mentioned in endnote 8, within the last few years there has been a growing body of literature detailing another side to Aristotle's political theory. Whereas in the past, the emphasis in Aristotelian scholarship has been decidedly on an aristocratic interpretation of the best society, this has shifted in recent years to include notice of Aristotle's positive treatment of democracy in books III and IV of the *Politics* to which I would now like to turn. This work is extremely difficult because of its denseness and terseness. Aristotle distinguishes between the three correct forms of constitution (*politeia*): kingship, aristocracy, and polity, or the rule by the one, few, or many and the three deviant forms: tyranny, oligarchy, and democracy, or the rule by the one, wealthy, or poor. What distinguishes the first group from the second is that in kingship, aristocracy, and polity, there is a concern by the citizens and rulers for the common good. There are statements throughout the *Politics* that could be taken as defenses for kingship, aristocracy, or polity as the ideal form of constitution. But throughout his work, there is also a strong indication of Aristotle's positive treatment of democracy. When describing the citizen in book III, Aristotle chooses the democratic constitution as his starting place; he argues in chapters 9, 13, and 15 that the democratic mass should be sovereign, favorably compares democracy to aristocracy and kingship, and in book IV equates the good form of democracy with the polity (one of the best forms of government). Whatever the ideal form of constitution is (and this is never really clear), democracy is a more important political form to Aristotle than has been traditionally recognized. If and when the debate over Aristotle's ideal and best forms is ever settled, the fact remains that Aristotle's description of the structures and ideals of Greek democracy and its various constitutional forms was invaluable to Marx.[16]

Aristotle begins book III by describing the general characteristics of the citizen as someone who participates in "giving judgements and in holding office."[17] By participating in the key offices of state (military, financial, ambassadorial, and so forth), in the deliberative functions of the assembly, and in judicial offices of the jury courts, the members of the political community manifest their citizenship. Aristotle begins with a participatory concept of democracy for "as soon as a man becomes entitled to participate in office, deliberative or judicial, we deem him to be a citizen of that state."[18] The citizen has a special status in society for he may share in the honors of state, that is, holding office. Another characteristic of the citizen is that he is sovereign and is capable of ruling and being ruled by, for the purpose of the good and noble life, individuals who are equal and alike. " 'Ruling and being ruled in turn' is one element in liberty, and the democratic idea of justice is in fact numerical equality, not equality based on merit; and when this idea of what is just prevails, the multitude must be sovereign, and whatever the majority decides is final and constitutes justice. For, they say, there must be equality for each of the citizens."[19]

The final goals are happiness (*eudaimonia*), virtue (*arete*), and wisdom (*phronesis*)—the just society. Citizenship is part of the wider network of friendship. The polis was organized to foster moral and intellectual virtue among its sharing members; to develop their potential and capabilities to perfection. This is accomplished through participation in the political process. In turn, citizens privately own property through the *oikos*, but hold it for the common use and benefit of the full community. It is certainly not private in the modern sense of the term. In book VII, Aristotle states, "We do not agree with those who have said that property should be communally owned, but we do believe that there should be a friendly arrangement for its common use, and that none of the citizens should be without means of support."[20]

According to Aristotle, "justice is equality; . . . but only for those that are equal."[21] The basis of the polis is equality and justice, that is, giving what fairly and rightfully belongs to persons on the basis of their citizenship. The actual criterion of merit and equality rests with birth (king), virtue (aristocracy), or free citizenship (democratic polity). Aristotle is continuing the argument raised in the *Nicomachean Ethics* about the criteria of merit, sovereignty, and citizenship. Who should hold office in society: the one, the few, or the many? Which criterion should be the basis for making this determination: wealth and family, virtue, or numerical superiority? He concludes that they are all bad and unjust. All eventually lead to one form of tyranny or another: the democratic tyranny of the majority, the tyranny of the single ruler, and even the oligarchic tyranny of the virtuous.

The dilemma is temporarily resolved in book III as Aristotle carefully and cautiously moves toward democracy as being the best form of constitution. Seven times in the course of this book he articulates his reasons for viewing democracy as the best possible alternative.[22] First, the mass of people are better judges than the few because collectively they are able to perceive and judge more comprehensively and completely. In body and spirit, mind and character their collective wisdom is greater than that of a few individuals.

For it is possible that the many, no one of whom taken singly is a sound man, may yet, taken all together, be better than the few, not individually, but collectively in the same way that a feast to which all contribute is better than one supplied at one man's expense. For even where there are many people, each has some share of virtue and practical wisdom, and when they are brought together, just as in the mass they become as it were one man with many pairs of feet and hands and many senses, so also do they become one in regard to character and intelligence. That is why the many are better judges of works of music and poetry: some judge some parts, some others, but their collective pronouncement is a verdict upon all the parts. And it is this that gives sound men their superiority over any individual man from the masses.[23]

The many are better judges of music and poetry than the few. As in the case of a feast, it is better when all contribute than when it is given by one man. Second, democracy provides for the structural stability of society. Third, *praxis* or political experience itself creates an expertise for forming opinions and making judgments in the same way that the user of a house will be a better judge of its quality and utility. Fourth, since the deliberative and judicial processes require the participation of many people, it is necessary that a numerical majority should be citizens of the polis. Fifth, the corporate body of democratic citizens are collectively stronger, richer, and better. They share more power, wealth, and virtue as a group than any other small minority in the polis. The sixth justification for democracy rests on the virtue and practical wisdom of the members of the polis acting in harmony. In their collective deliberation and participation, the full citizen body possesses a virtue and wisdom surpassing even the best of its members; collectively it is more just. Finally, the many are not as easily corrupted by fame or wealth as the few. Nor is their judgment as corruptible. They are also, for Aristotle, less likely to fall victim to passions or bad temper. By their very numbers, they will be able to contribute more to the military, financial, and political well-being and stability of the state. Even among the many citizens, each shares virtue and wisdom to some degree that, when added to the collective deliberative and judicial bodies, makes a qualitative difference.

Aristotle defended a conception of the democratic polity seven times in response to seven different types of issues he raised in book III: who is sovereign and what are the intelligence and character qualifications necessary for rule; what is the nature of political stability; should experts rule and should they be held accountable to the mass of people; who should participate in the council, jury courts, and assembly; should contributions of wealth, nobility of family heritage, and moral and intellectual virtue be factors in the claims to justice and sovereignty; who can make legitimate claims to political honors and offices; and should man or the law rule in the polis? As Aristotle moved from one series of questions to the next, he continued to make the case for the necessity of a participatory democracy. However, this issue is complicated by Aristotle's references to nobility of character and a life of virtuous excellence before the first and after the fourth defenses of democracy.[24] What is the relationship between an aristocracy of virtue and a democratic polity? Why does Aristotle seem to defend democracy at one point and aristocracy at another? Certainly, the fact that this work is not a book, but a collection of Aristotle's notes may contribute to the confusion.[25] After the second reference to the virtuous and noble life, why does Aristotle return to defend democracy three more times? He could be anticipating his later defense of a mixed government in book IV. One explanation that seems to correspond to changes in the text is that Aristotle moves between different levels of analysis without giving the reader fair warning. At times, it appears that he is talking about pure or ideal states (kingship, aristocracy, and polity), and at other times, he is referring to more complex societies with a mixture of classes. There seems to be a tension within his methodology between his idealism and his empiricism. More on this in the subsection entitled "Epistemology and Politics in Aristotle's *Politics*."

If the locations of his defenses of aristocracy in the middle of his consideration of democracy are not accidental, then it is interesting to note that after the second reference there is a change in the type of discussion about democracy itself. This leads me to suspect that the tension between democracy and aristocracy is merely apparent. The first four defenses of democracy are based on Aristotle's view of sovereignty and the centrality of political participation. After the first defense of democracy, he introduces the concept of the "spheres of sovereignty" by distinguishing between two forms of democratic participation: the exercise of official duties and responsibilities and participation in the courts, council, and assembly.[26] By distinguishing between these two types of participation, Aristotle has structurally differentiated between the spheres and types of participation appropriate to the virtuous few and the many. The majority has sovereign responsibility for deliberating, deciding, and judging issues. They make the laws, enforce them, and adjudicate disputes about them. The virtuous have the responsibility and honor of holding the offices necessary for the maintenance of the polis: military generals, ambassadors, financial experts, and so forth. Sovereignty lies in the hands of the majority of citizens, while the official duties of implementing policy lie in the hands of the aristocracy.

The majority also has the obligation of enforcing its sovereignty by means of periodic review and the procedures of accountability of officials in office. In book II, there appears to be a recommendation for the relative equalization of property as being essential for a just and stable society. "It is clear, therefore, that it is not enough for a legislator to equalize property: he must aim at fixing an amount midway between extremes."[27] To an equal and moderate amount of property, Aristotle also thought that there had to be an equalization and moderation of appetites. But to this egalitarian element in popular sovereignty, Aristotle also introduced an element of aristocratic inequality of honors and offices. In a similar approach, as found in the example of Solon, Aristotle called for an inequality of status and hierarchy of political power in the more technical offices of the polis. Thus, there is relative economic equality with differential political status. All this, however, presupposed the popular sovereignty and participation of the majority in the deliberative and judicial processes of the state. Each group in this integrated society would get its fair economic and political share.[28]

Chapter 11 contains the first four defenses of democracy. In chapter 12, Aristotle returns to the issues of justice, equality, and virtue found in chapter 9. Here he talks about the appropriate distribution of fine musical instruments among a variety of different pipe players with different skills:

> The use of the better instrument ought to belong to the better performer. If one man is outstandingly superior in pipe-playing, but far inferior in birth or good looks (even supposing that birth and good looks are each a greater good than the skill of pipe playing, and its superiority to them is greater in proportion than the superiority of this player's ability to that of the rest), even then, I say he should still get the best pipes.[29]

In the last paragraph of this chapter, Aristotle claims that noble birth and wealth have legitimate claims to the honors and offices of the polis. However, in the last sentence of this same paragraph he returns to the issue of citizenship. It is this distinction between those who are the citizens and those who are the officeholders that offers us the best possibility of resolving the conflict between virtue and freedom, individual excellence and collective wisdom, and aristocracy and democracy. In the next chapter, Aristotle begins to examine democracy from a new perspective. That is, his model of society is now more complex: "Now suppose all these to be present in a single city—that is to say the good, the rich, and the well-born, and beside them a mass of citizens—will there or will there not be dispute as to which should rule?"[30]

Aristotle seems to be moving away from a consideration of ideal types to an examination of historically more real political situations. Scattered through this chapter are references to another issue that deserves mention here: it is law that is ultimately sovereign.[31] The question of whether the best man or the law decides is important since it is another way of determining between the few and the many. Sovereignty of law implies the existence of a good constitution and citizens. But throughout this chapter, Aristotle has already defined the citizen and the mechanism of sovereignty as participation by the many in the legislative and judicial process.[32]

> The fourth alternative, that the respectable should rule and have sovereign power over everything, means that all the rest must be without esteem, being debarred from the honor of holding office, under the constitution. . . . Is then the fifth alternative better, that one man, the most worthy, should rule? But this is yet more oligarchical, because it leaves still larger numbers without honor. It might be objected that it is a bad thing for any human being, subject to the affections that enter the soul, to have sovereign power, which ought to be reserved for the law.[33]

The law and constitution are sovereign because they are the result of citizen participation in the political process. The law delineates the general framework and principles that guide the constitution, but in the course of their application and implementation, citizens must decide and judge the manner in which universal principles are applied in particular cases. "A man will give sounder counsel than law in individual cases."[34] It is the constitution that sets the pattern for the types of law created. Mary Nichols argues in her work *Citizens and Statesmen* that the distinction between the good citizen and the good man in chapter 4 is a "rebuke to the one who claims absolute rule for himself." She continues, "We have also seen that he [Aristotle] defines the citizen so that it includes the many." The characteristics of the good citizen are moderation, justice, and prudence, as well as the ability to deliberate and judge. Claims to autonomy from citizenship and the constitution, that is, self-sufficiency and its corresponding inability to be ruled, as well as rule, transcend political goodness.

Throughout his analysis, the clear distinctions between the three correct forms of constitution and the three deviant forms are constantly shifting for the pure forms themselves contain elements of their own perversions. At the political level, theoretical purity may even be a form of deviation itself. This would certainly place Aristotle's political theory in conformity with his epistemological assumptions found in the *Nicomachean Ethics*. In a rejection of Platonic political philosophy, Aristotle views politics as incapable of being a science with universal and objective validity (*episteme*) and unchanging categories. Rather, it is a form of political wisdom (*phronesis*) that attempts to find the universal within the historical and empirical particular. This becomes much clearer in book IV of the *Politics*.

Aristotle is concerned about a constitution founded on the rule of one (kingship or tyranny) or a few (aristocracy or oligarchy) because with so few individuals being citizens, the state cannot function in the manner he described at the beginning of the chapter. It would not be the product of citizen deliberation within the council, assembly, and jury courts. Aristotle also argues that there would simply not be enough members to maintain the best constitution. The polis would not be constituted by individuals who are equal and alike, nor would legislation and jury decisions "apply only to equals in birth and capacity."[35] He even says that the superior men of "superlative virtue" and outstanding character are, in fact, beyond the law—they are more like gods. This characterization of the truly virtuous, who are beyond the boundaries of the polis, would then supply justification for the exercise of ostracism and social unrest. In spite of this, he consistently returns to the argument that a numerical majority will be less corruptible; will contribute more to the functioning, stability, ideals, and goals of the polis; have collectively better political judgment; and, ultimately, will be more compatible with his notions of citizenship, constitutionalism, and law. He concludes his defense of democracy with the unusual statement that if the majority are good men, then democracy itself is a form of aristocracy.

Aristotle is very aware throughout his analysis that his political categories are fluid and changeable. Aristocracy is characterized by a political community in which the highest honors and offices are determined by merit and virtue, that is, by the "best of citizens."[36] He does not say that they are the only citizens, just the best. There is no mention in this definition of aristocracy of the broader issues of citizenship and constitutionalism: participation, deliberation, and judgment in the assembly, courts, and council. There is one time when Aristotle equates polity with aristocracy and another where the mixing of elements in a democratic polity creates an aristocratic component.[37] The real differences between the ideal and the real, aristocracy and democracy, are less clear. There appears to be an effort to mix not only democracy and oligarchy in the polity, but also democracy and aristocracy in order to form the best constitution.

When examining the merits of each claim to sovereignty by wealth, noble birth, virtue, or the multitude, Aristotle concludes in book III by saying, "All these considerations seem to show that none of these criteria is right by which one set of men claim that they themselves should rule and the rest be subject to them."[38] Aristotle seems to tire of approaching the issue of sovereignty from the perspective of who should rule and shifts his focus to the issue of how one should rule. He returns to his initial definition of citizen: "So far as the best constitution is concerned, he is a man who is able and who chooses to rule and be ruled with a view to a life that is in accordance with virtue."[39] In the final analysis, the deciding criterion is not simply which group should rule, but which group should rule given the political goals of friendship, citizenship, constitutional integrity, and the rule of law that he examines throughout book III.

Without a democracy, a participatory form of government based on deliberative rationality and broad citizen participation would be impossible; so, too, would be the realization of fundamental human capabilities and virtues, and the fulfillment of human nature—man as a political animal. If a large segment of the population were excluded from political rule, the definition of rationality as speech, deliberation, and discourse, citizenship as participation in judicial and legislative organs of state, and human essence as political animal would all be made impossible. The collective has capabilities and merits beyond that of even the best individual or small group. Together in a democratic constitution, the people have collectively more virtue, wisdom, and character than the best individuals; they have better opinions and judgments; maintain the sovereignty and integrity of the constitution; permit the widest possible citizen participation; make the most contributions to society as a whole; collectively act more justly and rightly for the common good; and are more honest and moderate as a group. But probably the most important reason for his defense of democracy is his defense of the constitution and law, since they "if rightly established ought to be sovereign."[40]

It is interesting to note that Aristotle, in book IV of the *Politics*, moves in a different direction. Instead of detailing the absolutely best form of government, he directs his attention to the best under the circumstances, the constitution from the given conditions, or the constitution most generally acceptable to all societies. He turns to the polity or participatory democracy as the constitutional system that synthesizes the various claims to merit and equality: freedom, wealth, virtue, and good birth. It is a moderate, middle-class democracy that Aristotle claims is the best form of government for the majority of states and the majority of men.

> Virtue is a mean, and the happy life is a life without hindrance in its accordance with virtue, then the best life must be the middle life consist-

ing in a mean which is open to men of every kind to attain. . . . Since therefore it is agreed that moderation and a middle position are best, it is clear that, in the matter of the goods of fortune also to own a middling amount is best of all.This condition is most easily obedient to reason and following reason is just what is difficult both for the exceedingly rich, handsome, strong and well-born, and for their opposites, the extremely poor, the weak, and those grossly deprived of honor.[41]

Aristotle continues the argument from book III when he states that the state consists of those who are "equal and alike." That is, when they are moderate in spiritual virtue and material means. "Among those who are equal and alike, it is neither just nor expedient that one single man should be sovereign over all the rest."[42] Democracy is grounded in the principles of freedom, equality, sovereignty of the majority, and the rule of law. The state is constituted so as to eliminate, as far as possible, psychological, economic, and political extremes. Among the rich, arrogance, crime, contempt, injustice, and abuse of power are the general rule, whereas the injustice of the poor is expressed in their envy, wickedness, pettiness, and subservience. In a society where one extreme has political power over the other, we get one of the following scenarios: either power is tyrannically held by a small minority who do not understand rulership, submission to others, or power sharing, but only contempt for the poor and maintenance of their own status and positions in society, or the poor exercise political rule, but they know only slavery to authority. "For the greedy grabbing of the rich does more harm to the constitution than that of the people."[43]

Extremes lead to factionalism and the tyranny of the few or the many—what Aristotle calls the "unmixed oligarchy" or "extreme democracy." Thus, it is only among the middle group that equality, similarity of character, moderation, prudence, economic sufficiency and security, and political understanding are the general characteristics. The two extremes of class antagonism are to be avoided since they make friendship, sharing, partnership—the cornerstones of a moral community—impossible. A moderate constitution is framed in order to create the "best" and "natural" political community, free from internal dissention, strife, and civil war. Only in this form of legal system do we fulfill the requirements of a moral community found in books VIII and IX of the *Nicomachean Ethics* and book I of the *Politics*. Finally, for Aristotle, it was from this middle group within society that the great lawgivers Solon, Lycurgus, and Charondas came.

Epistemology and Politics in Aristotle's *Politics*

Perhaps one of the most interesting questions about the organization and structure of Aristotle's *Politics* is the relation among chapters 1, 2, 3, and 4. Or to put it more clearly, what is the role of Aristotle's defense of democratic polity in this work? Is democracy the best and most natural form of polis; or does democracy represent a perversion and deviation from the ideal? Is it only a second or third best form of political constitution? What is the relation between absolutely ideal constitutions (books II, III, VII, and VIII) and best actual constitutions (books IV, V, VI) in Aristotle's political theory? These have been hotly debated questions. I would like to argue that the apparent answer (if there really is a final answer) lies in seeing these chapters in the broader context of Aristotle's *Nicomachean Ethics* and *Metaphysics*. It is his epistemology, metaphysics, and ethics that place the political discussion in a better and more subtle context of discourse. That is, it is more helpful to view Aristotle's theory of the best constitution within his analysis of intellectual virtue (*episteme* and *phronesis*), friendship and moral community in his ethical work, and form and matter and potency and act from his treatises on physics and metaphysics.

Turning from political *episteme* to political *phronesis*, political science to practical wisdom, the ideal to the real world, thought to action, and Platonic utopianism to political pragmatism, Aristotle examines the issues of sovereignty, justice, citizenship, and the best constitution from the perspective of the concrete and historical world. This is a world of ordinary virtue and character abstracted from the realm of biological luck of natural abilities and birth. Though most states do not have the constitution and individuals to be an aristocracy, the democratic polity does come the closest in the real world.

> If one group of persons were as far superior to all the rest as we believe gods and heroes to be superior to men, and if they had both bodies and souls of such outstanding quality that the superiority of the rulers were indisputable and evident to those ruled by them, then it would obviously be better that the same set of persons should always rule and the others always be ruled, once and for all. But since this is not a condition that can easily be obtained, and since rulers are not so greatly superior to their subjects as Scylax says the kings are in India, it is clear that, for a variety of reasons, all must share alike in the business of ruling and being ruled by turns. For equality means giving the same to those who are

alike, and the established constitution can hardly be long maintained if it is contrary to justice.[44]

The relationship between the ideal state in books II and III and the best state among the actual communities is not a simple juxtaposition-ing of the best and second-best societies, but a profound argument within Greek political theory about epistemology and politics. The crucial question is not only the best state, but also what kind of knowledge is appropriate to political theory and is knowledge of an ideal state even possible. Is it a science giving us knowledge of universal principles and structures? Or does it provide for an entirely different form of political knowledge based on an understanding of diversities of opinion, the weakness of science (*episteme*) when applied to politics, a critique of abstract rationality and political idealism, and an understanding of moderation, prudence, and deliberative action.

After book III, Aristotle tells the listener that the discussion about the best constitution has been completed and that now the topic of discussion will move to an examination of how and why the best constitution develops. He immediately turns in the first chapter of the next book to a consideration of the various forms of knowledge given within "political science": the absolutely best constitution, the best under the circumstances, the given constitution, and a generally adopt-able constitution. The first form of knowledge gives us three forms of correct polities, whereas the last three give us many different forms of constitutions. There is an epistemological shift from a contemplative Neoplatonic philosophy searching for unchanging universal standards and forms to a political *phronesis* searching for the best constitutions within the limits established by history, tradition, and the actual structures and circumstances of society. "This same practical wisdom enables one to discern both which laws are best, and which of them suit each constitution. For one ought to lay down laws to fit constitu-tions (as indeed is always done), not constitutions to fit laws."[45] This shift in Aristotle's thinking from political *episteme* to practical wisdom in book IV is reflected in a new political topology of "well-formed constitutions": oligarchy and democracy. The combination of these two produces the best polity.

In book II, Aristotle turns to a study of some of the legal opinions about the best constitution by prominent Greek thinkers: Socrates, Phaleas, and Hippodamus. In the first half of this book, he runs through his analysis and critique of Plato's communism, his theory of class and property, and his ideas about a community of wives and children, Phaleas's egalitarian society and the equalization of property ownership, and Hippodamus's social engineering and mathematical ideal of the best society.[46] The second half of the book is devoted to an examination of some proposed forms of good constitutions in Sparta, Crete, and Carthage. What is at issue in this discussion is the type of knowledge appropriate to "political science," which is the very same question Aristotle raised at the beginning of his *Nicomachean Ethics*. In the latter work, he contends that there is a great diversity and fluctuation of opinion. Politics can achieve a level of truth that is imprecise and in outline form only. "We must be content, then, in speaking of such subjects and with such premises to indicate the truth roughly and in outline, and in speaking about things which are only for the most part true and with premises of the same kind to reach conclusions that are no better."[47]

Throughout the *Politics*, Aristotle recognizes that the discussion about the "best constitution" is a false topic because of the epistemological limitations about the nature of political knowledge. Politics strives not for an unchanging knowledge of universal principles and institutions, that is, political science. Rather, it deals with a variety of opinions, deliberation, judgment, and action about the best constitution—political *phronesis*. The heart of politics, for Aristotle, is not philosophical contemplation but political action (*praxis*) in particular cases.[48] His ideas on this subject represent the most articulate critique of rationalism and science in ethics and politics in the history of Western thought. About this aspect of Aristotle's political theory, Mary Nichols writes:

> While a critique of political idealism aims at a moderation of political activity through understanding the limits of politics, Aristotle's political science aims at political activity through understanding the potentialities of politics. . . . Phaleas fails to consider how the human desire for distinction would thwart his egalitarian property arrangements. And Hippodamus proposes organizing cities according to mathematical principles and constant change. All such schemes fail to recognize the complexity of politics that Aristotle points out. . . . His [Aristotle's] criticism of his predecessors is a criticism of an *abstract* rationality that attempts to impose schemes while ignoring the context of human life. Aristotle's suggestion that political philosophy look to the "deed"—to "what happens"—is a recommendation that reason focus on particulars.[49]

In the *Nicomachean Ethics*, Aristotle corrects the limitations of legal justice for being too abstract, absolute, unbending, and removed from the particular circumstances that require equity and just action; in the *Politics*, he is concerned that the laws be treated as sovereign and that the citizens and officials act properly in order to interpret how the law should be justly applied in particular cases not covered by universal principles and general regulations. Aristotle moves from a consideration of the opinions about the politically ideal form of polis in book II to an articulation of the best constitutions (kingship, aristocracy, and polity) in book III. But in book IV, he moves further toward a reflection on the more pragmatic consideration of the best constitution for actually existing political communities and the variety of constitutional options available for consideration. It is not the case that the distinction between the ideal and the actual is a question of settling for the second best or "modest and middling" political system; it is not a question of resigning oneself to a lower standard of distributive justice and civic virtue.[50] This gives too much weight to a Platonic reading of Aristotle. Rather, the emphasis should be on Aristotle's theory of law, constitution, and sovereignty; his theory of citizenship, statesmanship, political participation, and the best way of life as political rule and activity; the theory of the deliberative, judicial, and executive functions of the constitution; and his theory of knowledge and distinctions between contemplation and action, *episteme* and *phronesis*, and abstract rationality and deliberation. These elements of his ethics, politics, and epistemology lead Aristotle to a position that emphasizes moderation and prudence over theoretical tyranny, political action over political idealism, opinions over universal knowledge, and political *praxis* and democratic participation over social engineering from above. These are the ingredients of his democratic imagination. The movement from a consideration of political ideals to the constitutional and legal potentialities within the real world is a product of Aristotle's whole philosophical orientation and not the inability to conceptualize or realize political ideals.[51]

Martha Nussbaum in *The Fragility of Goodness* outlines Aristotle's position on *phronesis* as a critique of the Platonic view of the good life and political *techne*. Plato attempts in his writings "to make ethics into a *techne*."[52] On the other hand, practical deliberation involves a rejection of scientific knowledge, a rejection of universal principles removed from the particular, from commensurability and quantitative measuring, from perception and insight through experience, and from rough guidelines and indeterminacy of judgment. Aristotle states that "practical wisdom is not scientific knowledge."[53] Ethics and political theory must adjust to the particular circumstances that are met in the everyday world.

> Practical wisdom, then, uses rules only as summaries and guides; it must itself be flexible, ready for surprise, prepared to see, resourceful at improvisation. This being so, Aristotle stresses that the crucial prerequisite for practical wisdom is a long experience of life that yields an ability to understand and grasp the salient features, the practical meaning, of the concrete particulars. This sort of insight is altogether different from a deductive scientific knowledge, and is, he reminds us again, more akin to sense-perception.[54]

The state cannot be engineered into existence using external and universal formulas about the "best constitution," because this only imposes a formal structure on political experience without becoming part of the habit, personality, and reason of the citizens. Aristotle, by moving toward a moral community in which deliberation and judgment, equality and freedom, sovereignty and participation are the defining characteristics of the citizen, moves away from the Platonic view of the good life and truth. He develops toward a practical wisdom based on knowledge of different theoretical and historical constitutions in a democratic polity. By rejecting the ideal form of political construction, Aristotle makes his political theory conform to his earlier epistemology and ethics. In the final instance, the best society is the result of a consideration of a diversity of political opinions, deliberative rationality, debate, and moral choice. This ideal also comes about by the realization of the potentialities incorporated into the formal structure of the polis. That is, its form is not an abstract entity existing outside the state, but is the life of the state itself existing *in potentia.*[55] This is the reason why Aristotle articulates his theory of the best moral community and participatory democracy out of the deviant forms of polities.

Thus, polity is an integration of democracy and oligarchy, but in such a fashion as to incorporate even the ideals of an aristocracy and the life of political virtue.[56] The ideal comes from the development of the potentialities that lie within the formal principles and structures of concrete particular societies. They are not imposed (*techne*) from above by a technological or philosophical elite or from the outside in the form of mathematical or scientific (*episteme*) engineering. They come from the potentialities of the actual constitutions, however underdeveloped, as they evolve according to their own immanent principles implicit in their particular political forms.[57]

Greek Ideals and Democratic Imagination in the Athenian Assembly and Paris Commune

Unlike the relationship between Aristotle's critique of commodity exchange and the market in the *Politics* and the development of Marx's economic theory in *Capital*, there is no explicit reference to Aristotle's political philosophy in Marx's analysis of participatory democracy in the Paris Commune. However, I agree with those authors who have argued that Marx, in his later writings, is using the Commune to expand his own earlier themes of the common good, species being, and human needs. The themes were initially developed by Aristotle: his concept of the political nature of man and his notions of deliberation, freedom, needs, and citizenship.[58] As in the case of his economic theory, Marx's political thought represents a retranslation of Aristotle's ethical and political theories adjusted to reflect the issues and structures of modernity. The *Politics* supplied Marx with a wealth of detail about the history of Greek legislation from Solon and Kleisthenes to Ephialtes and Pericles, the history and forms of various constitutional arrangements, including Sparta, Crete, Carthage, and Athens, the principles of popular sovereignty and participatory democracy, structural analysis of Greek society, a theory of moral economy and ethical community, and a comprehensive theory of ethics and political life. However, there is no direct reference to this political material in Marx's text. In spite of this, after a careful reading of Marx's works, the Aristotelian ethical and political influences are not difficult to see.

Marx's analysis of the Paris Commune is one of the few discussions in which he details briefly his views on the just society. It was a grand experiment of working-class politics that lasted for seventy-two days from March 18 to May 28, 1871. The Commune, as the governing body of Paris, was made up of municipal councillors, chosen by universal suffrage from the smaller districts throughout the city and was constituted mainly by members of the working class. As in the case with Aristotle's theory of democracy, Marx stresses participation in the administrative, judicial, and educational spheres, universal participation, and close scrutiny of public officials and recall for abuse and misuse of power and position. Remuneration for officials was tied to workers' wages and a limited tenure of office was instituted to prevent "place-hunting," "careerism," and a professor elite. His critique of parliamentary democracy and the old French republic lies in its nonparticipatory elements. "Instead of deciding once in three or six

years which member of the ruling class was to misrepresent the people
in Parliament, universal suffrage was to serve the people, constituted
in Communes."[59] Democratic liberalism permits participation within
the very limited parameters of plebiscitary elections. Marx is echoing
the thoughts of Rousseau, who in his *Social Contract* also rejected
parliamentary liberalism as being nondemocratic.[60]

In his analysis of ancient and modern democracy, M. I. Finley
emphasized political participation in deciding public policy, judging
civil and criminal cases in private and public arenas, and electing
officials as the main characteristics and superiority of classical Greek
democracy. "Freedom meant the rule of law and participation in the
decision-making process, not the possession of inalienable rights."[61]
Marx's analysis of the Paris Commune parallels his earlier negation
and transcendence (*Aufhebung*) of egoism, economic liberties, natural
rights, and political emancipation in *On the Jewish Question*. His
views of participatory democracy as outlined in his address on the
Paris Commune to the General Council of the International Working
Men's Association are certainly related to his earlier discussions
about political and human emancipation, happiness and human needs,
freedoms and liberty, political and economic rights, egoism and the
common good, and species creativity and social beauty.

The old mechanisms of oppression—the police, standing army,
clergy, and officials of Bonaparte's government—were to be dissolved.
In his theory of popular sovereignty, Marx is critical of these forms of
tyranny manifested in the centralized state and its organs of oppression. To him, the state was an extension of the interests of civil society
and market rationality and was to be dismantled.[62] The unity of France
was to be maintained by a Communal Constitution and National
Delegation to Paris. A French federation of communes would perform
those functions of government that required some central direction
and national unity.

> In reality, however, the state is nothing but a machine for the oppression
> of one class by another, and indeed in the democratic republic no less
> than in the monarchy: and at best an evil inherited by the proletariat
> after its victorious struggle for class supremacy, whose worst sides the
> victorious proletariat, just like the Commune, cannot avoid having to lop
> off at the earliest possible moment, until such time as a new generation,
> reared in new and free social conditions, is able to throw the entire
> lumber of the state on the scrap-heap.[63]

The Commune articulated in its brief history Marx's criticism of the
parliamentary republic with its hierarchical power, state bureaucracy,

political division of labor, and centralized state control. He sees these institutions as mechanisms for ensuring and maintaining the "national power of capital over labor, public force organized for social enslavement, and the engine of class despotism."[64] Reacting to the "class terrorism" of the French republic of Louis Bonaparte and the later government of Thiers, Marx holds up the Commune as an example of a working-class government containing the possibilities of a future moral community resting on universal suffrage, political responsibility, and direct democracy. The political, military, and ideological power of the republic was dismantled and replaced by popular sovereignty, integration of the executive and judicial branches of government, broad worker participation in the Commune, payment for public services, but at worker's wages, the transformation of the professional standing army into a national militia, and a federation of decentralized communes throughout France.[65] With this political emancipation, there also came the economic emancipation of labor.

There would be a total restructuring of the social organization of production and a redistribution of social wealth based on human needs and not class power. With this dismantling of the state bureaucracy and army, the costs of maintaining the state would have been greatly lowered and the possibilities for majority participation greatly increased. Only when there is a public sphere for participation and deliberation, grounded in the political community and based on equality and social justice, is there real democracy.[66] The goal of the Commune was to radically transform the economy to rid it of class inequality, alienated labor, and the oppression of private property as the society moved from political to human emancipation. As Marx says, "The Commune was therefore to serve as a lever for uprooting the economic foundations upon which rest the existence of classes, and therefore of class rule."[67] It created local producer cooperatives run and owned by the workers themselves—the "self-government of the producers" and "republic of labor"—for the common good and social needs of the political community.

> If co-operative production is not to remain a sham and a snare; if it is to supersede the capitalist system; if united co-operative societies are to regulate national production upon common plan, thus taking it under their own control, and putting an end to the constant anarchy and periodical convulsions which are the fatality of capitalist production— what else, gentlemen, would it be but communism, "possible" communism?[68]

As in the case of Aristotle and reflecting his manner of connecting democracy and epistemology, Marx also raises the issue that the Commune has "no ready-made utopias to introduce *par decret du peuple*" and "no ideals to realize, but to set free the elements of the new society with which old collapsing bourgeois society itself is pregnant."[69] Aristotle maintained that in a democracy, the collective experience, judgment, and practical wisdom of the majority outweighed the disadvantages of transferring sovereignty from the few best virtuous men to the many free citizens. Participatory political institutions would provide the training ground for the further education and nurturing of the virtuous citizen and good life. Though Marx's position is different, he, too, sees a connection between epistemology and politics. Rejecting the Platonic alternative of social engineering of revolutionary change from above by an elite group, he does not accept the notion that there are specific ideals to be realized. Ideals may focus attention on the present situation, and ideals may be part of a general vision, imagination, and hope for things to come, but they do not appear to be part of Marx's thinking about the future. They are too inflexible, abstract, and universal to act as base guidelines for social action; they reify and fetishize the future.

As with Aristotle, Marx is faced with the dilemma of the relationship between universals and particulars, abstract ideals and particular history. It seems that in this context the term "ideals" refers to particular transhistorical blueprints for an ideal society presented to the working class by "bourgeois-doctrinaires" with "their ignorant platitudes and sectarian crotchets in the oracular tone of scientific infallibility."[70] It is very reminiscent of Aristotle's critique of Platonic utopianism, the philosopher king, and class structure of Socrates' communism. For Marx, workers need "a full consciousness of their historical mission." They need the practical wisdom that results from a participation in the creation of their own history and social institutions. In turn, social analysis and moral critique must come from within the historical conditions of political economy.

There is another reason why there are no ideals to realize at this stage of historical development. In his statement *Critique of the Gotha Program*, Marx argues that in the transitional stage toward communism, what he called "socialism," society would institute the principles of liberalism in exchange and distribution: rights, equality, and fairness.[71] This means that socialism would actually be the highest stage of liberalism and the beginning of communism. There would be equivalent exchanges in the marketplace based on equal contributions of labor and production. Communism would transform the last vestiges of liberalism and its inequality of ability and contribution into a social system based on political and economic emancipation and human needs. It would be an historical transition based on economic and political realities and not on abstract social ideals and movements.

Years earlier in the *Communist Manifesto*, Marx expressed similar reservations about utopian socialism. He feared that utopian calls for socialism would not be connected to any historical and structuralist analysis of capitalism and therefore not tied to a knowledge of historical reality and the realistic possibilities for social transformation and revolutionary change. Emancipation of labor requires that the workers' class consciousness and initiative be cognizant of the real economic conditions of society and that the proletariat be aware of and ready to take advantage of any serious structural crises within the system. With utopian socialism there is no materialist understanding of history and no knowledge of economic institutions and structures. One result is that these socialists created artificial and fanciful ideas about revolution and socialism that were unconnected to the real possibilities that lay within the historical moment. "Historical action is to yield to their personal inventive action, historically created conditions of emancipation to fantastic ones, and the gradual, spontaneous class organization of the proletariat to an organization of society specially contrived by these inventors. Future history resolves itself, in their eyes, into the propaganda and the practical carrying out of their social plans."[72] These socialists had an inadequate understanding of history, economic conditions, class antagonisms, and political activity and revolutionary potential. They created a new social gospel with its laudatory, but misplaced and ill-conceived ideals. These abstract ideals of political fetishism were imposed upon society from above by political reactionaries and were not the product of the working class coming to its own rational self-consciousness in an historical and democratic struggle for human emancipation.

There is a split between theory and practice, thought and reality. Morality is overlaid upon economics and social critique condemns capitalism from abstract moral principles without understanding the structures of political economy or principles of society that the individual is rejecting.[73] This is just another form of natural law perpetuated by a theology from above. It is reminiscent of Hegel's critique of the moral abstractionism and indifference of Kant's self-imposed categorical imperative and the terror of the French Revolution, and Marx's critique of Kant (*Paris Manuscripts*), German Idealism and Left Hegelianism (*The German Ideology*), Proudhon and the neo-Ricardian socialists (T. Hodgskin, P. Proudhon, W. Thompson, T. R. Edmonds, and J. R. Bray in *The Poverty of Philosophy*), and commodity fetishism (*Capital*).[74]

On the other hand, the Paris Commune created a revolution in the very act of creating a new democratic society based on the principles of participation, freedom, equality, liberty, and self-determination. These are the same principles outlined in Aristotle's discussion of his best society. There was a clear tendency toward "a government of the people by the people."[75] But when Marx turns to clarify this idea, he uses examples such as the elimination of night work for journeyman bakers; the elimination and prohibition of wage increases by means of workplace fines; and the take-over and running of factories by associations of workers. There would be compensation to all former owners and capitalists, even those who decided to side with Thiers, the National Assembly, and the old Bonapartist army at the gates of Paris. The power of capitalists to determine the length of the working day, the appropriate level of wages and fines, and the organization and management of the factory was, in fact, just another form of the exercise of political power that was to be democratically controlled in the future. Marx complains that the capitalist had executive, legislative, and judicial powers, which in a democracy should be reserved in the hands of the people. Economic institutions are forms of concentrated political and economic power that in an oligarchy are in the hands of those who own the wealth. Class property and class politics are to be transformed into a participatory democracy. In a democracy, the citizens will directly participate in the decisions that affect every aspect of their daily lives. In response, Thiers and the government at Versailles, what Marx called the "slaveholders' conspiracy," put down democratic communes all over France.

This short address is significant for it is as much an example of political philosophy as it is political history.[76] While the Commune was constituted mainly by followers of Blanqui, Proudhon, and the Jacobins, Marx sees it as potentially expressing the spirit of his view of socialism and democracy. The address itself is very interesting because the reader sees in it an attempt by him to define his own understanding of the new political community. It is a system that seems to flow out of the ideas he has borrowed from Aristotle (freedom, equality, and participation), Rousseau (egalitarianism and the common good), and the anarchists (decentralized power and small-scale democracy).

From Politics to Epistemology in Marx

Just as Aristotle's view of the nature of political knowledge influenced his understanding of the best form of political constitution, Marx's epistemology was affected by the development of his understanding of politics. We have seen above that Marx rejected social engineering, elitist decision making, and political *techne* as legitimate mechanisms for social change. Because of this, his social critique could not be imposed from the outside, but had to be the result of an internal process and immanent critique. Dialectical science evolves out of the logical and historical development of the concepts and laws of capitalism and the future is produced through democratic transformations. For both Aristotle and Marx, their understanding of political knowledge calls into question modern epistemology and the traditional forms of science and truth. Knowledge in the final analysis is the result of political *praxis* and democratic participation. Aristotle's politics and epistemology were very influential on the development of Marx's theory of knowledge and methodology in his later writings. Aristotle's theory of democracy and practical discourse also played an important role in Marx's own metatheoretical development. The next few sections of this chapter will investigate this relationship between politics and epistemology in closer detail.

In his doctoral dissertation, the *Paris Manuscripts*, and his other early writings, we can see already the beginnings of Marx's theory of consciousness and experience, subjectivity and objectivity, and concept and reality; his criticisms of traditional epistemologies, conceptual fetishisms, historical determinism, and theoretical mysticism; his juxtapositioning of materialism (Epicurus and Feuerbach) and idealism (Schelling and Hegel); his rejection of political ideology, economic abstractionism, and positivistic science; his distinctions between *Naturwissenschaften* (Democritus) and *Naturphilosophie* (Epicurus) and *Verstand* (Kant) and *Vernunft* (Hegel); the centrality of his anthropological ideas of *praxis*, human creativity according to the laws of beauty, and social epistemology; his dialectical view of science and immanent critique; and his notion of "theory and practice" based on a critique of philosophical scholasticism.[77] It is a cliché to say that Marx's methodology and theory of knowledge have their origins within the history of German Idealism and critical theory. From Kant's transcendentalism, Hegel's dialectical philosophy, Feuerbach's anthropology, and the Left Hegelians' critique of religion and ideology, Marx fashioned his critique of political economy. His epistemology was grounded in the evolution of German critical thought from Kant's constitution theory of objectivity and truth based on transcendental logic to Hegel's theory of cultural objectivity, historical reconstruction of Western values and institutions, and phenomenological method based on dialectical logic. Aspects of these theories have been used to explain Marx's economic crisis theory and labor theory of value.

The following sections will examine Marx's later economic theories as examples of his radicalization of Kant's critique of pure and practical reason and Hegel's dialectical philosophy. Horkheimer very nicely summarized this school's development in his *Eclipse of Reason*:

> Dialectical philosophy since Kant's day has tried to preserve the heritage of critical transcendentalism, above all the principle that the fundamental traits and categories of our understanding of the world depend on subjective factors. Awareness of the task of tracing concepts back to their subjective origin must be present in each step of defining the object. This applies to basic ideas, such as fact, event, object, nature, no less than to psychological or sociological relations. From the time of Kant, idealism has never forgotten this requirement of critical philosophy.[78]

Kant's theory of objectivity is also a theory of perception, understanding, and explanation. Objectivity (facts, events, experience), for him, is a constitutive process in which the knowing subject (transcendental consciousness) becomes part of the process in which the very objects of experience are created. That is, subjectivity is involved in the creation of objectivity, theory in the creation of empirical facts. His theory means that objects and facts do not exist autonomously from consciousness and the process of knowing. If this is true, then how does one come to understand facts or the objective world? German critical theory has argued that once the subject becomes a crucial ingredient in any theory of knowledge then a simple examination of the immediate facts is inadequate to express this creative process. Inductive reasoning, fact gathering, and empirical verification were important components of early nineteenth-century positivism. However, with Kantian epistemology, the subject too must be taken into account in this process of knowledge gathering. Both the facts and the constitutive process must be jointly understood within a holistic framework with special emphasis on the subject not just as a transcendental or static universal, but as a living product of history, culture, and social relations. Experience is predicated on a prior sociological framework within which the subject is historically and socially created. This means that to comprehend the object in time we must comprehend the subject in its biographical and historical context. Thus, we move from a theory of objectivity and subjectivity (Kant's transcendental subject), to a theory of history and culture (Hegel's dialectical subject), to a theory of economic contradictions and social crises (Marx's subject as class struggle). As the contours and content of the subject become more defined in terms of the categories of political economy (subjectivity), the meaning and relevance of economic facts and experience (objectivity) become better understood.

The nineteenth and twentieth centuries saw a radicalization of Kantian epistemology and moral philosophy, especially as they applied to social and political theory. Rejecting the claims of positivistic social science, Max Weber began to develop an historical sociology grounded in an interpretive science of society. Following Rickert, Nietzsche, and Dilthey, he expanded upon Kant's works in his own early methodological writings in *The Methodology of Max Weber* and Kant's transcendental logic in his later historical and economic works, especially *General Economic History*. Marx, too, before him, had been experimenting with different methodologies, which furthered the insights of Kant. The next three sections of this chapter will look at these influences through an examination of the relationships between time and method in Marx's *Capital* and how Aristotle's epistemology and political theory were used by Marx to resolve some of the dilemmas inherent in the Kantian theory of knowledge. What at first may appear to be widely different and even contradictory methodologies, on further investigation represent complementary approaches to the analysis of capitalism. With a change in the temporal horizons of his interests, there is a corresponding change in the *logic* (transcendental, dialectical, and consensual logic), *methods* (historical, dialectical, and discursive methods), and particular *institutional analysis* (historical origins of capitalism, contradictions and crises of capitalism, and structures of participatory democracy). This may help explain what appear to be inconsistencies and contradictions in Marx's approach to political economy.

When studying the past, present, and future, Marx raised different sets of questions that required different methods of approach. For the past, he used a transcendental logic, an historical method, and a structuralist analysis of the foundations of capitalism. In the study of the present, he used a dialectical logic, immanent critique of social contradictions, and economic crisis theory implicit in these contradictions. Finally, when his attention turned to the future, which was a very rare occurrence, he utilized an entirely different method consisting of a logic of consensus, a method of practical discourse, and an institutional examination of participatory democracy. Perhaps it would be too simplistic to argue that when his attention was directed at the past, Marx turned to Kant's transcendental critique of reason (as in the *Grundrisse*); when his attention was directed at the present, Marx turned to Hegel's dialectical phenomenology (as in *Capital*); and when his attention was directed to the future, Marx turned to Aristotle's ethic of practical and political discourse (as in the *Critique of the Gotha Program*). What makes the analysis of time and method in Marx's writings distinctive is the fact that the temporal dimensions are not static, but play into one another. This complicates the issue greatly, since one of the major points being made in the following sections is that Marx's notion of the future is intimately connected with his notions of the past and present. Time is not made up of discrete and unconnected moments, but its elements flow into one another in ways reminiscent of the view of time found in the Greek tragedies. Nietzsche will also interpret time as an integrated whole within the self-conscious awareness of the "eternal return" of being.

Both Marx and Nietzsche push Immanuel Kant's arguments and method of critique in their writings into new realms of study. They radicalized the treatment of the critical method well beyond its initial foundations in the critiques of pure and practical reason. Thus, Kant lies at the heart of both Marx's critique of nineteenth-century political economy and Nietzsche's critique of rationalism and nihilism. The question is, what is "critique" and how does Marx apply Kant's epistemology and moral philosophy to his analysis and rejection of liberal capitalism? How is critical science different from Weber's interpretive science and Durkheim's positivistic science? Chapters 5 and 6 will follow up on Nietzsche's rather different application of Kant to epistemology and moral philosophy, respectively. The next three sections of this chapter will systematically examine Marx's approach to the past (origins of capitalism), present (critique of capitalism), and future (social change within a free and democratic society).

Time and Method: Changing Views of Social Critique

The Past and Historical Method

As we have already seen in the third part of the first volume of *Capital*, Marx moves beyond Aristotle and the study of circulation and commerce to an examination of capitalist production. Here he emphasizes the production of absolute surplus value and lengthening of the working day. Part IV, which deals with the production of relative surplus value through the intensification and mechanization of labor, moves further beyond the study of chrematistic exchange. Industrial expansion, the social organization of the factory, mechanization of the division of labor, and modern science and technology become the basis for the production of more surplus value and profits. The method employed to study these structural conditions is not the same method he uses when undertaking an immanent and dialectical critique of capital or when dealing with the future. Rediscovering the past requires a different method grounded in historical sociology and structuralist methodology. Reminiscent of Kant's question about the conditions for the possibility of knowledge and objectivity, Marx searches for the key historical reasons for the rise of capitalist production in the structural foundations of capital itself.[79]

Part IV takes up over half of the first volume and contains Marx's examination of the social, technical, and historical foundations of the development of capitalist production. He centers his attention on the issues of the structural conditions necessary for capital accumulation: free and abstract labor, division of labor, urbanization, manufacture and labor specialization, development of machinery, modern science, and industry (factory system), concentration and centralization of capital, cooperation, agricultural revolution and enclosures (private property), commercial revolution, primitive accumulation of capital and the rise of the modern state with its taxation and fiscal policies, deficit financing, banking, international trade, protection of commercial and industrial interests, military expansion and colonialism, the socialization of labor and concentration and centralization of the means of production, the regulation of labor and wages (Statute of Laborers, Poor Laws, Factory Acts of 1861, 1864, and 1867, Workshops' Regulation Act, and so forth), and the maintenance of domestic peace and private property (Acts of Enclosure).

There is not space in this work to even briefly outline Marx's understanding of the history of capital. He traces the evolution of this new socioeconomic system from the early forms of cooperation and division of labor in the period of manufacture (sixteenth to eighteenth century) to the use of modern technology and machinery in the factory during the industrial period (eighteenth and nineteenth centuries). The main characteristics of the early period of capitalism are reflected in the decomposition of production into its simplest component parts and the formation of abstract labor (uniform, homogeneous, regular, and replaceable labor). Traditional and independent handicrafts are transformed into specialized, disconnected, and isolated functions located within one workshop. New forms of social production and cooperation are created during the manufacturing period, but they still rely on the old handicraft skills. Production is organized into a coherent and unified system of isolated handicrafts or detail laborers who function within very restricted limits of the production process. Labor is still performed by skilled laborers, but within a narrowed form of cooperation (concentration of means of production in one location under close and despotic supervision) and a capitalist division of labor. The result is greater differentiation, productivity, and efficiency of labor, but there is also greater intensity, exploitation, and distortion of labor. Though the traditional handicrafts are still in place, each worker becomes a "fractional detail." The result of this transformation of production during the manufacturing period is that the individual's "dexterity at his own particular trade seems in this manner to be acquired at the expense of his intellectual, social, and martial virtues."[80] There is, for Marx, a new differentiation of the instruments of labour (tools), which themselves are transformed into very specialized functions.

> By decomposition of handicrafts, by specialization of the instruments of labour, by the formation of detail labourers, and by grouping and combining the latter into a single mechanism, division of labour in manufacture creates a qualitative gradation, and a quantitative proportion in the social process of production; it consequently creates a definite organization of the labour of society, and thereby develops at the same time new productive forces in the society.[81]

The social organization of labor has produced an economic system in which men and women have become parts of mechanized production itself. During the manufacturing period with its decomposition of labor and the instruments of labor, there are further social forces on the move. With the increasing capitalist division of labor, there is greater concentration of property and the means of production in the hands of fewer and fewer capitalists; the subjugation of detail laborers to capital; increased competitive warfare in the artificially constructed state of nature in the market—a *bellum omnium contra omnes*; greater legitimation of the system through a defense of property, natural rights, and individual liberty; and, finally, greater need for new mechanisms of social control and workers' discipline within the workshop.[82]

The social and organizational principles and foundations for the Industrial Revolution are already in place. With the adaptation of machinery to social production, a new phase of capitalism develops in the industrial period that results in greater efficiency and productivity, elimination of the remaining handicrafts, further division of labor and specialization to the needs of machinery, and increasing control over the activity of workers. According to Marx, the chief characteristics of the Industrial Revolution are the transformations of the workshop into a factory, manufacturing into industry, labor motive power into natural power of wind, water, animals, and steam engine, handicraft skills into machinery, and individual tools into a mechanized production system. The cooperation of the detail laborers working with their individual tools and skills is replaced by an integrated and coordinated system of mechanized production in which machines replace handicrafts and in which labor is riveted to capital "more firmly than the wedges of Vulcan did Prometheus to the rock."[83] The detail laborer is replaced by the detail machine with the result that labor becomes more abstract, more mobile and fluid, and less tied to recognizable skills thus making the worker superfluous and redundant (industrial reserve army of unemployed). For Marx, manufacturing produced the machinery for the industrial period; however, its social foundations lay in handicraft production. This latter had to be changed in order for machinery to transform production. "Modern Industry was crippled in its complete development, so long as its characteristic instrument of production, the machine, owed its existence to personal strength and person skill, and depended on the muscular development, the keenness of sight, and the cunning of hand."[84]

In the capitalist system, the goal of the mechanization and scientization of production is not the alleviation of work, but rather its further intensification and expansion. Machinery replaces the need for labor power. However, Marx's theory of value presupposes that exchange value and surplus value can only be created by labor power. Thus, modern technology, the instruments of production, and the whole economic base of society must and does move in the direction of intensifying work, lengthening the workday, and increasing exploitation. The number of workers is reduced, while their work loads are increased. Competition and the drive to maximize profits requires that the revolution in production be separate from a revolution in the quality and standards of the individual's moral, social, and intellectual life. In the factory, the production process becomes "a lifeless mechanism independent of the workman" and "a miserable routine of endless drudgery and toil."[85]

In the last part of *Capital*, entitled "The So-Called Primitive Accumulation," Marx details the process by which initial sums of capital necessary for the development of the industrial apparatus are acquired. Money and commodities are transformed into capital only with the "polarization of the market," when one class has exclusive ownership of the means of production and the other class becomes "free workers" who own their own labor power. "Primitive accumulation" is the term for the actual historical process in which these classes are formed and the means of production become the exclusive right and privilege of the owning class. This required that all feudal restrictions on production, ownership, and attachment to the soil be dissolved. It also necessitated that the peasants be stripped of their lands, the feudal land tenure system be cleared away, and the guilds lose their power to determine the regulations of production and the rules of apprenticeship. Without these initial stages of precapitalist developments, the free wage laborer would have been impossible. This was accomplished by the Parliamentary Enclosure Acts of the late fifteenth and early sixteenth centuries.[86] The forcible expropriation of the land by the landlords depopulated many areas of the rural countryside, which provided the labor necessary for the new forms of cooperation and manufacture. All this was accomplished through the purposeful intervention and crucial oversight of the British state.

The Present and Dialectical Method

The "present," as a temporal mode in Marx's *Capital*, is commonly mistaken for the future for reasons that will become apparent. Though the term "economic crisis" with its concomitant forms of overproduction, stagnation, breakdown, and so forth, seems to imply a reference to a period that will come about because of some inherent defect in capitalist production, I will argue that this represents a misunderstanding of the nature of time in German Idealism and Marx's method of dialectical and immanent critique. In fact, to go out on an academic limb and bring my own chain saw for critics, Marx never really deals with the future in his economic theory. That, too, is only apparent.

What interpreters understand by Marx's unfolding of natural laws and hidden secrets of capital into the future, that is, the crystal ball and prophesying of Marx, is an invention of positivistic critics. These latter have failed to realize that what appears as the future in Marx's writings is only the working out of the historical dynamics, internal logic, and immanent principles of capitalist production in the present. He doesn't prove that capitalism is irrational, wasteful, or destructive by portraying the inevitable breakdown of the system, but rather by showing that its concepts and theories, its logic and principles, its structures and history are contradictory and flawed, irrational and nondefensible. Marx is developing a dialectical critique of the contradictions of capital, not an explanatory model of social behavior or historical transformations. Ultimately, it is not that the system inevitably and necessarily destroys itself, but that it destroys the ethical possibilities of humanity. *Capital* is not really about an economic crisis, but a moral crisis, though the former is certainly an important ingredient in this study. If there is a breakdown thesis, it is not an economic one but an ethical one. The precedent for such an analysis, as we have already discussed, lies not with Ricardo but with Aristotle. Marx is not viewing and judging modernity from the heights of the Exchequer, but from the Acropolis.

The present and future are probably the most interesting and complex temporal dimensions in *Capital*, but they are also the most misunderstood. Marx mentions three forms of economic difficulties in his crisis theory: the tendential fall in the rate of profit, overproduction, and disproportionality. The secondary literature is replete with exegesis over these topics with almost all interpreters assuming the temporal dimension as a given. However, the question arises as to which temporal dimension the crisis theory refers to: is it, in fact, the future? Is Marx predicting the future breakdown of the capitalist mode of production and its class structure? For this to occur, there would also have to exist the corresponding methodological and epistemological assumptions about the nature of a "science" of political economy. But do the prerequisites for a positivistic social science fit Marx's later economic writing?

Parts I and II of the third volume of *Capital* contain introductory chapters to the key section in this volume, "The Law of the Tendency of the Rate of Profit to Fall." This third part consists of three chapters on the general law itself, counteracting influences, and the contradictions of capital expressed in the law. Though not specifically laid out, there appears to be a movement in Marx's argument in this part from an analysis of the logic and concept of capital (pure theory), to the historical limits of the law and its counteracting influences, to the analysis of the contradictions of capitalism itself. I will argue that what is really going on here is the development of Marx's dialectic of capital from its concept or *Begriff* (Hegel's phenomenological method), to its history, to a final synthesis of Ricardo and Aristotle (economic crisis theory and critique of chrematistic production) in Marx's ethical critique of capitalism. It must be unequivocally stated that it is an ethical critique that does not devolve into abstract philosophy or moral theory, but incorporates and transcends economics. It empowers economic theory and places it within a broader intellectual and cultural tradition. All this is necessary to uncover the temporal dimension of the economic crisis theory.

By the time the reader has arrived at part III, Marx had already established a socioeconomic model of capitalist production that assumed the following: a constant intensity of labor exploitation, rate of surplus value, length of working day, and constant wages, as well as the fact that commodities are sold at their value. By holding these elements constant, he has constructed a model that will be able to show how changes in the organic composition of capital (relation between constant and variable capital) affect the accumulation of the mass of surplus value and the rate of profit. It is the social productivity of labor, its social organization and internal dynamic that Marx views as the hidden secret of capitalist production. The organic composition of capital reveals how much variable capital or living labor (materialized labor) is set in motion by a specific amount of technology and means of production. This relationship between labor and the means of production will help determine the rate of exploitation and the amount and rate of surplus value extracted from living labor. That is, it will help explain the nature of economic exploitation under capitalism. The organic composition is key to understanding differences in the rate of profit and, ultimately, the tendency of the rate of profit to fall in capitalist enterprises. Every indication is that Marx appears to be predicting the fall in the rate of profit and the subsequent economic stagnation and turmoil. Let's investigate further the law of the tendency of the rate of profit to fall.

Marx's thesis is that as capitalist production develops, so does competition, the technological development (technical composition of capital), and the productivity of labor. Since only labor can create value in a commodity, that is, the labor theory of value, there is a serious problem in capitalist production when there is a relative decline in labor (variable capital) and an absolute increase in the means of production (constant capital). In his theoretical model, the internal dynamics of production and competition result in a rising technical composition of capital. That is, there is an increase of constant in relation to variable capital. More and more technology is needed to put in motion the same amount of labor. This changing relation within the organic composition between constant capital and variable capital affects and highlights the crucial differences within Marx's economic theory between the rate of surplus value and the rate of profit. The rate of surplus value (s/v) is calculated on the basis of the ratio between the surplus labor and variable capital (wages). The rate of profit is determined on the basis of the total social capital (s/C), when the total capital C is equal to c + v + s or the total of constant capital, variable capital, and surplus value (profit). Changes in these variables will affect the rate of profit. In different areas of production, there is a different mix of the means of production and labor resulting in the use of different amounts of living labor, different surplus, and different rates of profit. In some firms, more industry is necessary to set in motion the same amount of living labor. For Marx, surplus can only be derived from the unpaid labor produced in each commodity. However, the rate of profit is determined by the ratio of surplus to the total expenditures on capital.

To refer to the example used by Marx:[87]

$$c = \ \ 50, \text{ and } v = 100, \text{ then } p' = 100/150 = 66\ ^2\!/_3\%$$
$$c = 100, \text{ and } v = 100, \text{ then } p' = 100/200 = 50\%$$
$$c = 200, \text{ and } v = 100, \text{ then } p' = 100/300 = 33\ ^1\!/_3\%$$
$$c = 300, \text{ and } v = 100, \text{ then } p' = 100/400 = 25\%$$
$$c = 400, \text{ and } v = 100, \text{ then } p' = 100/500 = 20\%$$

With the variable capital and surplus value held constant at one hundred, Marx adjusts constant capital from fifty to four hundred to correspond to the rising organic composition of capital. While the machinery, technology, and raw materials increase and labor is held constant, there is a decrease in the rate of profit from $66^2\!/_3$ percent to 20 percent. Why? According to Marx, this is the result of the increasing productivity of labor and the relative decline in variable capital in relation to the total capital. What this all means is that with the development of capitalism there is a logical tendency for the means of production to increase, thus reducing the amount of labor necessary to produce each commodity and, in turn, lowering the price of each one. Surplus value is measured by the extent of the exploitation of labor and the reduction of necessary labor (wages) to a minimum, but the rate of profit is calculated on the basis not only of variable capital, but also constant capital. Surplus value is recognized only in its relation to variable capital, while the rate of profit must also include the wider costs of production. The increasing need to expand the technology and means of production increases the cost, while the labor component remains the same. This expansion of capitalism results in less labor in each product, cheaper products, and a tendential fall in the rate of profit. As the system expands, larger amounts of total capital are necessary to put to work the same amount of labor power and produce the same amount of surplus value.

Another way of stating this point is that in a technologically advanced society, larger amounts of the means of production are necessary to maintain the same or decreasing amounts of labor. The system becomes more technologically dependent in order to remain more competitive. Less labor is required to produce each commodity and, thus, there is less surplus in each commodity. This is compensated for by the enormous extension of the productive apparatus. With the expansion of constant capital, the mass of surplus or profits derived from each commodity declines, but the total number of commodities produced increases. The conclusion, according to Marx, is that capitalism will produce greater amounts of profits at the same time that the rate of profit declines. This represents only an outline of his argument, but with expanding industrial capacity and technology, there is greater productivity and accumulation, falling commodity prices and need for labor power, decreasing amounts of labor in commodities, and increasing mass of surplus and profits. But concomitant with this rising organic composition of capital, there is also a tendency for the rate of profits to fall. This may, in turn, produce a situation conducive to serious economic crisis, stagnation of production, and, if left unchecked, eventual social breakdown.

Marx sees this process as essential to capitalist production and the logic of capital. There are, however, historically and structurally "counteracting influences" that can delay and postpone indefinitely these logical conditions. These structurally offsetting influences include the increasing intensity of exploitation, depression of wages below the value of labor power, cheapening the costs of constant capital, relative overpopulation, foreign trade, and increasing the capital stock.

This leads us back to the question of time. Is Marx really talking about the future when he develops his economic model? Or is he developing the notion of immanent principle (Hegel) or telos (Aristotle) contained in the logic of capitalist production? "It would seem, therefore, that here the theory of value is incompatible with the actual process, incompatible with the real phenomena of production, and that for this reason any attempt to understand these phenomena should be given up."[88] The argument in volume 3 of *Capital* is so abstract and philosophical that it would be difficult to accept the idea that Marx is outlining a real theory of economic crisis that could be used to explain and predict actual economic and historical behavior and happenings. What then is he doing? I would like to argue that he is blending together in a subtle and complex network of ideas a new dialectical and critical science. He is tracing the development of the concept or logic of capital in a manner similar to Hegel's phenomenological method for tracing the development of the spirit or pure concept.

> The progressive tendency of the general rate of profit to fall is, therefore, just *an expression peculiar to the capitalist mode of production* of the progressive development of the social productivity of labour. This does not mean to say that the rate of profit may not fall temporarily for other reasons. But proceeding from the nature of the capitalist mode of production, it is thereby proved a logical necessity that in its development the general average rate of surplus value must express itself in a falling general rate of profit.[89]

Nowhere in his writings does Marx say that the breakdown of capitalism is historically inevitable, only logically inevitable. Throughout this part of his study, there is constant reference to the Kantian and Hegelian categories of phenomena and essence. Even the reference to "necessity" should be placed within the context of Hegel's *Science of Logic*. Hegel sees necessity as part of the development of the "absolute" out of actuality and possibility. It is the temporal side of the unity of essence (possibility) and existence (being, immediacy, or appearance) in the concept (*Begriff*). Hegel says that "the contingent therefore is necessary because the Actual is determined as Possible."[90] The actual world consists of the contingent, the possible, and the necessity. Necessity must be viewed as part of this understanding of actuality.

> Real Possibility, since it possesses the other moment, Actuality, is already itself Necessity. What therefore is really possible can no longer be otherwise: under such and such conditions and circumstances something else cannot result. Real Possibility and Necessity are therefore only *apparently* different; this is an identity which does not *become* but is already presupposed and forms a basis. . . . But this Necessity at the same time is *relative*. For it has a presupposition from which it begins; it has its point of departure in the contingent.[91]

As the *Grundrisse* indicates more clearly than *Capital*, Marx is still wrapped-up in the terminology of nineteenth-century German metaphysics. The important point in all this is that Marx is using the concept "necessity" in ways entirely different from the traditional English usage. Here he means to say that the reality or essence of capital lies deep within its structures of political economy and the social organization of production. Reality is not a phenomenon immediately visible to surface science. Rather, a dialectical science seeks to uncover the structure or essence of capital that lies in its necessity—its potentiality or pure form. Thus Marx's phrase of "logical necessity" refers to the formal potential that lies within the concept of capital that reflects the reality of historical conditions and social formations. All actuality contains its own possibility, as content contains its own formal determinants. Marx displays the formal characteristics of capitalism, its essence or heart for all to see. But this is filtered through his own critique of Hegel's dialectical method.

> My dialectical method is not only different from the Hegelian, but is its direct opposite. To Hegel, the life-process of the human brain, *i.e.*, the process of thinking, which, under the name of "the Idea," he even transforms into an independent subject, is the demiurgos of the real world, and the real world is only the external, phenomenal form of "the Idea." With me, on the contrary, the ideal is nothing else than the material world reflected by the human mind, and translated into forms of thought.[92]

Marx assumed in the beginning of part III of volume 3 of *Capital* that the ideal and real world were the same. But he also recognizes that this is only a working assumption for his model. He has constructed a formal and historical model that, in reality, reflects the formal structures of capitalist production and the unfolding of its logical necessity. To check himself, there is constant reference throughout to the historical reality. But the two must be kept separate. Necessity in Marx's *Capital* is logical only, but does reflect a tendency within history—thus, the tendency of the rate of profit to fall. If this analysis is correct, then the temporal dimension Marx is working with is not the future, but the working out of the past (immanent and logical principles of capital) in the present. This means that there is a tendency for the rate of profit to fall because of the "formal necessity" built into the very structural and class contradictions of modern capitalism. The future then is not what we generally mean by the term today—something that has not yet come into existence.

For Marx, the "future" is a logical category in which the present concept and logic of capital develops within his economic model. It has no existence outside the model. This is not to say it has no relevance outside his theory or that it isn't part of the mechanism for the development of history and real social conflict. Marx clearly shows the historical ramifications of capital as it works itself out in history. It is just that his theory is not attempting to impose a logic on history, only on its structures. One cannot immediately apply Marx to explain a particular historical event or economic crisis. The law of the tendential fall in the rate of profit cannot explain a particular historical occurrence. This requires an in-depth empirical understanding of the event itself. Nor can it be used as a mechanism for predicting future events; it can only be used as an instrument for critically evaluating the present. We shall see in the next section that this analysis provides him with the foundation for his ethical critique of capitalism. The examination of the present also involves an immanent critique of utilitarianism and natural rights theory, as well as an ethical critique of capitalism resulting from lost moral, intellectual, and spiritual possibilities as a result of alienation, exploitation, and economic crises.

The Future and Method of Practical Discourse

When one views Marx's epistemology and methodology from a distance, one realizes his distance from the traditional interpretations of Marxism and positivism.[93] There appears to be no attempt on his part to establish an examination of political economy and history within the boundaries of a positivistic social science with its exclusive reliance on social facts, explanatory natural laws, causal relationships, deductivism, historical determinism, and scientific predictions. Its epistemological and metaphysical assumptions rest on a particular theory of objectivity that stresses a correspondence theory of truth, methodological distance and realist objectivity, naturalism, and ontological realism. According to Lenin, "Marx's theory of capitalism formulates the 'objective laws governing the development of the system of social relations,' and permits us to 'deduce the inevitability of the transformation of capitalist society into socialist society wholly and exclusively from the economic law of motion of contemporary society.' "[94] On the other hand, Marx's critique of both rationalism and empiricism, his immanent, dialectical, and critical science, his theory of objectivity (synthesis of subject and object) and *praxis*, his views on the relationship between theory and practice, his rejection of false universality, religiosity, commodity fetishism, alienation, and idolatry, his distaste for the tyranny of class and things (objects, laws, and groups), his theory of appearance and reality, and his concepts of temporality and history, all lead to a different epistemology and different theory of "science."[95] In order to develop a traditional view of Marx these ideas must in some way be explained away or ignored. This is not the place to get into the epistemological particulars of Marx's critique. However, his perception of the "future" can lead to an alternative and interesting direction in Marxian scholarship. For instance, why is there so little discussion of the future society, its economic structure, polity, laws, constitution, methods of distribution, and so forth, if Marx was so concerned with science, revolution, and the future society?

This is an extremely difficult question to answer. An adequate response must connect Marx's epistemology and metatheory with his politics. That is, the answer lies in his rejection of Platonic philosophy and social engineering by a political elite and his turn to Aristotelian epistemology and political theory.[96] Aristotle's view of epistemology and politics: his theory of politics and "political science," the distinction between *episteme* and *phronesis*, *techne* and *praxis*, universal knowledge and practical wisdom, and his ideal of the good life as deliberation and participation, all play a role in Marx's formulation of his theory of knowledge and its relation to politics.[97] The future is bounded by concrete historical conditions and the concepts generated by society. But society is pregnant with its own ethical and economic possibilities that lie inherent in its structures and principles—mores, traditions, and institutions. With the recognition of the material foundations for social life, the future lies open to the possibilities that exist in human imagination and moral vision, which are guided by its ideas about political and human emancipation, freedom and creativity, the vision of Winckelmann and the laws of beauty, and the good society. Marx's whole critique of idolatry, alienation, and fetishism, his rejection of positivistic science and its false theory of objectivity rest on this foundation that the future is to be an expression of human potentialities and not an expression of external, abstract laws of economic, political, and psychological development. It is men and women who can make their own history. When our lives conform to psychological and economic laws, we are alienated from our own self-consciousness and possibilities as human beings.

Thus, if the future is open, for Marx, what guidelines, ethical values, political truths, social institutions will steward us through the times of transformation and reaffirmation of our humanity? Where in his writings do we get the social blueprints and historical guides? The answer, of course, is that there are none. Obviously, this would be a serious and glaring mistake, unless we consider that he deliberately failed to deal with these issues because of his underlying epistemological assumptions about human freedom and creativity. His politics was constrained by his epistemological reservations about the nature of our knowledge and character. Marx cannot and does not say what socialism will look like when finally implemented. If access to the past is achieved through a Kantian structural analysis of the conditions that make capitalism possible, and access to the present is derived through an immanent critique of the social possibilities that exist (contradictions), the inadequacies of ideas when compared with historical reality (critique of ideology), and the social reality when compared to ideas (ethical critique), then the question arises of whether there is a way of dealing with the future without or beyond positivism. The answer, I believe, lies in Aristotle's *Nicomachean Ethics* and *Politics*, his rejection of positivistic knowledge (political *techne*), and his theory of participatory democracy.

For Marx, the recent past seems to have been controlled by immutable laws of exchange, such as supply and demand, money and prices; by laws of production, such as surplus extraction, profit maximization, division of labor, and technical control of the social organization of production; by laws of exchange based on private property, class ownership, and just distribution; and by the psychological laws of self-interest, unlimited desires, and maximization of pleasure and utility. These are the universal laws of political economy, which were rejected by Marx as he turned toward the development of an alternative theory of moral economy based on the insights of Aristotelian ethics and politics. But Marx's critique of political economy also has all the flavor of Hegel's rejection of the abstraction, externality, oppressiveness, and "terror" of Kantian morality and the French Revolution. The modern tyranny of capitalist morality has replaced the categorical imperative and political dictatorship that Hegel rejected.

Where the past is accessible through Marx's historical method and the present through immanent critique, the future is still to be created; it lies in the imagination, dreams, and visions of the members of society and is accessible only through rational discourse in the public sphere. Through democratic participation in our political, economic, and cultural lives, the future is something that becomes as a result of self-determination and self-realization. It is not imposed upon us by some unchanging social laws nor is it something that a philosophical elite can coerce its members into accepting as in utopian socialism. Rather, the future is open to rational discourse and democratic participation; it is open to society determining its own direction rather than following external laws.

Aristotle's Politics and Marx's Ethics

The concluding section of this chapter will look at the purpose of Marx's *Capital*. If there is a confusing variety of methods attached to different temporal dimensions, what holds the work together as a coherent statement about political economy? The answer actually lies in the subtitle of the book, *A Critique of Political Economy*. Marx, as we have already seen, rejects the epistemology, method, and content of classical nineteenth-century political economy. He does begin with many of the questions that they in fact raised including the theory of value, surplus value, nature of profits, class production, and so forth. However, Marx's critique of political economy is an attempt to provide the foundations for an ethics of moral economy. This is why the eight references to Aristotle throughout the first three volumes of *Capital* are so crucial. They represent a rejection of the approach by classical political economy and a return to classical Greece where economics had a role subordinate to the good and well-being of the community and the virtue and happiness of the citizen. In order to subordinate economics to its new role of providing the means for the material foundations of a democratic community, as well as part of the expression of humanity's ultimate purpose as a species being, there must first be a powerful critique of the concepts and structures of the existing political economy.

This explains why there was no use made of Marx's apparent references to the future. *Capital* is built upon the analysis of the natural laws and historical tendencies of capital to economic crises, overproduction of capital and commodities, disproportionality within the various branches of production, and a tendential fall in the rate of profit. But what appears to be clear statements about the inevitable and necessary future of capital are, in fact, analyses of the immanent principles working within the sinews and features of capitalism itself. At such a high level of theoretical abstraction, they certainly were not used by Marx as a basis for the prediction of the breakdown and fall of capitalism. There is no attempt to determine the structural arrangements, time schedule, or real historical possibilities for this momentous event. Marx's theory, as he presented it, has no predictive value, because it was never intended for this use. According to Marx, the future was tied to a complex web of temporal dimensions that included the historical past, contradictory and dialectical present, and open possibilities of the future. If Marx had any goal from his dissertation to his later economic writings, it was his calling into question the existence of the logical necessity and historical inevitability of certain social institutions that would determine and destroy the very possibilities of human freedom and creativity. To undertake this adventure, there first had to be a "critique of political economy." The values, theories, method, and epistemology of economists from Smith to Ricardo had to be critically and immanently undermined. When this was accomplished, the foundations would be in place for the development of a theory of moral economy.

Capital was an attempt at building a neo-Aristotelian ethical theory through a critique of liberal economics, especially Smith's labor theory of value and Ricardo's theory of the falling rate of profit. This helps to explain further the temporal and methodological arrangements in the work, as well as the apparent failure to predict the downfall of capitalism. After ranging through chrematistic exchange, the forms of capital as commodities, money, and capital, the fetishism of social and class relationships, and the destructive crises of a modern liberal economy in the first three volumes, Marx brings everything together in the last chapter of part III of the third volume on the tendency of the rate of profit to fall. This chapter entitled "Exposition of the Internal Contradictions of the Law" deals with the general structure and principles of the economic crises. It is followed by parts IV to VII which survey the nature of commercial capital, interest-bearing capital, banking, and ground rent. Though Aristotle is not mentioned by name, his critique of chrematistic exchange is present throughout. There seemed to be no need to repeat the comments made from volume 1.

An important question that has not been considered yet is, what role does Marx's crisis theory play in his overall design? That is, why is the law of the tendential fall in the rate of profit important? If it does not lead to an analysis of the breakdown of capitalism, to an analysis of the coming class struggle, to an anticipation of communism and its social formation, or to the creation of some universal philosophy of history similar to that found in the *Communist Manifesto*, what is Marx doing?[98]

The examination of the falling rate of profit and its counteracting influences develops into an analysis of the "internal contradictions of the law." Marx moves in a direction that could not have been anticipated if he was developing a positivistic and economic crisis or breakdown theory. His theory of value, surplus value, rate of profit, and natural law of the rate of profit instead leads to a consideration of the inner essence or contradictions of capitalism: the contradictory forces within society built on the production of use value and exchange value, material production and value production, accumulation and realization, production and consumption, production and sale, excess of capital and overpopulation, and expansion and concentration of property ownership and shrinking purchasing class. Here we find Marx's developed criticisms of capitalism—it wasted productive forces; it irrationally used technology and science; it turned economic means into social ends; it resulted in un- and underemployment of capital and the creation of a wasted, surplus population; it destroyed the material wealth of society; it produced economic stagnation; it mystified potential enlightenment and self-consciousness; and it alienated and exploited workers.

These are the phenomenal forms of the inner essence of capitalism. Again, we have Marx taking the economic issues of nineteenth-century political economy and placing them within a general context of Hegel's dialectical science. The importance of an analysis of the internal contradictions of capitalism lies in portraying the technological irrationality (industrial overproduction, social contradictions, economic crises, and material waste) and moral irresponsibility (exploitation and lost human possibilities and freedoms) of capitalism. It represents a reintegration of science and ethics, Ricardo and Aristotle, Kant and Hegel in a critique of political economy. It is interesting to note that, at the end of part III, Kant's moral philosophy and Aristotle's ethical theory are indirectly called upon again to provide the capstone for Marx's economic crisis theory.

As Marx delved below the surface phenomena into the "inner essence" of capitalist production, he concluded with his famous statement that the real barrier to further economic expansion lies in the heart of the economic system itself. But what is the real barrier? On the one hand, it refers to the very structure of capitalism, especially market competition and the transforming organic composition of capital that give rise to economic concentration and centralization along with the crisis of the tendency of the rate of profit to fall. The economic structure is its own worst enemy. It is the efficiency and rationality of production that undercuts its own future potentials for economic growth and industrial expansion. But there is another barrier that lies deeper in the meaning of the text. This barrier is a moral one. "The *real barrier* of capitalist production is *capital itself*. It is that capital and its self-expansion appear as the starting and the closing point, the motive and the purpose of production; that production is only production for *capital* and not vice versa, the means of production are not mere means for a constant expansion of the living process of the *society* of producers."[99]

If there is a moral imperative within capitalist production, it is the continuous self-expansion of capital and the productive forces. This natural law of market competition, however, results in creating the real barriers to further economic growth. With the development of the industrial activity of society, there is a backwash in the social conditions of production. The absolute development of capital results in the relative and artificial overpopulation of the workers who, in turn, are incapable of purchasing the commodities of the economy. In this passage, Marx mentions the distorted relationship established between means and ends. Material gain and the chrematistic economy have become their own motive; the creation of surplus value is the only purpose of production. Humanity has simply become part of this new economic machinery and, in the process, has reduced its human characteristics to serving the exploitation of labor and the production of surplus value. It has lost its potential for human rationality, creative production, democratic activity, and economic freedom. The economy no longer provides the material foundation for the development of the "living process of the *society* of producers." Marx has clearly placed his finger on the crucial issue of modernity. At both the micro and macro levels, at the level of the individual species being and society as a whole, there is no broader vision, purpose, or social potential to realize—no transcending values, hopes, or creative possibilities inherent in the individual or society, such as the fulfillment of species potential, the realization of social and political vision, the protection of civil and human rights, the articulation of individual hopes and aspirations, the development of human rationality and democratic participation, and the creation of an economic aesthetic of beauty and social justice. These are the ethical values of Marx upon which the economy must be built.

From his earliest works *The Difference between the Democritean and Epicurean Philosophy of Nature*, *Contribution to the Critique of Hegel's Philosophy of Law*, and the *Economic and Philosophic*

Manuscripts of 1844 to his later economic writings in the *Grundrisse* (1857–58) and *Critique of the Gotha Program* (1875), Marx continues to lay out the ethical foundations to his economic and scientific enterprise. In all the key sections of the first volume of *Capital*, Aristotle's critiques of chrematistics and lost human potential are prominent and in volume 3 at the end of sections dealing with economic crisis and breakdown, there is again reference made to the ethical critique of capitalism. Marx's theory of value and crisis ends with a restatement of the ethical imperatives that have grounded his thought from his first writings. There are social and technical limits to the further development of capitalism that Marx has detailed. However, the central point is that the real barrier to further economic activity is an ethical limit. By reversing the means/end relationship, modern society has undermined the fundamental teleology of all true economic systems—the realization of human potential and self-expansion of human capabilities and rationality. The exploitation of social productivity, the natural law of industrial expansion, and the resulting economic crises are condemned not only because they lead to war, revolution, social conflict, and economic chaos. Rather, they are condemned because they distort the essential social relations among human beings and rob them of their socially and individually defined possibilities. An exegesis of Marx that stresses the apparent centrality of economic theory is possible only by neglecting the purpose of the Hegelian dialectical and critical method, the moral injunction against treating humans as means to ends, and the failure to see Aristotle as a guiding principle throughout *Capital*. It should be stated that this doesn't relegate economics to a secondary position, it only places it within a broader philosophical and ethical context. It doesn't reduce economics to philosophy or sociology to ethics. As Aristotle clearly showed, ethics and philosophy cannot be undertaken without a detailed and empirical understanding of human surroundings.

Here again we have a return of the Kantian theory of the kingdom of ends and the critique of practical reason. Now, however, it is not applied to individual action guided by the categorical imperative within an abstract and moral philosophy, but rather is incorporated into ethical and political theory. In his earliest writings in Paris, Marx was very critical of treating individuals as means to ends in alienating economic relationships. Now he uses the same ethical critique but with reference to the whole structure of the economic system. That is, liberalism as a whole has no purpose or goal other than the self-expansion of surplus value and capital. This is also in direct conflict with Aristotle's ethical theory: the economy has reversed the relationship between economic means and social ends. That which was to provide for the material foundations of the good life has redefined happiness and virtue in terms of economic categories. That which was to be subservient to the principles and values of the community, political participation, and rationality has redefined reason, politics, and society in terms of efficiency, market rationality, and profit. Material production has no purpose other than its own moral imperative of economic expansion and growth. Industry, agriculture, and commerce have no transcending value system to provide society with a sense of values or ideals that could give meaning to life or purpose to human activity. It undercuts the possibilities of species being and incorporates the spiritual, intellectual, and political dimensions of human existence into adjuncts and extensions of the economic system. Humankind does not live to perceive a new sensuality and nature, imagine and create changing forms of beauty, or participate in the collective process of self-determination. It exists to continue the technical manipulation and control of nature, to maintain the inequality and domination of a class system, and to participate in turning life into a means of existence—"makes man's species life a means to his physical existence."[100] The later and earlier writings have now been integrated into one comprehensive perspective.

In the same chapter, there is another, longer passage that summarizes Marx's position on these matters and connects his historical/dialectical science with his ethical principles.

And as soon as formation of capital were to fall into the hands of a few established big capitals, for which the mass of profit compensates for the falling rate of profit, the vital flame of production would be altogether extinguished. It would die out. The rate of profit is the motive power of capitalist production. Things are produced only so long as they can be produced with a profit. Hence the concern of the English economists over the decline of the rate of profit. The fact that the bare possibility of this happening should worry Ricardo, shows his profound understanding of the conditions of capitalist production. It is that which is held against him, it is his unconcern about "human beings," and his having an eye solely for the development of the productive forces, whatever the cost in human beings and capital *values*—it is precisely that which is the important thing about him. Development of the productive forces of social labour is the historical task and justification of capital. This is just the way in which it unconsciously creates the material requirements of a higher mode of production. What worries Ricardo is the fact that the rate of profit, the stimulating principle of capitalist production, the fundamental premise and driving force of accumulation, should be endangered by the development of production itself.[101]

Again the emphasis is on the severed relationship between economics and ethics and the failure of a social system of chrematistic production to create a society in which the values of human development have priority over the values of industrial development and profit. Liberalism doesn't protect or even admire individual and human rights other than the rights to property, market liberties, and consumer freedoms. Every aspect of modern society, including individual consciousness and human rationality are defined by the parameters of chrematistics. Marx recognizes that classical political economists are interested in profits, economic expansion, and improvement in the productive forces. For him, however, they are not the ultimate purposes of human existence. There is no underlying metaphysics or teleology that could give direction and meaning to this type of society other than its own natural law of economic decline. As with Aristotle, it is this that is the most damaging and damning criticism against this modern Leviathan. There is no concern with the issue of happiness other than utilitarian pleasure, no concern with rights other than property and individual liberties, no concern with virtue other than hard work and saving, no concern with justice other than the distribution of consumer goods, no concern with democracy, participation, and freedom other than as a mechanism for political control and ideological distortions, and no concern with the common good other than the externalities and waste products of private interests. The ethical values, which form the foundations of Aristotle's politics, disappear with modern political economy. Marx is attempting to reestablish the values of a moral economy with his concern for species being, equality, freedom, creativity, political freedom, and direct democracy.

There is a barrier to production that lies deep within the structures of capitalism. But the most relevant barrier to political economy lies in the values of moral economy. That is, liberalism continues to press against its most profound contradiction—that it is a society that has no reason for existence. There is no purpose in production, no reason for economic expansion, no goal of human existence, and no ideals that transcend the material base of society. It is a society without ethics, and Marx is attempting to replace modern science with a modern form of ethical economics (*Wirtschaftsethik*). The nature of capitalist production is such that it will extinguish "the vital flame of production," undermine a "concern about human beings," produce commodities only when there is effective demand and realistic profit expectation, further develop the productive forces, but at the expense of species being, distort the social productivity of labor through economic crises, and undermine the material possibility for "a higher mode of production." To make these abstract points more forceful, Marx peppers this third volume with numerous references to exploitation, alienation, and mystification. And he does it within the framework of a comprehensive historical investigation into the history of the working conditions in England during and after the Industrial Revolution. With special emphasis on the health and work conditions in coal mining, the silk industry, tailoring, typesetting, dressmaking, and the cotton industry, Marx details the disease, poverty, and injustice of capitalist production. Though he remarks often enough about the material conditions within the workplace, his central focus always seems to be on the lost possibilities of a humanity living in such ethically and physically squalid conditions. He mourns for their spirits as much as for their bodies.

Toward the end of volume 3 in the chapter entitled "Trinity Formula," there is a famous passage dealing with the relation between the realm of freedom and the realm of necessity in a socialist society.

> Freedom in this field can only consist in socialized man, the associated producers, rationally regulating their interchange with Nature, bringing it under their common control, instead of being ruled by it as by the blind forces of Nature; and achieving this with the least expenditure of energy and under conditions most favorable to, and worthy of, their human nature. But it nonetheless still remains a realm of necessity. Beyond it begins that development of human energy which is an end in itself, the true realm of freedom, which, however, can blossom forth only with this realm of necessity as its basis.[102]

Though it appears that volume 3 of *Capital* focuses upon economic crises within developed forms of capitalism, it is in reality an uncompleted treatise on social ethics. Given his reservations and criticisms of moral philosophy as "absolute verbal rubbish" and "ideological nonsense" in the *Critique of the Gotha Program*, Marx had no intention of writing such a work, but his treatment of capitalism and socialism is very similar to Aristotle's treatment of chrematistics and economics. Marx never undertook a microanalysis of capital, nor did he develop the macro implications of his own economic writings. He didn't pursue the utilitarian and technical aspects of his theory of economic crises. On the other hand, his critique of political economy was used to provide the basis for his critique of the economic and political institutions of liberalism for not providing firm foundations for a realm of economic freedom and social justice. Throughout *Capital*, it is the ethical that surfaces within the debris left by the bankrupt ideas and structures of capitalism. The system is irrational not because of its constant tendency to crisis, though that is certainly present. It is not irrational because there is inefficiency and waste due to overproduction of capital and commodities and economic stagnation, though both are also present in his arguments. The system is rejected as irrational because it destroys human beings by turning them into the means for industrial development. It stunts their moral and political development; narrows their choices and possibilities for self-expression to market opportunities; turns communities and political constitutions into products of social contract rather than democratic participation and consensus; and turns species beings into species rivalry for the wealth of nature in a war of all against all. Marx's critique of political economy, in the end, is a critique of its failure to incorporate moral principles into its economic design. That is, political economy subverts the very possibility of a moral economy in which the goal of industry, agriculture, and commerce is the expansion, development, and realization of human potential and happiness.

Marx makes this very point in the *Grundrisse* when he states that the purpose of production should be the development of "individual needs, capacities, pleasures, and productive forces," "the absolute workingout of his creative potentialities," and the development of humankind as an end in itself. He concludes with the famous phrase, "This is why the childish world of antiquity appears on one side as loftier. On the other side, it really is loftier in all matters where closed shapes, forms and given limits are sought for. It is satisfaction from a limited standpoint; while the modern gives no satisfaction; or, where it appears satisfied with itself, it is *vulgar*."[103] Classical Greece created limits not from the barriers of capital, but from its own ethical ideals and imaginative vision that gave form and meaning to society. It informed its members as to the purpose and goal of human existence. Marx makes this point even more explicit when he states:

> The free development of individualities, and hence not the reduction of necessary labor time so as to posit surplus labor, but rather the general reduction of the necessary labor of society to a minimum, which then

corresponds to the artistic, scientific, etc., development of the individuals in the time set free, and with the means created, for all of them. Capital itself is the moving contradiction, [in] that it presses to reduce labor time to a minimum, while it posits labor time, on the other side, as sole measure and source of wealth.[104]

Capitalism creates barriers to the self-realization of human potential and it is this fact that lies at the heart of Marx's critique of the economic system and at the heart of his vision for an alternative future. For it is chrematistic capitalism that distorts the individual and social needs of all members in the community and undermines the development and self-realization of their productive powers and human capabilities.[105] The greatest sin of the market economy and industrial capitalism is that they replace Aristotle and Epicurus with Smith and Ricardo, Greek vision and inspiration with utilitarian calculus and pleasure, and the Athenian Pnyx with the London Stock Exchange.

Chapter Three

Storming Heaven and Liberating History: Marx and the Hebrew Prophets

Introduction

The three major traditions influencing Marx's intellectual development are German Idealism, British political economy, and French socialism. There are, however, two deeper and older cultural traditions that underlie his thought—Greek philosophy and the Hebrew prophetic tradition. These are difficult to uncover because they lie deep in the layers of Marx's thought. My contention is that the Greek and Hebrew traditions gave Marx his fundamental orientations and defined much of the parameters of his thinking, while the perspectives of nineteenth-century political economy, philosophy, and socialist theory provided the immediate substance and content of these theories. This chapter will examine the relationships between the social ethics of the Old Testament Hebrew prophets and the social critique of capitalism by Marx in order to show their theoretical and methodological similarities. The connections between Marx's notions of alienation and fetishism and the Hebrew ideals of social justice and critique of idolatry have been noticed by a variety of authors, including Erich Fromm, Karl Löwith, Paul Tillich, José Miranda, Enrique Dussel, Arend Th. van Leeuwen, José Bonino, and Murray Wolfson.[1] "The whole concept of alienation found its first expression in Western thought in the Old Testament concept of idolatry."[2] This connection will now be made more explicit and its implications for an understanding of Marx more concrete; it is this tradition that will give us a clearer insight into his critique of reified social relations and social categories (science and positivism). It will also further expand on the critique of positivism developed by Epicurus as we have already seen in Marx's dissertation.

That such a relationship exists would seem to strain the credulity of many readers, since there has been so much written concerning Marx's seeming anti-Semitism, his critique of religion in general, his rejection of the religious traditions of his forbears, and his radical secular philosophy.[3] Other reasons for rejecting the hypothesis of this chapter rest on the obvious differences between the prophets' critique of their society, their method, values, and orientations and Marx's political economy, his supposed economic and technological determinism, his materialism, and atheism. While Judaism is a religion whose emphasis is on the word of God, legal transgressions, the covenant, and morality, Marxism is a political economy, whose focus is on the material world and economic production, the critique of religion as the opium and cry of the people, and ultimately, on a rejection of the whole metaphysical foundations of the Hebrew and Christian traditions. Marxism and Judaism are incompatible and one would be hard-pressed to see any real connection between them.[4]

Though this is the generally accepted view with some variations, I would like to develop the thesis that this is a very limited (and limiting) understanding of the ancient Hebrew influence on Marx. Though the categorial frameworks within which they expressed their ideas—"religion" and "critical science"—are quite different, the substance of their ideas and the social goals they set for their societies were in many ways similar; but what is really important is that the Hebrew tradition offered Marx another classical justification for his rejection of traditional moral philosophy and his belief that morality is really a question of social ethics and moral economy. Though there is a profound difference between the Hebrews and the Hellenes, between prophetic social ethics and the *praxis* philosophy of Aristotle and the Greek polis, there is an agreement about the centrality of social justice. For the prophetic tradition, religion was the mechanism in which and by which they developed a sociological critique of their society, a critique of personal morality and personal sin, a condemnation of inordinate class inequality and concentrations of economic wealth, and the loss of social responsibility (the public good).

Ethics, for both the prophets and Marx, is joined to a critique of political economy; the issues of right and wrong action are centered not on individual conscience and consciousness, but on the concerns of distorted power, economic deprivation, and reified social relationships within the community. Thus, Marx can be viewed as returning to this form of ethical analysis as a reaction to the reduction of Christian morality to individual moral imperatives and universal rules, which began to develop during the sixteenth-century Protestant Reformation and received its most articulate expression in the writings of Kant.[5] While the Hebrew prophets were reacting to the reduction of ethics to the abstract formalism and rigid legalism in religion, cultic rites, and legalistic ceremonies, Marx was reacting to the loss of the historical and sociological components in morality with its acceptance of the abstract individualism and positivism of eighteenth- and nineteenth-century political economy. Both Marx and the ancients were attempting to reintegrate morality into the material world of political economy in the form of social ethics. They both attempted to validate and ground a deep humanistic understanding of social relationships, whose ultimate goals are human liberation and freedom. The following sections will examine the methodological and theoretical similarities between these two traditions with the goal of revealing aspects of the deepest foundations of Marx's social ethics in another ancient culture.

Nineteenth-Century German Theology and the Old Testament

In the 1830s, the University of Berlin was the international center of research in the Greek classics. In 1831 the Immanuel Bekker edition of Aristotle's works was published. Also at this time some of the most important and revolutionary investigations into biblical hermeneutics were being undertaken. In 1835, D. F. Strauss, a graduate of Tübingen Theological Seminary, published his famous *Das Leben Jesu* and caused quite a stir. The distinction was made within the life of Jesus Christ between the Christ of faith and the Christ of history with the central biblical issues being those of salvation and human freedom. Strauss argued that religion and philosophy had different ontological bases and that the former could not be transformed into the latter. The stories surrounding the life of Christ in the New Testament were mythic constructions of the early Christian church. Bruno Bauer would later radicalize this perspective and push the argument further by contending that the belief in Christ is itself a myth constructed by the gospel writers themselves.

With Strauss, Bruno Bauer's *Kritik der Geschichte der Offenbarung* (1838) [this is the first part of a larger unfinished work entitled *Die Religion des Alten Testaments in der geschichtlichen Entwicklung ihrer Prinzipien dargestellt*], and Feuerbach's *Das Wesen des Christentums* (1841), the debate over the criticism of religion had been settled for Marx. It also set the tone, framework, and method for the transition from the critique of heaven to the critique of earth.[6] It involved the constant unearthing of religious mythology to uncover the human element at the basis of religious thought. By revealing the reification of human experience in theological categories (the domination of abstractions), Marx was able to give historical and structural meaning to the issue of the "cry of the oppressed" as expressed in religion. "The basis of irreligious criticism is: Man makes religion, religion does not make man."[7] The foundation of the critique of political economy lies in the early criticisms of religion, since it is from the latter that the former arises.

These theological criticisms, which form part of the intellectual foundations of Marx's earliest thought, have been widely discussed.[8] During the last three years of his studies at the University of Berlin, Marx officially attended only two courses, according to the provost's account. As we have seen, one dealt with Greek drama and Euripides, but the other focused on the Old Testament and the Hebrew prophet Isaiah. The latter course in 1839 was taught by his friend and colleague Bruno Bauer, who the year before published a two-volume work on the religion of the Old Testament entitled *Kritik der Geschichte der Offenbarung*.[9] The first part examined the relationship between religion and society and stressed the Hebrew notions of law, marriage, family, land, property, and so forth. The second part dealt with the form and content of the prophetic tradition. Though the revolutionary works of Strauss and the Left Hegelians were important to the early methodology of Marx and his critique of Hegel, it was the Old Testament prophets who provided him with another component of his moral condemnation of modernity.[10] Also while still a student at the University, Marx had intensely read Benedict de Spinoza's *Tractatus Theologico-Politicus* making 160 excerpts in one of his notebooks from 1841 to 1842. This work provided Marx with a great deal of detail about biblical Judaism, Hebrew history, the prophets, divine and ceremonial law, and the political structure of the Jewish commonwealth.[11]

During a period in which the New Testament was interpreted by biblical scholars as a work independent of the Old Testament, during a period in which the formalism of Hebrew law came under close scrutiny and critique by Hegel in his early essay, *The Spirit of Christianity and Its Fate*,[12] and during a period when there was rampant anti-Semitism in German theology (Bauer's later works being a good example), this work by Bauer is a serious and scholarly analysis of the prophetic traditions. The work is part of a serious orthodox Hegelian analysis of the expression and development of the Absolute Spirit in the Hebrew laws, morals, and prophetic utterances. At this time there is no rejection of religion or critique of its form. Bauer is still under the Hegelian influence, which sees religion as an expression of the Absolute Spirit just below in importance its more rational expression in philosophy. Crucial to our examination of the social ethics of the Hebrew tradition and its influence on Marx is the section in the first volume dealing with property rights and the law.

Bauer stresses that land and ownership are inseparable in the Hebrew tradition. Ownership of property lies in the hands of God only. There is no concept of private ownership as it exists in modern political thought. The individual is a steward of the land and participates in its fruits only as a member of a family and only as result of the largesse of God. Access to the basic material means for the satisfaction of fundamental human needs is also the basis for the family and the foundation upon which it rests. There were concrete limits to the alienation of the land, which ultimately could never be truly alienated or sold from the family. This was the reason for the institutionalization of the sabbatical and the jubilee years. They were mechanisms used to reestablish the bonds between the family and nature. In the second volume, the prophets are seen as the objective manifestation (consciousness as posited in Hebrew social institutions) and self-consciousness of the Absolute Spirit (*"Jeway,"* i.e., *Yahweh*). They are "the historical appearances of God's goal."[13]

God has created the nation, but the unity between humankind and God has not been actualized in the totality (*"ist noch nicht die wesentliche"*). This unity is re-created through the mediation (*Vermittlichung*) of history, so that the nation becomes the "determination of the thoughts of Jehovah."[14] It is in history and through society that God objectifies and determines himself and expresses his being as self-consciousness. This is not to mean, however, that he is affected by this historical process since he is unchanging and eternal. It is through the community and the laws that God appears in history and it is also through the people that nature, the finite, and God are united. In the introduction to the first volume of his work, Bauer uses the term alienation (*Entfremdung*) to refer to the inner contradiction between the forms of the appearances of revelation in the finite and the absolute and infinite divine will.[15] He uses the term *fremde Gottheiten* when referring to false gods worshiped after the breakup of the initial unity between God and humanity. However, for the most part, the terms used in the second volume, when referring to this contradiction between history and the divine, are different: *Collision, Selbstsucht, Losgerrissenheit*, and *Widerspruch*.[16] The contradiction between the appearance of the transcendent divine will and goal of self-conscious determination in history results in God being driven back into his inner self.[17]

Here the emphasis, for Bauer, is on the failure of the people to realize the divine will in the covenant and the conflict between the divine and the human. Justice (*Gerechtigkeit*) involves the reunification of the two conflicting and opposing elements of the unity. The nation contains the inner determination of Jehovah's will, but doesn't recognize it as such. It does not have the self-consciousness that could restore this unity. The reconciliation and restoration of this unity from its contradiction (*Widerspruch*) is the goal of the prophets, guided by the picture of a new ideal world. Conflict arises, however, when the nation fails to perceive that it is an expression of the will of the divine, when there is a contradiction between *Gerechtigkeit* and *Wahrhaftigkeit*.[18] The son of man as prophesied in Isaiah 4:2 will ultimately reconcile the contradiction between human history and the ideal world as God returns to himself. The terminology and the construction of the biblical exegesis involves a reading of Hegel's *Phenomenology of Spirit* into the Old Testament.

Reconciliation is possible only after the destruction of the Hebrew nation and a new covenant with Jehovah is established. No longer bound to formal cults and institutionalized rituals, this new relationship will involve a new inner transformation of his people. Bauer's work on the Old Testament was a direct response to Strauss whom he believed guilty of the "sin of modern consciousness."[19] At the time, Bauer was much more an orthodox and conservative Hegelian and rejected Strauss's claim that the Bible was simply a historical document, a historical reflection of the early Christian community. He further rejected the argument that God himself was the product of the imaginative and mythological construction of this community. In both cases, he was defending the Hegelian notion of the Absolute Spirit. By 1841 and the publication of his *Kritik der evangelischen Geschichte der Synoptiker*, Bauer had moved to the left of Strauss and had radicalized his theological position on the New Testament gospels. They became a literary and mythological expression of writers and were not based on any historical reality. This also meant that he rejected the historical reality of Jesus. The foundations for his atheism were now set, as well as the claim that he was the "Robespierre of theology."[20]

With the emphasis on the objectification of the Hegelian Spirit in

Hebrew history and Bauer's exegetical writings on the Old and New Testaments, Marx became acquainted with the sociological foundations of Hebrew political economy and its theory of social justice. Along with this work, which stresses the movement of self-consciousness in history, Bauer also was the individual most responsible for Marx's choice of dissertation topic; it was Bauer who contra Hegel argued that, through the post-Aristotelian Greek philosophy of the Epicureans, Stoics, and Skeptics, self-consciousness became the supreme value in Western thought. Through their criticisms of the abstract formalism and philosophical system building of Plato and Aristotle, individual autonomy and freedom were reflections of this newly created self-consciousness. Just as Bauer saw the prophets as reacting to the alien subjection of reason to the particular and abstract legal codes of Hebrew society, he also saw post-Aristotelian philosophy as occupying a similar position with regard to the alien metaphysical systems of Greek thought.[21] These very ideas formed the heart of Marx's later critique of religion and theory of ideology.

Property, Justice, and Freedom in the Old Testament

As we have seen with Marx's analysis of Epicurus and Aristotle and their emphasis on self-conscious individualism and the political nature of mankind, respectively, there was a real tension existing within both Greek philosophy and Greek society between the needs of the individual and the demands of the community. The Greek striving for freedom and self-realization within the community provided the teleological and anthropological foundations for the whole question of social justice. The latter category was never dealt with in isolation from the broader questions about the nature and structure of society as happens in liberal social and political theory. For the Greeks, justice is simply the social basis upon which is built the economic and political foundations for the realization of human nature and happiness. Aristotle viewed justice as an end in itself, as an expression of self-realization within the political community. In the Hebrew tradition, there are two terms used to define different aspects of justice. The first is *mispat* (justice), which refers to justice, law, norms, and legal right. The second term is *sedakah* (righteousness), which refers to the internal nature and quality of the individual who is righteous. The latter category also implies a kindness, gift, or generosity.[22]

Whereas Aristotle also saw a relationship between the macro and micro aspects of ethics, that is, a relationship between justice and virtue, there appears to be a difference between the micro and macro in the Hebrew tradition. In the Old Testament, justice is always directed by kindness and mercy for the poor and the oppressed as a result of a divine command and covenant with God. While both the Greek and the Hebrew concepts of justice refer to the integration and preservation of the harmony of the community, the Hebrew concept is biased more heavily toward helping the lower classes in society and also involves a more metaphysical component. In fact, it is this latter that is central to Hebrew ethics and is contained in both the covenant between God and his people and in the very nature of the Hebrew perception of God as uniting the community in love, equality, and human dignity. The creation myth in the book of Genesis provides the anthropological foundations for the covenant and legal codes.

> Justice is not an ancient custom, a human intervention, a value, but a transcendent demand, freighted with divine concern. It is not only a relationship between man and man, it is an act involving God, a divine need. Justice is his line, righteousness his plummet (Isa. 28:17). It is not one of His ways, but in all His ways. Its validity is not only universal, but also eternal, independent of will and experience.[23]

Though injustice is done to individuals, the emphasis throughout the Old Testament is on the covenant between God and humanity; the critical focus is on the class nature of society and its social structures. Fundamentally, the Hebrew notion of justice is a social category, which is centrally concerned with the community, which, in turn, rests upon a covenant with the divine. This is not to be confused with the issues of charity and good works. The structures of political economy and the access to and stewardship over social wealth form the key components of the Hebrew theory of social justice.

The covenant is an historical act by which the community is established based on ethical principles and the divine. It also represented a return to the ethical precepts established during the long history of the Hebrew people and a recognition of their liberation from slavery at the hands of the Egyptians. Stephan Mott says, "Justice is not reduced to a formal principle of reconciliation or faithfulness to unspecified types of community relationships. It is restoration of that community as originally established by the justice of God; it is a community of equality and freedom from oppression."[24]

This is an interesting aspect of the Hebrew notion of justice; it has a religious, ethical, philosophical, and historical component. The latter includes the relatively egalitarian nature of early Hebrew society, the history of the developments of its legal and ethical codes, the admonitions against infringements on these earlier ideals, and a call for concrete historical redress by the prophets when either was broken. Centuries before the classical Greek period, the land tenure system had changed in Israel from a peasant society of equal and independent landholders to a class system based on concentrated economic wealth of the *latifundia*. The result was a greater disparity of wealth, poverty, suffering, and slavery.[25] There is a long history of the evolution of the legal traditions in the Bible and its call for the protection of human rights to home, property, and the community.[26] It establishes the material foundations without which a community could not exist— property (justice) and mutual trust (grace and love). Both the Hebrew and Greek traditions recognized that ethics and social justice were to be based on a real community of equals with a just moral economy cemented by love, friendship, and respect for human needs.

In addition to the Ten Commandments, there are more social rights established in the Mosaic codes of the Exodus, dealing with questions of interest, loan pledges, slavery, common rights of poor to fallow vineyards, and the proper dealings with the defenseless, poor, widows, and orphans (Exodus 21–23). Around the early seventh century B.C., there was a reiteration and expansion of the law of Moses, which included other specific recommendations to avoid a disruptive and unjust class society. This included the poor legislation of the sabbatical year (Deuteronomy 14–34). At a later historical period around the time of the Exile, there occurred a further expansion of these protections for the poor with the development of the jubilee year with its prohibitions against the maintenance of a slave and debtor class (Leviticus 17–26).[27] Leviticus 25 is the famous section in which the notion of the jubilee year is mentioned. The establishment of limitations on debt-servitude has, according to Robert North, its origins in another unknown ancient document; its structural elements can be found in Exodus 21, Deuteronomy 15, Nehemiah 5, Isaiah 5 and 61:2, and Amos.[28] Throughout these periods, the creation of the Hebrew legal tradition based on egalitarianism and a free peasantry took place. There occurred rapid social developments resulting in a new social system out of the nomadic and patriarchal society of the Exodus period. The result was a changing landscape of the economic and political system based on the *latifundia* and the growing inequality of the new class system. It was to this new social system, the breaking of the covenant, and the undermining of the ethical principles of social justice that the eighth-century B.C. prophets spoke.

According to Numbers 26, land was originally divided by God into relatively equal shares and given to families as their patrimonial right. These patrimonial land divisions were the basis for both the rights of the family and the foundation of the community. It was this view of society that became the vision upon which the later prophetic denunciations of social transgressions were directed. For the Hebrews, landownership always rested with God, while people were simply the stewards or hereditary tenants of the land (Leviticus 25). All alienation, changes of title, and debt-servitude were viewed as temporary and after a period of time, the land was expected to be returned to the family of the rightful ancestral owner. The social reform of the Hebraic law codes attempted to recall these ancient customs and legally institutionalize "the three demands for the remission of debts, the freeing of slaves, and the redistribution of the land."[29]After forty-nine years, all ancestral lands freely alienated or taken away in foreclosures or sharecropping arrangements were to be returned to their original owner (principle of redress);[30] land was to lie fallow for the poor; debts were to be remitted and slaves were to be freed; and there was also the usual prohibition against idolatry (false gods).

God's essence is justice and the essence of justice is a moral economy based on the solidarity of the community, human rights, equality, and love. God manifests and realizes himself in and through history and the social relationships of Hebrew society. The prohibition against idolatry is a prohibition against certain types of social relationships that undermine that community and, in turn, undermine the covenant and the ability of God to manifest himself and become real in history. Thus the issue of idolatry is an issue of moral economy and ethics. A spiritual or formalistic reading of these texts will miss these crucial points. "I hate, I despise your feasts, and I take no delight in your solemn assemblies. Even though you offer me your burnt offerings and cereal offerings, I will not accept them, and the peace offerings of your fatted beast I will not look upon. Take away from me the noise of your songs; to the melody of your harps I will not listen. But let justice roll down like waters, and the righteous like an everflowing stream."[31] These feasts and religious festivals are manifestations of idolatry as much as the belief in a pagan god or the veneration of golden idols, because the participants have forgotten that God and justice are social relationships and not things to be worshiped.

The development of the Hebrew legal codes and the corresponding covenant were certainly an attempt to institutionalize, at least ideally, the ethical principles of an egalitarian society in the ancient tradition in which there would be no poverty or economic oppression.[32] "But there will be no poor among you (for the Lord will bless you in the land which the Lord your God gives you for an inheritance to possess)."[33] There is throughout these writings constant need to remember that the God who liberated the Jews from bondage and oppression in Egypt is incapable of permitting the same type of social relationships to be established in Israel.[34]

From Amos to Isaiah, the Hebrew prophetic tradition beginning around the eight century B.C. developed a theory of justice and social ethics that stressed the socioeconomic component of morality, rather than a highly individualistic morality or a rigid legal formalism. The emphasis was not on individual behavior in relation to a set of universal moral or metaphysical norms, but rather on the nature and structure of society, especially in the areas of the concentration of economic wealth, power, and poverty. Unlike developments in the nonprophetic traditions and later developments of Christianity, moral transgression for the prophets was viewed as a social phenomenon, that is, as a social sin.[35] Morality was understood as a form of social ethics. Individual concerns, such as ritualistic and legal behavior, emphasis on individual conscience, the spiritual state of the individual, and personal sin, were not crucial to this ethic. Rather, the key issues centered around an examination of the types of social arrangements that impeded the organization of a community based on social justice. "Therefore because you trample upon the poor, and take from him exactions of wheat: you have built houses of hewn stone, but you shall not dwell in them; you have planted pleasant vineyards, but you shall not drink their wine. For I know how many are your transgressions, and how great are your sins—you who afflict the righteous, who take a bribe, and turn aside the needy in the gate."[36]

Inhumanity, economic oppression, poverty became those sins that precipitate the anger of God. From conspicuous palatial homes and concentrated agrarian landholdings of the wealthy, to bribery, slavery, legalized stealing through taxes, fines, charging interest on loans, and perjured judges, the prophets' charges of the corruption and immorality of the social system piled up. Isaiah says that the spirit of the Lord cries out, "Woe to those who decree iniquitous decrees, and the writers who keep writing oppression, to turn aside the needy from justice and to rob the poor of my people of their right, that widows may be their spoil and that they may make the fatherless their prey."[37]

Social justice became the watchword for the prophets as they measured their society against the humanistic ideals of an egalitarian vision. Religion for these men was not defined in terms of acceptable theological perspectives, metaphysical premises, or the correct understanding of the essence of God, but rather became defined in terms of the nature of the relationships within society—that is, the justice of that society. The sins of the community are measured by economic and social standards, such as the fine houses of the wealthy, and by how poverty is created and maintained by oppressive taxes, fines, and usury imposed on the poor. Amos argues that the hypocrisy of the wealthy at religious feasts and assemblies is anathema to God. Temple worship and religious practices meant nothing to the Hebrew God, only the justice of a nonrepressive society.

As José Miranda argues in *Communism in the Bible*, the poor person is not perceived as virtuous for being poor, nor is the rich person viewed as evil for his acts.[38] Rather, it is the relationship between the two caused by differentiated wealth that produces the condemnation. It is not wealth per se that is rejected, just the oppression and inhumanity caused by inequality of its distribution. It will only be later, when Christianity unites the concept of God to Greek metaphysics with its philosophical concerns for the essential and real that the nature of religion will be transformed into a formal theological system. Even when Isaiah prophesies the coming of the Messiah, it is expressed as the coming of justice in this life. "Of the increase of his government and peace there will be no end, upon the throne of David, and over his kingdom, to establish it, and to uphold it with justice and with righteousness from this time forth and for evermore. The zeal of the Lord of hosts will do this."[39]

Justice involves the moral condemnation of a whole society and its political economy based on the criteria of concern and love for one's fellow being. It is an ethical system based on the *halakhah*, "that man must act not only according to the general principles of justice, truth, and love, but that every act of life be 'sanctified,' becoming imbued with the religious spirit."[40] Sin was defined as a social transgression and ultimately tied to a very definite understanding of the nature of humanity and the quest for human freedom.[41] As with the concept of idolatry to be discussed shortly, the Hebrew perspective revolves around a social teleology that stresses human potentiality without naming or defining the final goals. As in the Greek and German traditions, ethics is tied to a critique of false universality, false claims to moral truth, and a critique of legalistic definitions of morality. Ethics is connected to both a theory of human potentiality and a theory of society that nurtures and maintains those historical possibilities. "Man, the prisoner of nature, becomes free by becoming fully human. In the biblical and later Jewish view, freedom and independence are the goals of human development, and the aim of human action is the constant process of liberating oneself from the shackles that bind man to the past, to nature, to the clan, and to idols."[42]

The Hebrew notion of the individual stresses the social being of people. Erich Fromm and José Comblin argue that to be free is to be free within the movement of the spirit and thus their concept of freedom is limited by their concept of God. Fromm deals with the issue by ultimately negating and transcending the concept of God, while Comblin ties the notion of God to the spirit of the community. In both these interpretations of the Hebrew tradition, there is an incipient notion of nontheism. Freedom, as it evolves in the New Testament and in particular the Pauline notion of freedom, is defined in terms of that community.

> To be free is to be with others, to enter into new human relations inspired by love. The actual content of freedom is the relation of reciprocal openness and mutual service between men. There is no such thing as a freedom of man on his own. From the time of the Renaissance modern western civilization has developed an ideal of individual liberation consisting of self-affirmation of the isolated and autonomous individual: freedom of the "conquistador." But to dominate is not to be free; it is to be related by the passion for domination and to be incapable of love, that is of being a man. There is liberation only in a new relationship between men and nature.[43]

It is this idea of the relationship between freedom and the community that is an essential characteristic of the Hebrew and early Christian perspectives on human liberation. What is missing from this perspective, however, is the importance of the political community and democratic participation as may be found in the Greek polis. Though the above quotation summarizes the Pauline view with its emphasis on openness and mutual service, it also summarizes the continuity between the Old and New Testaments. The idea that we are free to the extent that we are part of a wider social whole, committed to the good of the community, and expressing our individual selves in terms of the community is an idea that belongs to the classical Hebrew, Greek, and German traditions of social theory. It is explicit in both the Old and New Testament, but has been lost in modern liberal thought, especially since the developments in sixteenth-century Protestantism, seventeenth-century Catholic Jansenism, seventeenth-century natural rights tradition (i.e., Hobbes and Locke), and the eighteenth-century Scottish Enlightenment (i.e., Hume and Smith).[44] The cause of this lies not only in the rationalization of science and the secularization of society, but also in the changes in the orientations within the church and the exegetical reinterpretation of many key concepts and passages in the Bible. For example, the Hebrew concept of justice (*sedakah*) has been translated in later Christianity as almsgiving (*eleemosyne*) and as compassion (*eleos*).[45] The biblical concept of freedom has been interpreted in later times as spiritual freedom from the material world and the kingdom of God has been translated as a transcendent realm of spiritual bliss (the *Parousia*). The development of Western Christianity has dematerialized and depoliticized the very political and economic implications in the biblical notions of justice, freedom, and liberation. Within this broader biblical tradition, there is a fundamental split between the ancients and moderns.

What is truly interesting in the prophetic tradition is the rather complex relationship between religion and atheism. Both Ernst Bloch and Erich Fromm developed the thesis that the logic of the critique of idolatry and the Hebrew concepts of the community and justice pushed the Hebrew religion in the direction of atheism. That is, the principles of justice underlying the community required humankind to realize its own rationality within society even to the extent of the loss of God. For Bloch, the rejection of a belief in God is demanded by the belief in a God who stresses the rejection of all forms of idolatry and the acceptance of human freedom and rationality. If people are made in the image and likeness of God, then human freedom requires a radical social freedom from all forms of metaphysical coercions, that is, atheism.[46] Fromm argues that Judaism is not a religion, but an ethical system in which the very idea of God cannot be articulated. God's name is nameless, he is *Eheyeh*. According to Meister Eckhart, the more you seek the hidden God, the less chance you have of finding him. "You should seek Him in such a way as not to find Him."[47] The fear of making God into an object, into an idol, is later developed in the Talmudic tradition to the point where there is a trend to "make man completely autonomous even to the point where he will be free from God, or, at least, where he can deal with God on terms of equality."[48] Fromm traces the Hasidic literature to give examples of where Hebrew lawgivers challenged God and his interpretations of the law and *halakhah* in face-to-face discussions; it is the dynamic community that has final say even over the formal claims of God himself.

In the book of Amos, the idea is developed that social injustice is itself a form of idolatry. In chapter 2, Amos critically attacks the cultic religious ceremonies of the ancient Hebrews and in the process directly connects the issues of social justice and idolatry.

> For three transgressions of Israel and for four, I will not revoke the punishment; because they sell the righteous for silver, and the needy for a pair of shoes—they trample the head of the poor into the dust of the earth and turn aside the way of the afflicted; a man and his father go in to the same maiden, so that my holy name is profaned; they lay themselves down beside every altar upon garments taken in pledge; and in the house of their God they drink the wine of those who have been fined.[49]

This passage is similar to that in Jeremiah 7:5ff. where idolatry is directly connected to stealing, murder, adultery, and perjury. These various forms of oppression and violence are idolatrous in that they form the false framework for the worship of *Yahweh*; they are forms of false objectivity for they turn ethics into religion—a reified body of codes, formal prayers, and ossified ceremonies directed at a transcendent God. He requires justice and righteousness, and even when the cultic ceremonies are performed correctly, it remains a false homage when not related to social justice. The cultic prostitution, misuse of the pledged garments, and the drinking of the wine of fined individuals in the sanctuaries are all activities condemned by Amos as part of cultic religion and the worship of false gods. J. Lindblom argues that these cults were alien to the religion of *Yahweh*. When religious ceremony replaces concern for the poor and the oppressed, then social justice is replaced by idolatry.[50] Thus idolatry can be seen in this context as the formation of both a religion and named (reified) God.

Idolatry, False Universality, and the Hebrew Prophets

There seems to be a very close parallel between the prophet's condemnation of idolatry and Marx's critique of alienation and false objectification. In fact, Marx makes reference to the Old Testament to indicate that he, too, is aware of the parallels.[51] The notion of idolatry is the essential category of the Old Testament and, perhaps, as Fromm argues, higher than the worship of God himself. It deals not only with the critique of the false gods of Bethel, Gilgal, and Beersheba in Amos, but also with anything that would tend to undermine the integrity of human creativity and the community. As Isaiah says regarding the foreigners from the East, "Their land is filled with silver and gold, and there is no end to their treasures; their land is filled with horses and there is no end to their chariots. Their land is filled with idols; they bow down to the work of their hands, to what their own fingers have made. So man is humbled and men are brought low—forgive them not."[52]

Though both adultery and the worshiping of false gods with their altars and rituals are forms of idolatry for the prophets, the latter concept also included the false consciousness by which something that was created by people is mistaken for something divine or something particular and contingent is mistaken for something universal. This pathology of religion can be interpreted in a variety of ways: (1) the Hebrews were critical of calling anything divine that was the product of human hands—the idols, that is—mistaking the human for divine. (2) They were critical of the notion that anything created could lay claim to moral universality.[53] (3) The critique of idols was based on the belief of the freedom of the individual from all forms of religious coercion. (4) Idolatry, or the worship of a thing, also turns the worshiper into a thing.[54] The concept of idolatry includes a profound understanding of both ethics and human nature. The nature of God cannot be defined nor can the essential qualities of being human. Morality cannot be imposed from without nor can it be determined by scientific laws having universal certitude. Here there is an epistemological similarity to the ethical dilemmas raised by Aristotle.

The critique of idolatry running throughout the prophetic tradition is thus not really a metaphysical or theological issue about the existence or nonexistence of false gods, but mainly a moral issue, since an idolatrous creation or relationship shifts the locus of morality toward the transcendent and away from the moral economy of the community. Morality, for the Hebrews, Greeks, and Marx, was something that evolved from within the community. Just as there is no morality outside of the concrete historical situation in the Hebrew tradition, there is also no truth. The moral epistemology that underlies this tradition stresses that there is no epistemological split between knowledge and *praxis* as there is in the modern concept of truth with its correctness in mirroring reality. By not splitting concept and reality, the Hebrews saw truth as a form of ethical *praxis*.

As José Bonino has written, "There is, therefore, no knowledge except in action itself."[55] In a sense, one doesn't know the truth, one does the truth and it is social activity. In the very process of creating and acting upon ethical values within the community, God is known; the two are indistinguishable. God cannot be known directly, since he is nameless. Thus, the ancient Hebrew tradition emphasized that both morality and knowledge were part of society and history and thus part of social ethics. It is this synthesis of ethics and epistemology that forms the framework within which Marx himself will later develop his critique of political economy. According to Gregory Baum, this broad interpretation of idolatry was replaced by a more limited understanding of the meaning of idolatry as simply the critique of false gods. An appreciation of its broader meaning and its underlying moral epistemology results in a different view in which the condemnation of idols becomes transformed into a critique of all forms of ethical knowledge, which results in the "absolutizing of the finite and the elevating of a part to be the ultimate measure of truth."[56] The clearest statement of the nature of idolatry is in Isaiah 44:9–18:

All who make idols are nothing and the things they delight in do not profit; their witnesses neither see nor know, that they may be put to shame. Who fashions a god or casts an image, that is profitable for nothing? Behold, all his fellows shall be put to shame, and the craftsmen are but men; let them all assemble, let them stand forth, they shall be terrified, they shall be put to shame together . . . he plants a cedar and the rain nourishes it. Then it becomes fuel for a man; he takes a part of it and warms himself, he kindles a fire and bakes bread; also he makes a god and worships it, he makes a graven image and falls down before it. Half of it he burns in the fire; over the half he eats flesh, he roasts meat and is satisfied; also he warms himself and says, "Aha, I am warm, I have seen fire!" And the rest of it he makes into a god, his idol; and falls down to it and worships it; he prays to it and says, "Deliver me, for thou art my god!" They know not, nor do they discern; for he has shut their eyes, so that they cannot see, and their minds, so that they cannot understand.[57]

Humans take wood from the forest to make their fires and bake their bread, and from this same wood they make idols, which can neither see nor know. Idols neither perceive nor think, since they are not real. Only a fool would construct such images and idols and think that they are gods. Both John McKenzie and Edward Young argue that the sarcasm of this passage is best viewed in juxtaposition with the passage in Genesis 1:26–27 in which God makes humanity in his image and likeness.[58] The idolaters are *tohu*, a term that also comes from Genesis meaning waste and uninhabitable earth. In verse 9 of Isaiah 44, it is written that the images are all unreal and their makers do not profit from them. The makers do not recognize the "nothingness" of their creations.[59] People fall down before "a stock of wood." Idols seem to represent the passion for possession, for having the divine as an object of worship, and, therefore, present the possibility of potential control through ceremonial correctness. Idolatry turns the rationality and creativity of humanity into its opposite as they are used to create objects that limit its freedom, imprison its reason, and destroy its moral community. The latter is undermined since the community is no longer an expression of justice, nor the means through which God is known, but instead becomes the technical force through which the proper ceremonies are performed. The community, as the basis for ethics, is displaced by a distorted relationship with an objectified divinity. Morality as a form of social emancipation within the community is replaced by a personal relationship to the transcendent.

Fetishism of Objectivity: Marx on Alienation and Idolatry

For Marx, the concern with idolatrous relations indicates his interest in the various forms of false universality, that is, mistaking the particular for the universal in its various religious, psychological, political, and economic forms. These were generally expressed in the creation of universal and unchanging categories of human nature, political obligations, natural rights, and laws of the market; all these, in turn, were variations of the rationality, both structural and theoretical, of the marketplace. This is why the question of alienation is so important. While the content, direction, and method of Marx's analysis changes throughout his life, one of the underlying motifs, which colors and pervades everything he writes, is this issue of idolatry: the objectification of false truths that distort and hide humanity's potential and true social relationships (ideology). It is a theme that he also develops from his reading of the critical works of Feuerbach, especially his *Essence of Christianity*. *On the Jewish Question* represents a critique of religion and Judaism, in particular, but within the framework already established by the prophetic tradition. It is a work that is a microcosm of his own future intellectual development in his later writings on political economy.

Beginning with a rejection of religion, he will expand his critical perspective to encompass not only religion, but the political and economic spheres of life. Beginning with a response to the question of whether Jews should be granted civil liberties, he develops a critique of the natural rights tradition, the bourgeois state, and the conflicts between the state and civil society (economy). It is a more comprehensive view of alienation grounded in the Hebrew tradition. The essay may be divided into seven parts, which trace the evolution of Marx's thinking on political and economic idolatry: (1) the introduction of the question of Jewish civil liberties in terms of a contradiction between religious prejudice and political emancipation; (2) the response of Bruno Bauer, who demands political emancipation as the answer to the dilemma; (3) Marx's critique of Bauer for his inability to present an adequate and more sophisticated notion of emancipation; (4) Marx's articulation of the meaning and implications of political emancipation and the relationships between religion and politics—politics is viewed as simply another form of religious distortion and false universality; (5) Marx's critique of political emancipation as a false universality and distortion of people's species being; (6) analysis of the distinction between "the rights of the citizen"—civil rights and political liberties in the public sphere—and "the rights of man"—economic rights of property, security, liberty, and equality in the private sphere (the former he defends and the latter he criticizes); and finally, (7) his conclusions and statements on the distinction between political and human emancipation, political/economic rights and true human rights.

This relatively unknown and forgotten essay (mainly because it is so complex and controversial) is by far one of the most important pieces in his voluminous body of work. It gives us insight into the motivating force in his personal and intellectual life and is an articulate expression of his critique of modern liberalism based on the principles of idolatry and objectification. The false universality of religion is replaced in modern times by new forms of religiosity that continue to distort the relation between the universal and the particular. "The members of the political state are religious because of the dualism between individual life and species-life, between the life of civil society and political life. They are religious in the sense that man treats political life, which is remote from his own individual existence, as if it were his true life; and in the sense that religion is here the spirit of civil society, and expresses the separation and withdrawal of man from man."[60]

Religion created a split between the universal and the particular, between God and the finite, since the community failed to recognize that it was the creator of its universal values and the very notion of God itself. By the nineteenth century, religion no longer played such a central role in modernity, but the tensions and distortions that it introduced were taken over by the political sphere. Marx continues to argue that political liberalism is filled with the "creations of fantasy, dreams, the postulates of Christianity" because liberalism universalizes, like Christianity, the ideals of "man as he has been corrupted, lost to himself, alienated, subjected to the rule of inhuman conditions and elements, by the whole organization of our society."[61]

The state in modern society now holds the position formerly held by religion in that it constructs a "spiritual" relationship between concepts and reality, political institutions and the reality of a class society. It creates the image of social interaction and harmony based on the political values of liberty, property, security, and equality. The rights of man justify the universality of the modern state, but, in fact, what are justified are egoism, fragmentation, private interest, and the destruction of the real species being. The true social and communal nature of humankind is undermined by the idolatry of modernity. Politics and religion become affairs of the heart and limits on the application of reason as they retreat from any real social significance or efficacy in civil society. Both are creations of the mind that mask the underlying social reality; in the end, humans create objects that are "delectable things" from which they "shall not profit."[62] Marx concludes this section with the notion that the political emancipation from religion leaves the religious mentality in place, since religious consciousness and spirit of false universality still prevail within the political.

The reality of the religious spirit is masked by the ideology of political liberalism. The next step is to analyze the ideology and false consciousness of the market economy. There is a short essay in his next work *Early Economic and Philosophic Manuscripts* entitled "Alienated Labor." In it, he develops more explicitly the notion of objectification and alienation (idolatry) within the economic structures of liberalism.

All these consequences are implied in the statement that the worker is related to the *product of his labour* as to an *alien object*. For on this premise it is clear that the more the worker spends himself, the more powerful becomes the alien world of objects which he creates over and against himself, the poorer he himself—his inner world—becomes, the less belongs to him as his own. It is just the same in religion. The more man puts into God, the less he retains in himself. The worker puts his life into the object; but now his life no longer belongs to him but to the object.[63]

Thus, the externalized object (objectification) stands opposed to the individual and assumes a position of an autonomous and alien power over and against him. Contrast the above quotation from Marx with Fromm's description of idolatry in his work *Marx's Concept of Man*. "Man transfers his own passions and qualities to the idol. The more he impoverishes himself, the greater and stronger becomes the idol."[64] The idol becomes a thing, an independent force against which the individual loses the sense of self and freedom. It is a force that defines and limits the parameters of the individual's activity and being. For the Hebrews, it was the force that destroyed the community and set up false creations by the people thus leading to false consciousness and distorted religious practices. It ultimately reduced social relationships between individuals to relationships mediated by an object—in this case a religious object.

Religion is the product of this idolatry and false consciousness. To this extent, both the prophets and Marx were atheists; they were the critics of religion and their false gods. While the prophets rejected as idolatrous the worship of interests, accumulated and concentrated private property, differentiated wealth, and poverty, it is Marx who attempts to understand the ideological and structural components of this social critique. His venture into political economy and his examination of topics, such as the logic of capital, use value and exchange value, value and surplus value, the tendential fall in the rate of profit, and the immiseration of the working class, are ultimately based on this notion of alienated objectification. These are the systems and structures that modern society has created as its idols and that keep humankind from realizing its potential, as a species that constructs institutions for human emancipation. These institutions are wrapped in the ideology of universality, necessity, and rationality, thereby becoming unquestionable elements of nature. And there is no longer a self-consciousness about their historical origins or development, nor a self-consciousness about human control over their future. Rationality is transcendent to the extent that it lies in the structures and mechanisms of a market economy, but not in human control over the decisions, directions, and goals of this social system. Humanity is now ruled by immutable and godlike laws over which it has no control and no understanding.

Miranda has done an interesting job in reconstructing the relationship between Marx and the biblical tradition, especially in his chapters "The Gospel Roots of Marx's Thought" and "Marx's Thought as a Conscious Continuation of Early Christianity" in *Marx against the*

Marxists.[65] He has conscientiously traced Marx's references to the Bible in order to draw a closer connection between the two. He argues that Jesus is the first individual to have denounced money as a real idol. The reader can check the abundant textual notations from Marx, which Miranda feels clearly justifies the relation between fetishism and idolatry (*Theories of Surplus Value* 3: 470, 456, 494, 498, *Grundrisse* 221, 199, 222, 229, *Capital* 1:132, 133, 754, 751, 3:597–598, 392, 393; *Contribution to Critique of Political Economy*, 125, ftn. 3). In the many passages mentioned by Miranda, he has noticed that Marx used the German term *Machwerk* when referring to the artificial creations of human hands; this is the same technical term used in the German Bible to refer to false gods.[66] Throughout his writings on fetishism, Marx uses other terms to refer to the same point, terms such as Moloch, Baal, and Mammon; the last term is used only in the New Testament (three times in Luke, once in Matthew, and in all cases by Jesus). Miranda argues that Marx is making a direct link between his political economy and the biblical condemnation of money and capital. He believes that Marx is the best commentator and analyst of Jesus' pronouncements on money and wealth. Throughout his work, there is continuous documentation of those passages, which he believes are the product of Marx's debt to the classical Hebrew legacy.

Since the Reformation, the Enlightenment, the development of commercial and industrial capitalism, and other institutions of modernity, religion is no longer the integrative force it once was. The social relations have been transformed and, along with them, the forms of idolatry; its new objects of false consciousness and universality have changed from false gods to false theories of political economy.[67] In both cases, they are seen as reified and objectified, transcendent and independent of people. Whether they are the laws of gods or laws of the market, Marx is critical of all forms of objectification that leave people dependent on their alienated logic. This includes the fetishism of ideology and consciousness—the fetishism of metatheory. Beginning in his earlier works with a critique of objectification (alienation) in the workplace, his later writings mark a shift to the critique of alienated consciousness and the ideology of liberalism. "These metals (gold and silver) have been turned into idols. . . ." They have been transformed into "divinities."[68]

Demystifying Power and Social Amnesia

The modern theories of possessive individualism, liberalism, and classical economics, along with the institutions of the market economy, which they attempt to legitimate, have evolved into reified structures. They have become idolatrous creations, autonomous entities with their own independent laws, before which we are all humble supplicants incapable of either ethical appraisal or political action. Marx begins the section on the "Fetishism of the Commodity" at the end of chapter 1 in the first volume of *Capital* with the warning that a commodity appears to be a very trivial thing, but oddly enough contains "metaphysical subtleties and theological niceties."[69] The commodity has been vested with religious qualities, because it too has become an idol. Marx says that just as the prophets condemned the Jewish people for failing to recognize the human design in the idols, now commodities, the products of exchange in a capitalist society, have also taken on these same objective characteristics. "A commodity is therefore a mysterious thing, simply because in it the social character of men's labour appears to them as an objective character stamped upon the product of labour."[70] It represents the same failure to see the social and historical character behind these created objects (idols).

Generally, relations between individuals within an exchange economy are based on what are perceived to be universal laws of exchange, such as supply and demand. The price mechanism and consumer needs determine how and who will participate in a transaction and how the final distribution of society's wealth will occur. However, Marx believed that these ideas were the creation of a reified consciousness, which could not penetrate to the class and power relations in society. These social relations were most clearly manifested for him at the point of production with the extraction of surplus labor and surplus value. The apologists for the system could not see that profits were produced not by the efficiency of modern technology or by means of the entrepreneurial skills and commercial dealings of the trader, but were made only through the exploitation of labor itself.[71] Nor could they see that the wage contract concealed a systemic inequality in which the owner paid only for the rejuvenation of the physical energy of the laborer lost during the work period (labor power) and not for the labor itself. This is the great secret of capital, for in it lies the answer to questions surrounding the acquisition of surplus and profits.[72] It is not the invisible hand, but the unseen visible hand that defines and determines profits. The God and religion that Marx rejects are the same God and religion the prophets critiqued over 2,500 years before. This relationship is clearly seen by Marx when he writes, "It cannot be otherwise in a mode of production in which the labourer exists to satisfy the needs of self-expansion of existing values, instead of, on the contrary, material wealth existing to satisfy the needs of development on the part of the labourer. As, in religion, man is governed by the products of his own brain, so in capitalist production, he is governed by the products of his own hand.''[73]

With the further expansion of the theories of political economy, a sophisticated ideology develops that hides the underlying social relationships at the point of production—worker alienation. "Political economy conceals the estrangement inherent in the nature of labour by not considering the direct relationship between the worker (labour) and production."[74] This brief statement in the *Paris Manuscripts*, which Marx will later develop in his *Theories of Surplus Value* with his analysis of the classical tradition of political economy, indicates his starting point in relation to false consciousness. The categories used by classical political economists, such as production, consumption, credit, money, division of labor, and so on, simply reflect, for Marx, the mechanism by which production takes place, but not the historical origins or the social relationships within which they occur. He seeks to examine the sociological dynamics underlying the economic structures themselves. According to Marx, the mode of production always includes both sociological and economic components, the class and technical moments of any social formation—the social relations of production and the productive forces.

It is when we view these relationships within the framework of immutable and universal theories that they take on the appearance of "the movement of pure reason," natural law, and, ultimately, "applied metaphysics."[75] Profit is the product of land, rent, or interest. Productivity comes from the efficiency of capital viewed as a technical means of production. As an alien force, power is attributed to things and not to the social relations derived from commodity production and the creation of exchange value. Profits result from the mechanism of commodity production and not from the oppressive social relations, which tie the wage laborer to the control and dictates of the owners of capital. Economic categories take on a life of their own and then attribute supernatural powers to the technical means of production.[76] This same ideology exists in religion, which also conceals the alienation and injustice in society by radically limiting or eliminating the materialist and economic components from its morality. Moral philosophy is the ideological expression of ethics separated from social reality.

In turn, anthropology and psychology become expressions for an unchanging human nature. The historical relationships between individuals, the social issues of power and authority, control and domination are hidden under reified structures in which the social form of interaction created by capitalism appears to be universal. They not only represent the institutional expressions of human nature, individualism, aggression, and self-interest, but they also express the veiling and hiding of the created hand. No recognition of the artificial nature, the alien force, or the relations of domination within capital is possible, for they are hidden behind the curtain or fetishism of commodity relationships: power relationships take on an objectivity and neutrality of a relationship between things, money, and commodities. These latter bear the imprint of legal relationships between market equals or the exchange of particular commodities governed by the autonomous laws of a free market.

This market rationality anesthetizes the social actor and, thereby, undermines the freedom, consciousness, and being of humankind. This distorted rationality (value rationalization) is beyond the critical scrutiny of self-consciousness, because historical institutions have been immunized against the recognition of their inherent subjectivity. The truth of the reified market economy is the subjective or social relationships built around contracts, private property, and the class power that flows from them. Marx says that "the producers do not come into social contact with each other until they exchange their products."[77] It is only in the process of exchange that we see their universal nature. We see that they all have a value measured by a universal common commodity—money.

Marx is adamant that by only examining the objective or more visible components of exchange, the use value of objects (utility) and their money equivalent, classical political economists have missed the underlying relations of power and exploitation. They have, therefore, missed the creation of exchange and surplus value, which is the major focus of the early sections of *Capital*. First, the failure to view the social relations underlying commodity exchange and market rationality means that political economists have also failed to see that the quality and form of labor itself have been historically and socially shaped into abstract labor, that is, the labor of an average skilled individual who works within an average amount of time. The form of labor under capitalism is totally unlike that of any other historical period, both in terms of the organization and structure of the immediate workplace, and in terms of the systematic leveling and averaging of the quality of labor produced. This marks the crucial revolutionary aspect of the new economic system for Marx. It lies not in the new science and technology, not in the new factories, not in the new forms of transportation and communication, but rather, in the social power and class relations of abstract production. That is, the traditional emphasis on craft and quality of production is reduced to a point where "the equalization of the most different kinds of labour can be the result only of an abstraction from their inequalities, or of reducing them to their common denominator, viz., expenditure of human labour-power or human labour in the abstract."[78] A few years earlier he wrote,

> Only the conventions of our everyday life make it appear commonplace and ordinary that social relations of production should assume the shape of things, so that the relations into which people enter in the course of their work appear as the relations of things to one another and of things to people. This mystification is still a very simple one in the case of a commodity. Everybody understands more or less clearly that the relations of commodities as exchange-values are really the relations of people to the productive activities of one another.[79]

This is the heart of Marx's position—social relations begin to take on the form of relations between things. The economy, social relations at the point of production and exchange, general interpersonal relationships, and finally, the categories of social science themselves reduce the complex social and historical relations of the economy to relationships between things and universal laws of explanatory and predictable human behavior.[80]

These are the mysteries and theological niceties, the hidden gods, that inhabit the economic realm. The categories of classical political economy could not enlighten us to this reality, since they are infatuated with the empirical phenomena of this social process (positivism). The essential relations are hidden behind mere appearances of empirical science. This whole process is completed when, through "mutual consent" and within a judicial framework that protects contracts and private property, the exchange of commodities is completed in the market. It is after the realization of the value of commodities in sale that the utility of a commodity can be realized, since the key to this system is that the producers do not produce for themselves (use value), but for the market (exchange value). The importance of production can only be proved by the success of exchange, and this is why the emphasis has been on exchange and consumption and not the process of production itself. Society produces not for the satisfaction of human needs, but for the production of profits. This is the major lesson of the historical shift from a moral economy to a political economy.

In volume 3 of *Capital*, Marx argues that it is this that will ultimately cause overproduction and bring on the crisis of capitalism. Goods made for the satisfaction of humans needs (material rationalization) are not overproduced, but rather, only commodities produced for the creation of profits (value rationalization).[81] It is not simply human need and aggregate demand that lubricates the system, but effective demand that can pay the price of the commodities. This is why there can be poverty in plenty, that is, wealth and riches and economic stagnation, when there is both real need and enormous demand for further production. It is the contradiction inherent in the structural foundations of the class system.[82] This is a crucial point, for it marks the transition in Marx's thought from the fetishism of social relationships and forms of consciousness (categories of political economy) to the analysis of surplus value. This latter category involves his examination of the logical and historical mechanism through which surplus and profits are created in capitalist society.

Marx recognizes that the process whereby the "bodily form" of the universal equivalent or universal form of exchange (money) is created is similar in form to the worship of false gods. Near the start of the second chapter of volume 1 of *Capital*, he consciously and very clearly connects idolatry in the Bible to the fetishism of the commodity. Quoting in Latin from John's New Testament book of Revelation, Marx makes the parallels explicit.

> Thereby the bodily form of this commodity becomes the form of the socially recognized universal equivalent. To be the universal equivalent, becomes, by this process, the specific function of the commodity thus excluded by the rest. Thus it becomes—money. *"Illi unum consilium habent et virtutem et potestatem suam bestiae tradunt. Et ne quis possit emere aut vendere, nisi qui habet characterem aut nomen bestiae, aut numerum nominis ejus"* (*Apocalypse*).[83]

> [These are of one mind and give over their power and authority to the beast.[84] So that no one can buy or sell unless he has the mark, that is, the name of the beast or the number of its name.[85]]

What is interesting is that the quotation combines passages from two separate chapters: the first line is from Revelation 17:13 and the second is from Revelation 13:17. The first line is taken from one of the apocalyptic prophecies of John in which an angel tells him the secrets of the "great harlot who is seated upon many waters." At first John marvels in amazement and admiration at the wonders of the "woman drunk with the blood of the saints and the blood of the martyrs of Jesus,'' sitting atop a beast "which was full of blasphemous names" and wearing a purple and scarlet gown with many precious jewels, pearls, and golden ornaments. The angel remarks, "Why marvel? I will tell you the mystery of the woman, and of the beast with seven heads and ten horns that carries her."[86] The beast will make war against the Lamb and the saints, but will be defeated. The secret of the mystery is that the beast "was, and is not and is to come." The beast exists, yet is not. That is, the beast exists, yet is not real. The woman is an image (idol) of economic riches and the good life, but must be maintained by the power of the kings (beast with seven heads and ten horns). Both appear to be real, but, in fact, must be maintained by force and domination over the just. Marx seems to be indicating, especially when one relates this to the context in which it is written in *Capital*, that there is a similarity between this and the creation of the modern image of the "universal equivalent"—money and the market exchange. Though the market is shrouded in the jewels of the liberal ideals of equality, freedom, and individualism, it is a mystery ultimately structured and maintained by force and class domination.

In the second line taken from Revelation 13:17, Marx seems to be making the connection between money, as the bodily form of the exchange process, and the second beast mentioned in this chapter. This is not the first beast with seven heads and ten crowned horns (power of kings) previously mentioned, but a second beast, who appears coming out of the earth with horns like a lamb and who speaks like a dragon. This second beast forces everyone to worship the first by performing great wonders and by deceiving everyone with its miracles. It also forces them to make idols to the beast to which it then gives life, while in the process killing those who would not worship it. "And it was allowed to give breath to the image of the beast so that the image of the beast should even speak, and to cause those who would not worship the image of the beast to be slain."[87] It is difficult to determine all the possible subtleties Marx is intending here, but one plausible interpretation is that the first beast is the economic system with its political and economic power, while the second beast with its passive and unobtrusive exterior (lamb horns) has the power to create deception, false consciousness, and idols.

Following immediately on the heels of the analysis of fetishism, Marx seems to be making a strong link between the idea of idolatry and fetishism, since both create systems in which reality is hidden from view and in which artificial creations take on divine dimensions.[88]

Just as the earth is forced to worship the beast, so, too, do we worship the economic beast with its drive for power and domination, its assertion of an innate and objectified view of human nature, and immutable laws of economic development, which include poverty, human misery, wars, and alienated labor. In both cases, we fail to recognize the true reality of the beast behind the graven image. Both are metaphysical systems for they create their own ontological realms inhabited by appearances of life, reality, and objectivity. They are the shadows thrown on the walls by the fire in Plato's cave. It is in the short next paragraph, after the quotes from Revelation, that Marx mentions the contrast between use value and exchange value and the transition from "products" to "commodities"; the latter is expressed in the form of money.[89] It is money that is the beast. This, however, is not simply money as found in *On the Jewish Question*, where Marx sees it as the external manifestation of alienated powers of humanity. Here, too, he connects the idea of money to the being of a false god. But he has not yet developed the categories of abstract labor, exchange value, and surplus value, which will give him a more sophisticated sense of the structure and idolatry of the economy system.[90] Money has many forms: it is not only an alien power, but also represents the external expression of the conflict between utility and exchange value, products and commodities; it is also the universal measure of commercial intercourse and the expression of capital as surplus value; and, finally, money is a form of domination and the social relations of production. The idol or ideology hides all these aspects of its historical being.

The social character of the organization of the factory system, the mechanization and formalization of the rhythms and patterns of work, the structures of alienation studied by Marx in his early and later writings, and the privatization of ownership of the productive process result in a form of "abstraction," that is, all labor is reduced to a common denominator by the whole process and, therefore, can be measured by a universal yardstick such as money. Use value takes second place to the exchange value of a commodity. This requires the reduction of the quality of a product in commodity exchange to its socially necessary labor time. This involves the reduction of both production of use value and labor itself to the common denominator of abstract general labor. All the different products of the productive process are reduced to one common quality—value (abstract social labor). Marx continues by reflecting on the importance of the labor theory of value discovered by Locke and Smith, which for him is an "epoch in the history of the development of the human race." However, the political economists did not push their discoveries far enough, since they failed to see the historically specific social forms behind the objective forms created by labor. The price of commodities after time appear to result from the nature of the products and the circulation process itself.

The limits of the categories of political economy, while justifying a particular historical period, lie unveiled when compared to other preindustrial and peasant forms of economic production.[91] It is by means of this comparison that the distinctive historical nature of commodity production is made manifest with its historically specific forms of social relations: exchange value, abstract labor, and the social, economic, and legal organizations that structure these types of relationships. The production of commodities presupposes a structural framework in which historically specific forms of work, rhythm of labor, class institutions, and the division of labor produce a particular form of money exchange and a particular form of private ownership. Without this critical and historical method, the categories of political economy appear as universal criteria rationalizing the capitalist social system with its universal view of human nature, moral inversion, and judicial reductionism—social justice as fair market exchange. To move beyond the present social system, to anticipate a better future and common conscience, Marx relies on the wisdom and vision emanating from the ancient walls and moral economy of Jerusalem and Athens. It is from the ideals of the Hebrews and the Hellenes that he poetically reconstructs history, social institutions, and the aesthetic forms of work, according to the hopes and ideals of a just society.

Part II

Antiquity by Moonlight: Tragic Imagination in an Age of Nihilism

Chapter Four

Nietzsche and Classical Antiquity: Tragic Vision and Dionysian Creativity in the Abyss

Introduction

Nietzsche was born in Röcken, Saxony in 1844, the same year that Marx wrote his *Economic and Philosophic Manuscripts* in Paris. Of the two, Nietzsche was the more traditionally trained philologist. He entered the University of Bonn in 1864 to study classical philology and theology and after one year transferred to the University of Leipzig where he was a founder of the *Philologischer Verein*, a university classical society. It was here that he undertook his studies of Diogenes Laertius, Democritus, and Aristotle. His dissertation thesis began as an examination of the origins of the ideas of Diogenes Laertius, but was never completed. In spite of this, he received his doctorate from Leipzig based on the recommendation of his teacher and mentor Friedrich Ritschl. Much of the substance of his thesis later appeared as a chapter in a *Gratulationsschrift* at the University of Basel, entitled *Beiträge zur Quellenkunde und Kritik des Laertius Diogenes*. In 1869, he was offered a position at the University of Basel in Switzerland as professor of classical philology, which he retained until his early retirement ten years later. His lectures and seminars included topics on Greek and Latin poetry and rhetoric, grammar, Greek drama and religion, Platonic and pre-Platonic philosophy, and classical philology.[1] More specifically, he gave courses on Aeschylus's *Libation Bearers* and Sophocles' *Oedipus Rex*, Greek music drama, and Socrates and tragedy.[2] His earliest writings included detailed philological studies of Theognis, Diogenes Laertius, Simonides, Democritus, and an essay portraying a fictitious contest between Homer and Hesiod.

During this early period in his life work, he offered a course on pre-Platonic philosophers during the winter semester of 1869–70, summer semester of 1872, and again in 1873 and 1876. He also taught a course on the introduction to Plato's dialogues during the winter semesters of 1871–72 and 1873–74 and the summer of 1876.[3] His first published work *The Birth of Tragedy from the Spirit of Music*, was written in 1870–71, and over the next five years, he continued to work on the problem of the relations between pre-Platonic philosophy and the foundations of knowledge. In *The Birth of Tragedy*, he examined the role of drama and tragedy in Greek society, and in the process, revolutionized eighteenth- and nineteenth-century classicism. In his unpublished notes and fragments from 1872 to 1876, he focused his attention on early Greek philosophy and its relation to epistemology. These latter pieces comprised several hundred pages of short essays, partial beginnings of new works, and general outlines that provided important clues to our understanding of his later critiques of science and knowledge. These unpublished writings on pre-Platonic Greek philosophy of nature have become known as the *Philosophers' Book*.[4] Throughout this period of the early seventies, Nietzsche outlined a variety of projects on Greek philosophy with some of the following titles: *The Last Philosopher, The Philosopher, Philosophy in the Tragic Age of the Greeks, The Philosopher as Cultural Physician, The Justification of Philosophy by the Greeks, Plato and His Predecessors, On Truth and Lies in a Nonmoral Sense, Philosophy in Hard Times,* and *The Struggle between Science and Wisdom*. Though he never integrated this material into a comprehensive masterwork, never completed this project, and never published a volume in this area, these short essays, notes, and outlines constitute a wealth of material connecting his later epistemological insights with his early understanding of Greek society.[5] Daniel Breazeale, in his introduction to his translation of some of these early writings concluded:

> The published text of his lectures, as well as the notebooks . . . , show the extent to which he tried to relate Greek science and philosophy to modern science and the epistemological themes so central to modern philosophy. They furthermore demonstrate that he wished to use the history of Greek philosophy from Thales to Socrates to illustrate his own theoretical conclusions concerning the anthropomorphic character of all knowing and the ultimately nihilistic tendency of the knowledge drive.[6]

Thus, this period during the early and midseventies is important for understanding Nietzsche's attempt to grapple with early Greek philosophy and its relation to the issues of knowledge, truth, and wisdom. The full range of these early epistemological writings are to be found in *The Birth of Tragedy*, *Philosophy in the Tragic Age of the Greeks*, and the unpublished *Nachlass*. The issues discussed in these works include the origin of Greek tragedy, Nietzsche's theory of tragedy and aesthetic drives, examination of the pre-Platonic philosophers, and discussions about the nature of knowledge and science. These works on morality and epistemology are held together by a distinct, but transformed Kantian view of epistemology, whose radical implications are more fully developed in his later theory of perspectivism and critique of morality.[7] As he moves from these initial criticisms of science and rationalism to his later philosophy of nihilism, he expands upon his borrowing from Kant, Schopenhauer, and Lange. We saw in Chapter 2 that Marx also undertook to radicalize Kant's theory of knowledge toward a critique of epistemology and foundationalism, but with quite different intentions and results.

Evolving Eighteenth- and Nineteenth-Century Theories of Tragedy

Nietzsche's theory of tragedy in his *The Birth of Tragedy* was developed within the framework of the evolution of eighteenth-century German neoclassicism in the works of Gottsched, Lessing, Klopstock, Wieland, Voss, A. W. Schlegel, von Kleist, Goethe, and Schiller.[8] In particular, it was Lessing's expansion on the structure of tragedy from Aristotle's *Poetics*, Goethe's views on catharsis and reconciliation in Greek tragedy, and Schiller's adaptation of tragedy to his Kantian aesthetics that set the framework for Nietzsche's radical perception and interpretation of tragedy. The revival of Aristotle's *Poetics* during the German Enlightenment and the historical transformation of the German reading of this work created the context within which Nietzsche began to formulate his ideas about the birth and decline of Greek drama.

It was in the *Hamburgische Dramaturgie* that Lessing repeated Aristotle's principle that the goal of tragedy is the imitation of an action that constitutes a unified and complete whole within an appropriate magnitude or proper length of plot development. It is also an action that imitates fearful and pitiable incidents as in the case of the fall from power of a noble lord or family. Aristotle said that passions and pity are aroused only when the misfortune is not deserved. That occurs when the person is neither perfect in virtue or character, but falls through some miscalculation. Fear is expressed only when there is empathy with the misfortune of the main character.[9] This fear is evoked through the reversal of fortune and the hero's consciousness of change as in the case of Oedipus's recognition that the prophecy had come true. In a complex tragedy, plot action traces the change of fortune from good fortune to bad or from bad fortune to good. It is this that constitutes dramatic beauty. The two crucial structures for plot development include reversal and recognition.[10] He also stressed the overall unity of the plot and the subordination of the character to the totality of the action and structure of the story. Tragedy is built upon the unity of the plot and character, since the flawed character sets a chain of fateful events in motion that inevitably lead to the downfall of the tragic hero.

According to Lessing, the audience is involved in the unfolding of the tragedy and in the lives of its main characters through the fear (*Furcht*) and empathetic pity (*Mitleid*) produced by the work. This identification with the suffering of others, as our possible suffering, is a crucial element in the purification (*Reinigung*) and final moderation of these passions through "catharsis." We can see here the beginnings of the German Enlightenment and Weimar classicism and their stress on the balancing and harmonizing of reason and emotion: the eighteenth-century *Humanitätsideal*.[11] Robin Harrison argues that Lessing had added another dimension to this analysis in his play *Emilia Galotti*. After closely following the basic structure of the Aristotelian plot, Lessing introduced a new dimension of character development. Harrison calls this a creative adaptation and allegiance to Aristotle.[12] In view of his "*bürgerliches Trauerspiel*," Lessing adapts the character development and idea of the fatal flaw to a new type of character. The main character is not someone of noble birth, but is from the middle class. In this work, according to Harrison, Lessing has deviated from his initial ideas presented in the *Hamburgische Dramaturgie* by introducing a new element in German tragedy: the independent formation of character relations not immediately related to plot development.

In the nineteenth century, Johann Wolfgang von Goethe wrote about Greek tragedy and Aristotle's interpretation in two short essays: "On Greek Tetralogies" (1823) and "On Interpreting Aristotle's *Poetics*" (1827).[13] These essays correspond to Goethe's major theme found throughout his writings on the integrity and oneness of reality and the reintegration of all being back into nature. It was a vision of the Greeks that Goethe derived from Johann Winckelmann's classic works

Thoughts about the Imitation of Greek Works in Painting and Sculpture (1755) and *History of Ancient Art* (1764). Winckelmann saw the Greeks as representing the highest and purest ideals of beauty, that is, grace and charm, harmony and unity, and "noble simplicity and quiet grandeur." This was exquisitely expressed in the sculpture of the Trojan priest Laocoon defending his sons from the serpent.

> The most significant characteristic of the Greek masterpieces, finally is a noble simplicity and tranquil grandeur (*eine edle Einfalt und eine stille Grösse*). As the depths of the sea always remain calm, no matter how the surface may rage, just so does the expression of the Greek figures indicate among all passions a great and resolute soul.
>
> Such a soul is portrayed in the face of the Laocoon, despite the most violent suffering. The pain which appears in all the muscles and sinews of the body . . . nevertheless is not made manifest by any expression of fury. . . . Unlike Virgil's Laocoon, he raises no horrible cry. . . . Laocoon suffers, but suffers like Sophocles' Philoctetes: his misery . . . touches our very souls, but we would wish to be able to bear misery like this great man.[14]

In his earlier work "On Greek Tetralogies," Goethe views the *Oresteia* trilogy as the important example of reconciliation. In the first part, king Agamemnon is killed by his wife Clytemnestra on his return home from the successful completion of the Trojan War. In the second part, Agamemnon is revenged by his son Orestes, who kills his mother and her lover Aegisthus. In the third part, Orestes is pursued by the Furies avenging the matricide and is finally acquitted by the vote of the Areopagus (Athenian law court) and Athena. In "On Interpreting Aristotle's *Poetics*," Goethe pays homage to the "great master." He quotes from the *Poetics* that "tragedy is the imitation of a significant and complete action which has a certain length. . . . However, after a certain course of events which evoke pity and fear, the tragedy concludes by neutralizing those emotions."[15] While recapitulating the Aristotelian view of the structural components of tragedy and the nature of the tragic character, Goethe emphasizes the centrality of catharsis as the excitation and then "neutralization and reconciliation" of the spectators' emotions.

Catharsis and reconciliation will become less important in Nietzsche's own evaluation of Greek tragedy in *The Birth of Tragedy* as he stresses the creative role of the tragic artist and dramatist. Goethe summarizes Aristotle's view of pity and fear and argues that the end of tragedy is the neutralization or reconciliation of these empathetic passions of the spectators. According to Goethe, reconciliation is absolutely essential if "tragedy is to be a perfect work of art."[16] Goethe returns to *Oedipus at Colonus* as the quintessential example of catharsis and reconciliation. For him, it was Oedipus's daemonic drive and noble, but criminal, character that precipitated his fall into his miserable misfortunes. However, at the end of the tragedy "he is elevated to the company of the gods, becomes the benevolent guarding spirit of the land and is deemed worthy of the honor of a special sacrificial ceremony."[17]

Where Lessing and Goethe saw a preestablished harmonious world created by God in which humanity, through reflective reason, participates, Friedrich Schiller sees a world as potentially harmonious through the aesthetic and rational creativity of humankind. Where Lessing saw harmony and order from the perspective of eighteenth-century rationalism with its integration of reason and emotions, and Goethe, from the perspective of nineteenth-century neoclassicism with its integration of humanity and moral cosmos, Schiller sees them as overcoming Kantian dualism through a sublime reconciliation of sensuousness (*Sinnlichkeit*) and morality (*Sittlichkeit*), understanding (*Verstand*) and reason (*Vernunft*) through art and tragic poetry. Human reason has replaced the divine as the insurer of the universal moral order. It is only one step to Nietzsche's radicalization of Kant's and Schiller's insights, while rejecting their substantive moral philosophy. In turn, the German perspective on tragedy begins to move away from traditional neoclassicism and the strict adherence to the rules and structures of Aristotle's *Poetics* with the work of Schiller. Schiller incorporates Kantian epistemology, moral philosophy, and aesthetic theory into his reading of classical Greek tragedy.

Where Goethe saw the reconciliation between the gods and mankind through the reestablishment of the universal moral order as the final goal of tragedy, he was reaffirming the essential principles of Aristotelian tragedy within a neoclassical perspective of the Greek world. Schiller, on the other hand, reads Aristotle through the crystal of Kantian philosophy. He, too, dreamt of the possibility of harmony and reconciliation, but translates it into a union of conflicting elements in a modified Kantian universe. The conflicts and dualisms that produce a fragmented and alienated world are the result of the antagonisms between sensuousness and morality, inclinations and duty, pleasure and reason, beauty and the sublime, and grace and dignity. They were to be finally resolved and transcended in his *Humanitätsideal*. It is just this move from Goethe to Schiller, from neoclassicism to a form of

Kantianism that will set the stage for Nietzsche's radicalization of Kantian philosophy and his reinterpretation of Greek drama in *The Birth of Tragedy*.

Friedrich Schiller, poet, dramatist, and philosopher, has left us with an extensive amount of writing on drama and aesthetics.[18] During the 1790s, his reading of the *Critique of Pure Reason* (1781) and *Critique of Judgment* (1790) resulted in a flood of aesthetic works on the nature of tragedy: *Of the Cause of the Pleasure We Derive from Tragic Objects* (1791), *On the Tragic Art* (1792), *The Pathetic* (1793), *On Grace and Dignity* (1793), *On the Aesthetic Education of Man* (1795), *On Simple and Sentimental Poetry* (1795), and *On the Sublime* (appeared 1801).

In his essay *On the Tragic Art*, Schiller outlines a theory of tragedy that integrates a strong romantic and rationalistic, Aristotelian and Kantian perspective. In his desire to clarify the nature of the tragic hero or virtuous individual who struggles and suffers, Schiller develops many of the ideas that later become part of Nietzsche's work in a transformed way, including the concepts of the will, life, suffering, individuality, and universality. In this essay, Schiller integrates Aristotle's *Poetics* and Kant's *Critique of Pure Reason*, since the purpose of tragedy is to express and develop two different sides of the human experience. On the one hand, through the hero's suffering, sympathetic feelings and pity are produced in the sensuous faculty of the spectator. This precipitates and encourages the movement toward the development of the spiritual pleasure of moral reason. This attempted integration and reconciliation of passion and reason, emotion and the sublime, and sensual and spiritual pleasure prefigure a synthesis of the Greek view of tragedy and the eighteenth-century German view of morality and rationality. This perspective on tragedy also anticipates Nietzsche's view of the conflict between the Apollonian and Dionysian artistic drives. By means of tragic emotions stimulating individual enlightenment, a general harmony or supreme serenity is restored to the fragmented life of the individual. Universal moral laws are produced by means of the evolution of the individual in aesthetic experience and passionate involvement in sympathetic pain and suffering. Modern art brings together these contradictory elements of sensuousness and rationality, which makes it superior to Greek tragedy.

Schiller proceeds to summarize and repeat the same crucial Aristotelian elements of tragedy: a poetic imitation of human suffering by means of a succession of events or actions within a completed whole (plot) that awakens sympathy and pity. Its goal is to "prolong the torments of sense" and "the suffering of its sensuous nature" as the prelude to the development of moral sentiments of the sublime and noble, thereby "escaping the subjection of the senses."[19] Aesthetics moves beyond the sensuous to elevate our instinct for activity in moral reasoning. In the essay *On the Sublime*, he defines mankind as "the being who wills."[20] Schiller joins together emotional catharsis and moral enlightenment, individual suffering and moral harmony in a single theory of tragedy. "It is the union of these two that can only elicit emotion. The great secret of the tragic art consists precisely in managing this struggle well."[21] But it is a harmony and reconciliation resulting from the imposition and domination of moral law and universal principles on the "brutal instincts of nature" and the physical emotions of sensuousness. He expresses this in *On Dignity* in the following fashion: "The rule over the instincts by moral force is the emancipation of mind."[22] He continues to see the creation of moral excellence through suffering in political terms of rule, reign, independence, duty, and force. In his essay *Of the Cause of the Pleasure We Derive from Tragic Objects*, Schiller writes, "It follows that the highest degree of moral consciousness can only exist in strife and the highest moral pleasure is always accompanied by pain. . . . We here see the triumph of the moral law, so sublime an experience for us that we might even hail the calamity which elicits it. For harmony in the world of moral freedom gives us infinitely more pleasure than all the discords in nature give us pain."[23]

Throughout the aesthetic essays, there is a strong focus on the belief that the feelings of aesthetics, art, and nature represent only a stage in the development of the moral will and rational human being. Sometimes Schiller will emphasize the importance of moral over aesthetic judgments, reason over the sensuous, dignity over grace, the sublime over the beautiful, while at other times primacy is placed on aesthetics, the beautiful, and the sensuous.[24]

There is debate in the academic community over Schiller's intentions. Did he wish a reconciliation between the conflicting components of human nature or did he finally resolve on freeing the individual from the sensuous world through pure reason? In *On the Sublime*, he stresses the idea of reconciliation: "We are only perfect citizens of nature when the sublime is wedded to the beautiful."[25] In the work *The Pathetic*, Schiller emphasizes the differences: "After the rights of nature come those of *reason*, because man is a rational, sensuous being, a moral person, and because it is the duty for this person not to let himself be ruled by nature, but to rule her."[26] This tension between sensuousness and reason is expressed further on in this essay when Schiller contends that there are two laws of tragedy. The first law is to imitate suffering nature, while the second law expresses the resistance of moral reason to suffering. It is, however, the sublime and pathetic soul that can integrate both the physical and the rational in one person. Examples of this behavior in Greek lore are Laocoon and the Spartan king Leonidas at Thermopylae.

For Winckelmann, Lessing, and Schiller, Laocoon provided the symbol for beauty, simplicity, and nobility in the Greek spirit. At the moment when Laocoon's two sons seem to be succumbing to an attack by serpents, Laocoon doesn't flee the scene but fights the serpents in an ill-fated attempt to free his sons. The outcome is already determined, but the father through his love and duty overcame physical pain as he moved to a higher level of moral obligation. "It is this which calls forth our sympathy in the highest degree. It appears, in fact, as if he deliberately devoted himself to destruction, and his death becomes an act of the will."[27] Unlike the rationalist theory of tragedy, which argues that art is supposed to provide the spectator concrete examples for moral emulation, for Schiller, art is supposed to integrate physical suffering and moral development in creating a whole human being.

In *On Simple and Sentimental Poetry*, Schiller expresses the differences between the moderns and the ancients. He characterizes the Greek world in terms remarkably similar to Winckelmann in his *The History of Ancient Art*. "If we think of that beautiful nature which surrounded the ancient Greeks, if we remember how intimately that people, under its blessed sky, could live with that free nature; how their mode of imagining, and of feeling, and their manners, approached far nearer than ours to the simplicity of nature, how faithfully the works of their poets express this."[28]

Although Schiller experienced melancholy at the thought that the ancients represented the highest perfection in the ideal world, he also recognized that the break with the Greeks, accomplished with the rise of modern culture, was necessary to achieve a higher level of human development. Schiller, consciously leaning on Rousseau, views this movement from a "state of natural simplicity" to a "state of civilization" as an historical process of social evolution.[29] What had formerly existed as a fact is now raised to an ideal by the sublime soul. "Nature reconciles man with himself; art divides and disunites him; the ideal brings him back to unity."[30] For him, it means the progress and perfection of humanity. It is this dynamic treatment of the ideal, perfection, and humanity that can explain some of the apparent contradictions within Schiller. He is attempting to transcend the limitations of his Kantian perspective by introducing in his works the notions of personality, potentiality, and the surge to his own ideal.

In probably his most important and influential work, *On the Aesthetic Education of Man*, Schiller strikingly portrays humankind as constantly striving and carrying the potentiality for divinity within itself. He defines people in terms of their potential for becoming. In very Aristotelian categories, he argues that mankind "must make actual the potentiality which he bears within himself."[31] However, it is a potentiality whose realization lies in the distant future, for the present is characterized by the "dismemberment of their being" that is locked in a prison of disenchantment. Modernity is a fragmented and mechanical world constructed of lifeless parts. "Man himself grew to be only a fragment; with the monotonous noise of the wheel he drives everlastingly in his ears, he never develops the harmony of his being."[32] But there is optimism running throughout Schiller's words, an optimism that rejoices in the potential for human development and the possibilities of creating a harmonious union in life and return to nature. But in the aesthetic essays mentioned above, the goal was to transcend nature through escape or domination. In the letters on aesthetic education, Schiller argues that harmony is only an ideal. And this is precisely where tragedy and aesthetics have such an essential position in his thinking. These same conflicts are prominent throughout this work, which recapitulates this problem in dramatic fashion expressing his own inability to reconcile them in his aesthetics. Although Schiller recognizes that ideal harmony lay in reconciliation (*Aussöhnung*) of these Kantian antagonisms between epistemology and aesthetics, truth and beauty, he, like Kant, was never able to resolve the problem.[33] He did, however, uphold Kant's major philosophical premise that permeated all his writings that the essence of humanity lies in its aesthetic and creative abilities, since only in the latter is there freedom and self-consciousness: "Instead of abandoning himself to the world he will rather draw it into himself with the whole infinity of its phenomena, and subject it to the unity of his reason."[34]

Schiller integrated Aristotle's theory of tragedy, Lessing's views on pity, and Kant's epistemology into a modern theory of tragedy. One possible answer to the dilemma raised by Schiller lies in his distinction between simple or naïve poetry and sentimental poetry. It seems at times that Schiller views the dualisms as the product of historical development. That is, the Kantian dualisms between naïve and sentimental poetry are the result of a lost harmony that existed among the ancient Greeks. Through intense suffering caused by the tragedy of modernity, this lost period in the history of humanity can be recaptured. Reconciliation, or catharsis, can never be accomplished in the simple and immediate manner of the Greeks. But through conscious undertaking of human suffering grounded in the development of sublime emotions and the freedom of moral reason, the proper areas and limits of sensuousness and reason can be maintained in a new ideal of harmony.[35] Beauty is the most immediate type of harmony as it integrates matter and form, senses and intellect, but it is ultimately grounded in the physical. Tragedy, a human creation, though it begins with experience, ends with a higher reconciliation by producing the ideal of a sublime humanity.

Running throughout Schiller's works is the theme that humans give form to nature. Whether he is discussing the passions and human suffering, physical beauty and grace, the categories of experience and understanding; whether he is referring to morality, aesthetics, or epistemology, it is clear that creativity, freedom, and the realization of human potential expresses the meaning and rationality of the world. Reason provides a formal unity to the world without imposing a content on it. On this point, Schiller appears very clear. He begins to waver, however, when he discusses the interaction among these various elements in art and philosophy. However, according to Reginald Snell, there is a consistent pattern of inconsistency in his major work *On the Aesthetic Education of Man.*[36] In particular, what is the relation between truth and art, the sublime and the beautiful? It is here that Schiller becomes more and more unclear.

A more consistent theme begins to develop in the second half of *On the Aesthetic Education of Man.* In one of his most interesting remarks, he states, ''Through beauty the sensuous man is led to form and to thought; through beauty the spiritual man is brought back to matter and restored to the world of sense.''[37] He is making an attempt to bridge the gap between aesthetics and truth, which he was not able to do in his earlier aesthetic and philosophical essays. In fact, in the twenty-first and twenty-fifth letters, he contends that aesthetics is a higher form of reconciliation more compatible with the highest gift of humanity, since truth abstracts from the sensuous experience and thus further fragments the human. The realm of reason leaves behind the necessity of nature, by picturing the world as objects. In language that reminds the reader of Nietzsche, Schiller states that these objects are given form by reason with the result that ''man is superior to every terror of Nature so long as he knows how to give form to it, and to turn it into his object."[38] In the aesthetic essays, sublime reason took precedence over the sensuous, but in this work, beauty takes priority, since it returns to the physical world. In his essays *On the Sublime and The Pathetic*, Schiller portrays the rational, sublime soul as the higher form of development, which will reconcile the conflicts between art and truth. However, in *On the Aesthetic Education of Man*, he turns to beauty as the highest form of reintegration of the fragmented and alienated world.

> We must therefore be no longer at a loss to find a passage from sensuous dependence to moral freedom, after we have seen, in the case of Beauty, that the two can perfectly well subsist together, and that in order to shew himself spirit Man does not need to eschew matter. But if he is already free in association with sensuousness, as the fact of Beauty teaches us, and if freedom is something absolute and suprasensible, as its very concept necessarily implies, there can no longer be any question how he came to rise from the limited to the absolute, to oppose sensuousness in his thought and will, since this has already occurred in Beauty. There can, in a word, no longer be any question how he passes from Beauty to Truth, since the latter by its very nature lies in the former; the question is rather how he makes his way from an ordinary actuality to an aesthetic one, from a sense of mere life to a sense of Beauty.[39]

In the thirteenth letter on aesthetic education, Schiller calls the harmony achieved in reaching truth a premature harmony. It eliminates the tension between nature and reason by reducing the former to the latter. In Kantian fashion, he describes the process by which the mind through its categories gives form, appearance, and coherence to an incoherent world. The phenomena are given unity by the power of reason and the potentialities that lie therein. But it is the very authoritarian nature of the unification that bothers him, especially in light of the events of the French Revolution. In the final letter of the work, Schiller argues that the experience of the appearances and the striving for moral harmony in a general will are forms of existence based on the priority given to a fragmented aspect of the individual. Only in the contemplation of beauty is a harmonious whole and reconciliation possible, since only this unites sensuousness and reason, grace and dignity. "Only the perception of the Beautiful makes something whole of him."[40] During his lifetime, he saw it as an ideal, existing in few individuals, but nevertheless an ideal that defined the limits of the personality and human potentiality. The ideal exists not in the perception of appearances or in the moral determination of action, but in the realm of play: it exists in the imagination of sentimental poetry. This becomes, for Schiller, the arena for the highest expression of human achievement and free imagination.

Nietzsche on the Aesthetic Ideals of Greek Tragedy

Anyone who attempts to deal with the complexities and subtleties of Nietzsche's *The Birth of Tragedy* is faced with the difficulty of explaining the relationships between philology and philosophy in his work. Contemporary analysts tend to fragment their interpretations along narrow disciplinary lines in much the same way that Marxist scholarship has done in the past. With Nietzsche the divisions are even more pronounced. It also appears that individuals trained in philosophy and philology draw upon different parts of Nietzsche's work, as well as from different works themselves. In the end, the two fields have traditionally been kept quite separate. One result has been an apparent lack of interest in the classical component and theory of tragedy by philosophers. In turn, the classicists have been averse to unraveling the hidden mysteries and secrets of his philosophical orientation since this is viewed as interfering with their main work of interpretive exegesis.[41] Whether Nietzsche is discussing the Apollonian and Dionysian elements of tragedy, the birth of Socratic and scientific rationalism, or the formation of knowledge, his epistemology, philosophy, philology, and classicism should all be understood within a general framework that we can characterize as a radical Kantian theory of knowledge. The priority throughout his works is always on fundamental philosophical and cultural questions. The fact that he was trained in classical philology and not philosophy should not affect our perception of his intentions, nor affect the conclusions that may be drawn from his works. Understanding that his training in philology took a back seat to the primacy of broader philosophical and sociological questions about the nature of knowledge, truth, science, and modern Western culture is a necessary step in unraveling the spirit of Nietzsche's works.

Philosophy and philology are unquestionably interwoven in *The Birth of Tragedy*. When this is recognized, the title of the book becomes more intriguing. What is meant by the "birth of tragedy"? At first appearance, it looks as if Nietzsche is explaining the historical origins of Greek tragedy, the structural composition of tragedy in the conflict between Apollonian and Dionysian elements, a review of eighteenth- and nineteenth-century German theories of drama, and, finally, his interpretation of the ideas of conflict and resolution in Greek tragedy. In and of themselves, these issues are extremely important in clarifying Nietzsche's view of Greek tragedy, but this represents only part of the work. Classicists have for the most part dismissed the first part of the book as poor and sloppy classical scholarship and have not spent much time on the second half.

The notion of the "birth of tragedy" refers both to Greek tragedy and to the tragedy of modernity—the loss by the latter of the tragic vision of the Greeks. The disappearance of the Greek world is only part of the problem. The rise of Platonic philosophy, Christian religion, and modern science represent the real tragedy. Greek drama is only one character in this complex historical play. Nietzsche has used the term "tragedy" in the technical sense of the integration of Dionysian wisdom and Apollonian illusions, and in its everyday sense. The second refers to the decadence and passive nihilism of the modern world. The story is not just about the origins of Greek tragedy, but also about the birth of the modern tragic reality. Here again, as in his earliest writings about the pre-Platonic philosophers, modern philosophy and classical philology are intimately connected.

In an unpublished essay of 1875 entitled *The Struggle between Science and Wisdom*, Nietzsche very nicely summarizes his whole approach to the classics: "Greek antiquity provides the classical set of examples for the interpretation of our entire culture and its development. It is a means *for understanding ourselves*, a means for regulating our age—and thereby a means for overcoming it."[42] He uses the classics as a mirror by which to reflect his perception of the tragedy of modern nihilism and as a means for the transvaluation of the world. The first sections of *The Birth of Tragedy* are taken up with Nietzsche's examination of the origins of Greek tragedy from the Greek chorus with the union of Dionysian music and the plastic art of Apollonian images.[43] He discusses tragedy in terms of its origins in nature; reconciliation of the conflicting artistic forces of humankind (Dionysian and Apollonian dimensions); Schiller's theory of Greek art; the philosophy of art and objectivity/subjectivity of Kant, Winckelmann, Schiller, A. W. Schlegel, and Schopenhauer; a description of origins of tragedy in the dithyrambic chorus and lyric poetry; and, finally, an analysis of the Greek tragedies of Aeschylus and Sophocles. It is the interpretation of the natural, spiritual, and theatrical origins of Greek tragedy in light of eighteenth- and nineteenth-century German aesthetic philosophy. Nietzsche's ultimate goal seems to be the development of a general theory of human tragedy that includes an examination of the development of mythic poetry and tragedies of Aeschylus and Sophocles, the decline of the tragic age with the dramas of Euripides and the philosophy of Socrates, the rise and decline of Western Christianity, the anthropomorphic illusions of scientific enlightenment and philosophical rationalism, and, finally, the development of a Western culture characterized by moral and epistemological nihilism.[44] The conflict, reconciliation, and integration of dreams and intoxication, rationality and mysticism, Apollonian and Dionysian drives (*Kunsttriebe*) in artistic creativity provided Nietzsche's critics with grist for the mill.

But what interests us here is this integration of Greek drama and German aesthetics in a theory of the birth of Greek tragedy. This union of the ancients and moderns is important because by interpreting the Hellenes through eighteenth- and nineteenth-century German thought, Nietzsche is in an important position for the further expansion of a theory of the modern tragedy. In the process of examining the ancients, we learn more about the moderns. In the notes for his famous essay *We Philologists*, Nietzsche exclaimed, "Men have explained the ancient world in terms of their own experience; and from what they have in this way obtained of the classical world, they have *appraised* and evaluated their own experience."[45] This is not to mean that Greek drama is simply the basis for an introduction to the decadence of modernity, but it does mean that both parts should have equal weight with the interpreter.

The controversy and *Philologenkrieg* between Nietzsche and Wilamowitz-Möllendorff is well known,[46] but what has been investigated less is the connection between German philosophy and Greek tragedy. Theories of objectivity and alienation, essence and appearances, subjectivity and will, aesthetic reconciliation and creativity, reenchantment and harmony with nature, naïve and sublime art, and truth and illusion in the writings of German idealists are attempts to get at the issues of the relation between wisdom and knowledge, art and science. That is, in its epistemology, moral philosophy, and aesthetic theory, German philosophy provided the categories and theories necessary for Nietzsche to give life and meaning to the suffering, enlightenment, and eventual reconciliation of Oedipus and Prometheus within the natural order. Nietzsche's originality lies in his deviance from the classical tradition in German philology. By viewing the Greeks through the eyes of the German idealists, Nietzsche turns the orthodox interpretations on their head. Reconciliation is no longer viewed in terms of reestablishment of the natural moral order within the cosmos, but rather is now understood as a function of a narrower and more focused individualism whose origins lie in subjective will and individual creativity. Here he anticipates his later ideas on the individual as a "will to power."[47] These are the ideals of *The Birth of Tragedy.*

This Kantianization of Sophocles and Aeschylus provides Nietzsche with the vocabulary crucial for the development of his later expanded theories of nihilism, will to power, decadence, and critique of foundationalism. When philology is integrated with philosophy, when Greek tragedy is understood within the framework of German Idealism, when Greek philosophy and tragedy are viewed as part of a wider integrated whole, the parameters of our understanding of ancient and modern tragedy changes. Nietzsche's Greek experience is part of a more holistic and historical understanding of the distorted and constrained possibilities of human potential.

The Birth of Tragedy begins with an examination of three aspects of the Greek character that would help explain the nature and origins of tragedy: Greek spirituality (Dionysian drive), sensibility (theodicy, mythology, and pessimism), and sensuality (beauty, harmony, and aesthetics). A key to a reading of the work lies in the very first page where Nietzsche uses the phrase "the alleged 'serenity' of the Greek." The spirituality, sensuality, and sensibility of the Greeks were different forms of cultural illusions that hid the dark and unpleasant realities of everyday life—its terror, barbarism, cruelty, and injustice. In fact, he calls these cultural expressions forms of "metaphysical solace" (*der metaphysische Trost*).[48] From the very first page, he challenges the traditional views of ancient Greece established since Winckelmann and Goethe stressed the nobility, simplicity, and beauty of the Greek world. But the challenge lies within the classical German model of transcendence (*Aufhebung*). That is, he incorporates German aesthetics with this Dionysian perspective of intoxicated frenzy, spiritual rapture, enchantment of the world, reconciliation with humankind and nature, and love of existence. This is what Nietzsche called "a plethora of health, plenitude of being" expressed in art for the express purpose of reintegrating the fragmented world of people and nature.

> Man now expresses himself through song and dance as the member of a higher community; he has forgotten how to walk, how to speak, and is on the brink of taking wing as he dances. Each of his gestures betokens enchantment; through him sounds a supernatural power, the same power which makes the animals speak and the earth render up milk and honey.

He feels himself to be godlike and strides with the same elation and ecstasy as the gods he has seen in his dreams. No longer the *artist*, he has himself become a *work of art*.[49]

The Greeks inhabited a world of gorgons and monsters, terrors and Titans. Nietzsche himself says that it is a world of the Furies and horrible punishments (Prometheus), of incest, pain, and family curses (Oedipus), of fate, matricide, and flight from retribution (Orestes). This forbidding and dangerous world required a symbolic overlay that gave a different picture of the meaning and purpose of life and that reconciled its antagonisms. This is the world of Greek art, music, and poetry, and especially Greek tragedy. Art reconciles individuals to others and nature, reestablishes a harmony within the world, overcomes the fragmentation of the universe, elevates humanity to a higher moral level, and creates a new existence based on justice, beauty, and serenity. For Nietzsche, art provides humanity with the cultural illusions necessary to "make life possible and worth living."[50] Aesthetic experience makes life meaningful and reintegrates and reconciles the individual into the natural moral order. This interpretation is essential both for an understanding of Greek tragedy and also for the insight it offers into the spirit and soul of ancient Greece. The latter is especially important in that it provides the moderns with an alternative to the mediocrity of the modern Christian world. "From the very first, Christianity spelled life loathing itself, and that loathing was simply disguised, tricked out, with notions of an 'other' and 'better' life. A hatred of the 'world,' a curse on the affective urges, a fear of beauty and sensuality, a transcendence rigged up to slander moral existence, a yearning for extinction . . . had always struck me as being the most dangerous, most sinister form the will to destruction can take."[51]

Schiller, Schopenhauer, and Greek Tragedy

Nietzsche is fascinated by the juxtaposition in Greek society of the Olympian gods and the Titans, joy and fear, beauty and terror, and harmony and horror. "It was in that sphere of beauty that the Greeks saw the Olympians as their mirror images: it was by means of that aesthetic mirror that the Greek will opposed suffering and the somber wisdom of suffering which always accompanies artistic talent."[52] In order to help explain the role of art, Nietzsche turns to Schiller's aesthetic theory of näive and sublime art. In the essay *On Simple and*

Sentimental Poetry, Schiller distinguishes between the simple or näive poetry of the ancients and the sentimental poetry of the moderns. For him, the näive poet is in direct contact with nature, that is, with the essence, unity, and eternal laws of nature. It is a direct contact with life itself. The emphasis is on the object: nature in its simplicity, existence, and necessity. For the sentimental poet, however, nature has become an ideal toward which he strives. It is already a more distant and indirect reality. This is important for Schiller because the very essence of nature represents our lost identities, "the image of our infancy," and an "image of our highest perfection."[53] The individual obeys the dictates and necessity of nature out of a feeling for the simplicity and harmony of nature itself. Sentimental poetry stresses the subjective feelings of the writer as the poet attempts to recover in a new, integrated, and transformed artistic expression the lost simplicity and harmony with nature. It is a mediated relation, but ultimately one that allows for the modern accomplishments of moral freedom and self-consciousness, thereby going beyond the simplicity of feeling, natural serenity, and childlike sincerity of the Greeks. In fact, nature is not imposed upon the individual but becomes part of his or her moral constitution and inner necessity. This sentimentality produces a melancholic longing to return to this ideal world, which is not the result of intuition or beauty, but rather the moral and rational apprehension of the real. This sublime feeling of moral awakening transcends childlike innocence and ingenuousness of the Greeks, as well as a direct sensuous and emotional contact with nature, because nature and reason are reunited under the universal laws of moral reason. The Kantian division between inclination and duty, understanding and sensibility, the physical and the moral, instincts and reason are negated in Schiller's view of humanity as longing for the pleasure and happiness of moral integration and rational harmony. The moral individual is reintegrated into the harmony of natural necessity freely created by the poet. "While we were still only children of nature we were happy, we were perfect: we have become free, and we have lost both advantages. Hence a twofold and very unequal longing for nature: the longing for happiness and the longing for the perfection that prevails there. Man, as a sensuous being, deplores sensibly the loss of the former of these goods; it is only the moral man who can be afflicted at the loss of the other."[54]

Where Kant required the split between personal inclinations and universal moral imperatives based on a formal logic of the law of noncontradiction, Schiller turns to an immediate feeling of natural simplicity to create the correct moral action. There is no longer a split in this particular essay between the heart and the mind. This feeling is also a means to get beyond the depravity and artificiality of human existence to a renewed state of individual calm, moral innocence, and pleasure. Civilization has become a land of Kantian exile and anti-nomic alienation. Reason longs for the harmony of its lost moral self; it wishes to become a moral instinct and feeling, thereby losing the deadening artificiality, formal universality, and oppressive objectivity characteristic of Kantian moral philosophy. The moral laws are to become simple human feelings producing moral harmony, universality, and freedom. Schiller, however, shares with Kant a belief in morality that is divorced from a social ethic, which, as Hegel and Marx had recognized, had serious consequences for the creation of an ethical philosophy. For Schiller, there is no return to this ideal, which he believes was evident in ancient Greece. The Greeks provide us with a sublime model of a lost ideal, which reason and culture must reconstitute in a new way. But Greece will always remain a goal we can strive for in this world.

> Civilization with them [ancient Greeks] did not degenerate, nor was it carried to such an excess that is was necessary to break with nature. The entire structure of their social life reposed on feelings, and not on a factitious conception, on a work of art. Their very theology was the inspiration of a simple spirit, the fruit of a joyous imagination, and not, like the ecclesiastical dogmas of modern nations, subtle combinations of the understanding. Since, therefore, the Greeks had not lost sight of nature in humanity, they had no reason, when meeting it out of man, to be surprised at their discovery, and they would not feel very imperiously the need of objects in which nature could be retraced. In accord with themselves, happy in feeling themselves men, they would of necessity keep to humanity as to what was greatest to them, and they must needs try to make all the rest approach it.[55]

Schiller succinctly summarized the distinction between the ancients and the moderns when he said that "the ancients felt naturally; we, on our part, feel what is natural." It is sentimental poetry that attempts to keep this moral experience with nature intact in an exiled and depraved world through a poetic ideal. Schiller writes that sentimental poetry and the striving after nature began with the works of Euripides, Horace, Propertius, and Virgil. This ideal world of the Greeks was lost due to the rise of modern civilization, but it will only be through civilization that we will regain the natural instincts at a higher level of

moral unity. This *Humanitätsideal* of the moderns is superior to the
ancients, because of its very self-reflective and free nature. Sentimental poetry recreates natural harmony through the imagination as it
reintegrates reason and sensibility.

In *The Birth of Tragedy*, Nietzsche expands upon Schiller's aesthetic
theory and ideas on sentimental poetry, but with ironic and fascinating
twists.[56] Where Schiller views the alienation of modernity as an expression of Kantian dualisms, Nietzsche takes Schiller and, in turn, German theory of art and places it within a revised Kantian framework
that emphasizes the distinction between essence and appearance. In
his attempt to explain the nature of Apollonian art, Nietzsche turns to
Schiller's theory of simple poetry. But as is usual for Nietzsche, the
turn is always one that incorporates the material into his overall
schema. He mentions the nostalgia of naïve art and the will to return
to a harmony with nature within the framework of the "beauty of
appearance." But Nietzsche is very much aware of the philological
weaknesses of this approach to the study of ancient Greece. In the
notes for *We Philologists*, he contends, "They imitate something
wholly chimerical and pursue a fabulous world that never existed."[57]
Classical philology had become a romanticized image juxtaposed
against the pessimism of modernity. The values of noble simplicity and
beauty were created as aesthetic ideals to counterbalance a world
of scientific rationalism and technological mechanization.[58] Art, for
Nietzsche, is an illusion or aesthetic deception of the appearances for
the purpose of recreating a naïve identity and harmony with nature as
occurs in the works of Homer and Rousseau. The Apollonian will
creates a world of beauty, joy, and reconciliation, but it is a deception
to mask the underlying essence of a horrible and terrifying reality.

> In the case of the Greeks it was the will wishing to behold itself in the
> work of art, in the transcendence of genius; but in order so to behold
> itself its creatures had first to view themselves as glorious, to transpose
> themselves to a higher sphere, without having that sphere of pure contem-
> plation either challenge them or upbraid them with insufficiency. It was
> in that sphere of beauty that the Greeks saw the Olympians as their
> mirror images; it was by means of that esthetic mirror that the Greek will
> opposed suffering and the somber wisdom of suffering which always
> accompanies artistic talent.[59]

Nietzsche has transposed Schiller's theory to fit his Kantian view of
the world. Art is made to conform to his underlying metaphysics,
which also contains strong elements from Aristotle's worldview. The

Kantian distinction between essence and appearance and the Aristotelian distinction between form and matter are important ingredients in Nietzsche's aesthetic theory. The antinomic character of artistic representation is maintained when he wishes to stress the chasm between the Apollonian plastic harmony and beauty and the pain and suffering expressed in the Dionysian world. However, the two are irretrievably linked in the creation of Greek tragedy, which requires the presence of both artistic drives. The forms of beauty and serenity that are part of the German theory of art rest upon and are grounded in the knowledge of a dark and terrifying existence. Art does not transform that reality; it does not reconcile and reintegrate the world into a harmonious and beautiful whole; it does not transform the ugly into the sublime and graceful. Art creates illusory metaphors that give meaning and purpose to a meaningless world. In the process, it does not change or recreate reality. It redefines the moral base of the community, creates a theodicy in mythology and the Olympian world, and, finally, gives comfort and purpose to existence. But it all remains a dramatic illusion and grand lie. Beauty, joy, and harmony hide a world of terror, suffering, and pain. At the foundations of Nietzsche's theory of art are the remnants of an Aristotelian view of tragedy and the necessary unity between Apollonian and Dionysian art. But all this is expressed within a universe of irreconcilable Kantian dualisms and antagonisms.

It is clear from his aesthetics that there are profound anthropological and metaphysical assumptions at the heart of his thinking. It is here that he clearly joins his Kantian epistemology with Schiller's theory of art. Nietzsche writes that "since we ourselves are the very stuff of such illusions, we must view ourselves as the truly non-existent, that is to say, as a perpetual unfolding in time, space, and causality."[60] The empirical reality is itself an illusion since it is an appearance of reality created by consciousness. The mind gives the manifold of impressions from the external world a coherent form as it organizes these impressions within a temporal and spatial dimension. That which lies behind the appearances is the thing-in-itself or, as Nietzsche says, the original Oneness; it is this toward which art returns. But as we will see in Chapter 5, he later pushes this argument to deny the reality of the ego, material substance, and causality. For Nietzsche, then, experience is an "illusion" because it is a synthesis of impressions and consciousness. Art becomes an illusion of illusions, because it is built upon an already constructed empirical reality.

Schiller saw naïve art as a direct connection between the artist and nature where art is not seen as an imitation or ideal of nature, but an expression of nature itself. Nietzsche, on the other hand, uses the notion "naïve art" to stress, for him, what is the essence of Apollonian art. It is an illusion of an illusion. Where for Schiller there is an immediate contact between art and nature in simple poetry, for Nietzsche the artist is two steps removed from nature: consciousness and then art. Art as an illusion "is a reflection of eternal contradiction, begetter of all things."[61] Art reflects the inner tensions and contradictions of existence resting as it does on pain and terror as the ground of being, on the one hand, and the harmony and beauty created by art, on the other. There is a very ambiguous use of Kant's epistemology in this section of *The Birth of Tragedy*. In one sentence, he means to indicate that art is a second-level form of consciousness, once removed from the forms of the understanding and the appearances of sense experience. But within the same paragraph, he seems to indicate that Dionysian art reaches deep into the very ground and truth of being itself. First, it touches the depths of human despair and suffering, but "from this illusion there rises, like the fragrance of ambrosia, a new illusory world, invisible to those enmeshed in the first: a radiant vision of pure delight, a rapt seeing through wide-open eyes."[62] Nietzsche is very clear, however, on one point. The terror of the Titans, Prometheus, and Oedipus necessitates the world of Winckelmann, Goethe, and Schiller. He seems to be torn between Kant's epistemology and Aristotle's metaphysics. Here the traditional critics of Nietzsche's philosophy make an important point. He is moving too fast in his analysis to stop to unravel this apparent contradiction. He has other issues to present and a traditional philosophical discourse on metaphysics is not one of them. Rather, his goal is to establish the fundamental ground of our being in the conflict between the Apollonian and Dionysian spirits. Thus, for the Greeks, "their whole existence, with its temperate beauty, rested upon a base of suffering and *knowledge* which had been hidden from them until the reinstatement of Dionysus uncovered it once more. And lo and behold! Apollo found it impossible to live without Dionysus. The elements of titanism and barbarism turned out to be quite as fundamental as the Apollonian element."[63]

Apollo was the god of moderation (*sophrosyne*), self-knowledge, moral wisdom, and self-control. The Greek tragedies expressed this perspective of the cosmic order as they showed the various forms of transgressing the cosmic peace through human excess and *hubris*. That which had broken the peace and serenity of the Apollonian world would be punished whether it was the immoderate love of Prometheus for humankind or the immoderate knowledge and arrogance of Oedipus. Nietzsche develops a theory of the evolutionary stages of Greek art and places it within a philosophy of history characterized by conflicts between moderation and intoxication. He separates the Greek world into five stages of artistic development: the Iron Age (age of the Titans), the Homeric (Apollonian age of Olympian mythology of beauty), the Dionysian, the Doric (age of philosophy), and the synthesis of the Apollonian and Dionysian (age of Greek tragedy). It is with the creation of classical Greek tragedy that the two cosmic forces were for a short time united in one spirit.

Finally, there is an analysis of Nietzsche's philosophy of art and the structural components in the origins of Greek drama: lyric poetry (from Schiller), music (from Schopenhauer), and the Greek chorus (from A. W. Schlegel). There is no reason to examine Nietzsche here, as this material has been closely examined by others. However, what is of interest in these sections of *The Birth of Tragedy* are the references to subjectivity and objectivity, since they contain some of his earliest public statements regarding his underlying view of humans as creative beings. Lyrical poetry, for Nietzsche, is an artistic expression that lies somewhere between sculpture and music. It shares with sculpture the creation of objective images to express its subjective meaning, while like music it is a process of "unselving." That is, the subjective is transformed into an objective image expressing objective meaning. "The lyrical poet becomes his images, his images are objectified versions of himself."[64] Marx also played with the subjectivity/objectivity image of humanity.

What is interesting and different about Nietzsche is his notion of the "I." The very form of expression reminds one of Kant's transcendental unity of apperception. There is a phenomenal I and a noumenal I. Nietzsche refers to them as a personal I and an I that is the ground of being itself. It appears that he has again transformed elements of Kant's epistemology (noumena and phenomena, appearance and essence, and the transcendental unity of apperception) into a metaphysical and aesthetic theory of subjectivity and poetic objectification. The personal genius of the poet is objectified as the objective ground and spirit of being. The self as pure will expresses the underlying reality of the pain and contradictions of the world and in the process expresses the ultimate truth of reality.[65] In both lyric poetry and song, there is this synthesis of willing and contemplating of beauty and harmony. At this moment in the development of his ideas, Nietzsche's notions about creativity have not been freed from the epistemological and metaphysical baggage of Western philosophy. This will be attempted when he develops his critique of foundationalism (epistemological justification of claims to truth) and his moral nihilism. With these two components in place, he will radicalize and ultimately free his theory of will and creativity from Schopenhauer and Schiller, as well as from Kant and Aristotle. "But to the extent that the subject is an artist he is already delivered from individual will and has become a medium through which the True Subject celebrates His redemption."[66] It is in the act of aesthetic creativity that the individual derives his or her sense of dignity. Here, too, it is clear that the remnants of Nietzsche's metaphysics get in the way of his developing anthropology. In one line, he states that only as a work of art does the individual become dignified. The ontological priority is clearly given at this point in the development of his thought to a noumenal self, to his "true subject," to the ground of being. But he will also say that the self is the integration of both subject and object. It is the creator as well as the object of creation.

The darker, brooding, more emotional, pessimistic, and nihilistic side of Nietzsche—his creative and Dionysian spirit—comes partly from his interpretation and transformation of Arthur Schopenhauer's *The World as Will and Representation* (1819).[67] For Schopenhauer, "all life is suffering." This work, which is so frequently mentioned in *The Birth of Tragedy*, contains much that is important for the development of Nietzsche's theory of Greek tragedy. Nietzsche relied upon, but also strongly resisted and acted against, much that he found in Schopenhauer's theories of knowledge and dreams, representations and illusions, will and Neoplatonic sensibility and sensuality, art and tragedy, and theory of pessimism and resignation.[68] It was his radical Kantian epistemology that provided Nietzsche with the philosophical keys to his own theory of consciousness and objectivity.[69] Schopenhauer built upon the philosophical structures of Kant's thought to make his epistemology even more idealistic and subjective.[70] Access to the objective and external world, according to Kant, resulted from the linking of the material elements of sensation (sensible intuitions) with the categories and forms of human consciousness (forms of intuition and categories of the understanding). Individuals perceived a reality that they themselves played a part in creating through the relational categories of the mind. On the other hand, Schopenhauer took the logic of Kant's aesthetic and transcendental arguments one step further when he argued that our knowledge of objectivity is ultimately only a knowledge of the images of our perception. Our experience and our thoughts are reflections of our own representations. In effect, what we know is what we are and what we are is constituted by the formal structures and principles of rationality contained in abstract consciousness. We know only as perception and the mind represents the world to us. Subjectivity is not just a part of an integrated experience of objectivity; it is the full picture. As Schopenhauer said in the first line of his book, "The world is my representation."[71]

Representations are phenomenal experiences that reflect relational aspects of time, space, and causality in the world. They are the appearances of things, not their inner essence, or thing-in-itself. Schopenhauer moves beyond Kant by connecting these phenomena to the idealism of Platonism and Hinduism. Our experiences and the cognitive laws that govern them are really only sensory distortions and obscure shadows of reflected figures on the cave wall as Plato described empirical knowledge in the *Republic*. These same ideas are expressed in the doctrine of Maya found in the Hindu writings of the *Vedas* and *Puranas*. Schopenhauer summarizes these insights when he says, "For the work of Maya is stated to be precisely this visible world in which we are, a magic effect called into being, an unstable and inconstant illusion without substance, comparable to the optical illusion and the dream, a veil enveloping human consciousness, a something of which it is equally false and equally true to say that it is and that it is not."[72] The objective world of perception and understanding, experience and thinking governed by the principle of sufficient reason is an illusory veil of deception having no being or reality of its own, since it reflects only our relative representations of the world. We never really get beyond the individual knower in our understanding of objectivity.[73] The world contains in itself no meaning or value—it is a dreamlike existence that is "void and empty."

The individual's relation to the world is not only cognitive and joined by the forms of thought that condition knowledge of the world, but it is also a volitional, emotional, and sexual relationship. The world is also an expression of human will. There is, in fact, nothing but the will. This striving after existence with its motivations, desires and longings, hopes and fears, needs and expectations, and search for pleasure and happiness are all affirmations of life and the will-to-live. "All *willing* springs from lack, from deficiency, and thus from suffering."[74] In fact, the appearances are only the phenomenal forms of the objectivity of the will. For Schopenhauer, the will is the thing-in-itself. Since human desires can never be totally fulfilled, there is never any final satisfaction or end to the striving after pleasure. And thus, life is fundamentally only the experience of constant suffering and hardships, constant struggle and striving. In the end, "the subject of willing is constantly lying on the revolving wheel of Ixion, is always drawing water in the sieve of the Danaids, and is the eternally thirsting Tantalus."[75]

Access to reality and true being, to Kant's thing-in-itself and Plato's Ideas, according to Schopenhauer, is through contemplation and the removal of oneself from science and the principle of sufficient reason. Only the genius is capable of such direct and disinterested intuition and imaginative insight into reality. Contemplation requires enormous concentration, getting lost in the object, and forgetting the will and subjectivity in order to become pure knowing subjects who momentarily suspend emotions, passions, personality, impressions, and strivings. The constant movement and searching, the ever-present struggles and conflicts, the continuous quest for fulfillment and pleasure, the general restlessness and dissatisfaction with life are transcended in contemplative bliss. When this state is achieved, one has reached pure and blessed knowledge, spiritual and aesthetic peace, and the beautiful and sublime.

> This is why the man tormented by passions, want, or care, is so suddenly revived, cheered, and comforted by a single, free glance into nature. The storm of passions, the pressure of desire and fear, and all the miseries of willing are then at once calmed and appeased in a marvellous way. For at the moment, when, torn from the will, we are given ourselves up to pure, will-less knowing, we have stepped into another world, so to speak, where everything that moves our will, thus violently agitates us, no longer exists. This liberation of knowledge lifts us as wholly and completely above all this as do sleep and dreams.[76]

Contemplation of aesthetic beauty and the sublime transposes the individual out of and away from the torments and terrors of everyday life. Freed of the will and its torments and struggles in solitary contemplation, consciousness has escaped from the world of becoming and illusion into reality by conscious resignation. Schopenhauer has joined together Epicurus's search for pleasure and the Stoics' quest for peace and tranquility.[77] He turns his discussion of genius and will-less contemplation into an examination of his theory of aesthetics. In Christian and Indian art lies the access to the Platonic Idea and "perfect resignation," since its goal is "the giving up of all willing, turning back, abolition of the will and with it of the whole inner being of this world.''[78] Through tragedy, the horrors and sufferings of life are portrayed. ''The unspeakable pain, the wretchedness and misery of mankind, the triumph of wickedness, the scornful master of chance, and the irretrievable fall of the just and the innocent are all here presented to us.''[79] Through tragedy, the artist communicates the necessity for conscious resignation from life and the undermining of the will-to-live. Suffering purifies and enlightens the tragic character, and prepares for the moment when every spirit of life is surrendered.

According to Schopenhauer, the illusions of Maya are lifted from the phenomenal world and only resignation remains. To make his point, he draws upon scenes from the modern tragedies of Shakespeare, Voltaire, Goethe, and Schiller. The protagonists in their plays resigned themselves from life. There was no struggle and no attempt to impose ethical or political norms on the social chaos; there was no reconciliation with a higher moral order and no redemption of the individual at the end of the plays. In fact, Schopenhauer contends the most profound insight of tragedy is that individuals must atone for original sin or the "guilt of existence." In *The Birth of Tragedy*, Nietzsche will lean upon these ideas about the will, the veil of Maya and illusions of consciousness, and Kantian notions of phenomena and thing-in-itself. However, he will reject outright or substantially modify Schopenhauer's theory of tragedy and resignation, and will-less contemplation and pessimism. Though he will ultimately move beyond the traditional aesthetic categories of Schiller's reconciliation and Schopenhauer's resignation, their ideas inform every aspect of his own theory of art and tragedy.

According to Schopenhauer, the will is free and one of its main goals in life is to acquire a moderate character that knows its mental and physical powers and capabilities—to recognize the inner and outer necessities of life. (Variations of this theme of the relation between freedom and necessity also run throughout the works of Spinoza, Hegel, and Marx.) While the will is free, the phenomenal world appears as necessary and determined by fate. The knowledge of our personal strengths and weaknesses will protect the individual from immoderate desires and expectations. By knowing the limits and abilities of the will, by possessing self-restraint, we will not overestimate our talents and accomplishments and thus will avoid further suffering and humiliation. This form of self-knowledge is the "surest way to the attainment of the greatest possible contentment with ourselves."[80] The purpose of knowledge is to produce a state of fatalism, consolation, and contentment. Reconciliation is purchased with the price of life itself.

Life is a dark and forbidding place where humans are constantly searching for the satisfaction of their needs and desires while facing a threatening and hostile world. They are tormented from within by their needs and from without by physical dangers, wickedness, accidents, arbitrariness, and so forth. As people face every new day, they are alone, uncertain, cautious, anxious, fearful, and frightened that around each corner there is a new threat to their existence. Their lives are constituted by the contradictory moments of striving and suffering, satisfaction and boredom, happiness and despair. What forces humanity to continue daily is not the joy of life and exhilaration of existence, but the fear of death. In many respects, Schopenhauer appears closer to Hobbes than he is to Goethe and Schiller.

Life is truly tragic and unhappy as suffering is essential to it and cannot be avoided, but must be stoically accepted with moderation in our pleasures and pains.[81] "The never-fulfilled wishes, the frustrated efforts, the hopes mercilessly blighted by fate, the unfortunate mistakes of the whole life, with increasing suffering and death at the end, always give us a tragedy."[82] In order to avoid the emptiness and superficiality of life, the spirit creates a world of idols beyond the sensible with their hopes and visions to give support to this world. The self-conscious philosopher is capable of escaping the phenomenal world of change and will through a knowledge of the inner nature of the whole of life, by negating egoism and the *principium individuationis*, by developing a contemplative attitude to the transformation and suffering of the world, and by recognizing the bitterness and vanity of life, and the emptiness of its brief moments of happiness. Schopenhauer concludes that "we would like to deprive desires of their sting, close the entry to all suffering, purify and sanctify ourselves by complete and final resignation."[83] To escape from this world requires that we see through the dreams of Maya and the illusions of the appearances with their temptations and salvation of pleasure and happiness, hopes and desires, and meaning and purpose. There is no paradise and no hope in a beyond, there is no optimism of a final judgment or natural justice. This optimism in a better life is rejected as "merely the thoughtless talk of those who harbor nothing but words under their shallow foreheads."[84] He also rejects the validity of knowledge of the phenomenal world whose essence is the will-to-live and all vanity of possessions.

From here, Schopenhauer turns to a Neoplatonic asceticism and bodily renunciation that becomes indifferent to the pleasures of the physical and the affirmation of life in its silent and resigned sadness. Self-renunciation, bodily mortification, denial and suppression of the will, and withdrawal from and indifference to the world are its defining characteristics as we escape from our "miserable and desperate nature." Deliverance and salvation from the world are his ultimate goals and what remains is only the absurd and nothingness. He argues that similar positions are held by Christian saints, artists, and philosophers, as well as the Hindus and Buddhists by their negation of life. Nietzsche will reject this brooding pessimism and *ressentiment* as a continuation of Western metaphysics, since it undercuts the very wellsprings of life, human creativity, reconciliation, and happiness: it undermines human potentiality, the transfiguration of life, and the possibility of integrating the Apollonian and Dionysian spirit in the tragic vision.[85] Physiology, culture, and art, as well as the break between Schiller's views on reconciliation and optimism and Schopenhauer's resignation and pessimism must be healed in order to escape the nihilism and nothingness of modernity. Greek tragedy provides him with a model for such a sublime experience and a manifestation of the meaningfulness of life.[86]

Mythic Hope and Tragic Vision of Apollo and Dionysus

It seems that there has always been an intense, even vitriolic debate within philology and among the classicists about specific aspects of Nietzsche's theory of Greek tragedy: the origin of tragedy in the dithyrambic chorus, the conflict between Apollonian and Dionysian art, the critique of Euripides' comedies and Socratic rationalism, and so forth. What is of interest to us in this chapter is the philosophy that underlies his theory of tragedy. As we have already seen, Nietzsche's interpretation of Greek tragedy, and Aeschylus and Sophocles in particular, is filtered through Schiller's theory of poetry. In examining the different theories of the origins of tragedy, he briefly considers the ideas of A. W. Schlegel. However, he quickly returns to Schiller's aesthetic theory of sublime and naïve poetry. For Schiller, naïve poetry is a depiction of natural reality and truth. Nietzsche blurs Schiller's distinctions between naïve and sentimental poetry and never uses the latter term even when referring to its basic ideas. In his essay entitled *Sentimental Poetry*, Schiller makes the distinction between "sensuous unity" and "moral unity," and the "state of natural simplicity" and "state of civilization." These ideas become the basis of

Nietzsche's own theory of Greek tragedy as he uses terms such as the "truth of nature" and the "pretentious lie of civilization."

> The contrast between the truth of nature and the pretentious lie of civilization is quite similar to that between the eternal core of things and the entire phenomenal world. Even as tragedy, with its metaphysical solace points to the eternity of true being surviving every phenomenal change, so does the symbolism of the satyr chorus express analogically the primordial relation between the thing in itself and appearance.[87]

The role of tragedy is to fill the void of an existence that has no inherent meaning or purpose. The "truth of nature" is that life is a ghastly absurdity full of nausea whose real nature is one of suffering and hardship. But tragedy is to act as a palliative or metaphysical solace to give comfort by creating a world of metaphors and meanings. Poetry produces unity, solace, joy for life, recognition of the meaning of existence, and general reconciliation within nature itself. This reassertion of the power and joy of life, as well as the meaning and harmony of the world, is an aesthetic creation of the phenomenal and illusory world of appearances in Greek tragedy. The true reality of being or the essence of the world is hidden from view. Nietzsche is still ambivalent about the exact nature of this being. In section 4 of *The Birth of Tragedy*, he characterizes poetry as an illusion of illusion, while in section 8, he portrays it as the truth of nature. Is the Kantian idea of the thing-in-itself, as developed by Nietzsche, an artificial construct, an epistemological representation, or the essence of nature and a metaphysical truth? Is Nietzsche moving in the direction of Kant or Aristotle? Do the ideas of Winckelmann and Schiller about the simplicity, nobility, harmony, and beauty of the Greek world represent the truth of the Greek experience or only an aesthetic gloss over a more violent and horrible reality? Can it refer to both? What is the status of Nietzsche's reliance on the theories of the state of nature (Rousseau), the state of natural simplicity (Schiller), the thing-in-itself (Kant), and even the original Oneness (Schopenhauer)? Is the split between the phenomenal world of civilization and the noumenal world of truth or the split between the authentic person and the civilized individual an epistemological or metaphysical distinction or both? (Nietzsche's later writings will clearly fall on the side of the former, but for now, the issue is very ambiguous.)

The manner in which the issues surrounding Kantian epistemology are resolved ultimately will affect our reading of Nietzsche's interpretation of Schiller's philosophy of art and may help to explain the discrepancies within Nietzsche's own borrowings from him. Finally, does the juxtapositioning of the terror and joy, ugliness and beauty, chaos and harmony, and struggles and reconciliations within human existence reflect an aesthetic illusion or a metaphysical truth? What is the epistemological status of the works of Winckelmann and Schiller? These questions are important because they will determine how we are to read Nietzsche's appropriation of eighteenth- and nineteenth-century German aesthetics and his interpretations of *Oedipus* and *Prometheus Bound*. At this point in the development of his intellectual career, the answers to these questions appear to be very simple: there is no clear answer. This is not an equivocation, but rather a recognition that Nietzsche has not adequately dealt with these philosophical issues—at least not in any consistent and systematic fashion.[88] In the process of producing a new breakthrough in the analysis of Greek tragedy and the crisis of modernity, he, in fact, has glossed over some of these older questions in philosophy.

Whatever the answer to these questions, Nietzsche does argue that art provides an important role in the creation of an aesthetic universe in which humans recapture the world from barbarism and chaos. "Then, in his supreme jeopardy of the will, art, that sorceress expert in healing, approaches him; only she can turn his fits of nausea into imaginations with which it is possible to live. These are on the one hand the spirit of the *sublime*, which subjugates terror by means of art."[89] The terror is replaced by the mythology of the Olympian gods. Attic tragedy combined the Dionysian and the Apollonian elements, that is, the chorus and music, poetry, mythology, and drama in a glorious creation designed to heal a sick and tortured soul.

Nietzsche's approach to Greek tragedy and aesthetics is colored by his epistemological writings that will be examined more carefully in Chapter 5. By the time of *The Birth of Tragedy*, he interprets drama in terms of the categories of Kant's *Critique of Pure Reason* and Schopenhauer's appendix to *The World as Will and Representation* entitled "Criticism of the Kantian Philosophy." It is by incorporating Kantian categories into his aesthetic theory that Nietzsche is able to integrate the contradictory worlds of Apollo (and Schiller) and Dionysus (and Schopenhauer) in his works.[90] However, for Nietzsche, the noumenal world is knowable and supplies us with the secret keys to understanding Aeschylus and Sophocles. For example, on the surface, Nietzsche recognizes that Aristotle's *Poetics* does provide a powerful tool for an examination of tragedy, but concludes that Aristotle's moralism hides the underlying aestheticism and ultimate truth of art. Nietzsche mentions three important elements that make up the structure of tragedy: catharsis coming from within the story (excitation of empathy, pity, and terror and the consequent purging of emotions), the descent and elevation of the noble hero through sacrifice, and the reestablishment of the moral order.[91] Nietzsche does not seem to question the specific components or traditional interpretations of modern classicism. He does, however, reject Aristotle's theory of mimesis, catharsis, and emotions.[92]

> Our aestheticians have nothing to say about this grand return [sublime aesthetic joy in the heart of original Oneness], about the fraternal union in tragedy of the two deities, or about the alteration of Apollonian and Dionysian excitation in the spectator. But they never tire of telling us about the hero's struggle with destiny, about the triumph of the moral order, and about the purging of the emotions through tragedy. Such doggedness makes me wonder whether these men are at all responsive to aesthetic values, whether they do not respond to tragedy merely as moralists.[93]

The Winckelmann-Goethe-Schiller tradition represents the Apollonian aspect of tragedy that had not recognized a Dionysian component in its perspective. What Nietzsche wants is to get to its underlying foundations in the suffering and sublime reconciliation with life. Thus, the true significance and meaning of Greek tragedy is misplaced in its appreciation of only the tragic appearances. Beyond moralism is aesthetics, beyond knowledge is art, behind the Apollonian is the Dionysian, and, finally, behind the conscious symbols of the sublime and moral are the suffering, joy, and wisdom of the creative will—that is, behind Schiller is Schopenhauer, behind Winckelmann is Nietzsche.

Nietzsche's specific interpretations of the dramas of Aeschylus and Sophocles are framed within the theories, questions, and issues mentioned above. This makes his views more complicated and idiosyncratic. That is, his philology and studies of Greek texts are only part of his broader philosophy of history and critique of modernity. This means that his views of the Greeks must be understood and evaluated within his general philosophy and not isolated as simply another form of classical philology. But it does make it more difficult to get to the heart of Nietzsche's own ideas about these issues.

Nietzsche begins his analysis of the tragedies with a particular reference to the theory of forms and the cave in Plato's *Republic*. The characters and plot development in these tragedies are the appearances projected onto the cave wall, while the critical inquirer is blinded by the truth lying behind Greek drama and mythology. The two issues Nietzsche wishes to consider in this section are the reality of the "horror of nature" and the appearances of "serenity" produced in the plays. Behind the Apollonian masks of the individual characters, the definition and limits placed on morality and action, and the clarification of meaning through rational categories lies the universal experience of the Dionysian world, which seeks to shatter the determinant character and organized structure of the Apollonian moral universe. Behind the representations of the "shining fantasy of the Olympians" and their divine order of joy stands a painful dream of the "terror and horror of existence."[94] To reemphasize, the plays are formed around the Kantian antinomies of essence and appearances, rapture and serenity, and the Dionysian and Apollonian forces of art (*künstlerische Mächte*).[95]

What for the German philosophers of art reflected the underlying essence of the beauty and simplicity of the Greek world is turned upside down and inside out by Nietzsche, who sees the dialogue and tragic presentations as appearances and illusions hiding a deeper meaning of the Greek insight into the cosmos. The Kantian appearances are reflected onto the walls of the Platonic cave and a vision of reality is created that eventually reveals the Dionysian mysteries and a theodicy and metaphysics of life and death, suffering and purpose. From Nietzsche's perspective, the German philosophers were correct within limits, but only as they related to the "appearances" of the Greeks. The former failed to burrow into the depths of the collective unconscious of the ancients to uncover the "original Oneness." That is, not using a depth hermeneutics, they failed to uncover the primordial basis of their experience and their underlying psychological fears and emotional terrors. German philosophy and philology remained at a surface phenomenology, which only reflected their collective hopes, personal aspirations, and aesthetic values.

Beyond Resignation and Reconciliation in Aeschylus and Sophocles

Nietzsche pulls all this material together to form a comprehensive picture in his examination of two Greek tragedies: Sophocles' *Oedipus* and Aeschylus's *Prometheus*. These works share a common feature: they both objectify the conflicts between individuals, who strive after knowledge and wisdom and destroy the natural moral order. Nietzsche is quite explicit at the beginning of section 9 where he states that the concept óf serenity (*die griechische Heiterkeit*) has been misinterpreted to mean undisturbed complacence (*ungefährdetes Behagen*). He undertakes an alternative exegesis and inversion of interpretation of these two plays. This is certainly an early example of what he later calls the transvaluation of values. He undertakes a complete revision of Greek scholarship within the framework of his Kantian epistemology, Dionysian metaphysics, and Schopenhauerian pessimism. The traditional German interpretations of Greek drama and poetry stressed the adaptation, changes, conflicts, and resolutions within the moral universe resulting from individual transgressions. Whether it was the matricide by Orestes, the incest and murder by Oedipus, or the theft by Prometheus; whether it was the justice of Orestes, the immoderate knowledge of Oedipus, or the love of Prometheus; or whether it was the intrusion upon the natural order, ethical serenity, and aesthetic beauty of the Olympian gods, the results were the same for Nietzsche. The natural order was questioned, its conceptual and moral limits were undermined, and finally destroyed—and with it, Orestes, Oedipus, and Prometheus. Nietzsche looks at this as a positive step toward the development of self-consciousness, individual enlightenment, and freedom.

> This is the recognition I find expressed in the terrible triad of Oedipean fates: the same man who solved the riddle of nature (the ambiguous Sphinx) must also, as murderer of his father and husband of his mother, break the consecrated tables of the natural order. It is as though the myth whispered to us that wisdom, and especially Dionysiac wisdom, is an unnatural crime, and that whoever, in pride of knowledge hurls nature into the abyss of destruction, must himself experience nature's disintegration.[96]

All our previous discussions about the intellectual influences on the development of Nietzsche's thought come to focus on the relationship among the natural order, wisdom, destruction, and reconciliation. And it is in terms of these categories that he comprehends the meaning of the whole of Greek tragedy. In the end, his real revolutionary challenge to the classicist tradition centers on the notion of reconciliation. Up to that point, as he weaves his way through the structure and content of Greek tragedy, Nietzsche is well within the more traditional interpretations. However, it is at the point of reconciliation between the universal moral order and the individual that Kant, Schiller, and Schopenhauer take their prominent place in the evolution of Nietzsche's theory.

In *Oedipus* and *Prometheus Bound*, the natural ordering of nature is challenged by the arrogance and immoderate knowledge of Oedipus or the love of humanity of Prometheus. In both cases the natural law and universal ethics shared by the community are temporarily challenged and destroyed. This is the dialectical dilemma Nietzsche raises in the quotation above. It appears that individual striving toward wisdom and a "transcendent tranquility" requires the destruction of the universal relations established by nature. At the end of *Oedipus Rex*, Oedipus is stripped of his titles and property, blinded by his rage and recognition of his crimes, self-exiled from Thebes, and pitifully suffering because of his own fall and that of his family and city. But in *Oedipus at Colonus*, there is a radical transformation of Oedipus who changes from a pitiful and passive creature stricken by terrifying grief and misfortune at the end of the former play to a noble, wise, and serene character in the latter one. There even seems to be a reconciliation between the particular and universal, between Oedipus and the moral order of the gods. Oedipus has looked in the darkest abyss of human suffering, has transgressed the moral order, and has seen the meaninglessness of human life. He has risen from the cave to the sunlight. The gods are reconciled to the activity of this noble man who rises above his own misfortunes. And the audience experiences a profound joy at this reconciliation and reintegration of the divine and human. Nietzsche distinguishes between the "triumphant serenity" at the end of *Oedipus Rex* where the audience anticipates the creation of a new moral order after the shattering of Oedipus and the old order, and the "transcendent serenity" at the end of *Oedipus at Colonus*, which anticipates a new reconciliation.

Nietzsche uses the play *Prometheus* to expand upon his theory of tragedy and the role of the artist in its creation. He sees one of the formal themes as a reconciliation between the suffering of humanity and the gods joined together under the aegis of *Moira*, or "eternal justice." This would be the Apollonian component of Greek tragedy. Rather than develop a detailed philological analysis of this aspect of the play, Nietzsche turns to the Dionysian act of creativity on the part of the poet. It was the artist who created humankind with the new technology of light stolen by the Titan Prometheus from the gods themselves. In the process, the artist destroyed the supremacy of the divine Olympian order. For this, the artist too must atone for his wisdom and transgressions by suffering. In *Oedipus* and *Prometheus*

Bound, Nietzsche argues that both works do not exhaust the extent or depth of interpretation of the dialectic or the "extraordinary depth of terror" that the plays unfold. He is less interested in examining Greek tragedy as a literary production. Rather, he sees in it the profoundest insights and vision of the tragedy and joy of human existence. Where Oedipus is the "saint" who rises above the misfortunes of life into a state of serene activity, Prometheus is the artist whose activity becomes a metaphor for aesthetic production and creativity. This creative process is understood as a dialectic between Dionysus and Apollo, between the terror of life and the enlightenment and pleasure of human transcendence.[97] This is both a tragic vision of life and an emancipation of art.

In the very act of living and creating, the tragic hero, the artist, and even the spectator construct their own being and in the process transfigure the horrors of existence into a sublime justification and magnificent affirmation of life. The tragic experience liberates the individual not simply because it frees him from a debilitating fear and pity through dramatic catharsis. It helps to reaffirm the value and meaning of life.[98] "Thus through his acts, he brings into being his own perfection insofar as he completes all that of which he was capable, and is his own criterion so long as he is creative of what is."[99] The real tragedy lies in the negation of the dialectic, that is, when art disappears as a creative and transforming force and becomes reified in Platonic idealism, Christian theology, and scientific rationalism. It is then that the dialectic of the tragic spirit becomes transformed into the birth of another kind of tragedy. The tragedy of the Greeks was able to keep the tragedy of life at bay. When the Greek spirit died with the death of Hellenism, it unleashed an even more terrifying form of tragedy. This irony that lies at the foundation of *The Birth of Tragedy* is the key to an understanding of Nietzsche's view of modernity and the ancients and the Dionysian and Apollonian forces of nature.

The Apollonian drive or impulse is an aspect of human creativity that produces universal ethics, natural law, and formal order; it is the formative principle that creates ethics, law, polity, theodicy, and art that give meaning to human life; it also brings moral, legal, and political order to the universe. The Dionysian impulse is the creative principle of ecstasy and mystical rapture that brings wisdom, insight, and energy and which pushes and tests these limits and guidelines to human activity. Nietzsche viewed the Dionysian impulse as the artistic and creative drive expressive of human nature, which manifested itself in intoxication, sexuality, community, and ecstatic breaking of all forms of moral and conceptual limits. The Apollonian drive introduced the limits and boundaries that make up our everyday cultural and social world in the form of symbolic metaphors, cognitive frameworks, moral order, dreaming, and visual arts. The Apollonian drive produces our metaphysical, aesthetic, legal, and conceptual norms (and institutions), while the Dionysian impulse is the creative power constantly renewing our dynamic energies and drives toward a higher form of wisdom—the tragic vision.

The Dionysian powers—erotic, sensual, emotional, and cognitive—break down these conceptual and moral barriers to reveal the nausea and absurdity of human life: suffering, death, and tragedy. The tragic insight of the Greeks is the recognition of life's dialectic between the intoxicated rapture of the creative spirit and the ordered life of the cosmos. True creativity requires both production and order and destruction and development. The heroes of the Greek world, according to Nietzsche, are the saints who transcend the dialectic itself and the artists who are actively involved in using it for aesthetic creations.[100] He will make reference to the saints, philosophers, and artists throughout his whole intellectual life.

These descriptive categories in *The Birth of Tragedy* represent analytical distinctions within his general theory, which Nietzsche uses to present his interpretation of Greek tragedy. One difficulty is that he does not fully develop his theory or clarify the interrelations between and among these distinctive features. That is, within his overall ontology, the philosopher strives for metaphysical intoxication and Dionysian truth about the hollowness of existence and the primordial unity and joy of life. The saint attempts to reach for a state of metaphysical solace and Apollonian serenity in dreamlike illusions and reconciliation in natural beauty, law, and cosmic justice. And the artist necessarily pulls these together in an aesthetic creation of mythology and lyric poetry. Art is the force that makes life possible. "He feels himself to be godlike and strides with the same elation and ecstasy as the gods he has seen in his dreams. No longer the *artist*, he has himself become a *work of art*."[101] It represents the objectification of the suffering will. Pain and life are sublimated into joy; horror and terror into beauty and harmony. The integration of the three moments of Greek tragedy (i.e., fall of hero, aesthetic solace, and cosmic reconciliation) produces the Dionysian insight and Attic tragedy that subjugate the grotesque abyss by means of the sublime.[102] By losing ourselves (and our individuality) in the intoxicated ecstasy of the Dionysian experience, we participate in the very ground of reality (*das Ur-eine*), we become one with nature and at the same time create the possibility of our own redemption and salvation.

It seems that the residual trappings of Schopenhauer's metaphysics of art and music and Kant's theory of antinomies, especially the dualism between phenomena and noumena, appearances (myths and illusions) and thing-in-itself (original Oneness of Being and the primordial unity of life), have resulted in an inability to integrate these analytical moments into a unified theory of Greek art and tragedy.[103] (Note that these same themes will reappear in Nietzsche's analysis of pre-Platonic philosophy and physics, especially as articulated in Heraclitus's metaphysics of change and becoming and Parmenides' metaphysics of being.) How do the parts fit together? What is the ultimate purpose of the tragic vision? Is it to achieve reconciliation, the annihilation of the individual and reintegration into the primordial unity of life, or is it to produce the "will to power," and the creativity and strivings of human potentiality? Nietzsche says that the Dionysian and Apollonian moments of tragedy are necessarily linked in this transformation and revaluation of values. But the question is, how? And in what manner? The answer lies in Nietzsche's theory of activity and creativity.

It was in Sophocles' *Oedipus Rex* that Oedipus's boundless wisdom and moral *hubris*—his character—destined him to the break with the moral cosmos. But it was his nobility in the face of such enormous suffering after learning the facts that brought a reconciliation with the gods. For Sophocles, the new morality would come out of the challenge and reconciliation with the old law. For Aeschylus, the issue upon which he focused his poetic insight was the reconciliation of competing moral norms of social justice. Nietzsche took from both: from *Oedipus at Colonus* he found the serene and noble saint Oedipus, and from *Prometheus* he saw the active recreator of moral law in the form of the artist Prometheus who was able to rewrite the principles of justice for man and the Olympian gods. But they were transcending ethical principles under which nature and all living creatures must live. These principles are reconciled at the end of both works in the form of Olympian moral order in Sophocles and *Moira* or justice in Aeschylus. As Nietzsche says: "The artist's joy of life acts as a luminous cloud on the lake of sorrow."[104]

The goal of tragedy is not to produce an emotional catharsis or purging of the spectator's fear and pity or remission of his suffering. Rather, tragedy works when it confronts suffering within the abyss since it is from here the power comes to ignite the pleasure for life.[105]

Rather, the "tragic element" in Greek drama is the recognition and understanding of suffering and its relation to art.[106] The conclusion to his analysis of ancient Greece is that "life is at bottom indestructibly joyful and powerful."[107] What the spectator saw when he attended the festivals and plays was an aesthetic representation of the tragic vision. For a brief moment, he saw and heard the artist create a fictitious world at two levels: the first level was that of the Apollonian mythologies with their final reconciliation and harmony. The second level was the production of the play itself in which the artist through his Dionysian insight and creativity projected a world of meaning and purpose. "In the case of the Greeks it was the will wishing to behold itself in the work of art, in the transcendence of genius."[108] It was at that moment that the spectator felt a redemption and immense desire for life and existence. For Nietzsche, still relying on remnants of Schopenhauer's metaphysics, this was the means by which the Greeks experienced the ground of being—the original Oneness of pain and contradictions (world of becoming). Without suffering and pain, without struggle and overcoming, there was to be no creativity or self-becoming.[109] And without art there would be no *sophrosyne*, which mediated between the excesses and extremes of human passion and knowledge and Apollonian self-restraint and moral limits.

The wisdom of Silenus, that man's greatest good would have been not to be born, but having been born, it is better to die soon, is transcended in experiencing life as an autonomous, creative being. Tragedy transfigures life by its sublime objectification and transformation of human experience on stage and by the aesthetic experience itself. "We have every right to view ourselves as aesthetic projections of the veritable creator and derive such dignity as we possess from our status as art works. Only as an aesthetic product can the world be justified to all eternity."[110] And only in aesthetic creativity do the three moments of Greek tragedy come together in a unified whole. Only in artistic creation is the primordial ground and unity of existence present, only in artistic creation is transformation and self-overcoming possible, and only in artistic creation are the mythological illusions consoling.[111] These three moments of tragedy are present in unified form through the agency of human activity.

For humankind to grow, to experience life and joy, and to be creative, noble, and happy requires suffering and pain. The latter are necessary in order to break the established legal order and moral principles that bind the possibilities and potentialities of human existence. "Man's highest good must be bought with a crime and paid for by the flood of grief and suffering which the offended divinities visit upon the human race in its noble ambition."[112] Human guilt, sin, and suffering are the costs for human creativity, freedom, and dignity. This is the deep pessimism that lies at the heart of his view of the world. He counterpoises the Greek experience and mythology to the Semitic tradition's theory of the Fall. Individual striving and wishing to create a new natural law and moral universality produces suffering, but also future reconciliation and a new order.

Where the traditional interpretations stressed reconciliation between the existing order and humanity, Nietzsche emphasizes to the contrary the primacy of the striving individual who breaks down the old and replaces it with a new system of justice and morality. His focus is clearly on the destructive and creative process. Reconciliation is achieved on terms defined by individual activity. Though classical Greek tragedy has been interpreted through the intellectual lens of modern German philosophy, Nietzsche takes it beyond the issues of Schopenhauer's personal resignation and beyond Schiller's ideal of moral reconciliation to a higher level of human creativity. Where the latter stressed the Greek moral order, its beauty, harmony, and rationality, Nietzsche emphasizes moral ambiguities, judicial arbitrariness, and aesthetic irrationalities. For the representatives of classical aesthetics man was free because he was moral, self-conscious, and rational. Nietzsche, on the other hand, sees people from an entirely different perspective outside eighteenth- and nineteenth-century rationalism. As Martha Nussbaum has said,

> But then, by showing how life beautifully asserts itself in the face of a meaningless universe, by showing the joy and splendor of human making in a world of becoming—and by being, itself, an example of joyful making—it gives its spectator a way of confronting not only the painful events of the drama, but also the pains and uncertainties of life, personal and communal—a way that involves human self-respect and self-reliance, rather than guilt or resignation. Instead of giving up his will to live, the spectator, intoxicated by Dionysus, becomes a work of art, and an artist.[113]

Hubris is the sin of Dionysian wisdom and the titanic individual wishing to become Atlas bearing the whole world on his shoulders. History is the dynamic created by the dialectic between the Apollonian creation of new moral norms and the Dionysian breaking the bounds of these restraints. It is the metaphysical conflict within Hellenism between Dionysus and Apollo, creativity and order, renewal of life and social justice, the individual and the universal. The conflict is fought among the Hellenes in their art, philosophy, and tragedy, but it is also a conflict fought unconsciously within nineteenth-century German metaphysics and philosophy of art. The conflict between humanity and its gods represents an aesthetic expression of the conflict between the individual and moral order, the search for wisdom and subsequent human suffering. Pain and suffering are the prices paid for human development and the realization of human possibilities. Where the Germans played out their metaphysics in an indirect and often unconscious manner, for Nietzsche, the Greeks directly confronted these issues in the most sublime and clear fashion in their tragedies.

Greek tragedy thus explains this basic human phenomenon in terms of the fundamental question of human nature and potential. Without suffering, there is no development, since without suffering there is no challenge, conflict, and overcoming. Sin, guilt, *hubris*, and pain are part of the process of becoming individuals, since wisdom and growth are "always a crime committed on nature." Stephen Houlgate has written, "The core of tragedy thus remains the spectacle of human nobility and heroism crushed by cosmic forces. This spectacle is profoundly painful for us, but it also delights us because we gain through it a consoling feeling that we are essentially one with those cosmic forces."[114] With the coming of Christianity with its concerns for sin, guilt, and redemption in an afterlife in the kingdom of God and with the redemption of socialism with its anticipated reconciliations in a renewed historical beyond, the struggle for existence, the reality of the present, the human meaning of suffering, and the will to create life are lost. This becomes the foundation of Nietzsche's later critique of modernity. Modernity is seen as an attempt to escape suffering through denial of life and humanity. It hides behind the "casuistry of sin and the inquisition of the conscience" and its hatred of the spirit of freedom, beauty, the senses, and courage.[115] The moderns have lost the Greek experience of the tragic life with its struggle, courage, and accomplishments.

Whereas Schiller represented the Apollonian dimension in German thought, Schopenhauer expressed its darker, brooding, and pessimistic side. As we have seen, Nietzsche drew heavily upon Schopenhauer's Kantian epistemology and psychology of the mind, his theory of representation and will, his theory of art, illusion, and metaphysical solace, his views on nihilism and terrors of existence, and also his theory of dreams and original Oneness.[116] What he rejected was Schopenhauer's theory of tragedy, aesthetic contemplation and loss of self, and tragic spectatorship; his theory of guilt and resignation; his pessimism and rejection of life; his Hellenistic Stoicism, Neoplatonism, and Buddhist philosophy; and his notion of individual resignation in the face of the wretchedness of human life. From out of the abyss and the terrors of existence, Nietzsche saw the joys of human possibilities, creativity, and the pleasures of life. The meaninglessness and absurdity of life only express for him the meaningfulness of human creativity; moral arbitrariness expresses aesthetic and moral autonomy; the abyss only increases the range of human possibilities; and moral wretchedness only expresses the power of people to define themselves. By not being limited and restrained by a universe in which meaning is imposed from beyond, the world becomes the playground for unlimited possibilities and purposes. The meaninglessness of life means that human life is profoundly meaningful. Through aesthetic activity and the continuation of the dialectic between Apollonian and Dionysian needs, the individual is constituted as a free being. Art seduces, intoxicates, and saves us from looking directly into the abyss, while at the same time it provides the world with ethical and political order and thereby reaffirms the validity of human life.

Greek tragedy is a mythic construct and artistic illusion that saves us from the truth and permits us to approach the abyss without looking directly into the void. It constructs a world of meaning and values, while hiding the real horrors of existence from us. Tragedy permits ethical action without sickness and despair. However, Dionysian wisdom is itself a recognition of this tragic vision, for we are still aware that the myth is a falsehood that helps us transform the nausea and absurdity of existence into illusions through which we create and sustain life. Without the mythic illusions, life itself would be impossible since the truth would be too difficult to withstand directly. There would be no purpose or meaning to life. Everything would be empty, horrible, and absurd. This is the reason he will argue later that the doctrine of eternal return must be whispered and not spoken outright and only the strong are capable of withstanding the depths of despair to which it leads. One part of human nature drives humankind to greater wisdom (*Weisheit*), as the other part protects it from its own knowledge. Concerning this issue Benjamin Bennett has written, "The truth is absolutely horrible, and the only possible authentic relation to it, the only possible contact with the truth as truth, is the activity of struggling against it. . . . But the *purpose* of this repeated creative act is precisely to illude ourselves about our existence, to rescue ourselves from the knowledge of an absolute abyss in which nothing exists outside what we create."[117]

Dionysian wisdom pushes humanity to higher levels of mythic construction in order to survive and "suppress the truth."[118] For Bennett, there is "no existence outside of illusion" and thus there is a continuous dialectic in history between art and knowledge, myth and symbols, illusions and reality. As the Dionysian impulse pushes toward the horrible truth about reality, myths and illusions are created to unconsciously and artistically deceive ourselves in order to protect and preserve life. In turn, the Apollonian drive, as it becomes more symbolic and self-consciously reflective in Greek tragedy, drives the individual back to a recognition of the original tragic vision. By means of these dramatic and physiological conflicts, Greek tragedy commits suicide.[119] It reveals the very truth it was originally created to hide and in the process initiates the decadence of Socratic and Christian rationalism and the new mythical world of modern science.[120]

The tragic insight needs artistic illusions for protection, just as intoxication demands dreams, Dionysus needs Apollo as a mask, and music requires mythology as a vehicle for its true expression. With the intensity of tragic experience, the Greeks opened the way to a more self-reflective and critical insight into the nature of human existence. In the process, the mythic and the falsifying illusions began to loosen their grip on Greek consciousness and opened the way to a more reflective recognition of the meaninglessness of life and its concomitant experience of human futility and despair. The experience of looking at the contradictions and horrors of life became too direct. Greek tragedy began to affirm that which it intended to hide.[121] And a new mythology had to be created along with a new humanity—the theoretical individual of science. Nietzsche attributes the decline of Greek tragedy to the plays of Euripides.[122] The latter replaced the tragic vision and integration of Dionysian and Apollonian moments with formal dialectics and rationalist dialogue. Characters on stage became everyday, common figures, rather than masks of Dionysus and, in the process, the spectator was transported onto the stage. For Nietzsche, the ideals of classical Greece had been replaced by "bourgeois mediocrity" and a stultifying serenity that recognized neither ideal past nor ideal future. Plays merely mirrored the oppressive reality of the present, suspense and action disappeared, tragic compassion was lost, and there was no longer any Apollonian "redemption through illusion." All this was replaced by grand scenes of lyrical and passionate rhetoric, logical syllogisms, and optimistic dialectics in which action was to be explained and justified. Nietzsche called this new approach to drama "aesthetic Socratism."

Socrates directly attacked poetry, myths, and the Dionysian spirit by claiming that the world is knowable, absolute knowledge of the true forms is possible, and knowledge alone is virtue. The exiling of poets and the displacement of Dionysian wisdom turned the Greek ideal into scientific rationalism, logical syllogism, and metaphysical formalism.[123] A new metaphysical illusion was created by the "theoretical man" who grounded all reality in scientific concepts and theories, formal explanations, and absolute certainty. The world became bearable because it was theoretically comprehensible.[124] But the quest for knowledge, theoretical optimism, hostility to art, and struggle against illusions and fear of death would in the end "curl about itself and bite its own tail."[125] The veil of illusion created by Socrates produced a culture that was a preparation for death and a revenge upon life.[126] It is this view that would develop into the tragic resignation and metaphysical pessimism of Schopenhauer and, after Nietzsche, into Weber's "iron cage."[127]

But it was also to be Kant's and Schopenhauer's theory of consciousness and objectivity, and critique of epistemology, which would undermine Socratic and scientific values and prepare the way for a rebirth of tragic culture.[128] Within this culture there would be a recognition that the lot of mankind is suffering in a meaningless world where knowledge is only a surface appearance and false illusion. This theme will be expanded in Chapter 5. However, Nietzsche in this early work did not fall into the trap of pessimism, but rather saw the possibilities for a new tragic and sublime vision, and a new transfiguration of values in an integration of the music of Wagner and the philosophy of Schopenhauer. Socratic enlightenment had run its course and a new positive tragic age was on the horizon. It was Nietzsche's hope that the transcendence of nihilistic despair, moral nothingness, and scientific rationalism would eventually lead to a transformation and reaffirmation of life and creativity.[129] These same themes run throughout Nietzsche's lectures and unpublished essays during the early period of his work.

Pre-Platonic Physics from Thales to Anaxagoras

The early unpublished writings of Nietzsche provide us with an unusual perspective to view his appreciation of Greek philosophy and the inspiration it provides for the later development of his critique of science and modernity, as well as his understanding of the nature of knowledge and nihilism. In the preface to *Philosophy in the Tragic Age of the Greeks*, Nietzsche says that he is examining the philosophers of the sixth and fifth centuries B.C. in order to emphasize that part of their philosophical systems that "constitute a slice of personality."[130] By emphasizing personality over philosophy, subjectivity over objectivity, consciousness over formal theoretical systems, he seems to be stressing, from the very beginning of his project, a study of the intuitive insight and spirit of early Greek philosophy. This is not a typical introduction to the history of Greek thought, but a rethinking of Greek philosophy in light of the epistemology of Kant's *Critique of Pure Reason* and Schopenhauer's *The World as Will and Representation*. Beginning with the work of Thales and moving quickly through the philosophy of Anaximander, Heraclitus, Parmenides, and Anaxagoras, he contends that they excelled all men since their times. On the surface, the work focuses its attention on the central issue of the Eleatic philosopher's attempt to provide the foundation or "unmoved unity" of nature itself in a world that was constantly in flux. For this purpose, the work is built around an analysis of the pre-Parmenidian (Thales, Anaximander, and Heraclitus) and post-Parmenidian (Anaxagoras) philosophers.

The central metaphysical issue of the relation between thinking and being, concepts and the senses, provides Nietzsche with the opportunity of constructing his history of early Greek philosophy around issues that highlight the importance of both Kant and Schopenhauer. In fact, it is these two individuals who are the real focus of this work, since Greek philosophy's concern with metaphysics is slowly retranslated in his analysis into questions of epistemology. From concerns with reality and being through discussion about the primal, unchanging substance of nature and the process of its changing, or becoming, Nietzsche transforms these questions into those of consciousness and reality, objectivity and materiality. Questions about the reality of nature are transformed into questions about the nature of consciousness. This work then is as much concerned with "traces of Antiquity" as it is with interpreting issues of being and becoming in terms of Kantian categories of concepts and senses. Pre-Platonic philosophy is interpreted within the framework of Kantian epistemology and ultimately understood as a theoretical exposition about nature and consciousness. The real issues in this essay center around questions such as, what is reality? how do we know? and what is knowledge?

Nietzsche begins *Philosophy in the Tragic Age of the Greeks* by stating that there is a cultural disease of modernity, which he ultimately traces back to the rise of German metaphysics and the crisis of epistemology. By returning to the inspiration and vision of classical Greece, he hopes to re-create the philosophy of a "healthy culture," that is, a culture that is genuine, integrated, and harmonious within itself, without divisions between its philosophy and science, knowledge and the values of life, understanding and senses, insight and experience, culture and social institutions. This is what Nietzsche means by a "genuine culture" and "unity of style."

In later societies where these complementary aspects of human life became contentious antagonists, the philosophers became estranged in their own land: they became "exiles among barbarians." Though there is no analysis of the features of such a healthy society, since the insight is one of an intuitive glance at the ancients, there are hints that Nietzsche views the integration of philosophy and the polis as the basis for a rethinking of philosophy's role in modernity. To this extent, he views himself as a cultural physician whose purpose is to rediscover the role of philosophy within a healthy society. But he also recognizes that philosophy itself could never accomplish this reintegration. Nietzsche sees this as resulting from a free creative society, where philosophy becomes the cultural manifestation of an integrated whole, that is, an "artistically creative, self-determining power of the spirit."[131]

The "republic of creative minds" of pre-Platonic philosophy from Thales to Socrates will offer the reader a vision of a philosophy where nature and humanity, objectivity and subjectivity are spiritually united by the powers of consciousness. Classical antiquity provides insights into the foundations of a healthy integrated culture that Nietzsche believes will supply the antidote to a sick society that has lost its direction and values. This is the crisis of modernity that Max Weber will call "rationalization" and "the disenchantment of the world." It is a crisis that has its antecedents in the art of Greek drama and the rise of Platonic and Aristotelian scholasticism. The modern expressions of this crisis lie in German philosophy and scientific rationalism. The philosophical transition from Thales to Socrates and Plato parallels in a similar fashion the modern developments in German metaphysics and modern science. What is interesting here is that modern society is not a passive spectator in this process, since it is a transformed Kantian epistemology that provides the self-conscious rationality for interpreting the meaning of this early Greek experience. That is, it is through Kant that Nietzsche forces the Greeks to speak to the present crisis. Since the archetypes of all later philosophical reasoning already lie in the early Greeks, an examination of their contribution will have relevance even for those most distant from them.

Nietzsche undertakes a step-by-step analysis of these philosophers beginning with Thales. His focus of attention on early Greek philosophy is drawn from their unconscious understanding of nature as an expression of consciousness and rationality. It is through the harmony and beauty of the balance between humans and nature that they participate in the same cosmic law and principles of natural justice. At other times, this joint participation in the rationality of the universe is replaced by a more Kantian theme. In this context, nature is seen as an expression of the categories of human understanding. Each philosopher from Thales to Anaxagoras further develops this cultural integration between humankind and nature, as the categories that express natural relationships are also projections of consciousness itself. On the surface, Nietzsche seems to be outlining the philosophy of nature of early Hellenism, as he traces the development of their views on the primal origins of reality—whether it is water, the indefinite, fire, and so forth. In fact, he is attempting to come to terms with the epistemology and implicit theory of consciousness and truth hidden within each theorist. His philosophical analysis of Greek physics closely parallels the direction he took in his analysis of Aeschylus and Sophocles and aesthetic theory in *The Birth of Tragedy*. And by tracing the development of Hellenism through the eyes of a radical Kantian, he is attempting to come to terms with epistemology and philosophy in a healthy culture. At this stage in the development of Western civilization, empiricism and natural science are not antithetical to philosophical insight among the early Greeks. One complements the other.

Nietzsche compares the relationship between philosophy (i.e., intuition and creative imagination) and science (i.e., measurements, calculation, and principles of causality) to two mountain climbers—one who will not cross a wild mountain stream until a strong foundation has been built and the other who lightly jumps from rock to rock until safety is reached. Philosophy dares to cross over where the security of logic and empirical calculation will not. The latter leads the seeker of wisdom to a point beyond which only philosophical intuition may travel. From the empirical foundations of his natural science, Thales had ventured into a metaphysics that exclaimed: all reality is water.

For Nietzsche, even if later scientific experience destroys the validity
of this argument, there is a vision or insight that remains from which
future philosophers will be able to draw their inspiration. This insight
into the valid remnants of Thales' thought lies in the formal aspects of
Greek thinking that integrate an early acceptance of philosophy and
science. The Greeks had traditionally explained nature through myths
and allegories, resulting in Nietzsche's comments that

> The Greeks, among whom Thales stood out so suddenly, were the very
> opposite of realists, in that they believed only in the reality of men and
> gods, looking upon all of nature as but a disguise, a masquerade, or a
> metamorphosis of these god-men. Man for them was the truth and the
> core of all things; everything else was but semblance and the play of
> illusion. For this very reason they found it unbelievably difficult to
> comprehend concepts as such. Herein they were the exact opposite of
> modern man.[132]

It was not the specific content of Thales' thought that drew Nietzsche's
praise, but his critique of mythology and allegories, as well as his going
against the grain of ancient Greece. Though he did not follow his
thinking to the logical conclusion that "all being is one" because of
the cultural prohibition against abstractions, Thales begins the break
with the traditional mode of thought by searching for the essence of
all reality.

The art of philosophizing is a creative endeavor of the imagination
that objectifies the inner intuition and imagination—"the echoes of the
world symphony"—onto the external world. Rather than seeing truth
as the mirroring of the world in the mind of the philosopher, the
philosopher becomes the truth that mirrors consciousness back into
the world, since he projects onto this world the images of a dramatic
artist. "He grasps for it in order to get hold of his own enchantment,
in order to perpetuate it."[133] Nietzsche is playing off the ocular
metaphor used since the seventeenth century, but in a fashion that
undermines its empirical foundations. According to him, the philosophical mechanism for communicating Thales' insight about the harmony
and integrity of nature by means of the category of water was an error.
But it did initiate for him reflection on the nature of language as a
metaphor. This was a deeply felt, but extremely difficult idea about the
nature of reality to articulate. Thales thus became the archetype for all
future philosophical discourse and the foundation stone for Nietzsche's analysis of later Greek philosophy. But from the latter's perspective, it is an unconscious and unarticulated philosophy, which can

only result in alienation. The real value underlying the philosophy of nature in the pre-Platonic physics is the theory of knowledge and philosophy of language that it presupposes.

This philosophical abstractionism was continued by Anaximander in his attempt to explain the relationship between the one and the many, being and becoming, that is, to explain the transformation and sameness of nature. To this end, he introduced the concept of the undefinable "indefinite," which, like Kant's concept of the thing-in-itself, attempted to reach into the foundations of experience and nature. The indefinite was the unchanging ground of all changes in nature and was the material basis for explaining reality. Metaphysical dualism was assumed in order to explain the process of being and becoming. To explain nature, Nietzsche understood Anaximander's search for the primal being and the source of reality by means of "anthropomorphic metaphors" and ethical categories. Change, being, and reality were to be explained in terms of categories of human behavior. Anaximander was the first philosopher to make the value of existence problematic. The world has no inherent value, is a place of suffering, and is in constant flux.[134] That is, these metaphysical categories were seen as a projection of the values and perspectives of human society onto the panorama of nature. Nature's meaning and rationality was to be understood in terms of the values and rationality of the Greek polis. The dynamic process of change and diversity in nature was comprehended in terms of the ethical categories of Greek experience.

The two central figures in Nietzsche's analysis of pre-Platonic philosophy are Heraclitus and Parmenides, each of whom took archetypically opposing positions in their discussion about nature. Heraclitus rejected the distinctions between the metaphysical dualism of the indefinite and the empirical and further radicalized Greek philosophy by arguing that being (that which underlies all reality and experience and is itself unchanging) was not real. Becoming (coming to be and passing away) was not something to be explained away, but was the essence of reality. All objects were constituted by a union of their opposites. Nietzsche views Heraclitus's metaphysics as placing philosophical intuition on a higher plane than reason. He concludes that there are two main propositions for Heraclitus: multiplicity and diversity of the world result from the constant interaction of opposites within objects and "the conditions which alone make experience of this world possible are time and space."[135]

Further developing the perspectives of Schopenhauer, Nietzsche interprets Heraclitus as contending that all objects that are perceived in time and space are relational and relative to each other. Since there is no primal essence of reality in an unchanging substance and since all things exist in time and space, everything has an existence relative to everything else. Nietzsche here plays off the etymological relationships in Schopenhauer's distinctions between *Wirken* (acts), *Wirkung* (cause and effects), and *Wirklichkeit* (actuality).[136] Reality (actuality) is seen as an activity; materiality and objectivity are defined by temporal and spatial relationships as well as by relative interaction and reciprocal effects. Heraclitus does not take this position to its "terrible, paralyzing" conclusion, but instead returns to the "purest strings of Hellenism" in arguing that this constant change itself represents the eternal and just order of the universe. This becomes the inviolable and eternal substance upon which nature rests. Here, too, he expands upon Thales' physics by replacing water with fire as the primal substance of the universe. Heraclitus has returned to the wellspring of Greek thought after his break with its traditional values. But Nietzsche will not shrink from the "terror" lying behind the implications of this philosophy. However, this must wait for a later time when he develops the epistemological implications leading to nihilism and relativism.

   With Parmenides, Greek physics took a turn from metaphysical dualism and philosophical intuition to scientific rationality, calculating logic, and "bloodless abstraction." Parmenides' theory of being made a fundamental break with the previous philosophy of nature. Now the emphasis was on abstract logic and mechanical procedures, as he attempted to get beyond the dualism and contradictions between a natural and metaphysical world. Heraclitus, in his way, also attempted to get beyond the dualism of Anaximander's distinction between the definite and indefinite with his focus on the harmony and regularity of the eternal flux of nature. Nietzsche accuses Parmenides of having fallen back into mysticism and mythology as he explains the transformation of nature, that is, being and becoming in terms of the union of opposites through desire: the existent with the nonexistent, the positive with the negative. He relies on the metaphor of the relationship between men and women to explain this metaphysical principle.

   With the later development of his thought, Parmenides abstracts further from the empirical world to arrive at his final theory of being. He turned inward to lay hold of the subjective as the truth of objectivity. Nietzsche relates a story about the discovery of Parmenides' major insight. By transcending the conflicts between being and becoming, existent and nonexistent, and the one and the many, Parmenides sought refuge in logical tautology. Just as being cannot be nonbeing and the existent cannot be the nonexistent, so, too, Parmenides reasoned, according to Nietzsche, that A cannot be non-A. Only A = A. "Now, grasping the firm and awful hand of tautological truth about being, he can climb down, into the abyss of all things."[137]

Parmenides rejects the temporal and spatial dimensions of being, since nothing can come into being nor can something pass away into nothing. A unified whole could not have a diversity of appearances. Transitions from the past to the future become impossible because all being is both immobile and indivisible. All perceptions concerning apparent changes in time, place, or form are illusions and deceptions, since being itself cannot be broken down into discrete parts or undergo changes in its unified essence. All being is eternal, infinite, and incapable of undergoing change. This is a direct challenge to Heraclitus's position. By relying on a discussion of Zeno's paradoxes, Parmenides argues that distinctions between motion and rest, present and future, passing away and coming to be are all mistaken illusions of the senses. For Nietzsche, this view of time anticipates his own later theory of eternal return. Reality is reduced to logic and pure reason. Thinking and nature, concepts and reality, and the mind and existent were not understood as different types of being. Rather, Parmenides theorized that they were the same. Thus, by accepting the logical analysis of Zeno regarding motion and rest, time, and change, he could argue that logical conclusions represent true being. There was an underlying identity between thinking and being and an absolute separation of senses and concepts. Experience and perception were rejected as the foundation for knowledge and truth. The former could only give us semblance and appearances, but never reality. Only pure reason could occupy such a lofty position. However, at this point in his analysis, Nietzsche says that Parmenides' separation of senses and concepts, as well as his identity theory, are falsehoods. This interesting admission by Nietzsche will have importance later as his epistemology begins to unfold more fully in the theoretical side of his *Philosophers' Book*. In his severe criticism of Parmenides, one hears echoes of an attack on Hegel's metaphysical system very similar to Marx's.

In the dispute between Heraclitus and Parmenides, Nietzsche clearly sides with the former by accepting motion and change as the eternal foundation of reality. He raises the issues of the mobility of thought and reason and the origins of sense experience and semblance. Providing an unusual example of an immanent critique, he provisionally accepts the basic assumptions of Parmenides' theory of being, but concludes that the latter is unable to explain that thinking engages a multiplicity and diversity of ideas. He asks, how is this diversity and movement from one idea to another explained? Where do the illusions of the senses come from? Nietzsche's own questions lead him to Anaxagoras.

Anaxagoras accepted the basic structure of the argument found in Parmenides. At the same time, he rejected Parmenides' theory of semblance and illusions along with the Eleatic theory of primal substance. Objects are not derived from illusions, water, fire, or any other primal unconditioned being. The multiplicity of existence cannot be explained by one of the above substances. Anaxagoras returns the notion of the multiplicity of substances and their changes to a metaphysical prominence in his philosophical system. Passing away and coming to be are expressions of real being, not mere illusions. To explain motion, he postulated that nature was constituted by "thinking substances," that is, by the *Nous*. Nature was made up of substances whose essence were ideas and it is the latter that precipitated motion from within themselves. The substratum of nature was rational as ideas moved physical bodies. This eidetic motion, along with mechanical motion, was used to explain change and physical diversity in nature.

Nietzsche makes constant reference to Anaxagoras's scientific method and inductive reasoning. From empirical observation rather than intuitive insight, Anaxagoras concluded that the universe had its origins in a primal chaos consisting of an indistinguishable mixture of all things. Everything is contained in everything else in this cosmology: "Everything originates from everything." From within this primal mixture, opposites come from opposites. This also meant, for Anaxagoras, that all material objects contained elements of all the other elements in the universe. At a particular moment in time, distinct physical objects emerge, which are expressed in language by names. The constitution of particular material objects is the result of the circular motion of the universe. There is even an implicit theory of language in Nietzsche's analysis of this doctrine of universal chaos. Words refer to particular objects at a moment when there is a "preponderance of one substance."

This primal chaos is the ground of all explanation for becoming and motion. As motion churns this cosmic soup, like substances are united with like substances to form the essence of objects. This primal mixture is "like a dust-like mass of infinitely small filled points, each of which is a single specific, possessing but one property, yet in such fashion that each specific property is represented in infinitely many single points."[138] The formation of the cosmos from this chaos is the product of the rational law of the universe, which Anaxagoras viewed as beautiful and harmonious. The centrifugal force created by the rapid spiralling movement and circular whirling of the universe brings all similar materials together to form substances. That is, the dense materials join with other dense substances, the rare to rare, the moist to moist, and so forth. The ethereal and the earthly move together to form the structure of the universe.

Nietzsche describes this process of the formation of the universe in almost Hegelian terms. The *Nous* moves the chaos and alienates itself into different and opposing substances seeking to return to itself. The movement is the result of a rational decision of the *Nous* which has its own end in view. At this point, Nietzsche becomes critical of any Aristotelian or Hegelian teleology being read into Anaxagoras. The movement is orderly, purposive, and random and results in predictable laws of motion. Nietzsche expresses his praise for Anaxagoras who explains the creation of the universe in terms of mechanical and mathematical laws of motion rather than in the traditional terminology of mythological causes and anthropomorphic purposes.

Physics, Polis, Play, and *Praxis* as Aesthetics

Through his analysis of early Greek philosophy of nature, Nietzsche slowly developed the beginnings of his critique of objectivity and science in much the same way that Marx's analysis of post-Aristotelian philosophy of nature in his doctoral dissertation helped him to define his views on objectivity, ethics, and science. At each stage in the evolution of Greek physics from Thales to Anaxagoras, Nietzsche carefully supplied new categories by which traditional epistemology was being called into question. With Thales he introduced the distinction between creative imagination (i.e., philosophy) and calculating reason (i.e, science) and applied the concept of "metaphor" to the language of metaphysics. Anaximander's notions of primal being and the indefinite were described by Nietzsche as "anthropomorphic metaphors." Heraclitus too had distinguished between philosophical intuition and the logical concepts of science, as well as having described nature using anthropomorphic categories of polis activities and "cosmic metaphors." In the essay *The Philosopher*, Nietzsche says that "all natural science is nothing but an attempt to understand man and what is anthropological."[139]

But with Heraclitus came a qualitatively new addition. He was examined from within the framework of Schopenhauer's Kantian epistemology. A connection was being made between Greek physics and nineteenth-century German epistemology; the Greek notions of the cosmos and the law of reason begin to take on the characteristics of Kantian rationality and a praxis of aesthetics. Physics is understood as a form of aesthetics. A new interpretation of rationality that slowly transforms the Greek experience into a form of modern rationality is underway in *Philosophy in the Tragic Age of the Greeks*. This link between the Greek notion of rationality and truth is further connected to Kantian epistemology with the direct correlation between Parmenides and Kant. Anaxagoras's theory of *Nous* is, in turn, connected to Kant's theory of intuition of time and space from the "transcendental aesthetic" of the *Critique of Pure Reason*.

In the final section of Nietzsche's work, there is a more fully developed theory of artistic play that connects pre-Platonic construction of nature with Pericles' construction of the political constitution of Athens and the creative drive of the artist. Politics and physics provide the foundations for a new epistemology built on play and the polis—on the creative and imaginative artistry that goes into producing an aesthetic ideal, a political institution, or a poetic image. Nietzsche, in his study of early Greek philosophy, moves in the direction of the idea that art is the foundation of all reality. He is also making closer connections between his ideas developed while studying Greek poetry and drama and his new project on Greek philosophy of nature. There is thus an intimate interaction between Nietzsche's critique of knowledge, his theory of play and art in his epistemology, and his critique of traditional views of objectivity and rationality. At this point in his intellectual career, we have a primal mixture of the various ingredients that anticipate his later epistemology and critique of science with its crucial concepts of polis, play, and objectivity. Nietzsche continues to apply Kant's constitution theory of truth and a Kantian aesthetics to modern rationalism and empiricism as the basis for his reading of early Greek philosophy. In both cases of Kant's epistemology and pre-Platonic metaphysics, the world is a product of the synthesis of primal matter and consciousness.

Though Nietzsche had edited this unpublished work, it remains part of a broader project that was never completed. Some ideas are more developed than others. Some are only tantalizingly and provocatively stated, but never expanded upon. This is the case with his theory that scientific categories are only abstract metaphors for explaining nature.

Their forms of explanation are similar to that of artistic expressions used by Greek dramatists who attempted to get at the heart of the meaning of life in their plays.

> And just as for the dramatist words and verse are but the stammering of an alien tongue, needed to tell what he has seen and lived, what he could utter directly only through music or gesture, just so every profound philosophic intuition expressed through dialectic and through scientific reflection is the only means for the philosopher to communicate what he has seen. But it is a sad means; basically metaphoric and entirely unfaithful translation into a totally different sphere and speech. Thus Thales had seen the unity of all that is, but when he went to communicate it, he found himself talking about water.[140]

Because the scientific language of Thales and the other physicists was only an "unfaithful translation," there are lingering elements of Kant's inexpressible thing-in-itself. What is the reality that lies behind these metaphors? But even at this early stage in the development of his thought, language is not expressive of reality, but only of its appearances. According to Nietzsche, there is no privileged access to truth. There is no direct connection between the real world and sense experience and scientific categories. The immediate connection between concepts and reality has been broken, as we can only know nature indirectly through metaphorical language and experience. This idea is made more explicit when he likened Anaximander's theory of the indefinite to Kant's theory of the thing-in-itself.

The metaphorical nature of physics is developed even further in Anaximander. The natural process of change is characterized in ethical categories of melancholy, while the origins and diversity of the universe are understood in terms of natural justice and injustice. Ethical categories judging human behavior are projected onto nature, as the coming to be and passing away of the world are interpreted through categories of social justice. Heraclitus's theory of flux and eternal strife is also characterized by these same anthropomorphic categories of the law of reason and natural order. This application of "anthropomorphic metaphors" furthers our understanding of Nietzsche's view that language never gets to reality in itself, since the external world is only a projection of the subjective categories of human experience. This insight, developed so early in his intellectual career, will form the foundation stone for his later theory of knowledge, his radicalization of Kantian epistemology, his critique of science, and his theory of moral nihilism.

His seminal theory of knowledge is further expanded through his analysis of Heraclitus. It has already been mentioned that in this section of his work, Nietzsche expounds on his idea that objectivity (existence of perceived objects) is relational and relative. Things are not autonomous, but require the subjective forms of the intuition of time and space, which are the universal and transcendental conditions for the possibility of experience. Objectivity is made possible by experience and this latter is a condition of temporal and spatial relationships constituted by consciousness. Every object is relational and relative because it is formed by consciousness in time and space. To expand on this Kantian point, Nietzsche turns to Schopenhauer's distinctions between reality (*Realität*) and actuality (*Wirklichkeit*). What is real is the end result of the activity and causal interaction of the objects of nature. According to Schopenhauer, cause and effect are the only important categories for understanding nature. It is in the relational changes produced by causes and their effects that the world is known and judged. As the chief categories of human experience, they are the means by which consciousness constructs the relationships of nature in time and space.

The theory of knowledge generated by empiricism from the seventeenth century states that the reality of objects is mirrored directly in experience by a passive mind. Nietzsche is certainly challenging this epistemological thesis and beginning to explore the logic implicit in Kant's epistemology. That is, by referring to Heraclitus, even the reality of objects is questioned. With Thales and Anaximander, the implied role of consciousness was examined. Pre-Platonic philosophy was the earliest example of the idea that physics was formed through the synthesis of consciousness and the material world. As Nietzsche turns to Heraclitus and the latter's ideas about the eternal changing of the universe, language defining a particular object of experience only captures the momentary ascendancy of certain particular characteristics. Change is so fundamental to Heraclitus that opposites evolve from opposites. At one time an object may have one set of characteristics and in the future may have an entirely different set of features. There seems to be a dialectic working here. Elements of Kantian epistemology are used to help explain the revolutionary aspects of early Greek philosophy. However, when the implications of epistemology run out, Nietzsche turns to Greek physics to pick up the vision. Kantian philosophy and Greek physics are being dialectically fused with each other resulting in a new insight into the nature of epistemology and metaphysics. This would help explain why each new analysis of another physicist also incorporates a new ingredient into Nietzsche's theory of knowledge.

With the examination of Heraclitus, a new dimension to the puzzle is added. To physics and epistemology is added both ethics and aesthetics. Heraclitus is intent on answering the questions of theodicy: questions about guilt, innocence, and suffering. Since the world is in constant change, its coming to be and passing away are part of a universal law of reason. Fire, as the primal substance, consumes the world and then recreates it. Nietzsche asks whether this very process of cosmic change and universal destruction by fire is not itself the cause of guilt, suffering, and pain. His own response is that this view is shortsighted and only a philosopher like Heraclitus with his god-like powers of creative intuition can pierce the veil of change to see the order of the cosmos. The physical world is, in fact, grounded in the principles of rationality and justice. At this point, Heraclitus returns to metaphors to explain his vision. Fire is an aesthetic form that produces the universe through play. "Only aesthetic man can look thus at the world, a man who has experienced in artists and in the birth of art objects how the struggle of the many can yet carry rules and laws inherent in itself, how the artist stands contemplatively above and at the same time actively within his work, how necessity and random play, oppositional tension and harmony, must pair to create a work of art."[141]

Fire creates the world of water, earth, and air, the terrestrial and the celestial worlds from within itself in a playful innocence that is beyond moral categories of good and evil. This "ever self-renewing impulse to play calls new worlds into being."[142] Just as the child builds and rebuilds, creates and destroys its toy and fantasy worlds, fire creates a world through the dialectic of opposites: creation and destruction. The anthropomorphic metaphor of logos is connected to that of the artist to form a world characterized by reason, beauty, and harmony— universal justice and order. This is a perception gained through philosophical intuition rather than through the logical calculation of the scientist. After discussing the cold rationality of Parmenides' theory of being, Nietzsche turns to Anaxagoras who returns to more intuitive and mythological thinking. Rejecting the idea that the world is produced from nothing or from a particular substance, Anaxagoras searches for a new underlying substance of reality. Nietzsche characterizes this intuitive glance using the metaphor of the game of dice. The foundations of the material world are unchanging; eternal substances cannot change, but they can combine in new ways to alter their forms and appearances. Diversity and change can never result from opposites or from a single universal substance such as water or fire. As in a game of dice, the configurations are different with each roll of the dice. Though the essence of the dice does not change, it does take on different forms. It changes while remaining unchanged.

It has already been mentioned how Anaxagoras deals with these issues in his theory of chaos, motion, and *Nous*, and his critique of teleology. *Nous* sets the world in motion from within itself, after which mechanical laws of motion take over. In the initial phase of this process, the *Nous* creates the cosmos as a game. A metaphysical teleology consisting of external causes and ends would undermine the belief in the freedom that lies at the heart of this system. There are no prior ends for which *Nous* sets the world spiralling toward its orderly and rational form. Particular motion is self-determined by the blind randomness of the *Nous* determining itself from within. In the last section of this essay, Nietzsche takes more time to develop the implications of the themes of purposelessness, free will, and creative impulse running throughout his work. These are the characteristics of imaginative play. (They are also themes that excited Marx's imagination in his analysis of Epicurus's theory of the atom from his doctoral dissertation.)

> This seems to me to have been the final solution, the ultimate answer, that ever hovered on the lips of the Greeks. The Spirit of Anaxagoras is a creative artist. It is, in fact, the most tremendous mechanical and architectural genius, creating with the simplest means the most impressive forms and orbits, creating a movable architectonic, as it were, but ever from the irrational free random choosing that lies in the artist's depths. It is as though Anaxagoras were pointing to Phidias and—confronted by the enormous art object of the cosmos—were proclaiming as he would of the Parthenon, "Coming-to-be is not a moral but an esthetic phenomenon."[143]

Not only are we viewing Anaxagoras's primal material in play, but we are also experiencing Nietzsche's own coming to grips with the very issues of morality and theodicy. To the fundamental question of the value of human existence, Nietzsche turns to Aristotle's interpretation of Anaxagoras. Life is important because we are able to see the grand design of the whole universe. But Nietzsche radicalizes this insight of the Greek philosophers by giving it a Kantian twist. It is not that we stand before the cosmos and marvel at its beauty and rationality. Rather, following up on themes that run throughout this early work and *The Birth of Tragedy*, Nietzsche recognizes that life has meaning because we have given it meaning. Life has meaning and the world makes sense, because we are its architects; we give it meaning through our playful mythologies, metaphysics, and philosophy, that is, through our metaphorical language. The world is a projection of our own mind and expresses our essence as playful, conscious, free beings.

This playful creativity through which the rationality and objectivity of the cosmos are created is itself the projected image of the playful politics of Athenian Greece.[144] For this image, Nietzsche looks to Thucydides' Pericles whom he says represented the image and ideal of the cosmos created in play. "Pericles represented the visible human realization of the constructive, moving, distinguishing, ordering, reviewing, planning, artistically creative, self-determining power of the spirit."[145]

The *Nous* which permeated the ordered cosmos is the same rationality that participated in the creation of the Athenian polis. Anaxagoras and his pupil Pericles are expressions of the same spirit that pervades the whole of the cosmos; it pervades Greek metaphysics and politics in an integrated and unified culture. Just as the Greeks created a political order out of the chaos of its barbarian surroundings, so did its early philosophers create a representation of the origins of the cosmos using the metaphor of political interaction and play. Aesthetics and politics are uniquely joined together for Nietzsche in the harmony and beauty being created by a common rationality and primal substance that runs throughout its mythology and politics. Just as the order of the polis is created in the language, symbols, and metaphors of political rhetoric, the early Greek philosophers looked to a common spirit pervading its metaphysics and politics.

And just as the most miraculous and purposeful deed of *nous* had to be that wheeling primal motion, since just before it was made, spirit was still undividedly one, so surely the effect of a Periclean oration must often have seemed to the listening Anaxagoras a symbol of the primal revolution. For here too he felt first a whirl of thought, moving with orderly but terrifying force, gradually seizing, with its progressive spirals, first the near and then the far, taking them along and finally reaching its end by having re-formed the entire nation into a pattern of order and distinction.[146]

Within the framework of an interesting sociology of knowledge, Nietzsche understands that the unifying image of Greek culture lies in its political constitution. The whirling activity set in motion by the

Nous and the mechanical motion of cause and effect produced by the interaction of cosmic substances, he likens to the creative play of the artist's and child's games. He argues that in both instances there is no self-determined teleology that directs the artist or child toward any particular predetermined goal. It is this very point that will become the grounds of contention in the later philosophy of Plato and Aristotle.

Fine-tuning Epistemology through Greek Physics

What then does this all mean? A central theme in these early manuscripts is Nietzsche's attempt to come to grips with the issues of rationality and objectivity. Is the cosmos ordered and rational? What constitutes the substance and materiality of the world? How are the objects of perceptions formed and what constitutes the representation of the world in experience? As we have seen, metaphysical categories are intermixed with epistemological ones. Nietzsche attempts to come to terms with the world perceived though representations, anthropomorphic metaphors, myths, illusions, art, symbols, language, and imaginative creativity. Implicit in these discussions about the nature of reality and the role of consciousness in creating reality is an undeveloped theory of language.

The issue of play and games helped Nietzsche see the inner connections between early Greek metaphysics and the constitution of the polis at the macro level and language and reality (artificial illusions) at the micro level. But this very connection is also important for elucidating the nature of objectivity, Nietzsche's appropriation of the epistemology of Kant and Schopenhauer, and Nietzsche's radicalization of a theory of knowledge. This becomes more evident when considering Nietzsche's interpretation of Heraclitus. "Only a Greek was capable of finding such an idea to be the fundament of a cosmology; it is Hesiod's good *Eris* transformed into the cosmic principle; it is the contest idea of the Greek individual and the Greek state, taken from the gymnasium and the palaestra, from the artist's *agon*, from the contest between political parties and between cities—all transformed into universal application so that now the wheels of the cosmos turn on it."[147]

What was mirrored as the truth about the universe—its origins, activity, and purpose—are, in fact, a projection of the forms of relationships around which the polis organized its social life. The basis for understanding the objectivity of experience is the subjectivity of social experience. Nietzsche is here taking the foundations of Kantian theory of knowledge and turning them into a sociological theory of knowledge, which then will be further developed in his later genealogical and historical theory of morals. The perception of external reality is not a mirror of a pure objectivity (object of experience), but represents a synthetic union of consciousness and the manifold of the material world. According to Nietzsche, consciousness as conceived by the Greeks in the sixth and fifth centuries B.C. is joined to their representations and perceptions of nature. Nature is not an independent being made up of autonomous substances, but is itself a mixture with the forms of experience resulting from the molding of Greek consciousness and culture.

Throughout his analysis of Greek philosophy, there is one philosopher who is the focus of Nietzsche's criticisms, that is, Parmenides. Nietzsche is much more comfortable with Heraclitus and Anaxagoras—with the philosophers of motion and change. Parmenides' logical abstractions, his theory of the identity of being and thought, his critique of knowledge and rejection of sense experience as the basis of knowledge, his unconditional drive for knowledge, belief in the thing-in-itself (being), and his theory that experience results in semblance (illusion of objectivity) represented, for Nietzsche, the life-denying characteristics of his thought. While Heraclitus saw the world resulting from the law of reason and Anaxagoras saw it resulting from the eternal justice of the cosmos, Parmenides turns away from the excitement of life and its ethical justifications. To combat these elements, Nietzsche spends more time examining Parmenides than any other pre-Platonic philosopher of nature. However, despite this apparent rejection of Parmenides, there is another element in his thought that attracts Nietzsche. For example, when discussing Parmenides' critique of knowledge and sense experience, Nietzsche writes that it is "a critique as yet inadequate but doomed to bear dire consequences."[148] It pulls apart the senses from conceptual abstraction and ends the scholasticism of Platonic philosophy that "lies upon philosophy like a curse." This will become part of Nietzsche's later thought: sense perception results in illusions and mere semblance.

Nietzsche was understandably aggravated by Parmenides' denial of the validity of experience and his retreat into the philosophical abstractions of pure Being, which Nietzsche characterized as "reckless ignorance." Rejecting the Parmenidian and Platonic split of being and nonbeing, reality and sense experience, Nietzsche argues that all knowledge must be derived from experience, since without it we are simply dealing with ideas that offer no knowledge of the world. Parmenides had developed his identity theory in which the objective component of knowledge was replaced by the subjective, where being was reduced to consciousness. "For the mere logical criterion of truth, as Kant teaches it, the correspondence of knowledge with the universal and formal laws of understanding and reason, is, to be sure, the *conditio sine qua non*, the negative condition of all truth. But further than this, logic cannot go, and the error as to content rather than form cannot be detected by using any logical touchstone whatever."[149]

Nietzsche divided up Greek physicists into those who emphasized pure logical abstractions like Parmenides (and Plato) and those who used the scientific method of empiricism. In effect, the philosophical dualism of these early pre-Platonic philosophers was being used by Nietzsche to clarify the components of his own evolving epistemology. (Marx did the same in relation to post-Platonic philosophy.) He rejects Parmenides' turn to pure ideas as the foundation of truth by picking up Kant's critique of one-sided rationalism. While there is a strong criticism of Parmenides, there is also something new and intriguing in his thought at this time. There is the traditional defense of the Kantian synthesis of sensation and concept, matter and form, but with the addition of one added element. Those very aspects of being that Parmenides denies—motion, multiplicity, and succession—are, for Nietzsche, part of the consciousness of being.

> Words are but symbols for the relations of things to one another and to us; nowhere do they touch upon absolute truth. . . . Through words and concepts we shall never reach beyond the wall of relations, to some sort of fabulous primal ground of things. Even in the pure forms of sense and understanding, in space, time and causality, we gain nothing that resembles an eternal verity. It is absolutely impossible for a subject to see or have insight into something while leaving itself out of the picture, so impossible that knowing and being are the most opposite of all spheres.[150]

Kant is used as a corrective to the one-sided idealism and abstractionism of Parmenides. Nietzsche is moving from an analysis of the categories of the understanding, or causality, and the forms of pure intuition, or time and space, into the categories of language. Traditional Kantian epistemology is being amended by a new philosophy of language and metaphors. The result of this initial consideration of epistemological issues in the context of Hellenistic cosmology is a reaffirmation of basic Kantian principles of knowledge. But unlike Kant, Nietzsche also sought in this material answers to questions about the origins of the "constitution of things" in the playful activity of the artist and social life of the Greek polis. As consciousness was at the heart of forming experience, so too was consciousness as myth and culture making at the heart of early Greek philosophy. Even at this stage in the development of his thought, Nietzsche was viewing epistemology as a subdiscipline of aesthetics. Philosophy and philology would always be understood as forms of art.

Crisis of Epistemology in Modern Skepticism and Nihilism

Kantian themes are further developed during this period in Nietzsche's "theoretical writings" on the pre-Platonists. In these unpublished works, he not only further incorporates Kant's critique of pure reason into his writings, but also radicalizes the critical element of his epistemology to the point of skepticism and nihilism.[151] He radicalizes Kant by returning to the origins of Kantian epistemology and the dilemma of objective validity. The issues begun by Hume's critique of science and epistemology were taken up by Kant and later by Hegel in his dialectical method and immanent critique. This then became the focus point for Marx's ideas about "theory and practice" and the critique of political economy. When taken up by Nietzsche, they develop into a critique of science and all forms of knowledge and even the drive to knowledge itself. Marx had responded to the skepticism of Hume, by developing different methods and approaches that corresponded to different dimensions and categories of time. By this means, he developed his immanent critique of capitalism. In this way, the dilemma of relating social concepts to historical reality was overcome and with it the skepticism and relativism inherent in Hume's thinking. Nietzsche responded by further radicalizing Kantian epistemology in another direction. If all knowledge has a subjective element in the forms of time, space, and causality, then all knowledge must be subjective, relative, and ultimately illusory. This is one aspect of Nietzsche's interpretation of the crisis and tragedy of modernity: the loss of the foundations of knowledge.

In *The Will to Power* (1883–88), Nietzsche's unpublished writings from the last productive period of his life, we get a final statement regarding the centrality of the Greeks to his understanding of modernity.

German philosophy as a whole—Leibniz, Kant, Hegel, Schopenhauer, to name the greatest—is the most fundamental form of *romanticism* and homesickness there has ever been: the longing for the best that ever existed. One is no longer at home anywhere; at last one longs back for that place in which alone one can be at home, because it is the only place in which one would want to be at home: the *Greek* world! . . . all German philosophy derives its real dignity from being a gradual reclamation of the soil of antiquity.[152]

Greek philosophy of the post-Socratic period is interpreted as an attempt at a decadent restoration of Hellenic society and its dying institutions, values, and customs. Not being able to revive the past in reality, it is reconstructed in the ideal. Knowledge replaces action as the polis is transformed into political theory. Socrates, in particular, with his emphasis on logic, virtuous life, and happiness, manifested this rigid and static view of values. The diversity of the Sophists was replaced by the decadence of the Platonists. Throughout this section, Nietzsche juxtaposes science and philosophy, or morality. The pre-Platonic Sophists (Heraclitus, Democritus, and Protagoras) in their defense of becoming, relativism, and nihilism against moral dogmatism were attacked by the later Greek philosophers as a threat to their philosophical defense of moral absolutes. After the victory of the Platonists, science was incorporated into the philosophical quest for universality and truth. Nietzsche's critique of moral knowledge, which will be examined in Chapter 6, is merely the continuation of the Sophist's critique of morality. It is in this chapter that we move from Greek tragedy to the tragedy of modern nihilism.

Chapter Five

Decadence of Reason and Prison of Objectivity: Epistemology, Science, and the Tragedy of Modernity

Introduction

Nietzsche had returned to the Greeks in an attempt to resolve the crisis of modernity: epistemological skepticism and moral nihilism. The crisis focused on the problem of knowledge, science, and foundationalism. Traditional answers to the nature of truth and values no longer provided solid foundations for science and moral philosophy. Agnosticism, skepticism, and nihilism rose from the ashes of scientific rationalism and were the legacy of Western philosophical and theological thought since Euripides and Plato. "When one places life's center of gravity not in life but in the 'beyond'—*in nothingness*—one deprives life of its center of gravity altogether."[1] The philosophical idealism of the Greeks, the metaphysics and theology of the medieval period, and scientific rationalism of the modern age set the stage, according to Nietzsche, for the modern crisis of truth and morality. As in the case of Marx and other German scholars of the eighteenth and nineteenth centuries, Nietzsche's early writings on the Greeks and his philological studies provided him with the inspiration and vision for his analysis of modernity. Bernard Yack in his work *The Longing for Total Revolution* writes about the general relationship between the Germans and the Hellenes, "Like Rousseau's intoxication with ancient virtue, the enthusiasm for the Greek polis expressed by Schiller, Hölderlin, Schelling, and Hegel represents more than a mere infatuation with a mythical image of the past. They celebrate an idealized image of the polis with such enthusiasm because it suggests that the dehumanizing limitations of their own society are not inescapable."[2]

As we have seen in the previous chapter, Nietzsche responded to the discussions about knowledge and truth by further radicalizing Kantian epistemology, pushing its principles to their logical conclusion.[3] One aspect of the tragic insight offered by Greek drama was the recognition of the loss of foundations, that is, basic justifications and explanations for human existence and suffering. Nietzsche interprets Kant within this broad tradition as he expands upon the latter's contribution to the modern critique of knowledge. If all knowledge has a subjective element in the unifying forms of time, space, and causality, then all knowledge must in some way be subjective, relative, and ultimately illusory. If consciousness is the foundation of objectivity in the representations of objects in experience, then subjectivity is the foundation of all knowledge and truth rather than an access to the essence of reality (thing-in-itself).[4] This is the central point of Nietzsche's interpretation of the tragedy of modernity—the loss of the foundation and direction of knowledge.

At this point, Nietzsche recognizes that Kant has not answered the objections of Hume's criticisms of science. Thus, Kant's epistemology represents the modern form of the tragic art of the ancients. "Man's longing to be completely truthful in the midst of a mendacious natural order is something noble and heroic. But this is *possible* only in a *very rare sense*. That is tragic. That is *Kant's tragic problem*! Art now acquires an entirely *new* dignity. The sciences, in contrast, are degraded to a degree."[5]

According to Nietzsche, Kant's epistemology concludes by recognizing that all experience is an awareness of subjectivity and illusions, and prepares the ground for the modern form of the tragic art. Kant was warning us of the limitations of knowledge about the world and, in turn, about the limitations of the truth-claims of modern science. Thus, his philosophy about the nature of reason lies in a similar position to modern science as the pre-Platonic philosophers did to Socrates and Plato. Nietzsche views both as undermining the solid foundations of the scholastic and scientific claims to truth. Whether it is the ancient Greek metaphysical claims of the primal substance of water, fire, or the indefinite, or the modern epistemological claims of intuition and representation of the objects of consciousness in experience, both traditions built their knowledge of the world on artificial symbols and conventional metaphors. "Likewise the basic thought of science is that man is the measure of all things. Ultimately, every law of nature is a sum of anthropomorphic relations."[6] There is no direct or indirect knowledge of the essence of reality except through the mediation of human consciousness. "In their mythology the Greeks transformed all of nature into their own image. It was as if they regarded nature merely as a masquerade and a disguise for anthropomorphic gods."[7]

Greek drama, pre-Platonic physics, and Kantian epistemology are forms of tragic art since through them we realize that the world is a reflection of our own forms of consciousness. The world is a creation of language by which humans give meaning and value to their everyday experience and suffering. Kant's critique of pure reason is then a return to the forms of consciousness produced by the ancient Greeks. This chapter will examine Nietzsche's criticisms of science and epistemology from *The Birth of Tragedy* and his earliest writings in his 1872–75 unpublished manuscripts, to *The Gay Science*, and, finally, the unpublished works in *The Will to Power* (1883–88).[8]

Iron Cage and Exile of Reason in *The Birth of Tragedy*

Modern tragedy, according to Nietzsche, was born in the theoretical optimism of Euripides and Socrates. In his *The Birth of Tragedy*, Nietzsche attempts to integrate his philology and philosophy, that is, his theory of aesthetics and Greek tragedy, with his theory of science and pessimism (Kant and Schopenhauer) in tracing the decline of the tragic vision and the rise of the modern tragedy. By this means he introduces his main theme of the tragedy of modernity—the loss of mythology and a meaningful existence through the dialectic of knowledge. The Dionysian elements of joy, enchantment, and affirmation of life are lost beneath the weight of logical proof and explanations. The pleasures and mysteries of life are replaced by an unrestrained Apollonian vision of rhetoric, scholasticism, and syllogism. The death of Greek tragedy is placed at the feet of Euripides who replaced the Dionysian music and lyric poetry of Sophocles and Aeschylus with an inferior dithyramb and a dramatized epic; replaced the horrors of existence with the manipulation of illusions; replaced epic suspense and action with lyrical rhetoric and pathos; replaced mythological and cosmic conflicts with psychological character studies of intentions reminiscent of scientific analysis of human behavior, thereby reducing mythological questions to those of character analysis; replaced tragic compassion of pity and terror with rational understanding of motivations; and, finally, replaced tragic dissonance, metaphysical solace, and harmonious reconciliation with human success, recognition, and a "counterfeit Greek serenity."

Socratic rationalism completed this process of decadence with its search for the theoretical foundations of reality in forms of thought, the false optimism generated by the possibilities of unrestrained knowledge, and the replacement of Dionysian truth about being with false claims to technical knowledge and universal certainty. The reductionism of Socrates is manifested in his attempt to explain all existence in formal, logical categories of the mind; to reduce nature to categories of truth and falsity. The highest aspirations of humankind to beauty, nobility, and serenity are products of the dialectic of knowledge and not the integration of the Dionysian and Apollonian dimensions of human experience and art. Philosophy and not tragedy, theoretical optimism and not aesthetic pessimism win the day. Logic replaces tragic vision with a view of new illusions and resignations about the possibilities of life.

With Euripides, the poet of aesthetic Socratism, and with Socrates himself, with the loss of the conflict and integration of Apollonian and Dionysian spirits, the age of tragedy came to an end. As we have already seen in the last chapter, Apollo, who lives in the world of the appearances, represents the plastic art form that created the symbolic forms that gave meaning to the world through art: "Here Apollo overcomes individual suffering by the glorious apotheosis of what is eternal in appearance: here beauty vanquishes the suffering that inheres in all existence, and pain is, in a certain sense, glossed away from nature's countenance." On the other side, there is Dionysus, who lives in the inner world of true being as becoming. He is a powerful force destined to destroy the aesthetic illusions in order to uncover the inner truth of being itself.

> A metaphysical solace momentarily lifts us above the whirl of shifting phenomena. For a brief moment we become, ourselves, the primal Being, and we experience its insatiable hunger for existence. Now we see the struggle, the pain, the destruction of appearances, as necessary, because of the constant proliferation of forms pushing into life, because of the extravagant fecundity of the world will. . . . Pity and terror notwithstanding, we realize our great good fortune in having life—not as individuals, but as part of the life force with whose procreative lust we have become one.[9]

By the end of the fifth century, the aesthetic experiences that gave life to the tragedies of Sophocles and Aeschylus are gone and in their place are new forms of technical knowledge and scientific rationalism. Socrates was the harbinger of modern science, cultural rationalism, theoretical certainty, intellectual disenchantment, social optimism, personal happiness, misplaced security of mind, and a false affirmation of the world—all the things that Nietzsche calls "intellectual Socratism" and Max Weber will later call "cultural rationalization." Socrates was able to divide up the world into form and matter, truth and illusions, knowledge and opinions. Nietzsche also says that the nature of this rationalism was a technical form of knowledge derived from the unrestrained knowledge drive and the dialectic of knowledge oriented toward solvable problems, which could be passed on from individual to individual. These are all the characteristics of *techne*, which both Marx and Nietzsche find as potentially dangerous when misunderstood and misapplied.

Rationalism attempts to encompass the whole world of appearances and subsume that world under its philosophical forms. Nietzsche contends that ultimately that form of total rationalism will be unable to explain the periphery of human experience that lies outside of its reified and sedimentary prison of concepts. At the point where human suffering becomes problematic, imagination and human will are incapable of breaking out of this enclosed system of rational forms and scientific logic. Explanation about the world becomes useless. It is also at this point that the rationality of the world collapses leaving behind real possibilities for barbarism and nihilism with tragic resignation taking its place. It is important to note that this collapse of rationalism is not brought about by internal debate or an external onslaught on the ramparts of truth. Rather, the crisis of modernity is brought about by the scientific claims to absolute certainty themselves and their own inability to justify the full range of human experience that pushes humankind beyond the "periphery of science." Skepticism, nihilism, and decadence are products of the belief in a scientific culture, not its rejection.

To break through this iron prison of rationalism, Nietzsche looks back to the Greeks for help. "No one shall wither our faith in the imminent rebirth of Greek antiquity, for here alone do we see a hope for the rejuvenation and purification of the German spirit through the fire-magic of music."[10] The Hellenic ideal provides Nietzsche with insight and imagination to see through the interpretive illusions and falsifying appearances of science and logic. However, the moderns in their search for rational purity have perverted the Hellenic ideals of Greek beauty, harmony, and serenity by incorporating them into an isolated and reified Apollonian vision that forgets its Dionysian counterpart and its concomitant tragic vision. It turns them into the abstract formulas of classical Weimar.[11] Nietzsche gives praise to the aspirations and accomplishments of Winckelmann, Goethe, and Schiller. He is staunchly critical of those who followed these noble individuals since their philological attempts to recapture the Greek spirit using historical methods failed. They tried to reduce it to exegetical formulas, scientific methods, and formal truths: they attempted to reduce the Greeks simply to the conceptual appearances of Apollo.

Into this criticism of German classicism and abandonment and loss of Hellenic ideals come Kant and Schopenhauer to the rescue. They are the prophets of a new age of tragedy brought about through a revival of the Dionysian spirit in Kant's critique of pure reason and theory of knowledge, Schopenhauer's theory of the will and music, and Wagner's artistic productions. The claims to universal truth and scientific certainty began to unravel with the development of the arguments and principles first laid down by Kant. It was his theory of knowledge and its justification of Newtonian physics that contained its own immanent principle of refutation. The seeds of the destruction of intellectual Socratism were contained in Kant's own interpretation of reason and defense of science.

In the *Critique of Pure Reason*, Kant used "critique" as a philosophical method for the analysis of the limits of the concepts of the mind and their applicability to objective experience. In the process of clarifying the relation between science and metaphysics, he established the boundaries for theoretical knowledge. Nietzsche, however, interprets Kant as setting in motion the critical method that had unintended and more radical consequences than anticipated by Kant himself. The latter attempted to produce a new constitution theory of knowledge, a critique of empiricism and rationalism, a new theory of objectivity and subjectivity, and, finally, a rational and transcendental justification of modern science. But in the process of constructing a defense of scientific rationalism, Kant's epistemology provided Nietzsche with a tool to turn epistemology against itself, that is, to move from a critique of pure reason to a critique of science and epistemology.[12] What Kant actually accomplished, for Nietzsche, was to break through the limits of science, experience, and the regulative principles and categories of the understanding.

Kant intentionally called into question those intellectual and metaphysical endeavors that necessitated the mind's going beyond the chaotic raw data provided by sensibility (*Sinnlichkeit*). "Let us now recall . . . how Kant and Schopenhauer succeeded in destroying the complacent acquiescence of intellectual Socratism, how by their labors an infinitely more profound and serious consideration of questions of ethics and art was made possible—a conceptualized form, in fact, of Dionysian wisdom."[13] What he succeeded in doing was to call into question the limits of science itself and its claims to absolute and universal knowledge. With the distinctions between the noumenal and phenomenal, and the appearances and the thing-in-itself, the claim to the unknowability of that which lies behind objectivity and experience severely limits the range of that which is knowable. This, in turn, limits the applicability of the mind and its claims to truth.

By questioning the traditional theories of knowledge based on the existence of a privileged access to truth either through sense perception or self-reflection on innate ideas, inductive or deductive logic, Kant unintentionally developed an epistemological argument, which when used by Nietzsche would eventually turn its critical edge back upon itself. The laws of causality and the Newtonian universe, as well as the existence of time and space, are products of the principles, organization, and construction of the mind. Everything beyond the sensations and manifold of representations, and these relational categories are part of the unknowable thing-in-itself. "Whereas the current optimism had treated the universe as knowable, in the presumption of eternal truths, and space, time, and causality as absolute and universally valid laws, Kant showed how these supposed laws serve only to raise appearance—the work of Maya—to the status of true reality, thereby rending impossible a genuine understanding of that reality."[14]

Kant's *Critique of Pure Reason* had introduced a new age of the tragic vision because, according to Nietzsche, he undermined the optimism, universality, and objectivity of scientific claims to truth. Nietzsche recognizes in this work that there is now a serious crisis of knowing in the Socratic culture, but he neither develops its epistemological, existential, or moral implications at this point. The full implications lie in his unpublished material of this period. He has only drawn attention to the most obvious implications of Kant's epistemology. Over the next few years in his unpublished essays written between 1872 and 1875, he will develop these implications even further in a more critical direction, thus transfiguring and moving beyond Kantian epistemology. Nietzsche's own relation to Kant is still very unclear, as is his own theory of knowledge. At this point, he has not turned critique against itself, but only questioned the form of knowledge offered by science. Kant had shaken the foundations of the scientific culture from Socrates to Newton and had prepared the way for a new tragic vision based on the Dionysian wisdom of human suffering that lies behind the Apollonian appearances.[15] Kant's critique had prepared the ground for the birth of this new age of tragedy and the reappearance of an integrated Apollonian and Dionysian art form.

Nietzsche's *The Birth of Tragedy* is a story about the origins and decline of Greek tragedy, the rise of modern science and technological rationalism, and the possibilities of a rebirth of tragedy in the works of Kant, Schopenhauer, and Wagner. The book is built around a central critique of modernity that looks at the past and toward the future. It is in music that Nietzsche finds the direct access to the formerly inaccessible thing-in-itself: music provides access to the will and not a mere phenomenal form of the objectivity of the mind. (The concept of the thing-in-itself will play an increasingly smaller and smaller role in these early writings and disappear from Nietzsche's later material entirely.) Nietzsche recognizes that Kant had shown the illogical claims of modern science that will force this cultural form to perish. He characterizes the modern intellectual as "eternally hungry, the critic without strength or joy, the Alexandrian man who is at bottom a librarian and scholiast, binding himself miserably over dusty books and typographical errors."[16]

Dialectic of Enlightenment and Disenchantment of Science

This section will trace the evolution of Nietzsche's epistemology from the earliest stage of his belief in the knowability of the thing-in-itself in *The Birth of Tragedy*, to his continued, but more cautious use of Kantian vocabulary in his unpublished essay of 1872, *The Philosopher: Reflections on the Struggle between Art and Knowledge*, to a more sophisticated theory of knowledge that rejects the knowability of the thing-in-itself with the 1873 unpublished essay *On Truth and Lies in a Nonmoral Sense*. During this short period Nietzsche works through his own confusions and misunderstanding of Kant's critique of reason in order to develop a theory of knowledge that will help explain his own philological understanding of Greek tragedy. His goal is to place it within the broader philosophical context of the development of a decadent form of scientific rationalism, which constitutes for him the heart of the tragedy of modernity.

One of the more important of Nietzsche's earliest unpublished essays is the work written during the fall and winter of 1872 entitled *The Philosopher: Reflections on the Struggle between Art and Knowl-*

edge. It is a seminal piece, for it outlines, in however confused and sketchy form, a transformed Kantian epistemology. Beginning with some of the basic ideas of Kant, Nietzsche pushes his arguments to their extreme. His essay begins with a critique of science, then moves to Kant and epistemology, and finally expands toward a radical critique of foundationalism and the development of a theory of skepticism. This is all accomplished within a general analysis of the relationships among science, philosophy, and art, that is, among reason, will, and the imagination. This work also further establishes the importance of Nietzsche's early Kantian framework for his analysis of epistemology and moral philosophy. Even with his later rejection of Kantian categories, Nietzsche's radical critique of science and truth is placed within a transcendence (*Aufhebung*) of the former's insights rather than a complete rejection of Kant's critiques of pure and practical reason. The theories that argue that Nietzsche did not know Kant or that Kant was not important to Nietzsche have missed the point of how he appropriated, negated, and then incorporated Kantian philosophy into his own ideas.[17] This point is succinctly stated by George Stack when he says, "It is not the case that Nietzsche 'misunderstood' Kant. Rather, he understood quite well that Kant's critical philosophy sounded the death-knell of metaphysics and promoted an agnosticism about man's knowledge of actuality. Nietzsche's early formulating of a pragmatic or humanistic theory of knowledge, his emphasis upon the creative activity of knowing, as well as his stress upon 'conditional knowledge' or knowledge 'for us,' were shaped by Kant's philosophy. The notion that our basic categories of the understanding are 'fictions' was also suggested, in an indirect way, by Kant's critical thought."[18]

The essay *The Philosopher* begins with a statement on the limits of science and its relation to philosophy and art.[19] The clarification of the relationships among these three enterprises is necessitated by the changing importance and centrality of science. Modern philosophy has focused almost exclusive epistemological attention on the methods and truth-claims of science as the only legitimate form of knowledge. For Nietzsche, it is characterized by an unlimited and unrestrained drive for knowledge whose effect has been detrimental to culture, human needs, and the possibility of meaning in the universe. Science is incapable of creating norms, values, or meaning. He sees science as serving the "practical interests" of a utilitarian civilization. When science becomes the exclusive basis for truth, then society has produced a barbaric civilization that has lost its direction and purpose.

The philosopher and artist have the role of responding to this technical universe: the philosopher by conceptually and theoretically recognizing and explaining the situation and the artist by creating a new world of philosophical, aesthetic, or religious values and mythologies, or illusions.

Philosophy and art become objective expressions of self-consciousness and the will (*praxis*). Philosophy must regain control over science and supply it with the requisite value system necessary for human survival. Nietzsche says that "the philosopher should empathize to the utmost with the universal suffering, just as each of the ancient Greek philosophers expresses a need and erects his system in the vacant space indicated by that need."[20] Philosophy and mythology, as developed by the Greeks in their tragic vision, returned to the universal insight that suffering and pain lie at the heart of human existence. Through the works of the pre-Platonic metaphysicians and physicists and through the dramas of Oedipus and Prometheus, suffering provided the stimulus for human achievement and wisdom. According to Nietzsche, just as with the Greeks, modern philosophers should begin the process of creating a world around the sublime (ideal) and the beautiful. The model, vision, and imagination have been provided by the Greeks. It is very clear that later developments in German social theory owe a great deal to Nietzsche's critique of science, especially Weber and the Frankfurt School of critical theory.[21] Science left to itself—unrestrained by cultural values representing the highest ideals of humanity—has the barbaric effect of constructing a technological world geared to efficiency and control, a world locked in a disenchanted prison.[22] The Enlightenment has evolved into an age of "emancipation," but an emancipation that has dialectically turned into its opposite. (Horkheimer and Adorno will later call this process the "dialectic of the Enlightenment.")[23]

Because philosophy no longer controls and limits the knowledge drive in a unified culture integrating practical interests with aesthetic, ethical, political, and religious interests, science is left unrestrained in its universal claims to knowledge and truth. For Nietzsche, this results in an epistemological laissez-faire similar to that of an unrestrained free market in political economy. (Whereas Aristotle traced the implications and effects of market principles and structures on a moral economy and political community, Nietzsche outlines the implications of an unrestrained scientific and technological development on modern culture.) The goal of philosophy is to subdue and control the interests of the natural sciences and the unrestrained knowledge drive (*Erkennt-*

nistrieb) found in iconic historiography (cultural sciences that have aped the methods and theory of knowledge of the natural sciences). Modernity is a civilization run wild that has created an iron cage devoid of meaning and purpose. It forms a society bereft of transcending values of beauty and the sublime, nonresponsive to human needs for aesthetics and theodicy, split by an abyss between consciousness and will, unable to reply to the gnawing problems of the meaning of human suffering, and unable to provide the framework for the possibility of self-realization, self-transcendence, and self-creativity, that is, self-overcoming. These are the very aspects of Greek culture and nineteenth-century German aesthetics that inspired Nietzsche. The Germans provided the conscious recognition and theories about the loss, while the Greeks constructed a society in which individuals lived around these moral and aesthetic imperatives.

The striving (creative) individual who participates in the creation of his or her own self and culture is imprisoned in the modern world behind the bars of scientific metaphysics, instrumental rationality, and technological interests. Nietzsche's theory of art, and Greek tragedy and philosophy, his critique of science, epistemology, and foundationalism, and his critique of moral nihilism are all responses to his two great insights: his view of the inspiring heights and horrible depths of Greek culture and his critique of modern scientific and technological rationality. This is what ties together his earliest essays on epistemology from 1872 to 1875 and his later writings *The Will to Power*, as well as *The Birth of Tragedy* and *Philosophy in the Tragic Age of the Greeks* with *Thus Spoke Zarathustra* and *The Genealogy of Morals*.

Transfiguration of Greek Drama into the Tragedy of Modernity

Following his critique of scientific rationality, Nietzsche in *The Philosopher* expands upon his critical theory of knowledge by turning his attention to Kant and then epistemology as a whole. He picks up on themes he had already discussed in *The Birth of Tragedy*. According to Nietzsche, Immanuel Kant is an example of a modern "philosopher of tragic knowledge." The modern tragedy is prefigured in the work of Kant, since it was he who, in the process of examining the transcendental foundations of human experience and knowledge, called into question the very foundations and possibility of metaphysics and dogmatism. This is the tragedy of modernity, not the suffering and pain of the ancients. It is an experience in which suffering and pain reemerge in a world without epistemological and metaphysical foundations, without direction, truth, or values. Kant does, however, return to the world a renewal in life itself through a revival of the importance of art as a means for the establishment of norms and meaning.

Nietzsche opposes to the philosopher of tragic knowledge the positivist who searches for unrestrained knowledge: the "philosopher of desperate knowledge." It is interesting to note that Nietzsche is quite specific here when he states that a critical theory of knowledge does not necessarily lead to skepticism. This is not the goal of knowledge, but is the starting point for reestablishing the foundations and validity of a new form of aesthetic experience and wisdom. Again at this point in his analysis, Nietzsche develops a new twist to the dialectic of the enlightenment theme mentioned earlier. Kantian epistemology does lead to the critique of pure reason and the undermining of the basis of metaphysics, but it does not lead to skepticism. Rather, it points in the direction of a critique of epistemology and knowing itself. The tragic philosopher turns critical reason against itself at the behest of another imperative—life. In turn, the philosopher creates the illusions that give life meaning, as we have seen with the illusions and mythology of the Greek tragic artists and philosophers. However, we must remember that

> it is not possible for us to produce again a series of philosophers like that of Greece during the age of tragedy. Such a system remains possible only as *art*. Their task is now accomplished by *art alone*. Judged from the standpoint of the present, an entire period of Greek philosophy simultaneously belongs within the realm of their art. . . . The Greeks show us what art is capable of. If we did not have them, our faith would be chimerical.[24]

From one perspective, Kant's epistemology makes sense to Nietzsche only in a world that has gone through the experience of Greek tragedy. The limits of the knowledge drive are set by the values established in art. The moderns must establish similar boundaries on the unrestrained desire for knowledge as the Greeks had done over two thousand years before.

As Nietzsche oversees the development of modern culture with his priority on science and technological rationalism, he looks wistfully back to the Elysian fields at a time of myths, heroes, suffering, and universal moral order. The artistic experience of the Greek poets, dramatists, and philosophers created a world in which life was given value and meaning. That has been taken away in the formal logic and subjective rationality of modern science. Kant was extremely important because he took a closer look at the whole issue of this metaphysics and no longer accepted science in its forms of empiricism and rationalism. But by taking a closer epistemological look at the very foundations of science and by criticizing metaphysics as beyond knowledge, Kant prepared the way for Nietzsche. The latter, through his method of revaluation, moved beyond him when he recognized that "when carried to its limits the knowledge drive turns against itself in order to proceed to the critique of knowing."[25] Kant became a tragic philosopher when his critical method was transfigured and turned back upon itself in a critique of epistemology. In this 1872 essay, Nietzsche has not recognized the full importance of his own insight, or at least he has not developed it. There is one more step to be taken before this takes place. Nietzsche understands that Kant establishes the primacy of life not by creating a new metaphysics but through the justification of the role of art in creating a world of illusions. The metaphysical world, in turn, is not destroyed, but it is seen for what it is—an anthropomorphic projection of illusions and mystery.

Thus, the tragedy of modernity lies in a deeper understanding of the characteristics of modern society and the relationships among scientific rationalism, metaphysics, and art. Kant precipitates the modern tragic experience with his critique of metaphysics and science. He is the new tragic poet who places limits on the knowledge drive and the place of metaphysics in the world. With Kant, there is a new theory of knowledge, the traditional foundations of knowledge have been called into question; metaphysics has been undermined; limits have been set on science and the knowledge drive; and art and ethics have been given their place with a parallel importance to the critique of practical reason and judgment. While the rest of the world turns science into an idol and worships its claims to certainty and absolute knowledge, Nietzsche says that "all that philosophy can do now is to emphasize the *relativity* and *anthropomorphic* character of all knowledge, as well as the all-pervasive ruling power of *illusion*."[26] But with Kant came the other side of the modern tragedy: epistemology undermines the traditional claims to the status of knowledge and its universal certainty and metaphysics, but is itself incapable of replacing it with anything more than critical reason. Nietzsche is really playing with a subtlety at his command in his use and transformation of the concept of "tragedy." At one time, it represents a serious loss and deficit, and at another, it captures the break from belief and the metaphysics of natural science.

With a new epistemology, Kant questions the metaphysical foundations of knowledge and in the process creates the basis for a new modern tragedy. With the reduction of epistemology to critique, belief to critical reason, and metaphysics to anthropomorphism, Kant precipitates a new crisis and at the same time provides the context in which to escape the dilemma. By the time of his later writings and *The Will to Power*, Nietzsche will have pushed these Kantian themes to their limits—skepticism and nihilism, decadence and nothingness. Whether Nietzsche ever truly escapes from Kant is an interesting question, that has been less debated than pushed aside. It is clear in these earliest writings that Nietzsche's view of the role of the philosopher-artist is to enliven humanity's moral and aesthetic impulses and the means of expressing these insights in a transformed and radical Kantian philosophy. When he does criticize Kant in his later writings, it appears that it is not a rejection of Kant but a demystification and transcendence of his ideas. That is, he radicalizes Kant's theory of knowledge and critique of pure reason by turning critique against itself.

Beyond Skepticism in the Tragedy of Epistemology

Nietzsche has turned to a critique of epistemology for three reasons: First, his analysis of science and reason moved beyond the limits of traditional epistemology to a critique of subjectivity and the reflective process itself; second, the nature of knowledge for the tragic philosophers is not the accumulation of information and truth, but the creation of "a higher form of existence." Life, not certainty, is the goal of philosophical understanding. And third, Nietzsche maintains that the goal of culture is not happiness (utilitarians) or development of individual talents, but the creation of art, illusions, meaning, and joy in the exuberance of living. Greek tragedy and modern art were intended as mechanisms for reinvigorating life with new meaning, excitement, and purpose. "The *will to existence employs philosophy* for the purposes of a higher form of existence."[27]

The second half of *The Philosopher* outlines a new epistemology based on Nietzsche's theory of knowledge as a theory of language and illusions (representations, metaphors, metonymies, tropes, and concepts), a theory of sensation (perception and form, sense experience and categories of the understanding), and a theory of the understanding (noumena and phenomena, appearances and thing-in-itself).[28] This manuscript was not meant for publication and there are confusing statements and conflicting claims. In spite of this, it remains clear that Nietzsche is paralleling Kantian epistemology with his own version that incorporates his ideas about art, metaphysics, and language. The new section beginning with paragraph 50 starts with the claim that "we live only by means of illusions." In a manner similar to Hume in his *Essay Concerning Human Understanding*, Nietzsche argues that human knowledge in the fields of chemistry, physics, and architecture cannot penetrate to the underlying forces and laws of nature. What we know are the "schema."

Kant's split between the world of appearances and the thing-in-itself is also evident from the very beginning of Nietzsche's attempt at formulating a new theory of knowledge. In one paragraph, he has captured an important component of the debate between the empiricists and German Idealists. Kantian "appearances" become Nietzsche's "illusions." With this transformation, the seeds are sown for a more radical treatment of the implications inherent in Kantian epistemology. Humanity constructs its own experience and knowledge by synthesizing the cognitive forms of the mind (time and space, and the categories of the understanding) with the outside world of the manifold of intuitions. The objects of experience are formed by joining together the raw material of unorganized and incoherent sensations with the organizing structure and principles of the mind. Subjectivity creates objectivity and in the process our knowledge of the world. Marx, too, radicalized this insight with his theory of objectivity and *praxis*, as well as his dialectical method of critique. Nietzsche argues that the thing-in-itself is unknowable and the appearances are mere illusions. These epistemological comments are then integrated into his theory of tragedy and modern art. Knowledge is just another form of artistic construction that not only creates the objects of experience and the forms of knowledge, but creates a world of metaphysical illusions that give a semblance of organization, purpose, and meaning to life characterized by its apparent meaningless suffering and pain. The absurdity and meaninglessness of existence is forgotten in a world of illusions and ghosts. The nothingness of the world is hidden behind a veil of human imagination and creativity.

Nietzsche's critique of understanding reminds one of Hegel's distinction between *Vernunft* (reason) and *Verstand* (understanding). The former critically describes the understanding as the mental process of organization, systematization, categorization, and naming in a manner similar to that found in Hegel's *Phenomenology of Mind*. It is a subjective process because it only deals with the surface phenomena and does not delve below the surface to uncover what lies beneath. Nietzsche undertakes to outline a simple theory of knowledge by making the distinction between images and concepts. Images are the basis of human experience as the mind mirrors the phenomenal world of the appearances. Thoughts are developed from these building blocks of perception and create new forms for images. Though he begins with the traditional reference to the ocular metaphor of the Enlightenment, he quickly distances himself from its empiricist implications by introducing the aesthetic dimension as part of the understanding. Though the images reflect the world of experience, the understanding "must be an *artistic power*, because it is *creative*. Its chief creative means are *omitting*, *overlooking*, and *ignoring*."[29] Thinking emphasizes and organizes the images of sensation.

Where Kant had integrated empiricism and rationalism into a subtle and complex theory of knowledge combining what he saw as the most important elements of both, Nietzsche appears simply to juxtapose and combine images and concepts, and sensibility and understanding. Because the material is so sketchily laid out, one is hesitant about making more specific and concrete claims about his theory of knowledge. It does appear, however, that images (and language) are already formed objects by the time the understanding concentrates on certain aspects of experience by highlighting primary elements or deemphasizing other aspects of that experience. This position is the result of Nietzsche's early infatuation with Schopenhauer's theory of images and representations, but the latter's ideas are not systematically carried out throughout Nietzsche's work.[30] There is even a trace of the physiological component, which produces the forms of experience (para. 67). The combination of empiricism and rationalism is at times mechanical and awkward, with language placed somewhere between experience and thought.

Kant's theory of objectivity rested on the belief that the transcendental subject was involved in the construction of both the objects of experience and knowledge itself. Nietzsche, however, places the subject after the formation of objects in images and before the reorganization of the images in thought. Does Nietzsche split objectivity and subjectivity, perception and understanding to emphasize the split in modernity between the utilitarian world of self-interest and science and the Greek experience of tragedy? Even here he is not consistent, for in paragraphs 53 and 54, he refers to the mind as mirroring, and in paragraph 63, he continues this line of thought by referring to perception as a picturing of the world. However, in paragraph 64, he says that the artistic power itself produces images. Nietzsche seems to be saying that the power of these new images created by the understanding takes on the appearance of perceptions. In any case, there is either an inconsistency in the argument or else the distinction between perception and thought is not as great as he originally stated.

Science artistically creates a world of possibilities that have become reified over time ("residues of metaphors" and "sedimentation of belief"). The illusions are taken for real and the possibilities are mistaken for actualities. When Hegel said that the "real is rational and the rational is real," he was stressing the inherent possibilities that lay beneath the surface phenomena. His critical method uncovered the dialectical evolution of the Spirit. Like Marx, Nietzsche draws inspiration from Hegel's theory of objectivity and subjectivity, and, like Marx, he rejects its underlying metaphysics and broadens the scope of the application of the subject (self). The imaginative process of concept formation and theory creation, the creation of new experiences through conceptual intensity, and the strengthening or deemphasizing aspects of experience have freed Nietzsche's theory of human creativity from the straightjacket of Hegelian metaphysics. The imagination is freed from the dialectic and Absolute Spirit to form its own limits and possibilities.

A new ontology is grounded in the foundations of Western civilization with the conflict between Dionysus and Apollo in Greek art and mythology and, in turn, leads to the tragedy of modernity manifested in the critique of metaphysics, knowledge, and epistemology itself. It questions the grounds of the whole self-reflective process in science, epistemology, and ethics.

> It has to be proven that all constructions of the world are anthropomorphic, indeed, if Kant is right, all sciences. There is, to be sure, a vicious circle here: if the sciences are right, then we are supported by Kant's foundation; if Kant is right, then the sciences are wrong. Against Kant, it must always be further objected that, even if we grant all of his propositions, it still remains entirely *possible* that the world is as it appears to us to be. Furthermore, this entire position is useless from a personal point of view; no one can live in this skepticism. We must get beyond this skepticism; we must *forget* it![31]

This is a key passage in his essay. It summarizes Nietzsche's position toward Kantian epistemology along with its moral implications. Kant's use of the transcendental aesthetic (time and space) and the transcendental analytic (concepts of the understanding and schematization of the imagination) was intended to supply the needed justifications for Newtonian physics by establishing the foundations for experience and consciousness in the transcendental unity of apperception. But once the issues of the mental construction of reality and the subjective element in experiences become part of the public debate, Kant's logic takes on a life of its own for Nietzsche. What began as a justification for physics becomes transfigured into a questioning of science and epistemology. If the mind is actively involved in the construction of reality, then why must the laws and principles of physics be the final statement of its possibilities? If the mind is part of the process of constructing its own objects of experience, then why stop at a Newtonian worldview as the final form of knowledge? Nietzsche radicalizes the implications within Kantian epistemology and concludes that if Kant is correct, then science itself must fall beneath its own critical thought. There is no privileged position from which to examine and judge the construction of reality, for it is infinite. Science, too, falls beneath the critical eye of Nietzsche and loses its privileged position among the modern gods of knowledge.

To make his point even more emphatic, Nietzsche restates in one paragraph the history of pre-Platonic philosophy from Anaximander to Pythagoras. His purpose is to show that the whole of pre-Platonic philosophy is merely an anthropomorphic projection of human categories into metaphysics. The world is constructed according to key categories of ethical and logical thought: justice for Anaximander, law for Heraclitus, love and hate for Empedocles, being for Parmenides, mind for Anaxagoras, and numbers for Pythagoras. The Greek view of nature is a projection of the categories of human experience and knowledge and the historical reconstruction of Greek philosophy is a verification of the fundamental principles of Kantian epistemology. All knowledge is a production of the human mind. "Man is acquainted with the world to the extent that he is acquainted with himself; i.e. its depth is revealed to him to the extent that he is astonished by himself and his own complexity."[32]

Greek physics and metaphysics provided the ancients with a way of organizing their world not by going outward but by going inward. The categories for the organization of experience are provided by the inward-looking mind. "In their mythology [as well as their philosophy and art] the Greeks transformed all of nature into their own image."[33] Men and women explained the world in terms of their own wants and fears, pleasures and displeasures, and values and norms. Mythology and religion, morality and ethics, and physics and metaphysics are all explained though the subjective structures and mental forms of human experience. The objective world is a projection of subjective categories that give organization, purpose, and meaning to that world. What the Greeks knew was only the Greek mind; what they experienced was only their own thoughts. "The world has its reality only in man." The world they explored in their philosophy as they attempted to explain the origins of the universe in water, air, becoming, being, justice, and so forth was in fact the world of their own mind.[34] But even this does not transform the argument to its extreme: all knowledge, including science, is a creation of the mind, an anthropomorphic appearance and illusion. Kantian epistemology itself must fall victim to its own illusions, since it too is a creation of the mind. According to George Stack,

> Nietzsche understood that Kant's theory of knowledge led to the view that nature is a representation-world, that man does not discover laws in nature, but projects them into the natural world. . . . The outcome of Kant's theory of knowledge is that the world we know is primarily and essentially the world that we construct: that is, the world we have constructed, considered in its origins. With an irony that Nietzsche fully appreciated, the precise way to which Kant sought to lend support to natural science tended to generate skepticism about the objective validity of scientific knowledge.[35]

There is nothing that is not a product of the human imagination. Kant was right about the relationship between the manifold of intuitions (i.e., sensibility and sensations) and the categories of the understanding (i.e., structure of mind). But to go beyond Kant to see all knowledge as a creation of consciousness, Nietzsche radicalized the transcendental aesthetic and analytic and in the process came precariously close to a radical relativism and nihilism.

If epistemology is an expression of the mind, he saw all of this as a product of the creative and artistic dimension of humanity. Thus, he moves away from Kant, epistemology, and a concern with the central issue of objectivity to focus on aesthetics, creativity, and the will. As he says in note 455, the will to power represents a critique of objectivity. It was the imagination of classical antiquity that provided him further insight and justification for his view of the modern individual. Finally, he is well aware of the implications of this position: the possibility of skepticism. This is rejected as an alternative. Why? Because this is part of the tragic experience in modernity. As the

Greek dramatists dealt with suffering and pain in their tragedies, the moderns too must create a new metaphysical illusion that eliminates, or forgets, this experience of the nothingness and absurdity of the world.

Mirrors and Metaphors in Nietzsche's Early Theory of Knowledge

At the end of the essay, *The Philosopher*, Nietzsche begins to develop an expanded epistemology based on his theory of knowledge as metaphor. The theory still suffers from his initial dichotomy between its empiricist foundations and the subjective component, that is, between mirrors and metaphors, between picture thinking and conceptual thinking. He never truly distinguishes between its Humean and Kantian elements or between its Schopenhauerian and Kantian elements. Is Nietzsche's perspective fundamentally based on materialism, rationalism, idealism, or pure subjectivism? A good case may be made for each one of these positions. From paragraph 95 to the end of the essay, the basis of all knowledge lies in sensation and memory. Even Kant's forms of intuition (space and time) are moved from the subject back to the object. They are part of the act of sensing and its reflexive activity over time. The mind (memory) is only a storage area for these sensations. He refers to temporal and causal relations as the sensations of time and causality. In paragraph 102, he speaks of knowing as a process of acquiring more precise pictures of the world. In paragraph 114, he says, "Knowing is only possible as a process of mirroring and measuring oneself against *one* standard (sensation)"; and in paragraph 147, he says, "our senses imitate nature by copying it more and more." But lest one think he is reverting to an empiricist position, he shifts his ground again back to Kant. This dilemma and conflict between the two epistemological traditions in Nietzsche's writings is best summarized in two sentences: "All knowing is a mirroring in quite specific forms which did not exist from the beginning. Nature is acquainted with neither *shape* nor *size*; only to the knower do things appear to be large or small" (para. 123).[36] Nietzsche uses the image of the mirror reflecting a turn to Hume, but in the next sentence returns to Kant's emphasis on the subjectivity of all knowing. In the following paragraphs, time and space are viewed as forms produced by the subject.

Time, space, and causality are only *metaphors* of knowledge, with which we explain things to ourselves. Stimulus and activity are connected: how this is we do not know; we understand not a single causality, but we have immediate experience of them. . . . The most universal of all feelings is already a *metaphor*. The perceived manifold already presupposes space and time, succession and coexistence. Temporal coexistence produces the sensation of space.[37]

Concept formation is both a process of classification and abstraction produced in creating metaphors (transference from one object to another through relations, resemblance, and symbols), metonymies (false inferences in a definition where a particular predicate is mistaken for the whole of the object), tropes (poetic and rhetorical amplifications and embellishments based on likeness of one object to another), and metastases (improper generalizations and transitions from one area to another). Again, we have another manifestation of the split between the two schools of thought. This vacillation between Hume and Kant, empiricism and idealism, creates confusion when the reader attempts to make sense of Nietzsche's position. Part of the problem at least could be understood if Nietzsche is attempting to reconcile elements from both Hume's and Kant's philosophy. Another dimension of the interpretive difficulties is added when Nietzsche attempts to ground knowledge in the physiological process. In paragraph 98, he contends that all knowledge is ultimately reducible to pleasure and displeasure. This is why he argues that epistemology penetrates into the essence of nature. It seems as if he is attempting to resolve the conflict between empiricism and idealism by grounding both in a form of materialism. The issue is partially resolved when Nietzsche in *The Will to Power* makes metaphor and illusion the key categories describing his theory of perspectivism.

In his theory of knowledge as metaphor, Nietzsche develops his most sophisticated statement about the creation of concepts. We create both knowledge and even being itself. "We produce beings as the *bearers of properties* and abstractions as the causes of these properties. That a unity, e.g. a tree, appears to us to be a multiplicity of properties and relations is something doubly anthropomorphic: in the first place, this delimited unity 'tree,' does not exist; it is arbitrary to carve out a thing in this manner (according to the eye, according to form)."[38]

Whatever the problems Nietzsche may have in putting together a coherent theory about knowledge, concept formation, metaphors, and language, it is clear that his views of knowledge as illusions, anthropomorphism, and metaphors place the emphasis on the side of self-consciousness and subjectivity. The world is mediated by human consciousness and in the process transformed. What we know is not the world, but the projected forms of our own mind: linguistic anthropomorphisms and conceptualization of the world as abstractions and relationships: tropes, metonymies, and metaphors. The laws of nature expressed in chemistry, astronomy, and physics, no matter how mathematically elegant, precise, and predictive, are only the contours and structures of the mind projected into the universe. Therefore, for Nietzsche, there is, in reality, no chemistry, physics, or astronomy, but only anthropology. The various claims to truth and forms of knowledge so rearrange reality that we live in a constant state of illusion, false knowledge, and distorted consciousness. Finally, Nietzsche ends the essay with an appendix in which he states that natural sciences are products of the mind attempting to understand itself through its own anthropomorphic categories. This position is similar to that articulated by Marx in his doctoral dissertation.

The examination of the external world is an internal study of humanity; all natural science is anthropology. Nietzsche has returned to the fundamental insight of Protagoras that "man is the measure of all things." This question originally discussed by the Greek Sophists is again raised in Nietzsche's unpublished essay *Philosophy in Hard Times* (Spring 1873). Here, however, he is extremely agitated by the relativistic implications of this type of philosophical statement, since, for him, it has nowhere to go and leads to "totally barren soil."[39] On the other hand, in his essay written during the summer semester of 1873 entitled *On Truth and Lies in a Nonmoral Sense*, he philosophically uncovers another aspect of this issue. Whereas in *Philosophy in Hard Times* the concern was for the relativism inherent in Protagoras's maxim, in this other essay, it is not the subjective but the objective component that draws Nietzsche's attention. That is, the problem lies not in the attention given to "man," but in the concept of "thing." Nietzsche is further expanding and clarifying ideas that he originally developed the previous year. This new epistemological essay stresses the developments in his theory of language and metaphor. It is better written, philosophically more precise, and internally more coherent that his previous attempts. The residual empiricism of *The Philosopher* is no longer present. There is even a strong hint that perception requires the use of metaphors that would further eliminate the distance between the empirical and the rational, impressions and concepts, thus making an unbridgeable abyss between reality (the original nerve stimulus) and the metaphoric construction of that reality. Subjectivity would be part of the creation of objectivity, as well as knowledge.[40] The essence, or thing-in-itself, remains incomprehensible to us. Nietzsche says that the images themselves (impressions of sensation) require the use of illusions and metaphors for their constitution. This is an important advance.

Nietzsche's theory of objectivity is more developed, his relations to Kant are more distant, and his theory of metaphor now takes center stage. What he finds problematic in the Sophist maxim is the reference to "things," the implicit empiricism, and the copy theory of knowledge that lies behind the statement. He says the problem with this is that it mistakes objectivity for subjectivity, the thing for the metaphor of the thing. Nietzsche has by the spring of 1873 pushed Kant one step further and almost out of the picture. There is little or no reference to the antinomies of appearance and thing-in-itself, noumena and phenomena, and sensation and understanding. Even the complex balance and relationship between objectivity and subjectivity has evolved into a more radical emphasis on the role of consciousness and creativity. This disturbs the Kantian symmetry between object and subject, is a direct frontal assault on foundationalism, and is a further move in the direction of relativism, skepticism, and the critique of epistemology. If the remnants of empiricism have disappeared from Nietzsche's epistemology, the Kantian components are moving in the same direction. Nietzsche has outdone Kant; he has turned Kantian epistemology against itself by radicalizing its own implications lying deep within its epistemology. Whereas Hegel and Marx both turned to the dialectic as a way of criticizing Kant's theory of objectivity and in the process added the dimensions of history and society to his theory of subjectivity, Nietzsche turned epistemology against epistemology itself.

His [the philosopher] method is to treat man as the measure of all things, but in doing so he again proceeds from the error of believing that he has these things [which he intends to measure] immediately before him as mere objects. He forgets that the original perceptual metaphors are metaphors and takes them to be the things themselves. . . . It is even a difficult thing for him to admit to himself that the insect or the bird perceived an entirely different world from the one that man does, and that the question of which of these perceptions of the world is the one correct one is quite meaningless, for this would have to have been decided previously in accordance with the criterion of the *correct perception*, which means, in accordance with a criterion which is *not available*. But in any case it seems to me that "the correct perception"—which would mean "the adequate expression of an object in the subject"—is a contradictory impossibility. For between two absolutely different spheres, as between subject and object, there is no causality, no correctness, and no expression: there is, at most, an *aesthetic* relation.[41]

The Kantian theory of knowledge was finally used to overturn the very possibility of epistemology and knowledge. In *The Philosopher*, Nietzsche argues that Kant's *Critique of Pure Reason* undermined the possibility of metaphysics as beyond the conceptual. What first began with Kant as a critique of pure objectivity evolved with Nietzsche into a critique of all objectivity. There is no longer any epistemological basis upon which to justify or verify any claim to truth. The connection between the object and the subject has been severed and the verification of the latter by the former has been labeled a "contradictory impossibility." Both the correspondence and constitution theories of truth have been undermined and the traditional foundations for knowledge have been called into question. There is no longer a standard of measurement by which to juxtapose and compare the ideas of an object with its perception—the concept with the object itself. There is no basis in objectivity by which to ground subjectivity, no basis upon which to make truth-claims about the truth or falsity of perception. Apparent objects of perception are products of a habitual congealing of experience over time giving the semblance of permanency and objectivity. They are the "residue of metaphors" and the "graveyards of perception." The laws of nature (laws of causality and relationships) are abstract and reified products of language resulting in linguistic conventions, artificial constructions, subjective tautologies, asserted certainties, and reified regularities and relationships. This constructed false objectivity is usually unconscious, because the origins of metaphors have been forgotten. "That is to say, it is a thoroughly anthropomorphic truth which contains not a single point which would be 'true in itself' or really and universally valid apart from man."[42] With this critique of foundationalism, the whole of Kantian epistemology collapses and with it the possibility of epistemology itself. Where Kant had placed limits on and barriers between science and metaphysics, Nietzsche destroyed those limits and turned science into another form of metaphysics. All knowledge is appearance; all science is illusion; and all objectivity is art. Nietzsche has created a new form of idealism. By the time of this essay, the metaphors have won out over the mirrors.

In a manner similar to Marx's approach in the *Economic and Philosophic Manuscripts of 1844*, Nietzsche asks, what is the difference between humans and the bees? Both philosophers respond with the same answer: artistic creativity. For Marx, humankind creates its history and experience through *praxis* guided by the laws of beauty, whereas, for Nietzsche, we create, through an aesthetic language of metaphors and relationships. In both cases the truth of objectivity is an artistic subjectivity; in both cases, technical knowledge (whether of the productive forces or the knowledge drive) is not the basis for the distinction. What they both do with this insight is very different, but the epistemological and anthropological foundations of their ideas have similar roots. To clarify and emphasize his perspective, Nietzsche offers the metaphors and analogies of dreams, the Chladni sound figures, and astrology to convey his meaning.

The emphasis in his critique of knowledge doesn't lower the status of humanity in Nietzsche's eyes, but raises it to a new level. He sings praises of joy to the dignity, nobility, and beauty of humankind when he views the universe "as the infinitely fractured echo of one original sound—man; the entire universe as the infinitely multiplied copy of one original picture—man."[43] The universe is a cacophony of sounds and sights organized around the illusory and dissimulating metaphors that create the world of objects, things, and relations. It is a secular theodicy and *Weltanschauung* created to give meaning to the Dionysian reality of human suffering. Its grandest and most sublime expressions were in the tragedies of Aeschylus and Sophocles. Nietzsche updates his reference to human tribulations by referring to the darkest side of modern political theory in the work of Hobbes's *Leviathan* and his theory of the state of nature as a *bellum omnium contra omnes.*

The two drives that create the world of experience are the knowledge drive and the metaphor drive. Without an awareness of these drives and the habitual residues and reified experiences that remain after time, the world becomes, for Nietzsche, a disenchanted prison made up of forgotten perceptions and dried-up metaphors. It is a world of dreams and deceptions—"ghostly schemata"—abstractions and illusions, which become dangerous to the extent that they become unconscious. A discussion of these ideas is continued in Nietzsche's later work *Twilight of the Idols.*[44] The knowledge drive must be controlled and imprisoned because this decadent unrestrained drive kills culture and illusions, because it tries to make illusions disappear, ignores the aesthetic creativity at the heart of all knowledge and experience, hides the Dionysian reality of suffering and pain behind scientific rationalism and epistemological certainty, and denies the possibilities that make us human and free. It represses the reality of human existence and all attempts to transcend it. The world of consciously formed illusion is the world of happiness (*eudaimonia*). By transforming the Greek concept of happiness, Nietzsche has also eliminated the political context of Aristotle's key ethical category. The political dimension will be further eliminated in his later moral theory of self-overcoming.

Perspectivism in Nietzsche's Later Theory of Knowledge

By the time we read the unpublished notes in *The Will to Power* (1883–88), Nietzsche has developed his epistemological arguments in an even more unexpected direction from his initial "theory of science" with its criticisms of Socratic culture, scientific rationalism, and technological utilitarianism in *The Birth of Tragedy*, to his later development of a "theory of language and metaphors" in his early unpublished writings, to his transformation and final radicalization of Kant in this last creative period. In these writings, Nietzsche turns the full weight of Kant's epistemology back on Kant himself with his critique of epistemology and foundationalism in his "theory of perspectivism." He began his epistemological evolution with his early discussion of the relation between Hume (images) and Kant (concepts) and the development of a theory of objectivity based on the centrality of subjectivity. What is interesting in Nietzsche's development is that at the time of the unpublished writings of the 1880s, he had turned away from a transformed Kantian subjectivity toward a new form of objectivity: materialism and physiology. It is a materialism necessitated by the demands of his own radical critique of epistemology and the cutting of the foundations for all claims to truth and knowledge. It represents a retreat from the epistemological abyss created by the imminent development of Nietzsche's radical Kantian epistemology throughout his life.

Now he turns his critique of reason against both objectivity and subjectivity. At first, the objective world is perceived as a construct of human experience and the categories of the understanding. Objectivity has no independent reality of its own, but is a relational category created in the interaction between consciousness and the external world. It is an illusion based on the assumptions of the causal powers of the individual.[45] In *The Will to Power*, Nietzsche continues to permit his philosophy to roll over the remnants of traditional epistemology by claiming that subjectivity too must fall beneath the critical edge of the epistemological reaper. The phenomenalism of the "inner world" is a construct also. In an inversion of Kantian epistemology, Nietzsche contends that consciousness is a construction that reverses the process by which knowledge is created. This means that when the individual says, "I do," "I cause," and "I will," he or she is constructing a causal agent that is an imagined illusion. The Kantian critique of objectivity has now turned into a critique of subjectivity and consciousness. The articulation of temporal and spatial relationships, of successions of occurrences, of causal relationships between events, of an inner order to objective reality is the result of a misplaced concreteness that is attributed to the subject. Nietzsche's earlier theory of knowledge was the product of his working through his critique of pure reason and a Kantian theory of objectivity and epistemological antinomies: noumena and phenomena, appearances and thing-in-itself, illusions and truth. In his later writings, Kant's theory of subjectivity and the notion of the "transcendental unity of apperception" comes under Nietzsche's critical gaze.

Previously, objectivity was interpreted as a product of the imagination and schematism of the transcendental ego, whereas, in these later writings of Nietzsche, the ego is viewed as a necessary logico-metaphysical postulate. The organizational principle for human experience and the cause of objectivity is returned to the material world itself, since the self is a philosophical construction.

> Against positivism, which halts at phenomena—"There are only *facts*"—I would say: No, facts is precisely what there is not, only interpretations. We cannot establish any fact "in itself": perhaps it is folly to want to do such a thing.
>
> "Everything is subjective," you say; but even this is interpretation. The "subject" is not something given, it is something added and invented and projected behind what there is.—Finally, is it necessary to posit an interpreter behind the interpretation? Even this is invention, hypothesis.
>
> In so far as the word "knowledge" has any meaning, the world is knowable; but it is *interpretable* otherwise, it has no meaning behind it, but countless meanings.—"Perspectivism."[46]

Consciousness is not the cause of the concepts around which our experience is organized. He questions whether the concepts of subject, object, substance, causality are invented by the mind. According to Nietzsche, the actual sequence of events in experience begins with an agitation on nerve centers that consciousness then seeks to explain through an imaginary construction. Only those causes that the mind imagines enter the mind after the effect on the senses. Thus, according to Nietzsche, the effect comes before the cause. This analysis of the schematism of objects and forms of "erroneous causality" is a clear example of the critical application of Kantian epistemology, which is then turned upon Kant's basic categories themselves. Nietzsche now argues that consciousness or subjectivity is an invented category that is necessary to hold this imaginary construction together. What he has done is to introduce a more materialist component into the analysis of Kant's notion of the transcendental unity of apperception: epistemology is transformed into psychology. The transcendental ego is not a universal and necessary category that organizes experience, but, with Nietzsche, becomes the product of a utilitarian instinct for self-preservation and control over nature.[47] The categories by which we organize both objective and inner experience are created to give meaning and form to the original sensations.

The reader may detect here that Nietzsche's epistemology is catching up with both his aesthetics and theory of Greek tragedy with its emphasis on suffering, nothingness, and mythology creation. Thus, there is no objectivity or subjectivity, no things, objects, or substances, no causality, no will, and no consciousness. "There exists neither 'spirit,' nor reason, nor thinking, nor consciousness, nor soul, nor will, nor truth: all are fictions that are of no use."[48] The organization of experience around time, space, and causality, or objectivity, the creation of a static world of relatively unchanging objects, the ability to anticipate the future because of stored forms of experience in memory, the construction of value using aesthetic and moral categories of beautiful and good, and the ability to project meaning and regularity (aesthetics and knowledge) on the world through the forms and language of consciousness (subjectivity) are necessary tools for the instinct of human survival (a priori unconscious).[49] It appears that Nietzsche has revived the Dionysian spirit of rapture and ecstasy, passions and instincts, in this modern form of materialism and utilitarianism.[50] Perceptual emphasis and deemphasis, conceptual abstraction and simplification, and selective coherence and organization are prudent and expedient forms of falsification and appearances: this is what Nietzsche calls "perspectivism."[51] These artificial creations of the mind are helpful for knowledge and control over the world—will to power, that is, a will to error. Consciousness and the unity of experience are adaptive strategies for the survival of the species. "Trust in reason and its categories, in dialectic, therefore by the valuation of logic, proves only their usefulness for life, proved by experience—not that something is true."[52]

However, in order to stop the free-fall into complete nihilistic relativity, Nietzsche turns in another direction than philosophy for support. There is no substance, being, or ego, no objective or subjective world, no pure perception or experience, and no forms of intuition or categories of the mind that have any reality beyond the projections and horizons of the will to power. There is no universality or absolute certainty—there is no reality, only an abyss of nothingness, psychological drives, and instinctual needs. We continue to hold onto these epistemological categories because they serve another purpose than the representation of truth. We believe in time, space, causality, and the ego not because they represent apparent truths, but because we have to in order to survive. Ontology and realism have been replaced by psychology, biology, and utility.

> In short, the question remains open: are the axioms of logic adequate to reality or are they a means and measure for us to *create* reality, the concept "reality," for ourselves?—To affirm the former one would, as already said, have to have a previous knowledge of being—which is certainly not the case. The proposition therefore contains no *criterion of truth*, but an *imperative* concerning that which *should* count as true.[53]

There are no absolute truths or metaphysical entities, no being or essence, no reality or certainty. All is in a state of constant Heraclitean flux. But a semblance of stability, being, and self are created for security and preservation. In *Beyond Good and Evil*, Nietzsche writes, "It is finally time to replace the Kantian question, 'How are synthetic *a priori* judgments possible?' with another question: 'Why is it *necessary* to believe in such judgments?' It is time for us to comprehend that such judgement must be *believed* true in order to preserve creatures such as we are."[54] A priori synthetic judgments, categories of the understanding, and a unified and unifying ego are products of utilitarianism and an instinct for utility. They are not the causes of experience, but the effects of the struggles in life. As Nietzsche says, certain types of observations are necessary for preservation. Experience is constructed according to the criteria of predictability, calculation, manipulation, and control over all aspects of experience both subjective and objective. And just as objectivity is a construct, so too is subjectivity. The ego, as the cause of moral action or the cause of thought and experience, is a necessary lie and product of "our grammatical custom" in order to give semblance to a constantly changing world.

Nietzsche has challenged the very pillars of modernity from Descartes to Kant. It was the latter who recognized that our experience of a coherent and meaningful world rested on the foundations of a transcendental and noumenal subject. It was to this very point that Nietzsche directed his critique of subjectivity: an examination of the limits of subjective categories of experience and the notion of subjectivity itself. Nietzsche's early aesthetics and theory of anthropomorphism based on his interpretation of Greek tragedies of Sophocles and Aeschylus and Greek metaphysics, as well as his theory of nineteenth-century German philosophy, literature, and his early epistemology are integrated into a complex theory in these late unpublished writings. There are a multiplicity of selves, but the regularity of the world demands a unified consciousness. Ultimately the organization and stability of the world rests on the example and prior constructed unity of the self. In this sense, Kant's notion of the transcendental ego is also a prerequisite for knowledge, judgment, and being. But in the case of Nietzsche, the ego does not result from an examination of the underlying structure of pure reason and transcendental logic: the universal and necessary foundations of knowledge. It is just this knowledge that is problematic.

The underlying reasons for being and the ego are physiological and not transcendental, utilitarian not logical. Life demands that we live in a world of fabrications and mysteries that create the illusion of relatively stable beings and things, consciousness and reason, self and subjectivity. This permits us to master our universe, control our perceptions, organize our experience, anticipate our future, and create a world of essence and being. Logic, being, and consciousness are all fabrications that maintain the semblance of order and predictability. To think, to act, to create, and to master necessitate a fabricated world of essences, beings, inferential logic, time, space, causality, identity, and so forth. Being is fabricated on the model of the illusion of the existence of an ego and both together provide the foundation for logic and forms of rationality. "It is only after the model of the subject that we have invented the reality of things and projected them into the medley of sensations."[55] The world is constructed as a comprehensive appearance having a concrete reality, a conceptual unity, a relatively permanent identity, and logical order. For Nietzsche, these are clearly dogmatic and metaphysical assumptions—a dominant prejudice in modernity.

There is no true knowledge, no verifiable truth-claims, and no inner or outer world that can "objectively justify" claims to truth.[56] Everything is a swirl of forces brought together into a coherent unity by the creative power of the species to survive. It represents the pure utility of the drive to knowledge. There are no truths. And to be consistent, Nietzsche must argue that even his theory is an illusion created by the will to power.[57] Nietzsche has completed the Kantian epistemological exercise by arguing that epistemology is impossible. Philosophers cannot continue to generate theories of knowledge because there is no criterion, no ultimate basis for defining or determining reality or knowledge itself. "One would have to know what *being* is, in order to decide whether this or that is real."[58] Kant's critique of reason has been turned upon itself in a critique of epistemology and foundationalism. Nietzsche has taken the "back to Kant" movement of the nineteenth century well beyond Kant. Critical theory had raised questions about the limits of reason in its moral, epistemological, and aesthetic forms. It asked about the categorical imperative and moral values. Nietzsche, in his turn, asked about the limits of critique itself, about the meaning of values themselves. The transfiguration and revaluation process has been completed.

The postulates of experience also provide us with the metaphysical foundations of modern science and an insight into an important aspect of philosophy of science. The theory of the atom is a necessary lie and externalized illusion. It is interesting to note that Nietzsche quite explicitly rejects the concepts of thing-in-itself and the appearances as absurd and nonsensical: they are imaginative schematizations, theoretical abstractions, conceptual oversimplifications, and ontological fictions. With this criticism, the last remnants of the Kantian system have been overthrown and with them the belief in facts, objects, and things-in-themselves. (Also overthrown is Hegel's epistemology and his distinction between the thing-in-itself and the thing-for-us: see note 562.) "Not only did Nietzsche reject the 'pure facts' of positivism and the 'pure objects' (or things) of the Kantians ('things-in-themselves'), of the Platonists (immutable Forms or Ideas), and of the Cartesians ('substances'), he also rejected the 'pure subjects of knowledge' affirmed by Schopenhauer."[59] All the major schools of thought fell beneath Nietzsche's rejection of privileged positions and epistemological foundations, including positivism, phenomenalism, Kantianism, rationalism, and even Schopenhauer's pessimism. For Nietzsche, these schools of epistemology and metaphysics were an abuse of reason and escape from critical thinking. Concerns about being and reality, truth and science, objects and subjects, causality and laws of nature, and moral imperatives and universal absolutes were residues of discredited metaphysics and the "shadow of God."[60] And even this may be a relative interpretation and created perspective. There is only the movement between Parmenides and Heraclitus, being and becoming, Apollo and Dionysus: there is only constant flux in a whirl of the meaningless abyss and creative renewal. There is only self-overcoming or the decadence of "crude fetishism."

What remains are only interpretations and perspectives—the will to power as a form of the will to interpretation, meaning construction, and valuation. For Nietzsche, human beings are a species of liar that interprets; they are form creators, equalizers, systematizers, and concept organizers. This is the will to create—the will to art. Nietzsche pronounces in *The Genealogy of Morals* that the creative spirit would rather "will the void than be void of will."[61] The origins for the external world lie within the subject. What appeared as a latent inconsistency in his earliest writings becomes a crucial aspect of his thought in his later ones. The relation between Kant and Hume is more fully developed here. When it comes to the rational order and systematization of experience, it is reason that conceptually organizes the regularity and unity of the universe. But it does so for instinctual and physiological purposes. Is there a conflict within his own thinking between materialism and idealism, instincts and reason, psychology and creativity, science and wisdom, knowledge and art, Apollo and Dionysus?

Following Hume's *Enquiry Concerning Human Understanding*, Nietzsche theorizes that it is the will and passions that provide the power or cause for this imaginative organization, not reason. "Our needs have made our senses so precise that the same apparent world always reappears and has thus acquired the semblance of reality."[62] Reason provides the structure and principles of organization, but the active component in this process is the passions. It is clear that the simple distinction between images and concepts from his earlier writings has been replaced by a more subtle theory of knowledge, since he says in notes 500 and 517 that even the sense impressions are formed by a process of assimilation (incorporating new experiences into the old) and equalization (regularizing and integrating experience). Nietzsche rejects the simplicity of the copy theory of truth, but at times does seem to hold Hume's belief in the passive nature of reason at least when referring to utilitarian principles and imperatives of modern science.

Notes from the Margins

As is the case with Marx, Nietzsche returns to Vico's insight for part of his understanding of the world. He says that we can only comprehend a world we have in fact constructed. "The sense for the real is the means of acquiring the power to shape things according to our wish. The joy in shaping and reshaping—a primeval joy! We can comprehend only a world that we ourselves have made."[63] But it is a shaping done by the needs and will and not by the spirit or consciousness (note 526). At this crucial point in the development of his theory of knowledge, Nietzsche returns again to Kant and raises the question about the conditions for the possibility of knowledge, the conditions for synthetic a priori judgments. But already being well beyond Kant he also asks, what is knowledge? He repeats the latter's claims that the conditions for knowledge must contain necessary and universal validity, and cannot lie in experience. Nietzsche recreates the discussion about synthetic a priori judgments, and in a moving sentence reconfirms his whole response to the philosophical debate: "How does one know that the real nature of things stands in *this* relation to our intellect?—Could it not be otherwise?"[64] Other species perceive the world quite differently (note 565). Why would one think that human perceptions reflect metaphysical truths?

According to Nietzsche, the sentence "lightning flashes" contains a whole slew of dogmatic assumptions about the nature of reality. A concrete being is posited as real (such as lightning), which produces a definable activity (such as flashes) that has causes and effects. The sentence fabricates a metaphysical invention and theoretical fiction within the framework of laws of identity and causality. All of this is an example of the construction and workings of the will to error, but without this error, the world is incomprehensible. Lies are necessary for the construction of being, the preservation of life, and the mastering of reality. Logic and the semblance of reality would be impossible in a world that is constantly becoming. There would be no way to navigate through this world; life would become more problematic and precarious.

Nietzsche agrees with Hume that habit plays an important role in attributing causality and intentionality in the world. But as with Kant, he goes beyond Hume and argues that causality and intentionality are logical fictions. The real reason for this is not simply habit, which does play a role, but our needs and fears. Nietzsche attributes causality, necessity, and intentionality to the "fear of the unfamiliar." There is a danger in pushing this argument too far and Nietzsche must have seen it. Otherwise he would have developed this theme and its implications further. The psychology of preservation and personal security lies at the heart of the cult of objectivity. However, to continue in this direction would mean to move away from Kant and too far toward Hume. This means that the will to power would be simply a product of psychological and biological needs, thereby eliminating the real power and excitement of the "overcoming" force of creativity. Compare two short sentences. The first comes from note 526 of *The Will to Power*: "Consciousness plays no role in the total process of adaptation and systematization." The second comes from note 569: "The subject alone is demonstrable; hypothesis that only subjects exist—that 'object' is only a kind of effect produced by a subject upon a subject—a *modus* of *the subject*." Note 526 (as well as notes 521, 533, 581, and 584) makes room for a theory of the biological drive to knowledge and centrality of the passions, while notes 569 and 560 reinforce the notion of the creative, inventive, and constructive powers of the individual.

In the last years of Nietzsche's life, there is still a tension between the idealism of Kant and the materialism of Hume. Is it possible that the deeper underlying reasons for the forms of rationality and the laws of identity, causality, and contradiction are to be found in passions, but that within the drive to utility and self-preservation, consciousness and subjectivity continue to play an important dynamic and productive role? Are logic and rational categories and the phenomenal world simply adaptive strategies producing a consciousness that supplies the needed tools and mechanism for the regulation and systematization of nature and experience? Or is there still dynamic room for the active life of consciousness? Are the errors and illusions products of the mind or of the passions? Does biology completely replace idealism or only set a broader framework for the possibilities of subjectivity defined as becoming, as a "will to overcome" (note 552)? Where does perspectivism lie in relation to idealism or psychologism? Or are idealism and psychologism forms of perspectivism? Does Nietzsche distinguish a will to power as science and knowledge and a will to power as art? It is clear that life remains the basis for being and objectivity, but does the individual's will to power as interpretation, even though it is a response to deeper needs, still remain a creative process in the abyss of nothingness? These issues are not satisfactorily resolved and tensions remain throughout his published and unpublished works of this period.

As Nietzsche moves from Hume's nominalism and skepticism, Kant's agnosticism and critique of reason through Hegel's dialectic,

he creates a theory of perspectivism to replace traditional epistemology and dualistic metaphysics of the object and subject. It appears that
the *will* (self-overcoming, myth making, and will to power), the *body*
(human needs, desires, and instincts for survival), and *language* (categories of mind and forms of intuition) all play a role in the creation of
our worlds of experience.[65] Thus it would be wrong to emphasize one
aspect of his theory of perspectivism to the exclusion of the others.
This may account for the claims about Nietzsche's idealism, materialism, and metaphysics. What integrates these three moments is Nietzsche's focus upon human creativity through art, science, and linguistic
forms. Life is the will to power and expresses itself not only in a
biological need to survive, but also in the need for an Apollonian
organization of experience to form a unified and coherent world that
has meaning for its inhabitants. The will to power has utilitarian,
ethical, and existential elements, which in the end tend to the enhancement of life, the enrichment of human creativity, the opening up of
human possibilities, and the humanization of experience. A plurality
and multiplicity of worlds of experience are created that provide
endless horizons from which the world may be interpreted and given
meaning. Returning to a broader and more complete picture of pragmatism and thereby a more comprehensive notion of the will to power,
Rose Pfeffer has written,

> The new unified instrument of knowledge that Nietzsche introduces is
> the "will to power," of which both reason and instincts are
> manifestations. . . . It is a power that must be distinguished from that of
> Bacon and Hobbes or any utilitarian interpretation. It is not a power to
> control nature nor a power that serves as a tool of utility, but is a creative
> instinct, an inner drive toward growth and expansion which is not void of
> rational elements in their specifics.[66]

Though the will to truth and knowledge does have a strong utilitarian
component, Pfeffer's stress on activity and the creative dimension of
the will to power places the emphasis where it belongs—on the inner
drive and will to create. The exact status of Nietzsche's theory of
perspectivism with its key concepts of will to power, eternal return,
force centers, and self-overcoming has been hotly debated. Is the
theory of perspectivism simply another perspective or does it an-
nounce the foundations for a new metaphysics, poetic insight, or
mystical vision? Is it relative or does it possess an objective validity
not shared by particular perspectives in art, science, or philosophy?

The theory's apparent self-refuting claim is a contradictory "paradox of perspectivism."[67] For Nietzsche, the philosophical issues of nihilism and relativity are part of a traditional philosophy of foundationalism that he attempts to escape with his theory of perspectivism. He believes that he is beyond these questions, so to ask if his theory is relativistic is to apply standards that he, in fact, has rejected. He would claim that even his ideas are only mythopoetic forms that offer new horizons and bases for judgment.[68] They offer us a multiplicity of views, a plurality of metaphors and new conventions, and a variety of new forms of illusory objectivity, and thus ever new viewpoints and perspectives about the objects of experience—new myths—from which to interpret and comprehend the world and the creative potential and possibilities for freedom that lie within human beings to achieve and overcome again. In *The Genealogy of Morals*, Nietzsche says, "All seeing is essentially perspective, and so is all knowing. The more emotions we allow to speak in a given matter, the more different eyes we can put on in order to view a given spectacle, the more complete will be our conception of it, the greater our 'objectivity.' "[69]

Nietzsche seems to have come full circle from the concepts found in *The Birth of Tragedy* and his earliest writings at the University of Basel. By offering us new possibilities, his ideas enhance the power of the will, as well as the enjoyment of life itself.[70] The categories of will to power, eternal return, and self-overcoming are the modern forms of the Dionysian spirit and tragic vision, the modern forms of the striving against pain and suffering toward temporary reconciliation and serenity. But only the very strong will be able to tolerate nihilism and the "despair of all truth." This modern mythology attempts to rescue modernity from its own passive nihilism and decadence. It may not have the enormous power to elicit emotions or integrate an Apollonian mythology with the original source and oneness of life. But, for Nietzsche, it does present an alternative perspective to the metaphysics of modernity and the potential for escape from its oppressive logic, instrumental rationality, and eclipse of creative spirit.

Epistemology and moral philosophy are forms of "idealist dogmatism" that slander, distort, and undermine instinctual vitality and the joy of life. And life is ultimately both meaningless and creative. "The belief that the world as it ought to be *is*, really exists, is a belief of the unproductive who do *not desire to create a world* as it ought to be. They posit it as already available, they seek ways and means of reaching it. 'Will to truth'—*as the impotence of the will to create.*"[71] This is a very revealing passage, since it plays with the categories of epistemology and morality. Moral positivism in its forms of empiricism and idealism contends that the world as it ought to be does, in fact, exist either in empirical reality or in its conceptual possibilities. Nietzsche takes the position that this undercuts the very desire to construct morality—this explains his claims to immoralism. The belief in universal truths and absolute moral certainty destroys the will and its creative force. The will to truth and absolute standards must be seen as one form of interpretation of the possibilities of normative judgments, or will to interpretation.

Two of the more troubling and confusing issues that have occupied space in the secondary literature are that of nihilism and relativism in Nietzsche's writings. In Goethe's *Faust*, a bargain between Faust and Mephistopheles is made. The conditions of the agreement are such that, whenever Faust is satisfied with the moment, he will surrender his soul. When Nietzsche's individual is satisfied with a particular interpretation of nature or moral order, the creative process ends and nihilism begins. Thus, nihilism doesn't mean the absence of universal norms or absolute standards. Rather, it refers to the Faustian bargain in which people are satisfied with what is and don't question, challenge, or drive beyond the immediately given. When an individual becomes a will to truth or a will to morality, his or her nature as overcoming (overcoming self and previous interpretations in the realization of human potentialities) is lost, and with this nihilism demands its fulfillment of the bargain. People lose their souls "when no longer possessing the strength to interpret, to create fictions," they accept the validity, if not reality, of the present cultural forms in science, art, morality, and so forth. In moral idealism, the world is rejected and in its place another ethereal world is created in the forms, heavens, or dialectic. It depreciates life as it is by escaping to a transcendent metaphysics of the beyond. But someone who judges the present, meaningless abyss as possessing ultimate value distorts humankind's ability to transcend the moment and develop in the future. The former robs us of life and the latter robs us of the future possibilities of life; the former forces us to live in a world of ever-distancing goals, while the latter forces us to live where there is no life at all.

Nihilism, especially as developed in *The Will to Power*, is not a position of moral relativity and epistemological abandon. That is the normal state of human existence brought about by the collapse of Christianity, morality, and scientific optimism by Kant, Schopenhauer, Lange, and nineteenth-century philosophers of science. No, decadence and nihilism are states of losing one's soul to the moral objectivity of the present (empiricism) or to the reified subjectivity of the future (idealism), that is, to science and Christianity. The essence of Nietzsche's position lies in his underlying belief in humanity—its creativity (active nihilism as a critique of transcendental dogmatism and pessimism), its drive, its possibilities—its ability to create illusions and fabrications. "It is a measure of the degree of strength of will to what extent one can do without meaning in things, to what extent one can endure life in a meaningless world *because one organizes a small portion of it oneself.*"[72] This small portion is created through exertions of overcoming by the *Übermensch* (the self-overcoming and striving individual), belief in eternal recurrence and creative potential of individuals, and through the transfiguration and reversal of all values. This will be the focus of our attention in Chapter 6.

All forms of knowledge that claim being as their starting point, including morality, philosophy, and religion; all forms of knowledge built upon the cult of objectivity, the illusions of reality, and the errors of universality are expressions of decadence or life-denying and life-denigrating activities. Truth and dogmatism destroy the will to activity and the spirit of creativity. Decadence represents a domestication of the human spirit to outside forces. The goal of critical thinking is to reclaim our lost selves lying beneath these cultural idols of moral certainty, scientific objectivity, and epistemological truths. In a fashion directly reminiscent of Feuerbach, Marx, and the Left Hegelian critique of religion, Nietzsche criticizes the reversal of subjectivity and objectivity, the human and the divine. "All the beauty and sublimity we have bestowed upon real and imaginary things I will reclaim as the property and product of man. . . . His most unselfish act hitherto has been to admire and worship and to know how to conceal from himself that it was he who created what he admired."[73] Where Marx has transferred the critique of heaven into a critique of the earth with its political and economic relationships, Nietzsche directs his attention against traditional morality and epistemology. The false images are not only the ideology of liberalism and nineteenth-century classical political economy, but the illusions of Christian morality, Cartesian truth, and Kantian consciousness. Both men radicalized the implications immanently contained in German Idealism. Nietzsche recognizes this debt to German philosophy when he says that "the entire idealism of mankind hitherto is on the point of changing suddenly into nihilism—into the belief in absolute *worthlessness*, i.e., *meaninglessness.*"[74]

Nietzsche's criticisms of modernity also includes a direct attack on modern mechanistic science. As a technique for mastering nature, as a projection of utilitarian motives and needs, and as a construct of our creative drive, science both dominates and humanizes nature. It is a form of *"Herrschaftswissenschaft."* It has no inherent meaning, but neither does any other aspect of the world. The laws of physics, chemistry, biology, and mathematics are further manifestations of what is already implied in our grammar, language, and logic inherited from a distant past. They are all artificial illusions ultimately based on psychological necessity and prejudice to maintain a world of permanence and being. Necessity breeds ontology, psychology breeds metaphysics. There is no truth, only nothingness. However, because there is nothingness does not mean there is nothing. The physical laws of the atom, motion, causality, gravity, and so forth are perspectival inventions. What does not conform to psychological needs and the enhancement of life chances is eliminated from consideration and not made objective; it is not given a reality in the language of science. This theory of perspectivism and interpretation is a wildly exciting anticipation of the metaphysics behind quantum physics and the theories of Heisenberg and Kuhn, and the postanalytic philosophy of science of Popper, Hesse, Quine, Sellars, Feyerabend, and Rorty. On the other hand, it is also an anticipation of the terrors of ecological decadence.

Chapter Six

Morality and Art: Nietzsche's Deconstruction of Nihilism and Revaluation of Antiquity

Introduction

Having already examined Nietzsche's work on ancient philosophy and modern epistemology, it is time to turn our attention to his moral philosophy. As in the case of his other writings, many contemporary postmodern writers see only a montage of relatively unconnected soft ideas, feelings, insights, and so forth. I will argue in this chapter that Nietzsche is a child of nineteenth-century German education and intellectual training. Though his method of presentation goes to the heart of his critique of metaphysics and dogmatism, his underlying epistemological and moral ideas do, in fact, form a coherent and consistent whole throughout his life.

According to Nietzsche, nihilism is less a positive moral and epistemological position than an effect of the historical and metaphysical developments in science, religion, and morality. As we saw in the previous chapter, his critique of epistemology in *The Will to Power* provided a partial basis for his interpretation of epistemological nihilism. In this section, we will return to this work, while looking more closely at his critique of morality and religion. Since all knowledge is the result of interpretation and differing perspectives, there are only fabricated illusions, created opinions, and conceptual inventions. There is no truth or reality that corresponds to our theoretical constructs. Our perceptions, experience, judgment, and science reflect only the abyss of nothingness and not metaphysical truths. Everything produced by consciousness is error and lies. There are no meaningful coherent systems of values. The world is meaningless and empty.

However, for Nietzsche, this only represents the present devaluation of values. He views nihilism less as a philosophical position than as a continuous stage in the reevaluation of all meaning. This epistemological argument is supplemented in *The Will to Power* with a condemnation of Kantian moral philosophy and the Christian religion as leading to this state of affairs.

Nihilism at the Edge of the Abyss

Nihilism is a psychological state resulting from the insecurity, shame, and deception produced by traditional ideas about reality. Orthodox religion and morality share basic features including a belief in metaphysics, or unity, epistemology, or truth, and teleology, or aim. These are the conceptual underpinnings to all claims to religious and moral truths. Values are projected onto the world organized around these basic principles. The exterior and interior worlds are given the appearance of unity, purpose, and ultimate value. Finally, it is this struggle to organize religion and morality around categories of human rationality that precipitates Nietzsche's conclusion: "The faith in the categories of reason is the cause of nihilism. We have measured the value of the world according to categories *that refer to a purely fictitious world*. . . . All these values are, psychologically considered, the results of certain perspectives of utility, designed to maintain and increase human constructs of domination—and they have been falsely *projected* into the essence of things."[1]

Nihilism does not represent an ultimate truth about reality, since it, too, is only a stage in the development of humankind. The next level of development is that of the reevaluation and transformation of all values. Utilitarianism and pessimism are intermediate moments in which humanity has lost the willingness and ability autonomously to posit values in the world. Socratic rationalism, Christianity, modern science, and Kantian morality represent the underlying historical and cultural forces that have given rise to nihilism and despair. The search for the "beyond" and the "in itself" are modern illnesses. These different cultural forms are all variations of moral Platonism that force the implementation of foreign moral ideals from the outside. They express less the will to power than the power that wills. Loss of meaning and the resulting despair, resignation, and fear are only the effects of these broader changes. The philosopher "finds nothing behind all the ideals of man. Or not even nothing—but only what is abject, absurd, sick, cowardly, and weary, all kinds of dregs out of the emptied cup of his life."[2] Ideals are the moral equivalent of the Kantian "thing-in-itself."

However, there are deeper reasons for the decadence of modernity and these lie beneath the cultural appearances in the physiological and psychological foundations of nihilism, that is, in the loss of the instinctual drive for power, creativity, and life. Nietzsche calls this "physiological decadence."[3] Life is experienced as dead, as the glorification of nothing; the will is experienced as powerless, and its values as external, foreign, and meaningless. The source of the subjective drive and objective values has dried up. The negation of life is expressed in the scholasticism of values, in the reification of cultural forms, and in the mechanization of all social activity (religion, morality, knowledge, and so on). The resulting alienation and corruption of values, moral nihilism, pessimism (loss of meaning), and skepticism produce "the great nullity," which Weber will pick up on at the end of his famous work *The Protestant Ethic and the Spirit of Capitalism* when he examines the nature of rationalization and the iron cage.

It is important to note that nihilism is not the cause of modern decadence, simply its result. The search for pleasure replaces the search for meaning. Nietzsche holds that there are two kinds of nihilism: a passive and an active nihilism. The passive kind reflects the decadence of modernity in its loss of the joy of life and the pleasures of existence. Individuals are oppressed by reified and congealed structures of moral values that undermine their creative potential. "Existence is vulgarized." On the other hand, its positive form rejoices in the meaninglessness of the universe, because it places all meaning in the life-creating potential of humans. It is an expression of its will to power, a will to value and creativity, from which it takes its strength and dignity. "There is nothing better than what is good—and good is having some ability and using that to create *Tuchtigkeit* or *virtù* in the Italian Renaissance sense."[4]

There is in all this negative criticism of modernity a "new metaphysics," which Nietzsche terms "the eternal recurrence." If life has no meaning and everything is a subjective interpretation, then does the concept have any meaning? Nietzsche continues to push his critique of Kantian morality and practical reason to its limits when he contends that nihilism too is only a stage that must be radicalized and transformed. His critique of critique, or his critique of the limits of human rationality and moral action, of pure and practical reason, finally ends in his later unpublished writings with the acceptance and positive affirmation of existence as the only value and the only metaphysics. One must act as if the meaninglessness of the world is to be continuously re-created. What is being affirmed is not a particular value or even the valuelessness of the world. Traditional metaphysics or modern nihilism represent only aspects of the development of human potential. The true goal is the recognition of life and the valuation process itself. "There is nothing to life that has value, except the degree of power—assuming that life itself is the will to power."[5] Life has value because it expresses the life instincts and the will to power— it permits self-overcoming, self-form-giving, and self-legislation. Life is human potentiality.[6] In *Twilight of the Idols* (1889), Nietzsche remarks that though there are no moral facts and the world is meaningless, this does not mean that the world has no value. The world always has meaning to the extent that people create meaning in art, philosophy, religion, and science.[7] The world is nothing, while human beings are everything. This is the active form of nihilism that Nietzsche accepts, not the passive and pessimistic form that projects all meaning into an entirely transcendent mythological reality.

Dreams of Reason and Tyranny of Morality

Kant's moral philosophy draws special criticism in Nietzsche's later works, for he claims that the critique of practical reason, the categorical imperative, and the moral will lead not to dignity, freedom, and self-determination, but to their opposites. Kantian morality tyrannizes over the will because reason transforms the moral imperative to action into an imperialistic claim upon individual morality by an interior, alien force. Practical reason turns against itself and begins to impose moral order upon the subject in the same way that pure reason imposed being on becoming and substance on accidents. It refers to the relation between the subject and the categorical imperative. The moral individual must conform to the alien dictates of formal rationality. But it is a form of reason that lies outside the power of the individual. Self-legislation is transformed into imperial legislation as the Platonism inherent in Kant's philosophy is made explicit. Moral hypocrisy, declining spirit, loss of creative will, and the idolatry of pure forms turns morality into an external imposition rather than an internal celebration of life. The creative potential of the moral actor is replaced by the idolatry and conformity to the ideal moral forms that are external and oppressive. Kantian morality represents a form of the eclipse of reason (*Verdüsterung*) and an extension of the herd moral-ity.[8] It is an eclipse that eventually will lead back to Schopenhauer's pessimism. The categorical imperative becomes a form of the tyranny of reason over itself in a similar manner to the tyranny exerted by the "cult of objectivity" in science and metaphysics. In *The Antichrist*, Nietzsche calls the categorical imperative and its concomitant automa-tion of duty a "recipe for decadence, even idiocy."[9] However, just as in the case of epistemology and science, the way out of the dilemma is to transfigure the implications inherent in Kant's own ideas them-selves. The liberation of reason occurs when the categorical imperative is stripped of its formal characteristics while keeping in place the principles of self-determination and creativity.[10] "The fundamental laws of self-preservation and growth demand the opposite—that every-one invent *his own* virtue, *his own* categorical imperative. A people perishes when it confuses *its* duty with duty in general. . . . How could one fail to feel how Kant's categorical imperative endangered life itself!"[11]

Kantian moral philosophy stood outside of humankind as the arbiter of moral truth. It became an objective and foreign criterion to which the will to power was forced to yield. Morality became a formal procedure following logical rules and mechanical actions that flowed from the inevitable logic of practical reason. It closed off all other possibilities of morality and in the process reified the creative dimen-sion initially intended by Kant. Reacting to the one-side approaches of empiricism and rationalism, Kant integrated both traditions in his critique of practical reason. Morality would be the result of the individual's response to a real-life moral dilemma, while applying an a priori method of formal moral logic based on the principles of internal noncontradiction and universality. Morality would no longer be dic-tated from the external authority of religion, but would result from human rationality and its own moral imperatives. The creativity of the mind lent dignity and universality to the whole process. But, for Nietzsche, the process became objectified and reified and finally turned upon itself to where the individual had to conform to the imperialism of his or her own decadent rationality. Again Nietzsche simply pushed the principles inherent in Kant's moral philosophy to their extreme and reached beyond them. Humans would give themselves their own imperatives, but they would no longer be absolute and universal moral truths, since there is only nothingness and meaninglessness. When this is accomplished, Nietzsche can say, "Virtues are as dangerous as vices in so far as one lets them rule over one as authorities and laws from without and does not first produce them out of oneself, as one should do, as one's most personal self-defense and necessity, as conditions of precisely *our own* existence and growth, which we recognize and acknowledge independently of whether other men grow with us under similar or different conditions.''[12]

Of all the passages in *The Will to Power*, this represents one of the most important and powerful, since it reveals the heart of Nietzsche's position. Virtue and morality are not to be eliminated from social intercourse, but their nature will change radically. Human reason will maintain its position as the creator of values and norms, but the latter will not be permitted to claim universal and necessary status. Nietzsche, like Marx, but for different reasons, says that he has no political or social ideals to realize (note 80). The establishment of ideals of freedom, justice, and equality constructs boundaries around the constitutive element of the will. Nietzsche criticizes everything and everyone, from Luther to Schopenhauer, who eclipses or limits the possibilities and activities of practical reason. Moral objectivity sets reified standards and artificial boundaries that reduce the will to a formal, logical operation in order to determine the correct action. Objectivity eclipses and imprisons the will to power. Self-definition is replaced by the subordination of the individual to higher moral categories and standards of behavior.

Nietzsche calls Kant a dogmatist, moral fanatic, and tyrannizer. There are no true value judgments, and any attempt to impose them can only result in moral tyranny. "The will to a single morality is thereby proved to be a tyranny."[13] A single morality makes truth-claims to exclusivity based on a theory of knowledge that claims universality and absolute truth. This Nietzsche rejects, as we have already seen. A single morality fails to see the nothingness and meaninglessness of the universe. And, finally, its own claims distort and negate the creative spirit of humankind by seducing and leveling human potential to a fixed and static pure ideal. There is no longer a potential to be developed, no further ideals to be searched for, and no striving after future possibilities. Rather, there is only a technically efficient carrying out of the obligations determined by formal reason. There is, in effect, an eclipse of substantive rationality.[14] The claims of authority and law are simply ways of organizing society and moral order. There is, however, no effort to be made to make ontological and epistemological claims beyond the psychology that gives them life. Morality is necessary for life because it sets temporary limits, goals, and order. It gives a sense of direction and purpose and thus systematizes the infinity of possible moral choices. What is truly important about the process is that it expresses the creativity, will to power, and life instincts of humanity. Nietzsche draws from Kant the internal dynamic and power of asserting life through moral values. The emphasis is always on this creative component and not on the results achieved that are only ephemeral. Creativity is always beyond good and evil, beyond truth and falsity. Morality is always a handmaiden to life forces. In itself, it has no meaning, except as an expression of that life.

Though seemingly critical of morality as error and contradiction, Nietzsche does recognize that when morality expresses life and the will to power and when it is a reaction to the decadence and despair of modernity, it is a healthy instinct. When it serves the individual, morality manifests the dynamic side of people, but when it is a form of decadence, it simply becomes a means. Following Kant, he rejects moral action that reduces human behavior to a reflex of preestablished objectified norms and values. In the *Fundamental Principles of the Metaphysics of Morals*, Kant wrote, "He belongs to it as sovereign when, while giving laws, he is not subject to the will of any other. A rational being must always regard himself as giving laws either as member or as sovereign in a kingdom of ends which is rendered possible by the freedom of will."[15]

Compare this to note 269 in *The Will to Power* where Nietzsche states that "goals are lacking and these must be *individuals*. We observe how things are everywhere: every individual is sacrificed and serves as a tool. Go into the street and you encounter lots of 'slaves.' "[16] As we have already seen in many other situations, Nietzsche has accepted the underlying spirit of Kant's philosophy, while rejecting its metaphysical assumptions and superstructure. What is crucial throughout his discussions is the power of the will to determine and enforce its own moral guidelines without, at the same time, becoming caught in the web of a reified logic and formal rationality (principles of universalism, natural law, and noncontradiction), which only serve to undermine the substantive intentions of practical reason and the creative spirit of the moral will. Kant rejected any moral claim based on the suppression of the individual will or the treatment of the individual as a means to some higher moral purpose. Nietzsche simply recognizes that morality and religion have turned against their creators and made the latter into means for the maintenance of the former. In the process, humans become means for the realization of moral values, instead of morality being an expression of the dignity and sovereignty of humans. Morality has been degraded into a means.

Man has repeated the same mistake over and over again: he has made a means to life into a standard of life; instead of discovering the standard in the highest enhancement of life itself, in the problem of growth and exhaustion, he has employed the means to a quite distinct kind of life to exclude all other forms of life, in short to criticize and select life. I.e., man finally loves the means for their own sake and forgets they are means: so they enter his consciousness as aims, as standards for aims—i.e., a certain species of man treats the conditions of its existence as conditions which ought to be imposed as a law, as "truth," "good," "perfection": it tyrannizes.[17]

Marx had recognized this same point but escaped the problem by moving beyond morality to Aristotle's ethics and social theory. Nietzsche experiences the same problems but develops a new poetry and ethics of life. For both, ethics is *praxis*. For Marx, it is a *Wirtschaftsethik*, while for Nietzsche it is an *Überwindungsethik*. What is important is the process of self-determination, life preservation, and form giving in value constitution and system construction, not the particular form or value that is implemented. The illusions of a universal natural law created by the categorical imperative and principles of practical reason only confine and distort the moral will. Moral values not only dominate and control their creators, but also dominate all other values in society, including aesthetics, knowledge, and politics. Morality invents an artificial "authority of reason" and "metaphysic of unity" in an attempt to control the very interpretation and meaning of life itself. It turns reason away from the creation of principles of moral action through the operation of the categorical imperative. Duty to formal rationality is replaced by humiliation and obedience to the oppressive authority of reason. Reason and the will are turned against each other as impersonal forces that undermine their own life-sustaining functions. The rational determination of moral values turns into a tyranny of reason—the "categorical imperator," since the individual becomes incorporated into the herd mentality by the mass acceptance of transcendent values.

It is a relief to count oneself the same as others, to try to feel as they do, to *adopt* a current feeling: it is something passive compared with the activity that maintains and constantly practices the individual's right to value judgments (the latter allows no rest); in impartiality and coolness of judgment: one shuns the exertion of affects and prefers to stay detached, "objective"; in integrity: one would rather obey an existing law than create a law oneself, than command oneself and others: the fear of commanding—: better to submit than to react; in toleration: the fear of exercising rights, of judging.[18]

The instincts of life, individual striving, self-overcoming—self-realization by reaching beyond oneself—are replaced by obedience to an external authority, a conformity to a herd morality, and an adjustment and reconciliation to the norms of the community and the principles of a reified, objective, and formal rationality. Individual potential and free will are shattered by the centripetal forces of social mores, which turn them into mechanical automatons. In notes 397 and 398 of *The Will to Power*, Nietzsche states that this form of morality is a caricature of humans, an "iron cage of errors" (*ein eiserner Käfig von Irrtümern*) that will create an unhappy, sick, wretched, and hate-filled life. It produces an iron cage because it stultifies the desire to create a higher morality, a higher form of life, and a strengthening of the will to power.[19] But morality is still viewed by Nietzsche as an integral part in the creation of our world. He never rejects morality as such, only the exclusivity of its claims to absolute truth. Morality is only a stage in the further development of individuals. "Our strength itself drives us to sea, where all suns have hitherto gone down: we *know* of a new world."[20]

In a similar vein, Hannah Arendt was aware of these issues and their implications, as she used the term "the instrumentalization of action." The reduction of politics to instrumental categories for the purpose of maintaining the efficient functioning of a political system is something she sees as already developing with Plato's theory of justice and the Forms in the *Republic*. She argues that Plato transformed moral and political wisdom into a social technique. *Phronesis* (political wisdom through political participation and rational discourse) is replaced in Plato's writings by *poiesis* (making and using the tools of technical knowledge). The whole Greek emphasis on politics is replaced by the functional skills of the philosopher-king who engineers the social construction of the ideal world through the technical knowledge of the political craftsman. The disheartening implications lie for her in the fact that "we are perhaps the first generation which has become fully aware of the murderous consequences inherent in a line of thought that forces one to admit that all means, provided that they are efficient, are permissible and justified to pursue something defined as an end."[21]

This also accounts for Nietzsche's visceral attack on Christianity as the "most fatal seductive lie that has yet existed, as the great unholy lie" producing "these lying little abortions of bigots."[22] It creates a

moral ideal of obedience, psychological conformity, spiritual homoge-
nization, herd *ressentiment*, metaphysical dogmatism, and moral fanaticism. It replaces life with a "beyond this world." This is why
Nietzsche calls for immorality and atheism as a response to the
decadence of Western morality. Traditional morality has turned into
its opposite and only an opposite response—immorality—is adequate
to the problem. Christian theology with its theodicy of sin, evil,
sacrifice, immortality, guilt, repentance, forgiveness, and resurrection
produces a world that sacrifices individuality to the community of
believers. By rejecting true morality and the life spirit, these abstract
Christian ideals turn form making into a moral castration. "Life itself
is transformed into a defamation and pollution of life; the concept
'God' represents a turning away from life, a critique of life, even a
contempt for it; truth is transformed into the priestly lie, the striving
for truth into study of the scriptures, into a means of becoming a
theologian."[23]

Lest one think that Nietzsche is establishing another metaphysics to
replace the ideals of Christian theology, he states that his goal is not to
eliminate Christianity, but by applying the critical method, to undermine its ability to tyrannize and dominate. His goal is to have other
ideals expressed that would introduce moral and spiritual tensions,
conflict, and further attempts at self-transcendence.

Metaphysics of the Hangman and Politics of the Guillotine

Nietzsche wrote and published one of his last and best works,
written before his mental illness in 1889, entitled *Twilight of the Idols*.
Many of the themes mentioned in the unpublished notes of *The Will to
Power* are also discussed and developed in this work, especially those
criticizing morality, promoting the revaluation of values, and rejecting
the tyranny of reason. The book begins with a critique of the Greek
view of rationality, which assumes a universal form of knowledge
arrived at through the dialectic and which establishes an equation
between reason, virtue, and happiness. The degenerative sickness of
decadence has already begun with Socrates and Plato who "turn
reason into a tyrant." Its more modern versions are only variations on
the revenge of the post-Platonic philosophers. Nietzsche believes that
with the breakup of the delicate balance between the Dionysian and
Apollonian spirits during the age of tragedy, the Greek world began to
implode upon itself. The civil wars and the internecine fratricidal

conflicts between city-states required a radical solution—the fanaticism and dogmatism of a formal, moral rationality to hold the cosmos together. This situation also demanded that the Dionysian side of the Greeks was to be repressed into the unconscious, and with it, its exuberance for life. In the process, virtue and happiness were reduced to obedience to the dictates of practical rationality.

In order to survive in this world of the fifth century B.C., the perception of reality had to be re-organized in such a way that gave the appearances of permanency, universality, truth, and being. This line of thought continues his sociology of knowledge arguments from the earliest works, which stressed the relationships between social processes and conceptual arrangements. Rationality replaced joy in life as the key value articulated by this culture. And with this change came a newly invented world of being with its new ontology (the perfect), epistemology (the true), and morality (the good). But in its turn, a world of the gravediggers (rejection of the senses and becoming), tyrants (oppressive moral standards), and scholastics (reified categories of thinghood, substance, and causality) was fabricated. But it was a world that was alien to the mystery and life of self-overcoming and self-transcendence, a world that looked into the dark and passionate side of human existence. By having to conform to the new metaphysics, individuals lost their sense of self and purpose in the world. They lived in a world of fiction, which they no longer recognized as being a product of their own needs, creations, and logical conventions. "The prejudice of reason forces us to posit unity, identity, permanence, substance, cause, thinghood, being, we see ourselves somehow caught in error, compelled into error."[24]

Nietzsche articulates an ontology of language when he says that being is a product of human thought. He has not fallen back into a form of idealism, but rather he philosophizes that language has constructed a fiction that is believed to be universally true. As we have examined already in the analysis of his early writings, he begins by arguing that once the ego is viewed as a thing or substance, this impression is projected onto the whole world of experience. The thinghood of the world is a false product of the human imagination; its reality is only an illusion created by language and grammar. But this also means that language contains its own built-in metaphysical assumptions about the reality of being as opposed to becoming. "I am afraid we are not rid of God because we still have faith in grammar."[25] Nietzsche calls this a "crude fetishism" in which the image of the ego becomes the basis for interpreting reality.

The world is distorted by means of the theological categories of guilt, punishment, and salvation. Christianity constructs a world beyond the senses. It is presented as a thing, as having permanence and reality. A whole world is constructed in the kingdom of heaven, which stops the flow of becoming at every level and provides the foundations for Christian morality and theodicy. By the architecture of the theologian, the "innocence of becoming" is lost and replaced by the "metaphysics of the hangman." That is, morality and religion form a static and unchanging universe that destroys life and moral creativity by placing life and morality in an afterlife. It reduces morality to conformity and obedience to a preestablished normative order and natural law. It surrenders life to the executioner who works at the behest of the religious and moral establishment—those people who have fixed the laws of practical reason. But Nietzsche contends that there is no unity or order in the world—no judge, no standard of measurement, no universal values. Instead, the world (innocence of becoming), or life, is its own value and one of the most important expressions of life is the will creating its own moral universe.

The idea of the hangman has many expressions, among them a faith in an essential ideal, such as the ideals of humanity, happiness, morality, and salvation. The hangman is generally at the service of those institutions that require coercion as the basis for moral behavior. For Nietzsche, these ideals represent "the absurd wish to devolve one's essence on some end or other"[26] and thus subvert the creative dynamic of self-overcoming. According to Nietzsche in *The Will to Power*, the moral hangman is the "will to self-destruction" and the "will for nothingness."[27] In *Twilight of the Idols*, he attributes the development of these moral phenomena to the ancient priestly class's desire for domination and control. The latter could only be accomplished when the mechanism of guilt and punishment was established. This, in turn, could only be implemented when individuals were seen as having free will. The metaphysics of the hangman executes life by means of theological categories intended to establish social control by killing the "innocence of becoming."

True morality is ultimately not the end posited as the goal for human striving, whether established by utilitarianism (pleasure), neo-Aristotelianism (happiness), Christianity (God and salvation), or neo-Kantianism (categorical imperative and duty). Morality is one of the creative endeavors by which humans delineate and define the limits and meaning of human existence (Apollonian spirit) and overcome these limits (Dionysian spirit). It is a locus of the tension and dialectic between construction and destruction, reason and passion. The rejection of essence, moral truths, and final goals is not a manifestation of skepticism and moral nihilism. Just the contrary. Though there is a denial of moral facts, there is also a broader understanding of morality that encompasses human determination and self-definition. As with Kant, it is human dignity that ultimately underlies Nietzsche's critique of morality and religion. Traditional morality is denied so that morality and humanity (*Übermensch*) may live.

Christian and Kantian morality reflect the reduction of the process of devaluation to a technical method of applying correct standards to the proper situation. Just as Nietzsche had rejected an understanding of history in technical terms, so does he reject morality as *techne*. He even describes traditional morality as the taming of the beast and the improvement of humanity in a world where he is "stuck in a cage, imprisoned among all sorts of terrible concepts. And there he lay, sick, miserable, malevolent against himself: full of hatred against the springs of life, full of suspicion against all that was still strong and happy."[28]

What is interesting is that these same criticisms of Kantian morality were also leveled against Kant by Hegel in his essay "The Spirit of Christianity and Its Fate." There Hegel examined the Old and New Testaments in search of clues about the nature of true morality. He was critical of the Jews for what he perceived as their wretched and abject subservience to alien laws and the positivity of moral commands. Servitude, domination, and obedience to God's law reflected a moral community that, Hegel thought, produced the "nullity of mankind." Humans are moral only to the extent that they abjure the freedom of existence and subject themselves to the infinite. "Their life was subordinated to an end; it was not self-subsistent or self-sufficient."[29] This very subservience to God kept the Jews from reaching truth, beauty, and freedom, unlike the Greeks for whom freedom and equality were the source of life and power. After the conquest of their nation, the little independence they knew disappeared as they became a politically and theologically subjected people. Hegel finally states at the end of his analysis of the ancient Hebrews that their experience could not be considered a tragedy as was the case with the Greeks, because they produced no pity or terror. Over and against the Kantian Jews, Hegel sets the new spirit of Christianity. "Over against commands which required a bare service of the Lord, a direct slavery, an obedience without joy, without pleasure or love, i.e., the commands in connection with the service of God, Jesus set their precise opposite, a human urge and so a human need."[30]

The ideal was not to be a moral positivity, reified law, or external moral command. The conflict of opposition between the real and ideal was to be overcome in life itself. Hegel gives two examples of this: the first is the discussion about good works during the holy day of the sabbath and the second is the Sermon on the Mount. Rejecting claims of artificial absoluteness, Jesus showed the priority of need and love over law and guilt. "He made undetermined subjectivity, character, a totally different sphere, one which was to have nothing in common with the punctilious following of objective commands. Against purely objective commands Jesus set something totally foreign to them, namely the subjective in general."[31] Here Hegel is attempting to unite the Kantian antinomies of real and ideal, reason and desire, objective and subjective, and legal formalism and life. It was to be a general reconciliation of humankind within a moral community sharing common values of Christian love. Morality as the domination of the concept was to be transformed from an external, formal command and internal slavery to a subjective feeling of love.

Hegel's early turn to subjectivism and love as the means for transcending Kant's moral dilemma, caused by the opposition of law and inclinations, leads to problems in his later political philosophy. It was just this subjective component of virtue expressed as moral sincerity and certainty that formed the basis for a politics of the heart. An abstract politics outside the objective framework (structural supports and institutional networks) failed to give a social content and historical context to political activity. It was because of this subjective isolation and political abstractness that there were no limits and safeguards during the French Revolution and Robespierre's Reign of Terror.[32] There were no social guidelines to help form the will in its exercise of constructing a new political constitution. Between Rousseau's general will and Robespierre's terror lie Kantian subjectivity and the "dreams of reason." Without customs and traditions, without concrete institutions and specific criteria and standards of measurements, and without specific content to the political ideals of the general will and civic republicanism, the search for sincere, self-certain moral truths ended in the purges of the Terror. Mark Warren in his *Nietzsche and Political Thought* writes about Nietzsche's response in *The Genealogy of Morals* to this question. "The categorical imperative, he [Nietzsche] argues, is a metaphysical residue of violent political authority. As such it 'smells of cruelty.' "[33] The Kantian terror and resulting politics of the guillotine were viewed by Hegel and Nietzsche as a product of this subjective approach to morality.

Arendt also takes up this issue in her book *On Revolution*, when she discusses the differences between the American and French Revolutions.[34] The Americans had outlined the necessity for a free government, whereas the French had emphasized the natural rights of man and the citizen, which preceded the formation of the political realm. In Robespierre's "Principles of Revolutionary Government," there was a split between public virtue and private interests, public happiness and private pleasure, public freedom and civil liberties, and freedom and political power. Freedom, happiness, and rights became articulated within civil society and not the public sphere. These separations resulted in the split between freedom and power, which formerly had been viewed as part of the public sphere. Now, however, freedom was something private and power became the force used to realize the implementation of fundamental human rights of man and the citizen. The original meanings of these political categories became skewed, as did the whole institutional framework of the French Revolution. Power, which formerly was part of the constitutive process of forming the public realm, was turned into the violence of implementing natural rights as the revolution met resistance from the outside.[35] Nature itself became the justification for the revolution and, finally, the Reign of Terror, since the implementation of natural rights was immediate and unguided by social and political institutions designed to protect freedoms and liberty.

Steven Smith in his book *Hegel's Critique of Liberalism* also develops these insights of Hegel and Arendt on the French Revolution by showing the relation established by Robespierre between virtue and terror.[36] Within revolutionary conditions and a politics of virtue, the revolutionary was acting to realize these abstract universals without the moral and political guidelines of established traditions and customs. There are no social intermediaries between the particular political actor and the universal values. The former's criteria of political action lie in these absolutes and the intentions and purity of heart of the individual. Therein lie the basis and justification for the Terror.

Though Nietzsche transcends the subjective spirit of Kant, he does not see the dangers inherent in pushing this form of individualism too far. If there is a serious weakness in his thought, it is this lack of analysis of social objectivity. Though he shares similar concerns with Hegel about the oppressive nature of Kantian morality, his theory of herd morality and *ressentiment* weakens his concern about social issues. He does not take up a detailed analysis of the institutional structures of modernity to the extent that Marx does. Nietzsche sees the problems in Kantian morality with its metaphysics of the hangman, but misses sight of the dangers resulting from a politics of the guillotine. This requires that we consider Nietzsche's general critique of liberal modernity. In many respects, he fails to move beyond Kant and German liberalism and, in the end, falls back behind both.

Nietzsche's Critique of Liberalism and Socialism

Liberalism and socialism are the fullest development and expression in modern society of the social and political principles and values that began with Greek moral philosophy. From scholasticism and medieval Christianity to Protestantism and liberalism, there is a continuous effort to undermine nobility, personal differences, strength, power, and striving. Everyone is reduced to a common religious or political denominator. Nietzsche's critique of liberalism, though focused on the natural rights tradition, encompasses the full range of liberal values and institutions, including politics, economy, religion, art, anthropology, science, and natural rights and utilitarian ideals. Nietzsche states that both liberalism and socialism are variations of utilitarianism.

The liberal ideals of equality of rights, dignity, freedom, and justice originally were developed from the Christian values of modesty, patience, neighborly love, guilt and resignation, and submission and loss of self to God. Liberalism, like Christianity, "appeals to all the cowardices and vanities of wearied souls."[37] It blames human suffering on others. Someone must be guilty. The ideals represent a misplaced concreteness for the human dilemma of suffering and the political revenge of the underprivileged. Christianity with its last judgment and socialism with its final revolution share the common thread of a need for revenge, which is the other side of the utilitarian coin with its need for pleasure.[38] "Christianity presupposes that man does not know, *cannot* know, what is good for him, what evil: he believes in God, who alone knows it. Christian morality is a command; its origin is transcendent; it is beyond all criticism, all right to criticism; it has truth only if God is truth—it stands and falls with faith in God."[39]

Christianity undermines the very possibility of critique, of the search for truth, and of the development of a critical rationality. Life is negated, the will to power is endangered, and human creativity and possibilities are sacrificed on the altar of natural rights. Individuals are reduced to the embodiment of moral absolutes, as political ideals are transformed into immutable values that continue to tyrannize and coerce individuals to conform to a herd mentality. In *The Will to Power*, Nietzsche calls this "the politics of virtue": "Moralists need the *gestures* of virtue, also the gestures of truth; their error begins only when they yield to virtue, when they lose domination over virtue, when they themselves become moral, become true."[40] Morality, truth, and virtue replace becoming moral, truthful, and virtuous; morality ends with the loss of the will to power. There is a crucial difference between being moral and becoming moral. With the former, human-kind has lost the power of domination and control, its creative spirit and free will, and simply follows the herd instinct for self-preservation and social conformity. In the latter case, everything is becoming and there are no guidelines except the self-determining and self-legislating power of the moral and aesthetic will. This is why to be moral really means to be an immoralist—never accepting moral formulas and continuously striving beyond them.[41] Liberalism undermines the desire for individual freedom and produces a utilitarian, consumer-oriented society, which itself is antithetical to strong individuality and ulti-mately leads to slavery. "The democratization of Europe is at the same time an involuntary arrangement for the training of tyrants."[42] Like Marx, Nietzsche is extremely contemptuous of utilitarianism and the English shopkeepers' mentality of the need for pleasure. Liberalism, though its ideology is one of individual freedom, does not encourage or support individuality, but ends with the "last man" found in prologue to *Thus Spoke Zarathustra*.[43]

This is why Nietzsche sees Christianity as the model for modern liberalism. Religion reduces the individual soul to a common denomi-nator of original sin and its ultimate end to guilt, repentance, and salvation. All souls are equal and the liberal theory of equal rights is simply a secular expansion and projection of these ideas onto the state. "One has transferred the arrival of the 'kingdom of God' into the future, on earth, in human form—but fundamentally one has held fast to the belief in the *old* ideal."[44] The common liberal ideals of equality, rights, happiness, dignity, and humanization are all forms of political tartuffery and attempts to level individual distinctiveness, strivings, and noble attributes. Liberalism and Christianity are grounded in revenge and *ressentiment* for individual differences (egoism), the for-mer in society and the latter in the theodicy of sin and guilt.

Nietzsche's criticisms of liberalism rest on two distinct perspectives: the first is the critique of ideals and the second is the critique of leveling and abstraction. The former is consistent with his general epistemology and rejection of final ends and absolute standards. The second, however, is more problematic in that his rejection of liberalism, the market, democracy, and socialism is based on some ultimate standard of the nobility and self-overcoming of the individual. The issue is again raised in this context of whether Nietzsche is developing a new political metaphysics based on standards that are in contradiction to his own epistemological relativism. But throughout his works, Nietzsche is also aware that even revenge and *ressentiment* are prudent means of coping with survival and despair in underdeveloped cultures.[45] The result is a form of pleasure and happiness, security, community, and self-preservation. A danger develops when they are transformed into universal concepts and standards of moral measurement—into the iron cage of the moral menagerie and the will to nothingness.

In *Twilight of the Idols*, Nietzsche expands his critique of moral universalism and liberalism to include the democratization of education (*Bildung*) and reduction of education to a common, but fragmented standard of academic excellence. This also parallels the reduction of science to universal categories and methodology, along with the immunization of scientific objectivity from critical reflection and evaluation. Thus, these ideals—universalism, objectivity, science, religion, and morality—despise human beings and rob humanity of its creative powers and replace them with pretentious forms of mediocrity.

Nietzsche is also aware that the market molds individuals according to a common measure and value, where morality is bought and sold for exchange. Marx's labor theory of value is built around the insight that the market abstracts from individual differences and use values in order to create a common exchange value for the market. Though the interpretations and conclusions are different, they both recognize the leveling, moral inversion, and cultural reductionism that takes place in liberalism. All this occurs in contradistinction to the ideology that liberal society encourages individualism and self-realization. Nietzsche does not view socialism as a radically distinct political theory, but merely a further development of utilitarian values and ideals.[46] When referring to socialism in *The Will to Power*, he says,

> Socialism—as the logical conclusion of the *tyranny* of the least and the dumbest, i.e., those who are superficial, envious, and three-quarters actors—is indeed entailed by "modern ideas" and their latent anarchism; but in the tepid air of democratic well-being the capacity to reach

conclusions, or to finish, weakens. One follows—but one no longer sees what follows. Therefore socialism is on the whole a hopeless and sour affair.[47]

In *The Genealogy of Morals* (1887), Nietzsche undertakes an analysis of the psychology of liberalism by developing a theory of repression and sublimation in the state of nature. In a play with the ideas and apparent integration of Hobbesian and pre-Freudian psychology, he provides a psychological understanding of the herd mentality and the moral grounding of liberalism and modernity. Prior to the formation of law and society, humans lived in a state of constant struggle and warfare in a wilderness reminiscent of Hobbes's war of all against all. With the domestication of these warlike creatures, there occurred a devaluation of values, a pacification of aggressive instincts for domination, an avoidance and taming of sensuousness and physical desires, a repression of freedom, and invention of unhappy consciousness. This is what Nietzsche calls "the torture chamber" of moral guilt and bad conscience. He sees the socialization process as having provided important sociological, psychological, and cultural dimensions in the creation of this perspective.

In order to preserve and protect itself, society turned against these presocial instincts of aggression. At this point in his analysis, Nietzsche utilizes a vocabulary of the unconscious: social oppression, instinct repression, sublimation, and interiorization. Those instincts for war, freedom, aggression, and adventure, which were once necessary for survival and happiness, became socially disruptive with the creation of a commonwealth. The new social form required a different set of moral values which emphasized the status quo, common good, and social peace.[48] A leveling process began, which called into question just those values that recognized and rewarded individual distinctiveness and superiority. Nietzsche argues that conformity and mediocrity are now honored as the communal basis for solidarity. Combining Hobbes's social contract theory with a theory that anticipated Freud's theory of unconscious repression and sexual sublimation, Nietzsche develops his notion of bad conscience. In his work *Friedrich Nietzsche and the Politics of Transformation*, Tracy Strong writes that Nietzsche is using his genealogical method to examine the underlying values and foundations of European society in order to call them into question.[49]

As in the case of Freud's later analysis of instincts, Nietzsche argues that instincts can never be eliminated, only rechanneled and temporarily repressed into the unconscious. These repressed and unconscious instincts are turned inward upon and against the individual as "man began rending, persecuting, terrifying himself, like a wild beast hurling itself against the bars of its cage."[50] The will to power is turned against the self through the invention of life-negating religion and morality. Bottled-up aggression is repressed and turned inward by means of ideas of vengeance in which the self is the target. Sin, guilt, punishment, and damnation are ideational products of this self-directed violence. Nietzsche calls this a "sublime vindictiveness." Morality as a creative expression of the need to limit and delineate, to give moral boundaries and guidelines is turned into an accumulation of suppressed needs, inwardly turned hatred and violence, and a passive ego that does not act. The self is affirmed neither in its creative ability nor in its self-direction to legislate morality. It only passively receives and quietly reacts to traditional norms, reified values, and objectified ideals. The noble and beautiful virtues of the ancients are replaced by the weak and humble acceptance of moral givens. The pleasure derived from morality is only a form of "drugged tranquility."

When *eudaimonia* is separated from *praxis*, happiness from political activity, ethics from self-determination within the community, then morality itself is reduced to moments of fleeting private pleasure. What results is a further desire to inflict pain through resentment and revenge. This is accomplished, according to Nietzsche, by means of a passive and debilitating religion and morality that depreciate the accomplishments, abilities, and possibilities of the moral actor. As Nietzsche has said, "The building of heaven lies in everyman's hell."[51] This is the revenge of repressed and sublimated passions of hatred that, because of their very nature, cannot become conscious: this is the revenge of modern reason.

> Man, with his need for self-torture, his sublimated cruelty resulting from the cooping up of his animal nature within a polity, invented bad conscience in order to hurt himself, after the blocking of the more natural outlet of cruelty. Then this guilt-ridden man seized upon religion in order to exacerbate his self-torment to the utmost. The thought of being in God's debt became his new instrument of torture. He focused in God the last of the opposites he could find to his true and inveterate animal instincts, making these a sin against God.[52]

The psychology of liberalism stresses the revaluation of values in terms of aggression and passivity. It is people's very ethical passivity and suppression of needs that call forth their moral aggression against themselves. Christianity and liberalism are historical products of the distortion of human instincts and examples of the beast turning against itself. Even the calls for Christian love and liberal justice are reflections of this psychological process of inner decay. They are an expression of pity and loathing of humanity. Love and justice are to be given to individuals, imposed from the outside, offered to them as gifts for the just compensation and reward for their activity. They do not come from the inner reaches of the self. The stage has been set for bad conscience and the iron cage of modernity: Christian charity, liberal fairness, and economic redistribution require conformity to objective standards. The result of all this is to bring about "man's utter demoralization and, indirectly, a reign of nothingness." This situation "has conjured away one of their most fundamental concepts, that of *activity*, and put in its place the concept of *adaptation*—a kind of second-rate activity, mere reactivity."[53] The very categories of morality and politics reflect this underlying passivity and decadence of the modern world and reveal the distance we have come from the Greek experience of nobility, grace, and beauty, as well as from a resistance to and a striving against pain and the horrors of existence.

The political and social contract was formed not through rational recognition of needs, the fear of violent death, or the desire for material wealth and pleasure, but rather came from the external power of the tyrannical leviathan. The state was formed by the "hammer blows" of the political artists. With it there developed the distorted political ideals and moral values of modernity, the domestication of the self and the loss of the instinct for life, and the bad conscience of Christianity and liberalism. The suffering produced by this interiorization of the aggressive instincts and the repression of the desire for freedom was explained away in a theology of sin and guilt and the metaphysics of contrition, redemption, and afterlife. Though critical of modern values, Nietzsche does recognize in his revaluation of values that bad conscience is part of the process through which even beauty is created. Political despotism and moral aristocracy are the beginning points of Nietzsche's *The Genealogy of Morals*.

Transvaluation of Values and Critique of Moral Objectivity

Nietzsche's critique of morality and the striving to get beyond good and evil should not be interpreted to mean a rejection of moral values. He, in fact, calls for the revaluation of values and the recognition of the transformation of values into their opposites. Traditional morality, religion, and political philosophy had stressed the values of equality, dignity, duty, self-respect, moderation, industriousness, and perseverance. The values actually produced are obedience and subservience to moral duty; humility and fatalism before external, universal ideals; submission and *ressentiment* about the suppression of instincts of the spirit; self-mutilation and depreciation before alien idols; and the general "slandering and poisoning of human life." Thus, these moral values lead not to their explicitly intended ends, but to their contradictory opposites. Rather than leading to morality, they lead to the undermining of spirituality, moral becoming, and self-transcendence—they lead to decadence. Life is replaced by death, morality by immorality, strength by weakness, mastery by subservience and mediocrity, nobility and spirituality by the herd instinct, and creativity by conformity. "*All* the means by which one has so far attempted to make mankind moral were through and through *immoral.*"⁵⁴ All morality involves a process of revaluation, transformation, and recreation; all moral values represent the rejection of some previously accepted moral position. This is the moral life of becoming. What Nietzsche rejects is the turning of morality into being—into transcendent, unapproachable, and uncriticizable values. Nietzsche is still holding true to the basic Kantian position of the self-legislation and self-determination of moral values by the individual. However, "critique" must be turned into an historical and genealogical method.

Traditional morality has no place left for judging and valuing. These faculties are no longer necessary, since the absolute values have already been determined. The result is the iron cage of Christianity and Kantian morality, which must be replaced by a radical critique of practical values, that is, by that which challenges authority and ideals—by the immoral, which, in turn, will establish itself as the moral. And this, too, will be challenged in its turn as a form of false universality and objectivity. Nietzsche, therefore, rejects the formal rationality and substantive features of the technical application of the categorical imperative, but the spirit that underlies and animates Kant's critique of moral rationalism still guides his thought. What is truly moral is not the obedience to duty or subservience to being and objectivity, but the constitutive process of creating objects and moral ideals themselves. At this point, Nietzsche shares Marx's view that the danger in modernity lies in morality and religion becoming narcotics. This is the reason why nature can never act as a moral guide. It is designless and formless.

Nietzsche argues that true morality is an aesthetic experience in which concepts and forms are given to the natural world.[55] Through art and the aesthetic transformation of the world according to the forms of the human will, the world is enriched and "man enjoys himself as perfection." In one of his last clear statements toward the end of his productive life, Nietzsche again returns to the distinction between the Dionysian and Apollonian spirits. As expressions of the frenzies of the will that drive to give form and meaning to life, art is its highest achievement.

In the beautiful, man posits himself as the measure of perfection; in special cases he worships himself in it. A species cannot do otherwise but thus affirm itself alone. . . . Man believes the world itself to be overloaded with beauty—and he forgets himself as the cause of this. He alone has presented the world with beauty—alas! only with a very human, all-too-human beauty. At bottom, man mirrors himself in things; he considers everything beautiful that reflects his own image: the judgement "beautiful" is the *vanity of his species*.[56]

As Calvin once held that humankind honors God through work, Nietzsche contends that the artist honors life by his or her aesthetic response to human suffering. Individuals humanize nature to the extent that what they see overcomes the chaos and change and gives it a temporary form of beauty. "Nothing is beautiful, except man alone" and "nothing is ugly except the degenerating man."[57] This is a simple and naïve viewpoint that has validity to the extent that we abstract from other possible criteria of beauty. But as the present measure of all things, it is only the ugly that is truly beautiful, since it expresses the opposition to the stagnant and decadent values of modernity. But as we get closer to the end of this work and, in reality, to the end of his intellectual and scholarly life, Nietzsche, as many Germans eventually do, returns to the German saints of ancient Greece, especially Winckelmann. Nietzsche's critique of decadence, of the mediocrity of modernity, and the subservience of the herd is redeemed in the beauty and joy of the ancients—in their creative and tragic spirit.

Art has its own purpose and aims, since it is the aesthetic manifestation of the will to power and the forms that humankind has given to reality. Art must not be interpreted to mean a set of preestablished classical ideals to be emulated, but rather a spirit that animates our life and creativity. Ideals kill life, but the spirit invigorates our courage, strength, and will to beauty. Nietzsche calls the Greek ideals of beauty, perfection, the sublime, and harmony forms of "noble simplicity."

To smell out "beautiful souls," "golden means," and other perfections in the Greeks, or to admire their calm in greatness, their ideal cast of mind, their noble simplicity—the psychologist in me protected me against such "noble simplicity," a *niaiserie allemande* anyway. I saw their strongest instinct, the will to power. I saw them tremble before the indomitable force of this drive—I saw how all their institutions grew out of preventive measures taken to protect each other against their inner explosives.[58]

These ideals represent an unreflective faith and immediate attachment to the lost virtues of the Greek world. Though the above quoted passage is intended as a direct criticism of Winckelmann and classical Weimar, Nietzsche also recognizes the importance of the nineteenth-century German view of the classical experience. The mistake of idealism was to idealize the Greeks and turn their Apollonian forms into unreachable ideals as occurred within moral philosophy. Ideals are already desiccated expressions of a dead and decadent society. They occur after the fact that the life of the polis had passed away. As Hegel had said in *The Philosophy of Right*, the owl of Minerva spreads its wings only at dusk.[59] The modern philosopher must not imitate ideals, but distill the need and "will to life" behind them and recreate the original creative force of these ethical principles. The aesthetic drive of Apollo is necessary to revive the image of the ancients, but Nietzsche is also looking for a revival of Dionysus—the creative spirit and striving instincts that motivated their intuition and insights, not the particular substance of their cultural beliefs.

Hebrews, Hellenes, and the Revenge of Reason

Nietzsche's look into the mind of the ancient Hebrews and early Christians offers us an interesting insight into his critique of the evils of modernity. The Jewish and Christian traditions present us with one of the origins of the modern path that gave rise to the distortion of time through revenge. Christianity is seen as an outgrowth and development of Judaism, not its condemnation or rejection. The realization of the ideas and principles of Moses and the prophetic tradition lie in Paul and the New Testament. And it is just this tradition that Nietzsche juxtaposes to the nobility and strength of the Greeks. To the sickness and disease of Christianity, Nietzsche holds up the health and beauty of the ancients as a beacon.[60]

In Christianity, "God degenerated into the *contradiction* of life, instead of being its transfiguration and eternal Yes! God as the declaration of war against life, against nature, against the will to life."[61] This is a direct result of the creation of the pure fiction of the beyond, of the psychological need falsely to represent strength, pride, and sensuousness as moral transgressions, to falsely represent the affirmation of the values of perfection of the pure spirit as sickness, weakness, pity, and hope, and of the desire to avoid the feelings of displeasure. According to Nietzsche, it was the Jews who denatured all natural values, who falsified nature and turned it into its own contradiction. In a manner reminiscent of his critique of Greek moral philosophy as simply buttressing up a past society and its dead ideals, he approaches the Hebrews. His criticisms lie in the fact that after the Exile, the Jewish religion became an unrealizable and distant moral ideal— another form of moral tyranny. Between the time of the Exodus and the prophets, Jewish religion was an organic expression of its life. There was no abyss separating its moral norms, social behavior, and religious expectations. Its God was a symbolic expression of its own power and happiness, its material success and the bountifulness of nature, its real hopes and legitimate anticipations. There was an organic whole created between society, cultural values, and natural processes. Religion became the integrating feature in society, as well as its consciousness about itself and its past, present, and future. When the Hebrews lost their land and government through military defeat by the Assyrians, religion became divorced from society and nature, and began to project a falsifying vision of the beyond. The transcendent beyond was unconnected to reality. Nietzsche lets the Jews off the hook to the extent that he admits that their historical and social circumstances and environment left them with little option. He does not forgive Christianity so easily. The moral order created by the ancients with its will of God, holy scriptures, kingdom of God, sin, submission to the priests, redemption, and reconciliation are expanded in the New Testament.

In the place of the old God of Israel and prophetic justice, the new God of the priestly class took its position. This God was no longer an organic expression of the ultimate values of the Hebrews, but a falsifying God who suppressed their traditional values of strength and courage, graciousness and beauty, and sensuousness and spirit. A new religion was created that demanded obedience to abstract moral codes, formal laws and rituals, and submission to the priests. This was accomplished with a corresponding loss of natural instincts, creativity, imagination, and the will to power. "Morality — no longer the expres-

sion of the conditions for the life and growth of a people, no longer its
most basic instinct of life, but become abstract, become the antithesis
of life—morality as the systematic degradation of the imagination, as
the 'evil eye' for all things.''[62] The priests of the New Testament
with their theology of the cross, redemption through suffering, and
resurrected Christ merely perfected and further abstracted this religious orientation; their new metaphysics and formulas destroyed whatever reality remained in the Hebrew religion. Christianity was opposed
to worldly wisdom and science, sensuousness, pleasure, and happiness. The justification for its priestly control lay in the redemption and
creation myths (and myth of original sin) of the Bible. According to
Nietzsche, Christianity contains part of the truth about humanity. For
him, everything that suffers is divine.[63] But every attempt to explain
human divinity through the parasitic priestly class becomes a mechanism of error and terror, a distortion of the original idea and a rejection
of life.

What Nietzsche does is read back into history Hegel's rejection of
the Kantian critique of practical reason. Reading backwards into
history, one can see that Hebrew formalism, Socratic rationalism,
Christian scholasticism, modern objectivism and scientism, and liberal
abstractionism are all manifestations in one form or another of the
tyranny of the categorical imperative. In his *Phenomenology of Spirit*,
Hegel traced the evolution and development of the Spirit, which
concluded with the values of individuality and freedom in the French
Revolution and Kantian philosophy. Nietzsche is doing something
similar in that he is reading the whole of Western Enlightenment
and rationalism through the evil eye of Kantian metaphysics. The
metaphysics of the dialectic and moral freedom in Socrates, the
superstition of sin and redemption within Judaism and Christianity,
the metaphysics of individualism, equality, and rights within liberalism
and socialism are all expressions of the phenomena of logical abstractionism, formal rationality, and moral tyranny. As Nietzsche puts it so
succinctly and poetically in *The Antichrist*: "All that is solid kills."[64]

Whether it is natural law, religious faith, political ideologies, or
moral imperatives, formal rationality imposes a morality from the
outside that is alien to subjective consciousness. Nietzsche, as in the
case of Hegel, uses Kant's critique of practical reason as the symbolic
summarization and end point of the history of Western ethics. His *The
Genealogy of Morals* is simply an exposition of this process within the
framework of a genealogy and psychology of repression.

Historical Critique of Slave Ethics and Ideologies of *Ressentiment*

In his book *The Genealogy of Morals*, Nietzsche begins further to revise Kant's critique of practical reason and its underlying transcendental logic. Instead of raising questions about the formal and logical conditions of moral reason, he takes a decidedly more Hegelian approach.[65] Instead of grounding a moral natural law in the principles of pure reason, a priori synthetic judgments of the categorical imperative, and the maxims of formal rationality, he replaces the transcendental critique of Kant with a genealogical and historical critique of practical reason. Kant's moral abstractionism and his retreat into the formal conditions for moral action are rejected by Nietzsche. That is, he places the issue of the formation of moral consciousness and the principles of moral law within the context of a history of moral thought in general. It appears that he took Hegel's critique of Kant's moral abstractionism seriously.

Nietzsche constructs a psychology of utilitarianism and a sociology of knowledge within noble cultures. As with Hegel, he agrees that the origins of the principles of morality lie in the master-slave conflict. The determination of good and evil, beautiful and ugly, right and wrong is defined ultimately by their utility and their expression of the needs of the ruling class in society. They are expressions of the initial power relations of the aristocracy whose political and economic power is manifested in its ability to use language, define terms, and categorize human action as good or bad. Tracing the etymology of the concepts of the "good" and the "bad" in a variety of different languages from Greek and Latin, Gaelic, Iranian and Slavic, to English and German, Nietzsche contends that the words themselves reflect class power and prejudices. That which reflects the aristocracy is considered noble, good, and beautiful. That which comes from the common people is considered base and evil.

However, according to Nietzsche, there was a transfiguration of values within Hebrew society, which began a process of moral inversion. Whereas previously the strong, powerful, and noble in a pathos of distance defined the highest moral characteristics, among the Hebrews, it was the poor and weak victims of oppression who began to define an inverted and distorted value system. These ideals stressed a paralysis of the will, the passivity of the poor of spirit, the humbleness and impotence of the downtrodden, and a morality of meekness. This is the morality of the humiliated. And with the Hebrews came the impulse to level individual distinctions based on class power, strength of character, individual aggressiveness, and noble birth. Compassion, pity, and weakness became the new cultural norms reflecting a radical transformation of the accepted moral values in society. The Hebrews had taken revenge on their Babylonian captors and turned defeat and humiliation into the degradation of humanity. To justify and explain away their weaknesses, they projected their failings onto their conquerors. Nietzsche explains this through a psychology of rage, inverted cruelty, and unconscious projection of hatred and fear in the form of sublimated ideals at the pain caused by defeat and exile. It was the strong aristocracy that was seen as having all the bad characteristics. Nietzsche calls this slave revolt in morals "the sublimest hatred in human history."[66] This suppressed hatred and sublime vindictiveness, this moral domestication of the victors became part of the foundations of later Christian morality and the liberal politics of *ressentiment*, which, in turn, led to the madness of nihilism. The result is that

> The leveling and diminution of European man is our greatest danger, because the sight of him makes us despond. We no longer see anything these days that aspires to grow greater. . . . This is Europe's true predicament: together with the fear of man we have also lost the love of man, reverence for man, confidence in man, indeed the *will to power*. Now the sight of man makes us despond. What is nihilism today if not that?[67]

For Nietzsche, this slave revolt and herd morality of the Hebrews, as a "conspiracy of the sufferers," has infected the whole religious, moral, and political value system of the West. It has created a perverse social system in which the lowest common denominator in society, the meanest and most superficial values, and the most common and weakest individuals are placed first. Equality before God, before the law, or before scientific objectivity, as well as Christian rights to redemption or the natural rights of liberalism, all reduce moral excellence, personal effort and achievement, and individual struggle and suffering to deviant and unacceptable behavior. Power and strength are distrusted as religiously sinful, passionate intrusions on objectivity, or socially inegalitarian. Slave morality was able to hide its ideology by calling its retribution and vengeance "justice" in the kingdom of God or "justice" in a democratic society. The ideals of the Christian heaven and French Revolution, salvation and democracy became the ideologies of *ressentiment*. The weak were able to repay their military, political, and economic failures by capturing and defining the cultural values of society.

Willing History Backwards and the Redemption of Time

There is a very intricate and subtle relationship in Nietzsche's writings among his different views of history, temporality, the will to power, genealogical critique, and the myth of eternal return. "We have to realize to what degree we are the *creators* of our value feelings—and thus capable of projecting 'meaning' into history."[68] Just as Nietzsche rejected the existence of an independent objectivity, thing-in-itself, and ego, he also turned his critical method to the issue of human creativity and temporality. As has been noted by secondary interpreters, Nietzsche's theory of eternal return and will to power appear to be contradictory.[69] The former is apparently tied to the belief in an identical, continuous, and unchanging return of past events and experiences.[70] This may account for Zarathustra's nausea and horror at hearing this doctrine for the first time. It had to be whispered by the demon, since it was so unspeakable. "My formula for greatness in a man is *amor fati*: the fact that a man wishes nothing to be different, either in front of him or behind him, or for all eternity. Not only must the necessity be borne, and on no account concealed—all idealism is falsehood in the face of necessity—but it must also be loved."[71] The theory of eternal return is mentioned in the *Gay Science*, developed in *Thus Spoke Zarathustra*, and reaffirmed in *The Will to Power*. In the *Gay Science*, Nietzsche writes, "This life as you now live it and have lived it, you will have to live once more and innumerable times more; and there will be nothing new in it, but every pain and every joy and every thought and every sigh and everything unutterably small or great in your life will have to return to you."[72]

The theory of the will to power, on the other hand, stresses the openness and freedom of human willing in the future. Willing history, however, is made impossible if the past is monotonously and eternally being renewed in the same way each time. There would be no novelty, freedom, becoming, or self-overcoming: there would be no future, only the tiresome and burdensome repetition of the past into the present. And this same past is that of Christian slave morality with its *ressentiment* and revenge. If the past were to eternally repeat itself in the same manner each time, there would be no possibility of self-overcoming.

It is Alexander Nehamas in his work *Nietzsche: Life as Literature* who makes the interesting connection between the notions of eternal return and the thing-in-itself. Nietzsche has argued that there is no "will," "self," "causes," or "objects." In this critique of identity and substance, everything is related to everything else and it is impossible to wrench from the complexity of becoming specific loci of a distinct and separate faculty of mind or distinct objects and causes of experience. Nehamas has written, "The parts of these events are essentially connected with one another, and where one part ends and another begins is as undecidable an issue as the question of the nature of the whole event of which they are parts."[73] Consciousness has created a fictitious world of discrete objects, subjects, and causal relationships that appear independent of their effects and relationships.

In reality, there are only hypothetical interpretations and linguistic constructs. As Nietzsche has said, there are no underlying features, no universal essences, no foundations, and no enduring substances.[74] There is only nothing. As we have already seen, this represents a rejection of the whole metaphysical foundation of Western philosophy and psychology, and especially the Kantian notion of the thing-in-itself (independent objects or subjective faculties). He also treats "time" in the same way. Just as the subject is a multiplicity of its properties, relationships, effects, experiences, and actions, temporal dimensions are also integrated constructions. As he writes in *The Genealogy of Morals*, "There is no 'being' behind the doing, acting, becoming; 'the doer' has simply been added to the deed by the imagination—the doing is everything."[75] When we look at Nietzsche's *The Use and Abuse of History*, this point becomes even clearer.

> Yet it is a superstition to believe that the picture which things produce in man in such a state of mind reproduces the empirical essence of those things. . . . To think history objectively in this manner is the silent work of the dramatist; that is, to think everything in conjunction, to weave a whole out of the isolated: everywhere with the presupposition that a unity of plan must be put into things if it is not there. So man spins his web over the past and subdues it, so his impulse to art expresses itself.[76]

There seems to be an underlying coherent theme throughout Nietzsche's works on epistemology, history, and time. Just as there is no independent reality behind the appearances, there is no independent or objective time behind the present. History contains no inherent order, meaning, or telos: it, too, is nothing. Temporal and spatial objectivity is created by the form-structuring principles of the mind. Just as the self and objects are constructed according to their relationships, history is a construct and perspective of memory. Given Nietzsche's critique of metaphysics and Cartesian epistemology, there is no past to be eternally reconstructed or returned. Debra Bergoffen has written, "Thus there can be no such thing as a factual past, if by factual we mean independently objective. History is always the past in relationship to a subject. . . . For in the same way that perceptions are structured by the perceiving organism, memories are structured by the remembering subject."[77] There is no objectivity, only nothingness and a multiplicity of perspectives.

What Nietzsche appears to be doing is providing an argument similar to his critique of the thing-in-itself. In fact, the story of the eternal return is simply a rejection of reified time in the same manner that he rejected the existence of reified space. Eternal return is the temporal correlate of the issues surrounding the spatial concept of the thing-in-itself. Just as there is nothing behind the interpretations and perspectives of the objects of experience, there is nothing behind the present in the form of an objectified past.[78] The acceptance and affirmation of the present moment requires that all the relationships and actions that led to the present (the past) must be accepted also.

Nehamas responds to the apparent incomprehensibility of Nietzsche's thought by taking the position that though the occurrences of an action are given in the past, the interpretation, emphasis, and importance of that action from the perspective of the present can and do change. When reconsidering the past, living in the present, and accepting the theory of eternal return, we have, in fact, altered the past by giving it a new interpretation and meaning. By so changing the past, the future lies open to new narratives and discourses and thus to new modes of living. In this way, Nietzsche's historical transformations and reconstructions of moral history free the individual from resentment and despair. A new horizon of discursive and ethical possibilities opens up. This is certainly one of the main reasons behind Nietzsche's genealogical critiques. The future and present free the past of its reified and fetishized form. Present life is reaffirmed; the future is a creative and destructive process of constructing new forms of being and new modes of existence. The notion of eternal return reinforms and reinforces the temporal dimensions of Dionysian wisdom and tragic insight.

When looked at from the perspective of the reification and false objectification of time, Nietzsche's theories of *amor fati* and eternal return, of willing backwards and genealogical reconstruction (focus on the past), are integrated into his theory of the creative life force of the will to power that incorporates and frees the past, present, and future. Unless the past is revalued and transfigured into something that has been willed and justified by the acting individual, the present and the

future are weighed down by an unbridgeable abyss. And the individual
is always defined and determined by the past. To free the future, the
past must also be freed and transformed.

> But now learn this too: the will itself is still a prisoner. Willing liberates;
> but what is it that puts even the liberator himself in fetters? "It was"—
> that is the name of the will's gnashing of teeth and most secret melan-
> choly. Powerless against what has been done, he is an angry spectator of
> all that is past. The will cannot will backwards; and that he cannot break
> time and time's covetousness, that is the will's loneliest melancholy.[79]

However, the past is constantly being redefined and reinterpreted.
Nietzsche states, "I walk among men as among the fragments of the
future—that future which I envisage. And this is all my creating and
striving."[80] Nehamas has stressed that though Nietzsche rejected
Christianity and its ascetic ideal as a form of cultural decadence, it
still performed an unintended function of indirectly preserving and
enhancing the value of life. In a similar manner, Nietzsche reinterprets
the history of moral thought using his categories of master/slave
morality. The past is being continuously reconstructed and transfigured according to the perspectives of the present. History is reconstructed and rewilled: it is a temporal construct. The will has moved
from being a mechanism of folly, punishment, guilt, and revenge in the
theodicy of Christianity to becoming its own "redeemer and joy-
bringer." Since the past, present, and future are so tightly interwoven,
any new perspectives, series of questions, or interpretations change
the perception and experience of the past. According to Nietzsche, the
past can be rewilled. "All 'it was' is a fragment, a riddle, a dreadful
accident—until the creative will says to it, 'But thus I willed it.' "[81] By
this means, time is reconciled and redeemed. In fact, the individual
moves beyond time itself, since the latter becomes just another dimension in the creative process of the will to power.

Toward this end, Nietzsche develops his theory of eternal return as
a reaction to the nineteenth-century fervor of stressing the beyond and
ignoring past pains and problems, of ignoring existence and present
meaning, and of ignoring the necessity to struggle and create in life.
Never truly developed, he nevertheless argues that it is a response to
the use of universals and ideals among the Greeks and their continuation in modernity. The notion of an eternal return calls for a revival of
the orgiastic spirit of Dionysus and the continuous renewal of life and
return of the past. The infinite forms of renewal reflect not an accep-

tance of the recurrence of the past or even of particular events in the past. This would just be another form of idolatry. The principle of eternal return represents a critique of both the past and the future (death). It is a joyous celebration of the mysteries of life beyond good and evil and "beyond all death and change." It does not deny pain but includes past sufferings in the constant renewal of the present. Nietzsche is radically altering the temporal dimension so the past becomes a constant companion to the present and must be so recognized. Only then is the future rescued from moral and political ideals of the beyond. Humanity is finally turned into a being that creates beyond itself: "I am *that which must always overcome itself.*"[82] This is analogous, for Nietzsche, to the birthing process where pain gives birth to life and the "eternal joy of creating."[83]

In *Beyond Good and Evil* (1886), Nietzsche returns to this theme, which is not a form of fatalism or resignation to the past. This latter approach would again turn time into an idolatrous object. With his theory of eternal return, Nietzsche is able to distinguish between the different moments of temporality and history. That is, it represents a widening of his moral epistemology and history of moral reasoning found in *The Genealogy of Morals*, since it places history within a broader context of a philosophy of time. What this means is that the "genuine philosopher" must reappropriate all past events and experiences. The various claims to moral truth from eudaimonism, hedonism, pessimism, and utilitarianism to liberalism are incorporated into his or her overview of moral knowledge. He or she must move easily through the various forms of dogmatism, skepticism, fatalism, moral critique, and free thinking. If there are no facts or truths, and if the "in itself" of the world is nothingness and meaninglessness, and if the only value is creativity in the act of suffering, then the belief in an eternal return provides the philosopher with the opportunity to reconstruct the objectified past within the will to power and beauty— "to overpower the past." It means that all of human history can now come under the sway of the artist and be re-created according to his or her value judgments. "But they grope with the creative hands toward the future—everything that is and was becomes their means, their instrument, their hammer. Their 'knowing' is *creating*. Their creating legislative. Their will to truth is—*will to power.*"[84]

Future possibilities are opened up as the past is converted into an instrument of creativity. The past is not dead and gone forever, but becomes a living moment in the search for meaning and purpose in life. Time itself expresses the joy and exuberance for life. The moral ideals and political formulas of the past are salvaged from the abyss of nothingness and recreated to form a new meaning and life. The fetishism of past religions and philosophies, the claims of Christian moralism and scientific objectivism, the idols of the past are converted into the possibilities of the future. Former ideals and moral tyranny become means toward the furtherance of life. The moral hypocrisy and bad conscience of those who claimed universal knowledge and absolute truth are revealed. The fatalism and objectivism of the iron cage are overcome and what was once ossified in the past becomes an expression of people's will to power toward a new future. Creativity and moral self-legislation require that the individual incorporate past events into future possibilities. This alone makes it possible for humanity to be great, to be master of its own virtues, to define its own possibilities, and to create a moral universe that is beyond the static formulas of good and evil.

> Faced with a world of "modern ideas" that would like to lock everyone into a corner and "specialty" of his own, a philosopher would be forced to see the greatness of man, the very concept of "greatness," in all man's magnitude and multiplicity, in his "oneness in the many." He would determine human worth and rank by the amount and variety that an individual could carry within himself, by the *distance* his responsibility could span.[85]

The eternal return also has an exegetical and interpretive component, since it is part of Nietzsche's theory of critical hermeneutics. The past must be relived at least so that it is not lost beneath the interpretations of the weak and sick values of modernity. The strengths of the past must be saved for future generations.[86] In his critical hermeneutics, he views history as an important part of the interpretation of a text in which the past is recreated in the present and becomes part of the will to power's projection of future possibilities. The notion of the eternal return lessens the temporal distance between the past, present, and future and makes time itself a component in the fight for existence and meaning. That is why Nietzsche's theory of Greek tragedy in *The Birth of Tragedy* (1872) is placed within a wider critique of science and modernity. This is also why the Greek tragic vision and struggle within the abyss is part of the very joy and struggle for existence today. This connects Oedipus and Prometheus with a rejection of the "last man" and celebration of the *Übermensch*.

There is an even more radical treatment of the past in *Thus Spoke*

Zarathustra. In the second part of this work, Nietzsche contends that the past is a power over humankind, because it was never willed by individuals. Thus, liberation and freedom today require that we rewill the past, demand a return of the past, so that it can be made to conform to the will to power. It is not enough that we in the present be liberated, the past must be freed also. Since we cannot return to the past, the past must be forced into the present and rewilled. History must be created anew. "To redeem those who lived in the past and to recreate all 'it was' into a 'thus I willed it'—that alone should I call redemption."[87] Without this, the will is a prisoner to the objectivity of the past; in the same way, in Christianity and socialism, the will is a prisoner to the fetishism of the future. In fact, this apparent inability to change time results in a melancholy of the past and a revenge against time. Nietzsche sees this as a cause of the fixation upon and fetishism of the future. On the other hand, it is life, existence, and the present that must be liberated from a false temporality.

From the past, there are two crucial elements that are difficult to deal with: the first is the suffering associated with creativity, and the second is the inability to rewill the past. This is the temporal dilemma. While the past is unapproachable and the future lies in a "beyond," the present is depreciated into an arena of revenge, sin, and punishment that has no intrinsic worth and whose value is something always yet to be achieved until the will takes back its own history. In *Thus Spoke Zarathustra*, Nietzsche argues that the will must recognize the past as its own creation. This can be facilitated through a psychological belief that the past can return and can be recreated. In his later writings, this idea is developed into his theory of eternal return. In the early stage of its development, one can read a strong Hegelian element in his ideas. The truth of objectivity (i.e., past events and experiences) lies in subjectivity (i.e., self-consciousness and will). Whereas Hegel wanted to reconcile the Objective Spirit in the future realization of absolute truth, Nietzsche's goal is to reincorporate the past and future into a reconciled present. Hegel wished to liberate the mind from time; Nietzsche wishes to liberate time itself. His theory is another manifestation of the will to power.

Remembering Antiquity through Whispers of the Past

Both *The Genealogy of Morals* (1887) and *Twilight of the Idols* (1889) end with a recapitulation of Nietzsche's foundational themes from *The Birth of Tragedy* (1872). Humanity's possibilities lie in the recognition that it is a beautiful, spiritual being who suffers. *The Genealogy of Morals* concludes on a positive note that the breakdown of Christian ethics is necessary, since it has outlived its life function and because humankind is becoming more self-critical by examining the foundations of its own knowledge and will to truth. Even though Nietzsche has been critical of the humiliation and depreciation of human worth and dignity, traditional metaphysics with its core of guilt and punishment provided men and women some mythological protection from the nothingness of reality. Even in its distorting form, the will to power as the Christian ascetic ideal gave some expression to individual creativity and need for theodicy.

> Man, the most courageous animal and the most inured to trouble, does not deny suffering *per se*; he wants it, he seeks it out, provided that it can be given a meaning. Finally the ascetic ideal arose to give it meaning—its only meaning, so far. But any meaning is better than none and, in fact, the ascetic ideal has been the best stopgap that ever existed. Suffering had been interpreted, the door to all suicidal nihilism slammed shut.[88]

Though the Greeks are not mentioned, one can feel their eternal presence waiting in the background. They provided humankind with the noblest of reasons for enduring and persevering. The meaning of existences lies not in nature but in the very act of responding to the presence of human suffering. The decadence of Christianity, with its bad conscience and ascetic ideals of self-denial, rejection of sensuousness and sexuality, fear of happiness, reason, and beauty, and anticipation of afterlife, at least provided some respite from the anxiety and pain of everyday life. This is true in spite of the fact that Christianity "signifies a will to nothingness, a revulsion from life, a rebellion against the principal conditions of living. And yet, despite everything, it is and remains a *will*."[89]

It is not the particular form of the ideals of the will, but the will to life itself, the affirmation of life, and the self-affirmation of individual potential, that are the central defining ideas of Nietzsche. At the conclusion of *Twilight of the Idols*, it is just this exuberance for life that he expresses in his notion of eternal return. It is the affirmation of existence in its past, present, and future. It is here he also reconfirms his own insight into the nature of tragedy. Leslie Thiele contends that this represents a return to Heraclitus's view that truth results from rapture and intuitions and not logic and reason.[90] Rejecting Schopenhauer's pessimism and Aristotle's wish to be liberated from pity and terror through catharsis, Nietzsche reaffirmed the Greek struggle in the face of suffering: the continuous creation of new meaning and values, the attack on natural laws and the traditional moral order, the unquenchable thirst for knowledge and wisdom, and life as the possibility for power, beauty, and meaning.[91] Modernity has been revaluated, and with the eternal return, antiquity has been reincorporated into the present. The children of Oedipus continue to play out the meaning of their lives in a new age of Dionysian tragedy. But it is a tragedy with a purpose that is "to be *oneself* the eternal joy of becoming, beyond all terror and pity."[92]

Near the end of *Beyond Good and Evil*, Nietzsche states that humanity must retain four key virtues: courage, insight, fellow-feeling, and solitude. This unusual combination of virtues seems to parallel Aristotle's *Nicomachean Ethics*, as he moves from moral virtues (books II–V), to intellectual virtue (book VI) and friendship (books VIII and IX), to happiness and contemplation (book X). For Nietzsche, these are the values of superiority and strength of a warrior society, the Greek polis, and aristocratic morality. And they are opposed to those values of Christianity and slave morality that stressed the altruism of tolerance, pity, *désintéressement*, and modesty. They are the values that manifest human dignity and bring to a dialectical close the distinguishing values of both the genius of the ancients—Aristotle— and the genius of the moderns—Kant. And with the bridging of these two worlds, there is praise for the centrality, dignity, and even divinity of human beings. Nietzsche presents us with an ethics of moral striving and self-overcoming that is a Dionysian ethics. But it is ultimately an ethics that, in the process of breaking with traditional metaphysics and epistemology, created its own language and method of presentation.

Part III

Unbinding Prometheus: Expanding Classical Imagination and Vision in Nineteenth-Century Germany

Chapter Seven

Bridging Madness and Reason: An Untimely Mediation of Marx and Nietzsche

Though they are very different in approaches and conclusions, the very differences between Marx and Nietzsche will highlight their individual strengths and weaknesses, as well as possible areas for further development of their thought. Between them lies the possibility of removing the distance between ethics and science, politics and knowledge, equality and moral excellence; and between them we may map Thermopylae and its virtues and Parnassos and its wisdom. Whether defending their ideals and underlying values of autonomy, freedom, and creativity; or making a stand for human potentiality, self-realization, and individual development; or even searching metaphorically through the ethereal home of Apollo and Dionysus on Mt. Parnassos, the traditional distance between Marx and Nietzsche may be lessened.[1] They are both Promethean characters struggling against the moral limitations and lack of imagination in their societies.

They lived in worlds that they rejected, claiming that the appearances of reality were artificial illusions, scientific fetishisms, and political ideologies. One searched deep into the structures and layers of capitalist political economy, while the other sought his truth in the Dionysian terrors and horrors of human existence as expressed in Greek tragedy and the modern philosophy of Kant and Schopenhauer. During their searches one found the horrors of existence in social exploitation and economic alienation and the other found it in the suffering and pain produced by a meaningless world. In reaction to these realities, one turned to Aristotle's ethical and political criticism of the market economy and to Epicurus's rejection of Democritean

301

science and physics, while the other turned to the discussions about being and becoming in the works of Heraclitus, Parmenides, and Anaxagoras and to the tragic vision of Aeschylus and Sophocles.

Steeped in the classical tradition, they sought answers to the tragedy of modernity in the ancients. Marx interpreted the Industrial Revolution and the theories of classical political economy through the eyes of Aristotle's theory of unnatural chrematistics and moral economics found in his *Nicomachean Ethics* and *Politics*. We have seen that at every stage in the development of his major economic and sociological ideas in *Capital*, Marx evoked the ethical and political writings of Aristotle for moral enlightenment and critical direction. Aristotle's theory of social justice guided his vision and turned *Capital* into an ethical treatise. Throughout the first volume of *Capital*, Aristotle's theory of market equality and commensurability, economics and chrematistics, moral economy and political economy, household needs and market wants, use value and exchange value, commerce and profit making, merchants' capital and moneylenders' capital, and civic friendship and political freedom are used to help explain and critique ethically market liberalism and capitalist production. Marx's theory of moral economy and his rejection of liberalism is grounded in the insights and values of classical democracy and Greek society. Aristotle's conclusions that the market, profit accumulation, and class formation undermine friendship, the household, political stability and economic order, social equality and political democracy, and human happiness were incorporated directly into Marx's theory of social justice. He went beyond Aristotle to show that with these market developments under capitalism came labor exploitation, alienation, and economic crises that demand social change. Marx's theories of abstract labor, surplus value, and capitalist production were built upon Aristotle's understanding of the ethics of market behavior. And it is upon this foundation that his views of political and human emancipation, social justice, and economic democracy ultimately rest.

Nietzsche found the will to power, which inspired him to challenge life, realize self-potential, and create a meaningful world in all its cultural expressions, in the Greek tragedies of Oedipus and Prometheus. Rejecting the deep pessimism and resignation of Schopenhauer as well as the giddy and naïve reconciliation of Schiller, he moved into new territory to reestablish the primacy of individual aesthetic activity and self-overcoming. By means of a dialectical synthesis of the Dionysian and Apollonian artistic powers of creativity and redemption, he intended to recapture the divinity and nobility of humanity. Through dramatic illusions, the intoxicated rapture of creative spirits, the aesthetic transformation of human experience, and the triumphant serenity and metaphysical solace produced in artistic forms, life became joyful, meaningful, and worth living. Through the creativity and destruction, happiness and horrors performed in Greek tragedy, life became transformed into a noble and sublime experience of the tragic vision. Upon the moral abyss, the wretchedness and despair of human life, and the irrationalities of the world, the will to power constructed a world of beauty, harmony, and peace. Nietzsche's early work on Greek philosophy expanded these insights. According to Nietzsche's interpretation of pre-Platonic philosophy, the categories of Greek physics from Thales to Anaxagoras were projections of the forms of human consciousness itself. Physics, in its attempt to find the underlying essence of reality in being or becoming, water or fire, the one or the many, is a mixture of anthropomorphic metaphors and ethical categories. It is, in fact, the human mind searching for itself in nature. Nietzsche read the insights of German Idealism back into early Greek philosophy in his claim that the truth of nature and objectivity is subjectivity. Philosophy and drama are two means by which the Greeks brought order, meaning, and objective reality to their experience of nothingness within the void.

Marx and Nietzsche reflected the challenge of nineteenth-century Germany to the hegemony of the British tradition of science and morality in the face of the onslaught of modernity and liberalism. They represented different extremes held together by a common thread of interest in the issues of scientific objectivity and moral creativity. They challenged the orthodox epistemological views about the nature of objectivity, perception, and consciousness. By so doing, they challenged the very possibilities of traditional knowledge, as well as defended the centrality of the principles of the moral subject and human dignity.

Marx's critique of political economy evolved out of eighteenth- and nineteenth-century German philosophy: Kant's critical theory of objectivity and subjectivity, Hegel's theory of objective culture and history, and his own rejection of British positivism and economic theory. In the process, Marx forged a criticism of empiricism and rationalism in his theory of objectivity, developed truth-claims and a validation process through immanent critique and *praxis*, and finished his career with a daring recasting of political economy. By radicalizing Kant, Marx transcended traditional epistemologies and searched for alternative methodologies and theories of knowledge. In his *Early*

Economic and Philosophic Writings (1844), the *Theses on Feuerbach* (1845), *The Poverty of Philosophy* (1847), and his later economic writings, Marx's concept of *praxis* was turned into an epistemological category, which had important implications for his theory of the formation of consciousness (subjectivity) and the objects of experience (objectivity). There is no objectivity in the traditional sense of the category as defined by both rationalism and empiricism. That is, there are no pure objects unmediated by human consciousness and directly mirrored through sense experience. There are no preexisting, unstructured, pure facts, which are reflected onto the mind in a moment of intuitive self-examination or the act of perception. Objectivity is always a constitutive act involving social experience, understanding, and work. Thus, the methodology of the social sciences must reflect this more developed epistemology, which is critically aimed at the positivism of British political economists Smith, Ricardo, and Malthus.

Nietzsche, in turn, with the development of his theory of language and perspectivism, pushed the implications of Kant's *Critique of Pure Reason* to their logical conclusions in the form of a radical and creative individualism (*Übermensch*). Self-overcoming even overcomes illusory objectivity and truth. Science and metaphysics are shown by Nietzsche to be metaphorical constructs and conceptual perspectives whose purpose is to give the semblance of order and coherence to the world. This enables the will to dominate and survive in a constantly changing universe. By moving beyond and expanding the epistemologies of Kant and Hegel, Nietzsche expanded the application of the critical method toward a critique of epistemology itself (i.e., a critique of foundationalism). With the loss of objectivity and the foundations of knowledge, there is also a loss of subjectivity and consciousness. All reality becomes an expression of anthropomorphic constructs and mythological creations that attempt to give meaning and purpose in an otherwise absurd and meaningless world. Aesthetic, ethical, and theological categories shield us from the nothingness of reality, while supplying us with the artificial beauty, morals, and religion that make life worthwhile. All reality is an illusory and relative projection of the categories of the human mind and reflection of our own forms of consciousness. From the Greek tragedies, Socratic philosophy, Christian theology, and Newtonian rationalism, there is a continuous need to construct a world of objects, interrelationships, and morality into a coherent pattern of meaning, values, and order. They are ontological fictions, theoretical abstractions, and ghostly schematizations, but they also represent the continuous human will to power and physiological drive to overcome the terror, pain, and suffering, even for a brief moment of time, that it is human fate to endure. But in modern times, this world has collapsed, resulting in a decadent and nihilistic universe, which stands at a new age of tragic vision. That which inspires Nietzsche to move beyond the despair of the abyss is the striving and creativity of the individual. This is what makes us human and what gives life its ultimate purpose and boundless joy.

Schooled in the history of philosophy, Marx and Nietzsche reacted strongly to what they perceived as serious flaws in Kant's transcendental subjectivity and categorical imperative. They responded to his critique of the correspondence theory of truth (separation and correspondence of subject and object, knower and known) and the inadequacies of its replacement by his constitution theory of truth (synthesis of objectivity and subjectivity, sensation and understanding). Both returned to Hume's original problem of the dilemma of objective validity, and in the process, they moved beyond German Idealism. They picked up the central epistemological issue: how are concepts of the mind justified and philosophically related to reality? How do we know that our concepts reflect the external objective world as it really is? Kant's use of the categories of the transcendental unity of apperception and the critical imagination were viewed as an advance on traditional epistemology, but still remained tied to an absolute and orthodox metaphysics.

There was no longer a privileged access to truth either through sense perception or clear and distinct ideas. With the questioning of a belief in ontology and the existence of pure objects of perception as things-in-themselves, the possibility of a theory of knowledge that is objectively true also became problematic. Science or pure theory cannot be the foundation for knowledge and truth-claims, since the justification of any particular theory of knowledge as true becomes impossible. For Hegel and Marx, there are no foundations (epistemologies) for any possible truth-claims, because these foundations are also claims to absolute truth, which are themselves beyond justification. For Nietzsche, there are no objective (substance, causality, and so on) or subjective (ego or self) realities that can act as a reference or validation point for truth-claims. There is only the abyss of nothingness and absurdity. This explains Marx's move to immanent critique and a democratic ethics of participation (an ethics of discourse) and Nietzsche's theory of epistemological nihilism and perspectivism. However critical Marx may have been of traditional epistemology, he never pushed his arguments to the radical extremes of Nietzsche.

This is where the comparison of Marx and Nietzsche becomes even more fascinating. Hegel, too, had radicalized Kantian epistemology by arguing that a constitution theory of truth must be supplemented by a phenomenological reconstruction of subjectivity and objectivity: reconstruction of individual consciousness, the objects of cultural experience, and social institutions in history. This is what he meant by the "phenomenology of spirit." Marx and Nietzsche pushed Hegel's dialectical theory even further with the former's theory of the dialectical critique of capitalism and notion of "theory and practice" and the latter's theory of perspectivism (interpretive knowledge resulting from perceptual metaphors). Experience and knowledge are constituted in social and historical processes that involve the active participation of consciousness itself. The emphasis is clearly on the process of attaining knowledge (activity or *praxis*), not on reaching a final product (knowledge of being). In fact, it is the latter that has become questionable in their theories of knowledge.

Both stressed the creative and dynamic process by which the knower becomes actively involved in constituting objectivity, experience, and knowledge. They have deconstructed the work of Kant and have placed it within a broader understanding of the historical formation of Western consciousness with dialectical and genealogical critiques. According to Marx, the formation of consciousness is filtered through the institutions of the workplace, the structural and historical development of commodity production, and the ideology of political economy, whereas Nietzsche focused on the cultural development of Western metaphysics, religion, science, and nihilism. To accomplish their goals, they used the method of "critique" applied by the former in his critique of political economy and by the latter in his genealogy, or phenomenology, of herd morality. The traditional distinctions between subjectivity and objectivity, facts and values, theory and reality, truth and illusion are all called into question. Because the objects of experience are historical products or "perspectives," a full comprehension of experience is possible only by tracing its development from its origins. This critical approach of returning to the roots of objectivity (i.e., objects of experience), for Marx, involved a rethinking of capitalism through an analysis of the contradictions between use value and exchange value in market exchange and commodity production. For Nietzsche, it meant an interpretive study of the psychological and sociological origins of morality and religion with their beliefs in a transcendent truth. They began their writings with a high degree of skepticism, a radicalization of the phenomenological and dialectical method of Hegel, moved for a brief, but noticeable period of time into positivism, and then developed their later writings with an eye to the radical critique of science, positivism, and epistemology itself.

But lest the reader see too much of a consistent pattern here, it should be recognized that both authors also held contradictory positions on some of these epistemological issues. Unresolved within the thought of both thinkers are the apparent contradictions between their theories of knowledge and rejection of traditional epistemologies and their beliefs in certain objective moral claims, whether it is the Kantian or Aristotelian ethics at the heart of Marx's critique of capitalism or the ethics of self-realization and overcoming of the *Übermensch* at the heart of Nietzsche's philosophy. While Marx rejected traditional theories of knowledge and methods of verification, pure philosophy and theoretical abstractionism, and absolute claims to knowledge and truth, he spent most of his time in *Capital* examining the historical and empirical details of capitalist production and evolution. What was the metatheoretical basis for his claims to historical knowledge and understanding? He also criticized economic liberalism from Kantian and Aristotelian perspectives. These apparent contradictions between social critique and historical research have not been examined carefully in the secondary literature. In turn, Nietzsche's transcendence of Kantianism; his critique of epistemology and foundationalism; his theory of drama, language, and metaphors; as well as his epistemological nihilism must be confronted by the apparent contradictory claims of his theory of perspectivism and moral theory of self-overcoming. At times, their theories and conclusions do not match their underlying epistemological assumptions and methodological procedures.

By attacking the positivism of British political economy (Marx) and the natural sciences (Nietzsche), and their "cult of objectivity," they anticipated many of the arguments that developed in twentieth-century postanalytic philosophy of science. That is, they anticipated in their theories the postmodern criticisms of positivism. With the critique of science, they also turned their attention to the critique of universal and absolute ethical principles and moral imperatives. They rejected what they saw as the tyranny of moral rationality and its prison of objectivity, as well as its corresponding forms of universal moral and religious truths. Though different in their methods, styles of presentation, and general philosophical orientations and conclusions, they did wrestle with similar problems, returned to the lofty heights of the Acropolis to get better perspectives on the issues of modernity, and were prominent figures in the evolution of German skepticism and romanticism.

Marx, because of his theory of historical materialism, and Nietzsche, because of his theory of moral nihilism, have been criticized for
not having a theory of ethics. Ethics, according to their critics, would
result in either a "political ideology" or a "slave morality." In either
case, according to these interpretations, cultural products simply reflect the material, social, and psychological conditions of reality. This
is a form of crude materialism and does not reflect the complexity of
either author's view of ethics. From their perspectives, the reduction
of ethics to a cultural epiphenomenon undermines the possibility of
human dignity and respect for the "value-positing" nature of humankind that lies at the heart of their individual criticisms of reified
economic and moral systems. Instead, they have argued that people
are free when they transcend traditional morality based on the subjugation of individuals to the tyranny of external authority and the prison
of their own abstract reason. This is what Nietzsche called *decadence*:
a "subject without aim or purpose,"[2] which, in turn, has resulted in
the historical evolution of *moral nihilism*, reflecting a world without
meaning or values. Marx called it alienation.

Like Marx, Nietzsche was critical of idealism for he, too, recognized
that he had no ideals to realize, since ideals are disembodied forms
that are abstracted from existence and imposed upon individuals from
the outside. Marx and Nietzsche continued to move beyond Kant's
moral imperative that maintained that true freedom required the subject to become its own moral self-legislature; that is, it required the
subject to determine its own moral laws from within itself. Marx
emphasized this idea in the context of political and economic relations,
whereas Nietzsche stressed it in relation to morality and culture. In
the *Theses on Feuerbach* and *The Will to Power*, there was a general
condemnation of the "scholasticism" of theory and values in which
consciousness and thought are abstracted from the reality of *"praxis"*
and "existence." This represents a modern evaluation and use of
Aristotle's principle of *phronesis* found in his *Nicomachean Ethics*.
Theory, knowledge, and truth about the social and political worlds
cannot be abstracted from these worlds in the form of transcendent
moral, political, or scientific truths. For both German philosophers,
knowledge is something that develops through contact with the "practical world" in our everyday lived experiences. It is provisional without being relative, historical without being historicist.

Marx and Nietzsche, by rediscovering the value of Greek ethics
and political philosophy for modern thought, revived the power and
relevancy of Aristotle's distinctions among *phronesis* (practical wis-

dom), *techne* (technical knowledge), and *theoria* (philosophical contemplation). In their criticisms of alienation and decadence, in their understanding of theory and history, they returned to Aristotle's ethical writings for intellectual and spiritual guidance. Marx's discussion of political knowledge and action and Nietzsche's view of history and critique of traditional rationality and truth harkened back to these Aristotelian distinctions. They viewed ethics as a moral imperative to "overcome" and to transcend the blind objectivity and truth of positivism as individuals express their being in the process of the becoming and creation of their everyday worlds. Moral knowledge involves an interpretive act for the purpose of creating the self as a moral whole. From this perspective, modern forms of moral activity and knowing only result in fragmented experiences, alienated selves, and a rationalized universe without meaning or purpose. Toward this end, Marx turned toward Aristotle and the post-Aristotelian philosophy of nature of Democritus and Epicurus, whereas Nietzsche sought further inspiration from the pre-Platonists: Heraclitus, Parmenides, and Anaxagoras. Just as they sought to remake the objective and subjective worlds of experience, they attempted to recapture and remake the temporal dimension itself. Time and history would be reconstructed by means of a self-conscious recognition of the oppressive power of political ideologies, economic formulas, unconscious repression, and social institutions. Whether through dialectical science and immanent critique or through the myth of eternal return and *amor fati*, the past would be transfigured through a living *praxis* that would precipitate a new age of revolution and socialism or a new age of tragic vision and human dignity.

Both had returned to the ancient Greek philosophers in order to revitalize and reanimate their criticisms of liberalism and modern society. They found the isolation, terror, and loss of community within Kantianism and liberalism oppressive. Whether it was the ideology of British political economy and Left Hegelians or the decadence of Platonic rationalism and Christianity, their criticisms of modernity were filtered through their understanding of Greek social and aesthetic thought. Both had been suspicious of the mainstays of modernity and its philosophical underpinnings: Cartesian metaphysics, liberalism, individualism, the split between subject and object, the idolatrous belief in science and positivism, and the possibility of epistemological certainty and truth. They are the most prominent nineteenth-century critics of modernity; their works continue to influence those who came after them through the renewed inspiration of the ancients; and their ideas continue to be pushed beyond the present to a postmodern world.

They understood morality, philosophy, religion, and science as cultural expressions of the real material world and thus furthered the development of German materialism. They were raised in similar academic milieus and responded to many of the same epistemological and ethical problems generated during the mid to late nineteenth century. After their doctoral dissertations on Greek thought, they became marginal to their professional fields. Both have been vilified in the modern tradition as being anti-Semitic, antiphilosophical, materialistic, and atheistic.

Greek ethical thought acted as a cleansing agent by which they rethought modernity from a vantage point beyond modernity. The goal of ethics and knowledge is the self-realization of human potential, rationality, and sensuality: a reintegration of the mind and body in a free and self-conscious human being and the overcoming of distorted and reified truth-claims, false objectivity, and alienated rationality— what they both term fetishism. Epistemology and ethics were closely related for both philosophers, since the very possibility of creating and realizing oneself required the overcoming of false consciousness and of the illusions of science and liberal morality. Universal claims to truth and the corresponding metatheories were viewed by both as leading to dogmatism and the tyranny of reason, and both saw these as connected to the worst excesses of the French Revolution.

An appreciation of the fullness and richness of their ideas has been hampered by the piecemeal and slow publication of each's complete corpus of work. This, in turn, has resulted in a flood of questionable and distorted secondary interpretations. Marx has been read through the conceptual visors of Leninist communism, whereas Nietzsche has been interpreted through those of Nazism. This is beginning to change, but the general literature still remains fixed in reified philosophical categories.

Marx rethought and rejected the principles and institutions of modern liberalism because they failed to expand natural rights to include human rights, defined freedom and justice essentially in terms of market categories, and reduced freedom and imagination to fetishized social relationships. However, he saw politics as a process in which humanity expressed itself, created its own history, defined its own identity and future, opened up the possibilities of its own imagination and will, and emancipated both the individual and the species. Liberalism, on the other hand, limited human vision to consumer rights and commodity consumption, reduced imagination to improving profits and acquiring property, distorted reason to cleverness and calculations of domination, and replaced hope and happiness with market success and commodity pleasures. It inverted morality to marketable and alienated values, defined humanity through competition, self-interest, and profit maximization, and limited democracy to a defense of narcissistic rights, consumer liberties, class property, and plebiscitary participation. This is the liberal form of market chrematistics. And with the Greeks, Marx saw a deeper and more profound life, full of political purpose, human ideals, and economic freedom. He saw the possibilities of a meaningful life in a moral economy embedded in a political community.

By turning to the Greeks, Marx developed a theory of participatory democracy that reflected the ancient concerns for citizenship and friendship, equality and freedom, and a general participation in the Assembly, *Boule*, and jury courts. And from the ancient Hebraic tradition with its jubilee and sabbatical years, and its concerns for economic equality, freedom, and periodic land redistribution, Marx transcended the class biases, social inequalities, and theoretical weaknesses of Greek ethical and political thought. This helped in the development of the economic elements in his theory of radical democracy. He borrowed heavily from Epicurus and post-Aristotelian traditions in his doctoral dissertation in which he established his basic insights and principles concerning ethics, science, happiness, and truth. When supplemented with Aristotle's ideas about the intellectual virtues of practical wisdom and political *praxis*, his critique of political *episteme* and *techne* (political idealism and social engineering), and Hegel's dialectical method, the heart of Marx's epistemology and metatheory was formed.

According to Nietzsche, Kant's critique of pure reason undermined the foundations of all knowledge and led to a new tragic vision of the meaninglessness, as well as the possibilities, of existence. On the other hand, Kant's critique of practical reason and his categorical imperative led to a tyranny of morality, an eclipse of reason, and a new form of moral idiocy. It created a static, sick, and oppressive moral system that undermined the creative and self-overcoming powers of the individual. Nietzsche called this the "metaphysics of the hangman." Liberalism simply continued the nihilistic logic of Christianity by leveling individual potential, ability, and self-created differences through liberal fairness, political equality, and natural rights, the unnatural search for pleasure, utility, and security, the avoidance of pain and suffering in a "drugged tranquility," and the repression of individual freedom and self-expression. These new political ideals are expressions of the modern politics of *ressentiment*, social leveling, and herd morality. Nietzsche utilized Kant's ideas on epistemology, morality, and aesthetics by negating and transcending the critiques of pure reason, practical reason, and aesthetic judgment. He established his own thought by going beyond Kant's critical theory—that is, by going beyond noumena and phenomena, beyond good and evil, and beyond beauty and serenity.

Both authors shared this common heritage in Kant's three critiques of reason and art. Whereas Marx layered multiple levels of traditions, which only the most ardent of conceptual archaeologists could work through, Nietzsche proved to be an enigma pure and simple. Nietzsche had established himself in the tradition of Winckelmann and Hölderlin, in Kantian philosophy and in the skepticism and empiricism of David Hume, in the rationality of German Idealism and in the passions and instincts of British materialism, and, finally, in the rational world of Goethe and Schiller and in the mysticism of Schopenhauer. By transforming and sublimating idealism and materialism, rationalism and empiricism, and by integrating eighteenth- and nineteenth-century German romanticism, aestheticism, tragedy, and mysticism, he attempted to move beyond the categories of Western metaphysics.

Nietzsche's earliest works, *The Birth of Tragedy* and the *Philosophenbuch*, framed his whole intellectual career. They contained his major insights in undeveloped form. His theories of nihilism and self-overcoming in the *Übermensch* were connected with his theory of tragedy, since ultimately the universe and life possessed no grand meaning or teleological purpose, only existential suffering and despair, Promethean self-consciousness and struggle. "Tragedy gave its audiences comfort not by purging their emotions but by bringing them face to face with the awful truths of human existence and by showing how those truths are what makes heroism true and life worth living."[3] Nietzsche continuously pushed his categories and ideas beyond the realm of traditional philosophy and orthodox metaphysics.

Nietzsche also moved from Greek philology to German Idealism by way of Dionysian mysticism and the madness of the marketplace. Entering mysticism (the ecstatic unity of life and the original oneness of being) and madness (loss of foundations and nihilism), he recapitulated the history of modern German thought, which felt itself constrained by the limits of language and the abuse of reason. Whether in the poetry of Schiller, Heine, or Hölderlin, the thing-in-itself of Kant, or the "Absolute Spirit" of Hegel, the German poets and philosophers pushed language beyond self-consciousness into the realm of the ineffable. It is only when Nietzsche returned to the cavelike world of everyday life from the pure blinding images of his rapturous experiences about existence that we captured a glimpse of his intentions. That is, when he clarified his mysticism and madness in an understandable language, we get some glimpse of his journey. Waiting for those moments of illumination we are mesmerized by his will, his power, and his nobility. We are given the courage to wait by the intensity of his desire to express the inexpressible. In the process, the frequent discussions of contemporary philosophers about whether he had a moral theory, a cognitivist theory of knowledge, a metaphysics of nature, and so forth, show attempts to give some perspective and linguistic coherence to his Dionysian wisdom, tragic vision, and mystical raptures.

But in a deeper sense, Nietzsche was truly beyond morality, epistemology, and metaphysics and would himself have regarded these debates as false issues. This, however, does not get us off the hook. Those of us in the cave are still left with the need and obligation to make sense of him using the categories and experiences available to us. Our conceptual frameworks will always be inadequate because of what we have learned from Kant and Schopenhauer, but also because Nietzsche moved beyond the rationalist abuse of reason into a new level of experience and knowledge. For him, madness was the final response to the dialectic of the Enlightenment. And madness is not expressible in language, only in action.

But to his credit and our benefit, Nietzsche did attempt to will himself back from madness, both to rewill and to reconstruct his own intellectual and scholarly past. He did not wallow in decadence and nihilism, nor did he permanently retreat to his Dionysian raptures. He attempted to reconceptualize the inconceptualizable, to give objective meaning to his personal experiences, to revive the Greek vision, and to inform us about our own potential. In the end, this will always be a problem in the exegesis of Nietzsche. As we move back and forth between madness and sanity, mystery and art, chaos and knowledge, becoming and being, all we can get are limited perspectives and visions into the world seen by Nietzsche. We continue to use the categories of rationality to express the insights of the nonrational, which are always incommensurable. But however inadequate to the task, the attempt must be made, for the alternative to the nothingness and eclipse of reason is permanent pain, despair, madness, and suicide. Reason

(Apollo) must be tamed in order to serve life (Dionysus). At this point, some of the goals of Nietzsche and Marx come closer together and even seem to converge. This is the childlike experience of the Apollonian artist about which they both agree. "Oh, those Greeks! They knew how to live. What is required for that is to stop courageously at the surface, the fold, the skin, to adore appearance, to believe in forms, tones, words, in the whole Olympus of appearance. Those Greeks were superficial—*out of profundity!*"[4] Marx and Nietzsche are able to guide us through the farthest reaches of human imagination; and with them we rise with the lark and fly with the eagle.

There are many areas where the thought of Marx and Nietzsche overlapped, especially in their return to classical Greece for inspiration and vision; their critique of modernity and liberalism from the perspective of moral economy (Aristotle) or tragic vision (Dionysus and Apollo); their radicalization of Kant's critiques of pure and practical reason; their rejection of rationalism and empiricism; and their critique of epistemology and foundationalism in their respective criticisms of scholasticism and "theory and practice," on one side, and theory of language and perspectivism, on the other. In their thoughts about morality, further similarities included their development of an historical and sociological critique of morality; their negation of the decadence of moral fetishism and economic ideology as prisons of objectivity and dreams of reason; their rejection of Neoplatonic rationalism, political idealism and abstract formulas, and Kantian moral imperatives as forms of moral tyranny and political terror (i.e., their belief that there are no ideals to realize); their definitions of human potential in terms of self-realization and self-becoming; their viewing of the key human experiences as self-defining and self-legislating activity; their seeing life in terms of *praxis* and aesthetic creativity; and their critiques of the moral inversion, reductionism, and abstractionism of modernity and the mediocrity and leveling of liberalism. They also shared a deep and profound appreciation for the issues of temporality and change in their understanding of history in terms of Aristotle's concepts of *praxis* and *phronesis*; their interpreting *praxis* and aesthetic activity by rethinking the nature of time; their integrating humanity and nature, idealism and materialism in their common view of the humanization of nature and the naturalization of humankind; and their common rejection of crude communism and Marxism. Thus at the level of metatheory, social theory, aesthetics, and morals, there are common grounds for a joint discussion between Marx and Nietzsche.

There is no attempt here to underestimate or misrepresent the radical, substantive differences between the two writers. On the other hand, at a more formal and higher level of abstraction, there is an interesting similarity of directions. Both looked to a time when individuals would develop their moral and creative sides; when creativity and freedom would be defining characteristics of humanity. By returning to the pre-Socratic Greeks, Nietzsche had decided to emphasize the individual element in human nature. Though there is an obvious communitarian impulse in the Dionysian aesthetic drive, the ethical and political implications had not been worked out. Nietzsche's radicalization of Kant was accomplished within an understanding of the Sophist movement, which lent an important liberal bias and direction to his thought, which he was never able to transcend. Marx, on the other hand, returned to Aristotle and Epicurus to define human nature, the political process, and moral economy.

In the end, they shared a view of modernity that, by their very rejection, highlighted common classical roots and aspirations. They shared the same breath and spirit of the Greeks. And in the process, their differences become less important. Marx's understanding of democracy, equality, and freedom permits a much broader interpretation of the political community than has traditionally been offered. His politics is infused with aesthetics; his view of human nature with artistic creativity; his dialectical method with an epistemological nihilism and critique of epistemology; his egalitarian society with a quest for moral excellence (and a critique of crude communism); his ethical thought with a critique of fetishism and historicism; his economic socialism with a moral aristocracy; and his sense of democracy with achievement, individuality, and civic virtue. Just as Aristotle related epistemology and politics, knowledge and *praxis*, and aristocracy and democracy (in book IV of the *Politics* blending in a polity elements from both aristocracy and democracy), Marx's position lets an economic and political egalitarian society flourish along with an aristocracy of aesthetic and moral development. Individuality of merit and achievement of the species being presupposes social equality: aristocracy of political virtue and individual achievement presupposes and requires a socialist society, since in a market economy (as both Aristotle and Marx recognized) individuality, civic responsibility, and the general good are sacrificed on the altar of chrematistic exchange, economic liberty, and profit production. Equality and inequality are not opposites, but are mutually supporting elements in a free and democratic society; on the other hand, equality and liberty are incompatible principles.

Aristotle realized that, in the best possible society, equality, freedom, and democracy were essential for the development of individual and civic worth and merit—moral and intellectual virtues. This is social justice. Over two thousand years later, Marx called forth the same ancient ideas within the context of modernity. Marx turned to economics for the same reason that Aristotle's *Politics* began with economic theory. It provided the foundational building blocks for democratic politics and social justice. For this very reason, his later writings should not be read as attempting to invent a price theory, an economic development theory, or even a crisis theory. Rather, the critique of political economy provides the foundation for the building of a new theory of moral economy and an ethical critique of capitalism—a *Wirtschaftsethik*. By repressing the democratic connotations of the Dionysian mysteries that attack traditional institutions, orthodox values, and social stratification, Nietzsche radicalized, but never got beyond, the isolation and individualism of the Kantian moral imperative with his *Überwindungsethik*. When an ethic of self-overcoming and an ethic of economics are integrated, a bridge is formed between Dionysus and Athena (protector of democratic Athens), between individual madness, striving, and becoming, on the one hand, and an ethics of practical discourse, political rationality, and participatory democracy on the other. The world has no meaning other than that created through democratic participation in the life and soul of the community. The prison of reason and iron cage of objectivity are transformed into a *praxis* of social justice and political becoming. There are no fetishized ideals, no social formulas, no heavenly kingdoms, no scientific utopias to realize. There are only the possibilities contained in the constant striving and improvements of the human will and imagination. In this way, the micro and macro components of ethics are reintegrated, and, in the process, practical reason is expanded to include ethics, economics, and politics.[5]

And by challenging the modern organization of the liberal arts and expanding the range of questions we may ask, we get a picture of nineteenth-century German theory and social critique that lifts us to a commanding height where we may view the dark outlines of liberalism and the modern specter of industrial society. In turn, both Marx and Nietzsche helped form the heart of modern German thought and vocalized the echoes and whispers of antiquity well into the twentieth century in their call for a new humanity built on the values of aesthetic creativity and self-realization in the material world.[6] Both wanted to expand the range of rational possibilities and human freedom by defining humanity in terms of its highest moral and spiritual aspirations, by viewing humanity from the heights of the ancients, and by stirring humanity by touching its artistic and creative soul. They enchanted us by intoxicating our minds and enlightening our sensuality.

Notes

Introduction

1. Alasdair MacIntyre, *After Virtue* (Notre Dame, Ind.: University of Notre Dame Press, 1984), pp. 109ff.

Chapter One: Marx and Classical Antiquity

1. George E. McCarthy, *Marx and the Ancients: Classical Ethics, Social Justice, and Nineteenth-Century Political Economy* (Lanham, Md.: Rowman & Littlefield Publishers, 1990) and the essays by George McCarthy, Horst Mewes, David Depew, Steven Smith, Michael DeGolyer, Laurence Baronovitch, Martha Nussbaum, Philip Kain, William James Booth, Richard Miller, Alan Gilbert, Joseph Margolis, and Tom Rockmore in *Marx and Aristotle: Classical Antiquity and Nineteenth-Century German Social Theory*, ed. George McCarthy (Lanham, Md.: Rowman and Littlefield Publishers, 1992). There is an extensive bibliography on the subject in *Marx and the Ancients*, pp. 298 and 302–04. To this list should be added the following: Elisabeth Welskopf, "Marx und Aristoteles," *Antiquitas Graeco-Romana Ac Tempora Nostra*, eds. Jan Burian and Ladislav Vidman (Prague, Czechoslovakia: Academia, 1968), pp. 231–39, and "Wiederentdeckung und Weiterentwicklung Aristotelischer Gedanken über die Musse bei Marx und Engels," in *Probleme der Musse im Alten Hellas* (Berlin: Rütten & Loening, 1962), pp. 278–317; Reimar Müller, "Hegel und Marx über die Antike Kultur," *Philologus*, 116 (1972): 1–31; and Abram Ranowitsch, "Marx über die Antike," *Aufsätze zur Alten Geschichte*, Hrsg. von Gabriele Bockisch (Berlin: Akademie Verlag, 1961), pp. 25–34. There is also an interesting bibliography outlining the influence of Greek aesthetics on Hegel and Marx in Müller's "Hegel und Marx über die Antike Kultur," p. 3.

2. For an examination of Marx's academic records from the universities of Bonn and Berlin, see Karl Marx, *Marx Engels Collected Works*, vol. 1

(New York: International Publishers, 1975), pp. 657–58 and 699–704. See also Johannes Irmscher, "Karl Marx studiert Altertumswissenschaft," *Wissenschaftliche Zeitschrift der Karl-Marx-Universität Leipzig*, Gesellschafts- und Sprachwissenschaftliche Reihe, vols. 2–3 (1953–54), pp. 209–15.

3. Panajotis Kondylis, *Marx und die Griechische Antike: Zwei Studien* (Heidelberg: Manutius Verlag, 1987), pp. 7–39.

4. Karl Marx, "Notebooks on Epicurean Philosophy," *Marx Engels Collected Works*, vol. 1 (New York: International Publishers, 1975), p. 500, and *Marx Engels Werke*, Ergänzungsband, Teil 1 (Berlin: Dietz Verlag, 1968), p. 235. (Hereafter referred to as *MEW EB*.)

5. Kondylis, *Marx und die Griechische Antike*, p. 44.

6. Karl Marx, "The German Ideology: Critique of Modern German Philosophy According to Its Representatives Feuerbach, B. Bauer, and Stirner," *Marx Engels Collected Works*, vol. 5 (New York: International Publishers, 1976), pp. 136–44, and *Marx Engels Werke*, Band 3 (*MEW 3*) (Berlin: Dietz Verlag, 1962), pp. 119–27. See also Kondylis, *Marx und die Griechische Antike*, pp. 67ff., where he traces the evolution of Marx's thinking about the Greeks from the dissertation, to *The German Ideology*, to the introduction to the *Grundrisse*.

7. Karl Marx, *Grundrisse: Introduction to the Critique of Political Economy*, trans. Martin Nicolaus (New York: Vintage Books, 1973), pp. 471–514, and *Grundrisse der Kritik der politischen Ökonomie* (Frankfurt/Main: Europäische Verlagsanstalt, n.d.), pp. 375–413. See also Padelis Lekas, *Marx on Classical Antiquity: Problems of Historical Methodology* (New York: St. Martin's Press, 1988), pp. 55–104; E.J. Hobsbawm, "Introduction," to *Karl Marx, Pre-Capitalist Economic Formations* (London: Lawrence & Wishart, 1964); and Barry Hindess and Paul Hirst, *Pre-Capitalist Modes of Production* (London: Routledge and Kegan Paul, 1975).

8. Karl Marx, "The Ethnological Notebooks" in *The Ethnological Notebooks of Karl Marx*, trans. Lawrence Krader (Assen, The Netherlands: Van Gorcum & Company, 1974), pp. 196–241. These notebooks contain many excerpts from Lewis Henry Morgan's *Ancient Society or Researches in the Lines of Human Progress from Savagery through Barbarism to Civilization* (1877), from John Budd Phear's *The Aryan Village in India and Ceylon* (1880), from Henry Sumner Maine's *Lectures on the Early History of Institutions* (1875), *Village Communities in the East and West* (1871), and *Ancient Law* (1861), from John Lubbock's *The Origin of Civilization* (1870), and from Rudolph Sohm's *Fränkisches Recht und Römisches Recht. Prolegomena zur Deutschen Rechtsgeschichte* (1880). Marx also drew heavily upon the works of nineteenth-century Greek, Roman, and Germanic anthropology and history: J. J. Bachofen, *Das Mutterrecht. Eine Untersuchung über die Gynaikokratie der alten Welt nach ihrer religiösen und rechtlichen Natur* (1861) and *Versuch über die Gräbersymbolik der Alten* (1859), H. H. Bancroft, *The Native Races of the Pacific States* (1875), August Böckh, *Die Staatshaushaltung der Athener*

(1817), Fustel de Coulanges, *La cité antique* (1864), Otto Gierke, *Die Deutsche Genossenschaftsrecht* (1868–1913), George Grote, *A History of Greece* (1846–56), Carl Hermann, *A Manual of the Political Antiquities of Greece Historically Considered* (1836), Georg Maurer, *Einleitung zur Geschichte der Mark-, Hof-, Dorf-, und Stadtverfassung* (1854), *Geschichte der Fronhöfe* (1862–63), *Geschichte der Markenverfassung in Deutschland* (1856), *Geschichte der Dorfverfassung in Deutschland* (1865–66), Theodor Mommsen, *Römische Geschichte* (1854–56), J. W. B. Money, *Java, or How to Manage a Colony* (1861), B. G. Niebuhr, *Römische Geschichte* (1818–12), Georg Schömann and J. H. Lipsius, *Griechische Alterthümer* (1855), and E. B. Tylor, *Researches into the Early History of Mankind* (1865), *Primitive Culture* (1871), and *Anthropology* (1881).

To study the influence of these nineteenth-century examinations of ancient society on later developments in socialist works of Lafargue, Kautsky, Bernstein, and Cunow, see Krader, trans., *The Ethnological Notebooks of Karl Marx*, pp. 71–72. Some of the former writers will also influence the writings of nineteenth- and twentieth-century anarchists, psychoanalysts, political theorists, and anthropologists.

9. Frederick Engels, "The Origin of the Family, Private Property and the State. In Light of the Researches by Lewis H. Morgan," *Marx Engels Collected Works*, vol. 26 (New York: International Publishers, 1990), and *Marx Engels Werke*, Band 21 (Berlin: Dietz Verlag, 1962). See also "Die Mark," appendix to "Entwicklung des Sozialismus von der Utopie zur Wissenschaft," *Marx Engels Werke 19*, pp. 317–30.

10. Marx, *Grundrisse*, pp. 84, 91, 134, 160, 300, and *Grundrisse der Kritik der politischen Ökonomie*, pp. 6, 12, 53, 78, and 208. There are two references to Aristotle included in the German edition, but not in the English translation by Nicolaus, in the section entitled "Fragment des Urtextes von 'Zur Kritik der politischen Ökonomie,' " pp. 900 and 928–29.

11. Karl Marx, *A Contribution to the Critique of Political Economy* (New York: International Publishers, 1970), pp. 27, 42, 50, 68, 117, 137, 155, and "Zur Kritik der Politischen Ökonomie," *Marx Engels Werke*, Band 13 (*MEW 13*) (Berlin: Dietz Verlag, 1964), pp. 15, 28, 36, 52, 96, 115, and 131. The full, expanded version of *A Contribution to the Critique of Political Economy* is contained in volumes 30 to 34 of the *Collected Works*.

12. Marx, "Letter to Arnold Ruge, May 1843, Cologne," *Marx Engels Collected Works*, vol. 3 (New York: International Publishers, 1975), p. 137.

13. The references to Aristotle are found in the following parts, chapters, and sections of the first volume of *Capital*: Part I: Commodities and Money: Chapter I: "Commodities," Section 3: "The Form of Value or Exchange Value, 3. The Equivalent Form of Value" (he refers to Aristotle's *Nicomachean Ethics*, book V, chapter 5, 1132b22–1134a15, pp. 408–411, see trans. by W. D. Ross in *Introduction to Aristotle*, ed. Richard McKeon [New York: Random House, 1947]); Chapter I: "Commodities," Section 4: "The Fetishism

of the Commodities and the Secret Thereof" (refers to Aristotle's *Politics*, book I, chapters 3–7); Chapter II: "Exchange" (refers to Aristotle's *Politics*, book I, chapter 9, 1257a5–12, pp. 81–82); *Part II: The Transformation of Money into Capital*: Chapter IV: "The General Formula for Capital" (refers to Aristotle's *Politics*, book I, chapter 9, 1257b25–39, p. 84); Chapter V: "Contradictions in the General Formula of Capital" (refers to Aristotle's *Politics*, book I, chapter 10, 1258a38–b8, p. 86; *Part IV: Production of Relative Surplus Value*: Chapter XIII: "Co-Operation" (refers to Aristotle's *Politics*, book I, chapter 2, 1253a1 and 1253a7, p. 59); Chapter XV: "Machinery and Modern Industry," Section 3: "The Proximate Effects of Machinery on the Workman," b: "Prolongation of the Working-Day" (refers to Aristotle's *Politics*, book I, chapter 4, 1253b30–38, p. 65).

14. Karl Marx, *Capital: A Critique of Political Economy*, vol. 1, *A Critical Analysis of Capitalist Production*, ed. Friedrich Engels, trans. Samuel Moore and Edward Aveling (New York: International Publishers, 1967), pp. 59, 82, 85, 152, 164-65, 326, and 408, and *Das Kapital: Kritik der politischen Ökonomie*, *Marx Engels Werke*, Band 23, (*MEW 23*) (Berlin: Dietz Verlag, 1962), pp. 73–74, 96, 100, 167, 179, 345–46, and 430–31. An outline of Marx's first volume and a summary of some of its chapters reveal the central themes influenced by Aristotle's politics: Chapter 1: analysis of the nature of value and exchange value, equivalency and commensurability of commodities in the market; Chapter 2: issue of slavery, distinction between use value and exchange value; Chapter 4: distinction and contradiction between economics and chrematistics, nature of capital, circulation of money; Chapter 5: economics and chrematistics, distinction between moneylenders' capital and merchants' capital, origins of surplus value and capital; Chapter 13: origins of capitalism in social cooperation, philosophical anthropology: social nature of humanity; Chapter 15: analysis of industry, machinery, and productivity, slavery, and technology. Marx also wrote *Resultate des unmittelbaren Produktionsprozesses: Das Kapital.I. Buch. Der Produktionsprozess des Kapitals. VI Kapitel* (Frankfurt/Main: Verlag Neue Kritik, 1969) in which Aristotle is mentioned two more times.

15. George Wilson, "The Economics of the Just Price," *History of Political Economy*, 7 (1975): 57.

16. Marx, *Theories of Surplus Value*, vol. 2 (Moscow: Progress Publishers, 1971), p. 287 and vol. 3, pp. 534 and 535, and *Marx Engels Werke*, Band 26, Teil 2 (Berlin: Dietz Verlag, 1965), p. 259 and Band 26, Teil 3, pp. 522 and 524.

17. Marx, *Capital*, vol. 1, pp. 59–60, and *MEW 23*, pp. 73–74.

18. Scott Meikle argues in his essay "Aristotle on Equality and Market Exchange," *Journal of Hellenic Studies*, 8 (1991), that the only difference between the *Nicomachean Ethics* and the *Politics* is that the latter work examines the nature of commercial trade (M-C-M). Thomas Lewis, in his essay "Acquisition and Anxiety: Aristotle's Case against the Market," *Canadian Journal of Economics*, 11 (1978), contends that the real difference is

that the *Nicomachean Ethics* analyses natural exchange (C-M-C) between mechanics, whereas the *Politics* studies the exchange between households. Meikle fails to see that the exchange relation between the builder and shoemaker and the interhousehold exchange represent different economic forms. He contends that both are forms of barter. The latter, however, is the ideal of exchange as an expression of grace and reciprocity (C-C) and the former is a form of commodity exchange (C-M-C). It is from commodity exchange that the real dangers to the polis arise, since from it eventually evolves the commercial exchange of the market.

19. Aristotle, *Nicomachean Ethics*, book V, chapter 5, 1133b7, p. 409.

20. Cornelius Castoriadis, "Value, Equality, Justice, Politics: From Marx to Aristotle and from Aristotle to Ourselves," in *Crossroads in the Labyrinth*, trans. K. Soper and M. Ryle (Cambridge, Mass.: MIT Press, 1984), pp. 294ff. In this section of his work, Castoriadis shows the relation between Aristotle's theory of proportional equality, distributive justice, and equity in the *Nicomachean Ethics* and Marx's theory of needs and geometrical equality in the *Critique of the Gotha Program*.

21. Lewis, "Acquisition and Anxiety," p. 79. The art (*techne*) of acquisition is understood within an ethical and political framework of economic sufficiency, human or household needs, natural order and activity, and civic friendship. For a discussion of the relation between economic *techne* and natural acquisition see Wayne Ambler, "Aristotle on Acquisition," *Canadian Journal of Political Science*, 17, no. 3 (September 1984): 497–502.

22. Aristotle, *The Politics*, trans. T. A. Sinclair (Harmondsworth, England: Penguin Books, 1981), book II, chapter 5, 1263a38–39, p. 115.

23. Karl Polanyi, "Aristotle Discovers the Economy," in *Trade and Market in the Early Empires: Economies in History and Theory*, ed. K. Polanyi, E. Arensberg, and H. Pearson (Glencoe, Ill.: The Free Press, 1957), p. 80.

24. Aristotle, *Politics*, book I, chapter 8, 1256b26ff., p. 79.

25. Castoriadis argues that Aristotle never answers the question of the appropriate standard (*axia*) for distributive and reciprocal justice ("Value, Equality, Justice, Politics," p. 299). In fact, he contends that Aristotle proposed two answers to the question but never resolved it. According to Castoriadis, one standard of measurement for a fair distribution was proposed in book V, chapter 3 of the *Nicomachean Ethics* as the value and dignity of individuals defined by constitutional law, and one standard in book V, chapter 5 as *chreia*, or need. Are the standards of distribution and reciprocity citizenship or need?

26. M. I. Finley, "Aristotle and Economic Analysis," in *Articles on Aristotle*, vol. 2: *Ethics and Politics*, ed. J. Barnes, M. Schofield, and R. Sorabji (New York: St. Martin's Press, 1977), p. 142.

27. This explains why Aristotle was not concerned with developing a theory of market prices. See M. I. Finley, "Aristotle and Economic Analysis," in *Articles on Aristotle*, vol. 2: *Ethics and Politics*, ed. J. Barnes, M. Schofield, and R. Sorabji (New York: St. Martin's Press, 1977), p. 149; Polanyi, "Aris-

totle Discovers the Economy," p. 87; and Scott Meikle, "Aristotle and the
Political Economy of the Polis," *Journal of Hellenic Studies*, 99 (1979): 69.

28. Aristotle, *Nicomachean Ethics*, book V, chapter 5, 1133b15–24, p. 410.
Finley in "Aristotle and Economic Analysis," pp. 146–47, recognizes that the
market mechanism makes exchange possible and objects commensurate but is
not sure if it is based on the parties involved, their skills, their labor, or their
labor costs. Polanyi in "Aristotle Discovers the Economy" (p. 88) views it as
a question of the status of the worker. See also Wilson, "The Economics of
the Just Price"; Lewis, "Acquisition and Anxiety"; and J. J. Spengler,
"Aristotle on Economic Imputation and Related Matters," *Southern Economic Journal*, 21 (1955). There is a useful history of the debate in Meikle,
"Aristotle on Equality and Market Exchange," in which he gives an analytical
and theoretical framework for understanding the relationship between the
house builder and the shoemaker as developed in the works of R. Williams, A.
Grant, H. Rackham, J. Burnet, R. L. Meek, J. Soudek, D. G. Ritchie, W. D.
Ross, W. F. R. Hardie, J. Schumpeter, B. J. Gordon, H. H. Joachim, M. I.
Finley, T. L. Heath, and R. A. Gauthier–J. Y. Jolif and in Meikle's "Aristotle
and the Political Economy of the Polis," *Journal of Hellenic Studies*, 99 (1979).

29. Marx, *Capital*, vol. 1, p. 60, and *MEW 23*, p. 74.

30. Aristotle, *Nicomachean Ethics*, book V, chapter 5, 1133a1–32, pp.
408–9.

31. Lewis in "Acquisition and Anxiety" distinguishes between the needs of
the household and the lower needs of those involved in commodity exchange.
In the former (*Ethics*), the concept of needs is based on a broader understanding of the social and political relations of the community, while in the latter
(*Politics*), it is his theory of the just price that defines the nature of tradition
and custom surrounding economic exchange.

32. Polanyi says, "The sole purpose of the exchange is to draw relationships
closer by strengthening the ties of reciprocity" ("Aristotle Discovers the
Economy," p. 73).

33. Aristotle, *Nicomachean Ethics*, book V, chapter 5, 1133a3–4, p. 408.

34. Ibid., book V, chapter 5, 1132b31–32, p. 408.

35. Lewis, "Acquisition and Anxiety," pp. 83–84.

36. Ibid., p. 86.

37. The debate over Aristotle's economic analysis has been as frustrating as
it has been fascinating. Joseph Schumpeter in his *History of Economic Analysis*, ed. E. B. Schumpeter (New York: Oxford University Press, 1954) treated
Aristotle as if he were attempting to write a neoclassical treatise on price
determination and market rationality; and Josef Soudek, in "Aristotle's Theory of Exchange: An Inquiry into the Origin of Economic Analysis," *Proceedings of the American Philosophical Society*, 96, no. 1 (February 1952), reads
Aristotle as if he wrote from the perspective of marginal utility analysis.
Others such as Polanyi, "Aristotle Discovers the Economy," and Finley,
"Aristotle and Economic Analysis," viewed Aristotle as developing a theory

of mutual sharing, reciprocity, and moral economy. On the other hand, Meikle in "Aristotle and the Political Economy of the Polis" recognized the weaknesses of Schumpeter and Soudek, but rejected the thesis of Polanyi and Finley that he was simply a "philosopher of the *Gemeinschaft*." Meikle argues that Aristotle's major concern, especially in the *Nicomachean Ethics*, was in seeking answers to the issues of price and commensurability of commodities in market exchange. He contends that it is this problem that Marx turns to in the first volume of *Capital*. If both Aristotle and Marx recognized the split between *oikonomia* as the natural exchange of the household based on needs and reciprocity and *chrematistike* as commercial trade based on profit and unnatural accumulation (or a moral economy and political economy), then Polanyi, Finley, and Meikle could all be correct. Aristotle was concerned with the continuance of a moral economy as he watched the nascent growth of a market economy and Marx examined its developed form while attempting to develop a "critique" of political economy based on a theory of democracy and needs. Castoriadis, in "Value, Equality, Justice, Politics," states that Marx, by emphasizing exchange value and abstract labor, missed Aristotle's main issue of the determination of the standards for distributive and reciprocal justice. I disagree.

38. See Patricia Springborg, "Aristotle and the Problem of Needs," *History of Political Thought*, 5, no. 3 (Winter 1984): 419.

39. Of course, Marx is begging the question here. At the very least he is overemphasizing one aspect of Aristotle's analysis of the commensurability of exchange products. An argument could be made that Marx is playing too freely with Aristotle at this point in his argument. Aristotle's goal was not to explain market commensurability (*chrematistike*), but the commensurability of exchange (*oikonomia*), which he does in terms of his theory of needs and friendship. Marx concentrated in his critique of modernity on abstract labor and does not return to a theory of needs until the *Grundrisse* and *Critique of the Gotha Program*. However, the issue is always present in his distinction between use value and exchange value. (See Springborg, "Aristotle and the Problem of Needs," pp. 419–24.)

40. Marx, *Capital*, vol. 1, p. 38, and *MEW 23*, p. 53.

41. Ibid., vol. 1, p. 39, and *MEW 23*, p. 54.

42. Ibid., vol. 1, p. 46, and *MEW 23*, p. 61.

43. It is clear that Marx at this point in his analysis is pushing Aristotle's argument too far. Aristotle was not interested in determining the nature of market prices, but the just price. The former would require understanding the market mechanism that was only just forming in Athens, while Aristotle is more concerned with the influence of needs, friendship, and community on the formation of prices.

44. Marx, *Capital*, vol. 1, p. 47, and *MEW 23*, p. 62.

45. Ibid., vol. 1, pp. 57–58, and *MEW 23*, p. 72.

46. Ibid., vol. 1, p. 70, and *MEW 23*, p. 85.

326   *Notes*

47. McCarthy, *Marx and the Ancients*, pp. 226–29.
48. Marx, *Capital*, vol. 1, p. 72, and *MEW 23*, pp. 86–87.
49. Ibid., vol. 1, pp. 81–82, and *MEW 23*, p. 96.
50. Ibid., vol. 1, p. 85, and *MEW 23*, p. 100.
51. Following Marx, Scott Meikle defines barter as C-C; natural exchange based on needs as C-M-C; unnatural *kapelike* as M-C-M'; and usury as M-M' in his article "Aristotle and the Political Economy of the Polis," pp. 61–64.
52. Aristotle, *Politics*, book I, chapter 9, 1257a25–26, p. 82.
53. Herman Daly and John Cobb, Jr., *For the Common Good: Redirecting the Economy Toward Community, the Environment, and a Sustainable Future* (Boston: Beacon Press, 1989), pp. 138–158.
54. Aristotle, *Politics*, book I, chapter 9, 1257a30, p. 82.
55. Marx, *Capital*, vol. 1, pp. 92–93, and *MEW 23*, pp. 107–8.
56. Ibid., vol. 1, p. 132, and *MEW 23*, p. 146.
57. Ibid. Sophocles, "Antigone" in *The Three Theban Plays*, trans. Robert Fagles (New York: Penguin Books, 1984), 335–341, p.73.
58. For a comment about the effects of industrial technology, factory division of labor, and modern machinery on intellectual and moral virtues, see Marx, *Capital*, vol. 1, pp. 362 and 530, and *MEW 23*, pp. 383 and 552.
59. Ibid., vol. 1, p. 152, and *MEW 23*, p. 167.
60. Many of these ideas, especially the critique of moral inversion and mistaking ends for means, were developed by Marx in some of his early manuscripts from 1844, including, "Private Property and Communism," "Needs, Production, and Division of Labor," and "Money" in the *Marx Engels Collected Works*, vol. 3.
61. Mary Nichols, *Citizens and Statesmen: A Study of Aristotle's Politics* (Lanham, Md.: Rowman & Littlefield Publishers, 1992), pp. 26–27.
62. The first book of the *Politics* deals with economics and the last books of the *Nicomachean Ethics* examine friendship. Before Bekker's edition in the nineteenth century, the two books were part of one work. The relationship between Aristotle's theory of friendship and political economy could have been very important if it were not for the fact that the organization of the books is an open question. There is a good deal of debate about the organization of the chapters of Aristotle's *Politics*. Werner Jaeger has argued that books VII and VIII were early Platonic works ("Reviser's Introduction," by T. J. Saunders in Aristotle's *Politics*, p. 34), whereas Josiah Ober contends that they were later products influenced by the rise of the empires of Philip and Alexander of Macedon in his *Mass and Elite in Democratic Athens: Rhetoric, Ideology, and the Power of the People* (Princeton: Princeton University Press, 1989).
63. Polanyi, "Aristotle Discovers the Economy," p. 69.
64. Aristotle, *Politics*, book I, chapter 9, 1257b29, p. 84.
65. Ibid., book I, chapter 9, 1258a13, p. 85.
66. Marx, *Capital*, vol. 1, p. 153, and *MEW 23*, p. 168.

67. Ibid., vol. 1, pp. 164–65, and *MEW 23*, p. 179.
68. Aristotle, *Politics*, book I, chapter 10, 1258a36, p. 87.
69. Ibid., book I, chapter 10, 1258a40, p. 87.
70. Ibid., book I, chapter 11, 1258b35–36, p. 89.
71. Marx, *Capital*, vol. 1, p. 163, and *MEW 23*, pp. 177–78.
72. Ibid., vol. 1, p. 249, and *MEW 23*, p. 263.
73. Ibid., vol. 1, p. 326, and *MEW 23*, pp. 345–46. See also the reference to Aristotle and the species nature of humanity in the "Economic and Philosophic Manuscripts of 1844" in *Marx Engels Collected Works*, vol. 3 (New York: International Publishers, 1975), p. 305, and *Marx Engels Werke*, Ergänzungsband, Teil 1 (*MEW EB*) (Berlin: Dietz Verlag, 1968), p. 545.
74. Aristotle, *Politics*, book I, chapter 2, 1253a16–17, p. 60.
75. Marx, *Capital*, vol. 1, p. 364, and *MEW 23*, p. 386.
76. Ibid., vol. 1, p. 354, and *MEW 23*, p. 375.
77. Ibid., vol. 1, pp. 365–67, and *MEW 23*, pp. 387–89.
78. Ibid., vol. 1, p. 329, and *MEW 23*, p. 375. Krader comments in his introduction to *The Ethnological Notebooks of Karl Marx* that Aristotle's reference to the political nature of man appears after his discussion about the nature of social life in the family, village, collectivity of villages, and the city-state. He remarks that, unlike Marx's earlier writings in the *Communist Manifesto* and the *German Ideology*, there is no historical connection between the ancients (Aristotle) and moderns (Benjamin Franklin)—no historical determinism between historical periods (pp. 19–20).
79. Marx, *Capital*, vol. 1, pp. 408–09, and *MEW 23*, pp. 430–31.
80. Aristotle, *Politics*, book I, chapter 4, 1253b30, p. 64.
81. Ibid., book I, chapter 4, 1253b36, p. 65.
82. Marx, *Capital*, vol. 1, p. 408, and *MEW 23*, p. 431.
83. Ibid., vol. 1, pp. 320–21, and *MEW 23*, pp. 339–40.
84. Ibid., vol. 1, p. 394, and *MEW 23*, p. 416.
85. Ibid., vol. 1, p. 396, and *MEW 23*, p. 418.
86. Ibid., vol. 1, p. 407, and *MEW 23*, pp. 429–30.
87. Ibid., vol. 1, p. 447, and *MEW 23*, p. 471.
88. Ibid., vol. 1, p. 488, and *MEW 23*, p. 512. This theme is also developed in *Capital*, vol. 1 on pages 506 and 530, and in *MEW 23*, pp. 529 and 552.
89. Marx, *Capital: A Critique of Political Economy*, vol. 3, *The Process of Capitalist Production as a Whole*, ed. Friedrich Engels (New York: International Publishers, 1967), pp. 384–85, and *Marx Engels Werke*, Band 25 (*MEW 25*) (Berlin: Dietz Verlag, 1964), p. 398.
90. Marx, *Capital*, vol. 1, p. 176, and *MEW 23*, p. 189.
91. Ibid., vol. 1, p. 271, and *MEW 23*, p. 287. See also *Capital*, vol. 1, p. 302, and *MEW 23*, p. 320.
92. McCarthy, *Marx and the Ancients*, pp. 247–96.
93. Max Weber was another nineteenth-century social theorist who was influenced by classical antiquity in his writings: *The Agrarian Sociology of*

Ancient Civilizations (London: Routledge, Chapman & Hall, 1988); *Ancient Judaism*, trans. Hans Gerth (New York: Free Press, 1967); *Die Römische Agrargeschichte in Ihrer Bedeutung für das Staats- und Privatrecht* (New York: Arno Press, 1979), reprint of 1891 edition published by Verlag von Ferdinand Enke, Stuttgart; *General Economic History* (New Brunswick, N.J.: Transaction Books, 1981); and *Economy and Society*, vol. 1, part 2, ch. 3 (Berkeley: University of California Press, 1979). The Greeks also had an important influence on the French Enlightenment, which later had a direct impact on Emile Durkheim's work *Montesquieu and Rousseau: Forerunners of Sociology* (Ann Arbor: University of Michigan Press, 1960).

94. Marx, "Difference between the Democritean and Epicurean Philosophy of Nature," *Marx Engels Collected Works*, vol. 1 (New York: International Publishers, 1975), pp. 30–31, and *Marx Engels Werke*, Ergänzungsband, Teil 1 (*MEW EB*), (Berlin: Dietz Verlag, 1968), p. 263.

Chapter Two: Ancient and Modern Democracy

1. Jennifer Roberts, *Acknowledged Folly: The Anti-Athenian Tradition in Western Thought* (Princeton: Princeton University Press, forthcoming 1994); R. K. Sinclair, *Democracy and Participation in Athens* (Cambridge, England: Cambridge University Press, 1988), pp. 191–222; and Ellen Wood and Neal Wood, *Class Ideology and Ancient Political Theory: Socrates, Plato, and Aristotle in Social Context* (Oxford, England: Basil Blackwell, 1978).

2. For the most comprehensive treatment of the Athenian Assembly see Mogens Hansen, *The Athenian Assembly: In the Age of Demosthenes* (Oxford, England: Basil Blackwell, 1987). In the introduction to the work, Hansen makes an unusual discovery during his review of the literature on the Assembly. He states that the most recent work on the subject was Georg Schömann's *De Comitiis Atheniensium* written in 1819. The relevancy of this fact for Marxian scholarship is striking, since Marx, too, relied on Schömann's material.

3. Alan Gilbert, *Democratic Equality* (Cambridge, England: Cambridge University Press, 1992), pp. 268, 284, and 287.

4. To this material would have to be added his later readings in nineteenth-century anthropology including L. H. Morgan, H. S. Maine, J. Lubbock, J. B. Phear, M. M. Kovalevsky, and G. L. Maurer. See Padelis Lekas, *Marx on Classical Antiquity: Problems of Historical Methodology* (Sussex, England: Wheatsheaf Books, 1988), chapter 3 and appendix.

5. Herodotus, *The History*, book 3, chapter 80, trans. and ed. George Rawlinson (New York: D. Appleton and Company, 1893), p. 394.

6. Thucydides, *The Peloponnesian War*, book 2, chapter 37, trans. Rex Warner (London: Penguin Books, 1972), p. 145.

7. M. I. Finley, *Democracy Ancient and Modern* (New Brunswick, N.J.:

Rutgers University Press, 1988), pp. 3–37; Josiah Ober, *Mass and Elite in Democratic Athens: Rhetoric, Ideology, and the Power of the People* (Princeton: Princeton University Press, 1989), pp. 53–103; Martin Ostwald, *From Popular Sovereignty to the Sovereignty of Law: Law, Society and Politics in the Fifth-Century Athens* (Berkeley: University of California Press, 1986), pp. 3–83; and David Stockton, *The Classical Athenian Democracy* (Oxford, England: Oxford University Press, 1990), pp. 19–56.

8. There is a growing body of literature that recognizes, though not necessarily endorses, the "democratic interpretation" of Aristotle's *Politics*. For a collection of many of these secondary interpretations and an analysis of this thesis, I am indebted to Mary Nichols who, in the introduction to her work *Citizens and Statesmen: A Study of Aristotle's Politics* (Lanham, Md.: Rowman & Littlefield Publishers, 1992) examines the debate between the democratic and aristocratic interpretations of Aristotle. The democratic interpretation is discussed in the following: Hannah Arendt, *The Human Condition* (Garden City, N.Y.: Doubleday and Company, 1959), p. 30; Ernest Barker, *The Political Thought of Plato and Aristotle* (New York: Dover Publications, 1959), pp. 295, 350–53, 421–22, 460, and *The Politics of Aristotle* (Oxford, England: Oxford University Press, 1946), p. xxxi; William Bluhm, "The Place of 'Polity' in Aristotle's Theory of the Ideal State," *The Journal of Politics*, 24, no. 4 (November 1962): 746–50; John Davies, *Democracy and Classical Greece* (Stanford, Calif.: Stanford University Press, 1978), p. 36; Mary Dietz, "Citizenship with a Feminist Face: The Problem with Maternal Thinking," *Political Theory*, 13, no. 1 (February 1985): 28 and 34; Jean Bethke Elshtain, *Public Man, Private Women* (Princeton: Princeton University Press, 1981), pp. 52–53; Brian Fay, *Social Theory and Political Practice* (London: George Allen and Unwin, 1975), pp. 53–54; Thomas Lindsay, "Aristotle's Qualified Defense of Democracy through 'Political Mixing,' "*Journal of Politics*, 54, no. 1 (February 1992); R. G. Mulgan, *Aristotle's Political Theory* (Oxford: Oxford University Press, 1977), p. 114; Martha Nussbaum, "Nature, Function, and Capability: Aristotle on Political Distribution," in *Marx and Aristotle: Nineteenth-Century German Social Theory and Classical Antiquity*, ed. George E. McCarthy (Lanham, Md.: Rowman and Littlefield Publishers, 1992); J. G. A. Pocock, *The Machiavellian Moment* (Princeton: Princeton University Press, 1975), p. 550; Steven Salkever, "Women, Soldiers, and Citizens: Plato and Aristotle on Political Virility," *Polity*, 19, no. 2 (Winter 1986): 232, "The Crisis of Liberal Democracy: Liberality and Democratic Citizenship," in *The Crisis of Liberal Democracy*, ed. Kenneth Deutsch and Walter Soffer (Albany: The State University of New York Press, 1987), and *Finding the Mean: Theory and Practice in Aristotelian Political Philosophy* (Princeton: Princeton University Press, 1990); Sinclair, *Democracy and Participation in Athens*, pp. 20–23 and 215–26; Stockton, *Classical Athenian Democracy*, p. 177; William Sullivan, *Reconstructing Public Policy* (Berkeley: University of California Press, 1984), p. 181; Delba Winthrop, "Aristotle on Participatory Democracy," *Polity*, 11,

330 *Notes*

no. 2 (Winter 1978): 162–64; W. von Leyden, *Aristotle on Equality and Justice: His Political Argument* (New York: St. Martin's Press, 1985), pp. 12–13 and pp. 59–61; Gilbert, *Democratic Equality*, p. 287; and Sheldon Wolin, *Politics and Vision* (Boston: Little, Brown, and Company, 1960), pp. 57–58. See also Cynthia Farrar, *The Origins of Democratic Thinking: The Invention of Politics in Classical Greece* (Cambridge, England: Cambridge University Press, 1988), who sees the foundation of democratic theory in the works of Protagoras, Democritus, and Thucydides.

Communitarians and socialists have also used Aristotle and the ancients to frame their critiques of liberalism. Some of these major authors include Robert Beiner, *Political Judgement* (Chicago: University of Chicago Press, 1984), pp. 91ff.; Robert Bellah et al., *Habits of the Heart: Individualism and Commitment in American Life* (New York: Harper and Row, 1985), p. 285; Alasdair MacIntyre, *After Virtue* (Notre Dame, Ind.: University of Notre Dame Press, 1981); Benjamin Barber, *Strong Democracy: Participatory Politics for a New Age* (Berkeley: University of California Press, 1984); Charles Taylor, *Sources of the Self: The Making of the Modern Identity* (Cambridge, Mass.: Harvard University Press, 1989), p. 82; Chantal Mouffe, "American Liberalism and Its Critics: Rawls, Taylor, Sandel, and Walzer," *Praxis International*, 8, no. 2 (July 1988): 193–206; and David Held, *Models of Democracy* (Stanford, Calif.: Stanford University Press, 1987), pp. 18–20.

9. Aristotle, *The Politics*, trans. T. A. Sinclair (Harmondsworth, England: Penguin Books, 1981), book IV, chapter 4, 1291b34–38, p. 250.

10. Hansen, *The Athenian Assembly*; Sinclair, *Democracy and Participation in Athens*, pp. 24–34, 77–84, and 115–27; Stockton, *Classical Athenian Democracy*, pp. 67–84; and Ellen Wood, *Peasant-Citizen and Slave: The Foundations of Athenian Democracy* (London: Verso, 1988).

11. P. J. Rhodes, *The Athenian Boule* (Oxford, England: Clarendon Press, 1972); Sinclair, *Democracy and Participation in Athens*, pp. 84–114; and Stockton, *Classical Athenian Democracy*, pp. 84–95.

12. Stockton, *Classical Athenian Democracy*, pp. 90–91.

13. Mary A. Glendon, *Rights Talk: An Interpretation of American Political Discourse* (New York: Free Press, 1991).

14. Stockton, *Classical Athenian Democracy*, pp. 186–87.

15. George E. McCarthy, *Marx and the Ancients* (Lanham: Md.: Rowman & Littlefield Publishers, 1990), pp. 199–205.

16. In his work *The Class Struggle in the Ancient Greek World* (Ithaca, N.Y.: Cornell University Press, 1981), G. E. M. de Ste. Croix, who calls Aristotle "the great expert on the sociology and politics of the Greek city" (p. 79), outlines Aristotle's contribution to an analysis and theory of the class structure of ancient Greece, the political relevance of private property, a theory of law, "theory of mixed constitution," and theory of types of democracy (pp. 69–80). Ste. Croix then states, "The Marxist character of Aristotle's sociology has not escaped notice." Marx would probably be very critical of

the limits of Aristotle's theory of "mixed democracy" and his critique of radical democracy in Athens, but he does provide an important structural analysis of the workings of democracy.

17. Aristotle, *Politics*, book III, chapter 1, 1275a22, p. 169.

18. Ibid., book III, chapter 1, 1275b20–21, p. 171.

19. Ibid., book VI, chapter 2, 1317b3–8, p. 362.

20. Ibid., book VII, chapter 10, 1330a1–2, p. 419. See also book II, chapter 5, 1263a21–39, pp. 114–15.

21. Ibid., book III, chapter 9, 1280a9, p. 195.

22. Ibid., 1281a39–b10, 1282a16–23, and 1282a34–35 in book III, chapter 11; 1283a40–41 and 1283b27–34 in chapter 13; and 1286a25–35 in book III, chapter 15.

23. Ibid., book III, chapter 11, 1281b1–10, pp. 202–3.

24. Ibid., book III, chapter 9, 1281a2–8, p. 198 and chapter 12, 1282b14–1283a2, pp. 207–8.

25. Trevor Saunders, "Revised Introduction," in Aristotle's *Politics*, p. 34, outlines the argument of Werner Jaeger who contends that books II–III and VII–VIII were written from an earlier Platonic perspective, which stressed the idealism and utopianism of the ideal state, whereas the other books have a non-Platonic and more mature, pragmatic, and empirical character.

26. Aristotle, *Politics*, book III, chapter 11, 1281b22–31, p. 203.

27. Ibid., book II, chapter 7, 1266b25–26, pp. 128–29.

28. Ibid., book II, chapter 7, 1267a37–b12, p. 131 and book VI, chapter 4, 1318b27–1319a3, p. 369.

29. Ibid., book III, chapter 12, 1282b33–1283a1, pp. 207–208.

30. Ibid., book III, chapter 13, 1283a42, p. 211.

31. Ibid., book III, chapter 10, 1281a32–34, p. 200; chapter 11, 1282a41–b4, p. 206; chapter 15, 1286a7–21, pp. 221–22; chapter 16, 1287a10–21, p. 226; and chapter 16, 1287b16–24, pp. 227–28. Reference to the sovereignty of laws occurs before the first defense of democracy, and after the fourth, sixth, and, finally, seventh defenses.

32. Nichols, *Citizens and Statesmen*, p. 61.

33. Aristotle, *Politics*, book III, chapter 10, 1281a28–35, p. 200.

34. Ibid., book III, chapter 15, 1286a20, p. 221. This argument resonates with echoes of his earlier discussion about law, equity, and the Lesbian molding in book V, chapter 10 of the *Nicomachean Ethics* in *Introduction to Aristotle*, ed. Richard McKeon, trans. W. D. Ross (New York: Random House, 1947).

35. *Politics*, book III, chapter 13, 1284a14–15, p. 213.

36. Ibid., book IV, chapter 8, 1293b40, p. 259.

37. Ibid., book IV, chapter 9, 1294b12–13, p. 262 and chapter 11, 1295a33, p. 266.

38. Ibid., book III, chapter 13, 1283b27–28, p. 212.

39. Ibid., book III, chapter 13, 1284a1–2, p. 213.

40. Ibid., book III, chapter 11, 1282a42, p. 206.
41. Ibid., book IV, chapter 11, 1295a35–b4, p. 266.
42. Ibid., book III, chapter 17, 1288a1–2, p. 229.
43. Ibid., book IV, chapter 12, 1297a8, p. 272.
44. Ibid., book VII, chapter 14, 1332b14–30, pp. 431–32.
45. Ibid., book IV, chapter 1, 1289a11–12, p. 237.
46. Though Aristotle favors "private ownership" of property, he calls for its communal use; though critical of Phaleas's egalitarianism, he calls for its inclusion in a broader understanding of justice and needs; and, finally, he is critical of the level of class inequality in Sparta. In her essay "Nature, Function, and Capability" in *Marx and Aristotle*, Nussbaum sees this as part of a more positive treatment of democracy by Aristotle.
47. Aristotle, *Nicomachean Ethics*, book I, chapter 3, 1094b20–23, p. 310.
48. Aristotle, *Politics*, book II, chapter 5, 1264a5–6, p. 117; book II, chapter 8, 1269a11, p. 138; book III, chapter 11, 1282a41–b4, p. 206; *Nicomachean Ethics*, book V, chapter 10, 1137b10–35, pp. 420–21.
49. Nichols, *Citizens and Statesmen*, pp. 42 and 45.
50. E. Barker, *The Political Thought of Plato and Aristotle* (New York: G.P. Putnam's Sons, 1906), pp. 473–74.
51. Bluhm, "The Place of the 'Polity' in Aristotle's Theory of the Ideal State," p. 744, argues that the state pictured in books VII and VIII represents an extension of the structural principles of the ideal state from books I–IV and concludes that "some kind of democratic rule is the ideal government of the *polis*" (p. 746).
52. Martha Nussbaum, *The Fragility of Goodness: Luck and Ethics in Greek Tragedy and Philosophy* (Cambridge, England: University of Cambridge Press, 1986), p. 291.
53. Aristotle, *Nicomachean Ethics*, book VI, chapter 8, 1142a24, p. 433.
54. Nussbaum, *Fragility of Goodness*, p. 305.
55. Bluhm, "The Place of the 'Polity' in Aristotle's Theory of the Ideal State," pp. 743 and 750.
56. Nichols, *Citizens and Statesmen*, p. 121.
57. This type of reasoning becomes part of the thinking of both John Stuart Mill and Marx. In his book *The Political Thought of Plato and Aristotle*, Barker traces the Aristotelian influence on medieval and modern authors from Marsilius of Padua, Machiavelli, Spinoza, Rousseau, and Hegel. They were particularly impressed with Aristotle's theories of the state, democracy, popular sovereignty, virtuous life, and justice.
58. Gilbert, *Democratic Equality*, pp. 268 and 287. Gilbert also lists other egalitarian movements that influenced Marx's understanding of the Paris Commune, including the slave revolt of Spartacus, the German-Peasant War, the Levellers in the Puritan Revolution, and the sans-culottes in the French Revolution (p. 267). In his earlier work *Marx's Politics: Communists and Citizens* (New Brunswick, N.J.: Rutgers University Press, 1981), p. 111,

Gilbert saw a connection between Aristotle and the Paris Commune. Also Horst Mewes, "On the Concept of Politics in the Early Work of Karl Marx," *Social Research*, 43, no. 2 (Summer 1976): 291–92.

59. Karl Marx, *Civil War in France: The Paris Commune* (New York: International Publishers, 1968), p. 59, and *Marx Engels Werke*, Band 17 (*MEW 17*) (Berlin: Dietz Verlag, 1962), p. 340.

60. Jean Jacques Rousseau, *The Social Contract and Discourses* (New York: E. P. Dutton and Company, 1950), pp. 94–95. See also Finley, *Democracy Ancient and Modern*, pp. 11–12.

61. Finley, *Democracy Ancient and Modern*, p. 116.

62. Marx in *The Civil War in France*, *The Eighteenth Brumaire of Louis Bonaparte*, and in a letter to Dr. Kugelmann (April 12, 1871) and Engels in the preface to the English edition of the *Communist Manifesto* of 1888, changed their original position on the seizure of state power by the proletariat as expressed in the *Manifesto*. Instead of the workers seizing state power from the capitalists, the legislative, judicial, executive, and military organs of the state must be destroyed, because they are implements of class oppression. The very nature and essence of politics must be democratically transformed and new institutions created that reflect the new democratic principles of economic participation.

63. Marx, *Civil War in France*, p. 22, and *MEW 17*, p. 625.

64. Ibid., p. 55, and *MEW 17*, p. 336.

65. For a discussion of the nature of Marx's mature political views, especially his views on the "dictatorship of the proletariat," the extent of state power, representative government, and the relationship between Marx and anarchism, see Richard Hunt, *The Political Ideas of Marx and Engels: Marxism and Totalitarian Democracy 1818–1850* (Pittsburgh, Pa.: University of Pittsburgh Press, 1974), pp. 319–328. See also David Felix, *Marx as Politician* (Carbondale, Ill.: Southern Illinois University Press, 1983), pp. 176–80.

66. In *Democracy Ancient and Modern*, Finley makes note of John Stuart Mill's reliance on George Grote's *History of Greece* for his analysis of Athenian democracy and for his view of modern participatory democracy. Grote also had a strong impact on Marx's political perception of ancient democracy. For Mill's understanding of the Greek polis see the *Edinburgh Review* (October 1840) reprinted in *Dissertations and Discussions*, vol. 2 (London: 1859), pp. 1–83. Mill in *Considerations on Representative Government* states,

Notwithstanding the defects of the social system and moral ideas of antiquity, the practice of the dicastery and the ecclesia (Assembly) raised the intellectual standard of the average Athenian citizen far beyond anything of which there is yet an example in any other mass of men, ancient or modern. . . . He is called upon, while so engaged, to weigh interests not his own; to be guided, in case of conflicting claims, by another rule than his private partialities; to apply, at every turn, principles and maxims which have for their reason of existence the common good.

67. Marx, *Civil War in France*, pp. 60–61, and *MEW 17*, p. 342.

68. Ibid., p. 61, and *MEW 17*, p. 343.

69. Ibid., pp. 61 and 62, and *MEW 17*, pp. 342–44. This idea also appeared in the *Communist Manifesto* in 1848 on pp. 20–21: "Theoretical conclusions of the communists are in no way based on ideas or principles that have been invented, or discovered, by this or that would be universal reformer. They merely express, in general terms, actual relations springing from an existing class struggle, from a historical movement going on under our very eyes." [*Marx Engels Collected Works*, vol. 6 (New York: International Publishers, 1975), p. 498, and *Marx Engels Werke*, Band 4 (*MEW 4*) (Berlin: Dietz Verlag, 1964), pp. 474–75.]

70. Marx, *Civil War in France*, p. 62, and *MEW 17*, p. 343. Marx's own ideas have been rejected for being utopian and thereby totalitarian. See Maurice Meisner, *Marxism, Maoism, and Utopianism: Eight Essays* (Madison, Wis.: University of Wisconsin Press, 1982), pp. 15ff.

71. Karl Marx, "Critique of the Gotha Program," *Marx Engels Collected Works*, vol. 24 (New York: International Publishers, 1975), pp. 86–87, and *Marx Engels Werke*, Band 19 (*MEW 19*) (Berlin: Dietz Verlag, 1962), pp. 20–21.

72. Karl Marx, *Communist Manifesto*, p. 515, and *MEW 4*, p. 490.

73. Karl Marx, *The Poverty of Philosophy* (New York: International Publishers, 1963), pp. 11, 51, 121, and 124, and *Marx Engels Werke*, Band 4 (*MEW 4*) (Berlin: Dietz Verlag, 1964), pp. 83, 140, and 142.

74. Patrick Murray, *Marx's Theory of Scientific Knowledge* (Atlantic Highlands, N.J.: Humanities Press International, 1988), pp. 37–38, 63 (critique of the moral abstractionism of German Idealism), 94–96 (critique of Proudhon's socialism), and 199.

75. Marx, *Civil War in France*, p. 65, and *MEW 17*, p. 347.

76. David Felix, in *Marx as Politician*, quotes Marx as privately writing that the "majority of the Commune was in no sense socialist, nor could it have been." Felix says, "Within the city limits of Paris Marx had seen the model, imperfect and a failure, of successful revolution on a national *and* international scale. His achievement was to transform the model into myth—and make it real" (p. 175).

77. For a more detailed study of these issues see McCarthy, *Marx and the Ancients*, pp. 19–55, 142–43, and 172–75.

78. Max Horkheimer, *Eclipse of Reason* (New York: Continuum, 1974), p. 92.

79. Daniel Little in his work *The Scientific Marx* (Minneapolis: University of Minnesota Press, 1986), p. 18, outlines some of the major empirical themes in *Capital*. He rejects the view that Marx held to a naturalistic and positivistic view of science. However, his critique of the naturalism in which *Capital* "is intended to provide a unified deductive theory of capitalism" (p. 11) leads him simply to list the various areas of empirical investigation such as a description of property system, labor theory of value, capitalist production, economic

crises, social foundations of capital, historical account of capitalism, description of the working day, and so forth. Because of his rejection of one overarching theoretical orientation, he does not ask whether all these empirical studies can be viewed from a more comprehensive and inclusive perspective. This is partly supplied by the ancients.

80. Marx, *Capital: A Critique of Political Economy*, vol. 1, *A Critical Analysis of Capitalist Production*, ed. Friedrich Engels, trans. Samuel Moore and Edward Aveling (New York: International Publishers, 1967), p. 362, and *Marx Engels Werke*, Band 23 (*MEW 23*) (Berlin: Dietz Verlag, 1962), p. 383.

81. Ibid., vol. 1, p. 364, and *MEW 23*, p. 386. Classical political economy attempts a justification of this new division of labor by stressing declining costs, efficiency, and productivity of exchange value and commodities. Marx juxtaposes this modern perspective to the values of Greek writers such as Homer, Archilochus, Thucydides, Plato, and Xenophon who, when discussing the division of labor, stressed the quality and utility of the products made and the development of the talents of the artisans. "Hence [in the ancient world] both product and producer are improved by division of labor." But Marx is also very critical of both Plato and Xenophon who make the worker subservient to the needs, logic, and function of the production process.

82. In industrial societies, the division of labor will turn into a radical split between the anarchy of competition and the despotism of the factory. For a discussion of this distinction between the logic of markets and firms see William James Booth, "Households, Markets, and Firms," in McCarthy, *Marx and Aristotle*, pp. 250–259.

83. Marx, *Capital*, vol. 1, p. 645, and *MEW 23*, p. 675.

84. Ibid., vol. 1, p. 382, and *MEW 23*, p. 403.

85. Ibid., vol. 1, p. 422, and *MEW 23*, p. 445.

86. Marx stresses the enclosure movements of the fifteenth and sixteenth centuries. However, two-thirds of the arable land in England was expropriated during the second enclosure movement of the eighteenth and nineteenth centuries. [See Phyllis Deane, *The First Industrial Revolution* (Cambridge, England: Cambridge University Press, 1979), pp. 42–52; J. L. Hammond and Barbara Hammond, *The Village Labourer: A Study of the Government of England Before the Reform Bill* (Wolfeboro Falls, New Hampshire: Alan Sutton Publishing, 1989); E. J. Hobsbawm, *Industry and Empire* (Harmondsworth, England: Penguin Books, 1969), pp. 97–108; Eric Hobsbawm and George Rudé, *Captain Swing: A Social History of the Great English Agricultural Uprising of 1830* (New York: W. W. Norton, 1968), pp. 23–71; Paul Mantoux, *The Industrial Revolution in the Eighteenth Century* (New York: Harper & Row, 1961), pp. 136–185; Karl Polanyi, *The Great Transformation: The Political and Economic Origins of Our Time* (Boston: Beacon Press, 1944), pp. 77–102; and E. P. Thompson, *The Making of the English Working Class* (New York: Vintage Books, 1963), pp. 213–233.]

87. Karl Marx, *Capital: A Critique of Political Economy*, vol. 3, *The*

336   *Notes*

Process of Capitalist Production as a Whole, ed. Friedrich Engels (New York: International Publishers, 1967), p. 211, and *Marx Engels Werke*, Band 25 (*MEW 25*) (Berlin: Dietz Verlag, 1964), p. 221.

88. Ibid., vol. 3, p. 153, and *MEW 25*, p. 162.
89. Ibid., vol. 3, p. 213, and *MEW 25*, p. 223.
90. G. F. W. Hegel, *Science of Logic*, vol. 2, trans. W. H. Johnston and L. G. Struthers (London: George Allen & Unwin, 1966), p. 176.
91. Ibid., pp. 181–82. See also Herbert Marcuse, *Hegel's Ontology and the Theory of Historicity*, trans. Seyla Benhabib (Cambridge, Mass.: MIT Press, 1987), pp. 89–102.
92. Marx, *Capital*, vol. 1, p. 19, and *MEW 23*, p. 27.
93. See Karl Popper, *The Open Society and Its Enemies*, vol. 2, *The High Tide of Prophecy: Hegel and Marx* (Princeton: Princeton University Press, 1966), pp. 84–86. For an overview of this issue and a discussion of positivist interpretations of Marx see Daniel Little, *The Scientific Marx*, pp. 11–16.
94. Quote from Lenin taken from Little, *The Scientific Marx*, p. 11.
95. For an analysis of the German view of science as *Wissenschaft* and not the predictive knowledge of the positivist interpretation see Murray, *Marx's Theory of Scientific Knowledge*. Murray also emphasizes the historical specificity of Marx's method by distinguishing between the logic of history (capitalism) and the logic of capital. See also Russell Keat and John Urry, *Social Theory as Science* (London, England: Routledge & Kegan Paul, 1975), pp. 97–100.
96. Arendt, *The Human Condition*, pp. 225–30.
97. McCarthy, *Marx and the Ancients*, pp. 57–119.
98. There is an implicit recognition of this in Marx, *Grundrisse: Introduction to the Critique of Political Economy*, trans. Martin Nicolaus (New York: Vintage Books, 1973), p. 750, and *Grundrisse der Kritik der politischen Ökonomie* (Frankfurt/Main: Europäische Verlagsanstalt, n.d.), p. 636. Here he refers to the economic crises, explosions, and cataclysms that lead to the "violent overthrow" of the system. This implies some element of class conflict and self-direction, but he does not develop this line of argument.
99. Marx, *Capital*, vol. 3, p. 250, and *MEW 25*, p. 260.
100. Marx, "Estranged Labor," in the "Economic and Philosophic Manuscripts of 1844," *Marx Engels Collected Works*, vol. 3 (New York: International Publishers, 1975), p. 277, and *Marx Engels Werke*, Ergänzungsband, Teil I (*MEW EB*) (Berlin: Dietz Verlag, 1968), p. 517.
101. Marx, *Capital*, vol. 3, p. 259, and *MEW 25*, pp. 269–70. For an examination of Marx's further ethical statements in this volume see *Capital*, vol. 3, pp. 85–86, 88, 250, and 820, and *MEW 25*, pp. 95–96, 99, 260, and 828.
102. Ibid, vol. 3, p. 820, and *MEW 25*, p. 828.
103. Marx, *Grundrisse*, p. 488, and *Grundrisse der Kritik*, pp. 387–88.
104. Ibid., p. 706, and *Grundrisse der Kritik*, p. 593.
105. Ibid., p. 708, and *Grundrisse der Kritik*, p. 596. For an analysis of

Aristotle's theory of human capabilities and needs see Martha Nussbaum, "Nature, Function, and Capability: Aristotle on Political Distribution," in *Marx and Aristotle*; Patricia Springborg, "Aristotle and the Problem of Needs," *History of Political Thought*, 5 (Winter 1984); and Agnes Heller, *The Theory of Need in Marx* (New York: St. Martin's Press, 1976).

Chapter Three: Storming Heaven and Liberating History

1. José Bonino, *Doing Theology in a Revolutionary Situation* (Philadelphia: Fortress Press, 1975), pp. 112ff.; Erich Fromm, *Marx's Concept of Man* (New York: Ungar Publisher, 1966); Karl Löwith, *From Hegel to Nietzsche* (Garden City, N.Y.: Doubleday, 1964); Paul Tillich, *Der Mensch in Christentum und im Marxismus* (Düsseldorf, Germany: Ring Verlag, 1953); Arend Th. van Leeuwen, *Critique of Earth* (New York: Charles Scribner's Sons, 1974), pp. 217–33 and *Critique of Heaven* (New York: Charles Scribner's Sons, 1972); José Miranda, *Marx against the Marxists: The Christian Humanism of Karl Marx*, trans. John Drury (Maryknoll, N.Y.: Orbis Books, 1980); José Miranda, *Marx and the Bible*, trans. John Eagleson (Maryknoll, N.Y.: Orbis Books, 1974); Enrique Dussel, "Domination—Liberation: A New Approach," in *The Mystical and Political Dimension of the Christian Faith*, ed. Claude Geffré and Gustavo Guttiérez, trans. by J. D. Mitchell (New York: Herder and Herder, 1974), and "Historical and Philosophical Presuppositions for Latin American Theology," in *Frontiers of Theology in Latin America*, ed. Rosino Gibellini (Maryknoll, N.Y.: Orbis Books, 1979); Murray Wolfson, *Marx: Economist, Philosopher, Jew* (New York: St. Martin's Press, 1982), p. 196; There is also a further extensive bibliography of works relating Marx and Judaism in Albert Massiczek, *Der menschliche Mensch. Karl Marx' jüdischer Humanismus* (Wien, Austria: Europa Verlag, 1968). Here he stresses the relationship between Marx and the prophets as examined in the works of N. Berdiajew, P. Bigo, W. Blumenberg, Th. Brauer, H. Diwald, S. M. Dubnow, G. Ferrero, F. Heer, R. M. Heilbrunn, R. Kayser, A. Liberman, Gustav Mayer, W. Rathenau, F. Rosenzweig, J. A. Schumpeter, E. Simon, Th. Steinbüchel, P. Tillich, C. Tresmontant, Th. Zlocisti, E. Fromm, R. König, K. Löwith, and E. Thier (pp. 476–77); the relationship between socialism and Judaism is examined in the works of Leo Baeck, Ernst Bloch, Jochanan Bloch, Rudolf Kayser, Moses Hess, Robert Michels, and Theodor Zlocisti (p. 489).

2. Fromm, *Marx's Concept of Man*, p. 44.

3. For an analysis of the inflammatory and possibly anti-Semitic language and Marx's defense of the civil liberties and emancipation of the Jews see Shlomo Avineri, "Marx and Jewish Emancipation," *Journal of the History of Ideas* (July 1964): 446 and 450; Julius Carlebach, *Karl Marx and the Radical Critique of Judaism* (London: Routledge and Kegan Paul, 1978); Emil Fackenheim, *Encounters between Judaism and Modern Philosophy: A Preface to*

Notes

Future Jewish Thought (New York: Basic Books, 1973), p. 250; Louis Harap, "The Meaning of Marx's Essay 'On the Jewish Question,'" *The Journal of Ethnic Studies*, 7, no. 1 (Spring 1979): 43; Eugene Kamenka, "The Baptism of Marx," *The Hibbert Journal*, 56 (October 1957–58): 346; Michael Maidan, "Marx on the Jewish Question: A Meta-Critical Analysis," *Studies in Soviet Thought*, 33 (January 1987): 28; Henry Pachter, "Marx and the Jews," *Dissent* (Fall 1979); Joel Schwartz, "Liberalism and the Jewish Connection: A Study of Spinoza and the Young Marx," *Political Theory* (February 1985): 72–74; and Marx Wartofsky, "Marx on the Jewish Question: A Review," *The Philosophical Forum*, 19 (1961–62): 85.

    4. Arthur McGovern, *Marxism: An American Christian Perspective* (Maryknoll, N.Y.: Orbis Books, 1981).

    5. Richard Tawney, *Religion and the Rise of Capitalism* (Gloucester, Mass.: Peter Smith, 1962).

    6. Karl Marx, "Contribution to the Critique of Hegel's *Philosophy of Law*: Introduction," *Marx Engels Collected Works*, vol. 3 (New York: International Publishers, 1975), p. 176, and *Marx Engels Werke*, Band 1 *MEW 1* (Berlin: Dietz Verlag, 1961), p. 379.

    7. Ibid., p. 175, and *MEW 1*, p. 378.

    8. For an appreciation of the history of the broader philosophical context of the issues surrounding biblical hermeneutics see Hans Frei, *The Eclipse of Biblical Narrative: A Study in Eighteenth and Nineteenth Century Hermeneutics* (New Haven: Yale University Press, 1974), p. 225.

    9. F. Lichtenberger, *History of German Theology in the Nineteenth Century*, trans. and ed. W. Hastie (Edinburgh, Scotland: T. and T. Clark, 1889), pp. 374–78.

    10. Edmund Wilson, *To the Findland Station: A Study in the Writing and Acting of History* (New York: Harcourt, Brace and Company, 1940), pp. 306–7.

    11. Benedict de Spinoza, *A Theologico-Political Treatise*, trans. R. H. M Elwes (New York: Dover Publications, 1951); Maximilien Rubel, "Notes on Marx's Conception of Democracy," *New Politics* 1, no. 2 (1962): 80–81; and Sigmund Krancberg, "Karl Marx and Democracy," *Studies in Soviet Thought*, 24 (July 1982): 27.

    12. Georg Hegel, *On Christianity: Early Theological Writings*, trans. T. M. Knox (New York: Harper and Brothers, 1961).

    13. Bruno Bauer, *Kritik der Geschichte der Offenbarung*, Band 2 (Aalen: Scientia Verlag, 1983), p. 347. Part I of *Die Religion des Alten Testaments in der Geschichtlichen Entwicklung Ihrer Prinzipien Dargestellt*.

    14. Ibid., p. 348.

    15. Ibid., Band 1, p. 25. For a further analysis of the meaning of the term "contradiction" in this work see John Toews, *Hegelianism: The Path toward Dialectical Humanism, 1805–1841* (Cambridge, England: Cambridge University Press, 1985), pp. 300–1.

16. Ibid., pp. 352–53.

17. August Cornu, *Marx und Engels. Leben und Werk*, Band 1 (Berlin: Aufbau-Verlag, 1953), p. 143.

18. Bauer, *Kritik der Geschichte der Offenbarung*, Band 2, p. 354.

19. Toews, *Hegelianism*, p. 295.

20. William Brazill, *The Young Hegelians*, Dissertation, Yale University (Ann Arbor: University Microfilms, Inc., 1967), p. 199.

21. Zvi Rosen, *Bruno Bauer and Karl Marx: The Influence of Bruno Bauer on Marx's Thought* (The Hague, Netherlands: Martinus Nijhoff, 1977), p. 150.

22. Abraham Heschel, *The Prophets* (New York: Harper and Row, 1969), pp. 200–1.

23. Ibid., p. 198.

24. Stephan Mott, *Biblical Ethics and Social Change* (New York: Oxford University Press, 1982), p. 67.

25. Ibid., p. 66.

26. Martin Buber, *Moses: The Revelation and the Covenant* (New York: Harper and Row, 1958), p. 133.

27. Walter Pilgrim, *Good News to the Poor: Wealth and Poverty in the Luke-Acts* (Minneapolis, Minn.: Augsburg Publishing House, 1981), pp. 19–32.

28. Robert North, *Sociology of the Biblical Jubilee* (Rome: Pontifical Biblical Institute, 1954), pp. 2–3.

29. Martin Hengel, *Property and Riches in the Early Church: Aspects of a Social History of Early Christianity* (Philadelphia: Fortress Press, 1974), p. 15.

30. Mott, *Biblical Ethics and Social Change*, p. 67.

31. Amos, *The New Oxford Annotated Bible with the Apocrypha*, ed. Herbert May and Bruce Metzger (New York: Oxford University Press, 1977), 5:21–24, p. 1112. All further references to the Bible will be from this edition.

32. North, *Sociology of the Biblical Jubilee*, p. 1.

33. Deuteronomy, 15:4, p. 234.

34. Deuteronomy 12, pp. 230–31 and Leviticus 25, pp. 153–56.

35. Peter Berger, *An Invitation to Sociology* (Garden City, N.Y.: Doubleday, 1963), p. 27.

36. Amos, 5:11–12, p. 1112.

37. Isaiah, 10:1–2, p. 834.

38. José Miranda, *Communism in the Bible* (Maryknoll, N.Y.: Orbis Books, 1982), pp. 28–29.

39. Isaiah, 9:7, p. 833.

40. Erich Fromm, *You Shall Be As Gods: A Radical Interpretation of the Old Testament* (Greenwich, Conn.: Fawcett, 1966), pp. 44–45.

41. Robert Coote, *Amos among the Prophets: Composition and Theology* (Philadelphia: Fortress Press, 1981), especially analysis of class structure of Israel and concept of justice, pp. 24–42; E. Hamilton, *The Prophets of Israel* (New York: Norton, 1936), dealing with the issue of religion and politics and economic justice, pp. 21 and 194; E. W. Heaton, *The Old Testament Prophets*

(Atlanta: John Knox Press, 1977), especially concerning social sin, pp. 65–70; Hengel, *Property and Riches in the Early Church*; Roy Lee Honeycutt, *Amos and His Message* (Nashville, Tenn.: Broadman Press, 1963); John Paterson, *The Goodly Fellowship of the Prophets* (New York: Scribner's, 1948), especially concerning the church as the vehicle for economic oppression, p. 22; Gerhard Von Rad, *Deuteronomy: A Commentary* (Philadelphia: Westminster Press, 1966), chapter 15; Martin Noth, *Leviticus: A Commentary* (Philadelphia: Westminster Press, 1965), pp. 181–92; Michael Walzer, *Exodus and Revolution* (New York: Basic Books, 1985); James Ward, *Amos and Isaiah* (Nashville, Tenn.: Abingdon Press, 1969).

42. Fromm, *You Shall Be As Gods*, p. 57.

43. Joseph Comblin, "Freedom and Liberation as Theological Concepts," in *The Mystical and Political Dimension of the Christian Faith*, ed. C. Geffré and G. Guttiérez, trans. J. D. Mitchell (New York: Herder and Herder, 1974), p. 99.

44. C. B. MacPherson, *Possessive Individualism: Hobbes to Locke* (Oxford: Oxford University Press, 1962); Thomas Spraegens, *The Irony of Liberal Reason* (Chicago: University of Chicago, 1981).

45. Miranda, *Marx and the Bible*, p. 15; John Donahue, S.J., "Biblical Perspectives on Justice: Examining Christian Sources for Social Change," in *The Faith That Does Justice*, ed. John Haughey (New York: Paulist Press, 1977).

46. Ernst Bloch, *Atheism in Christianity: The Religion of the Exodus and the Kingdom*, trans. Swann (New York: Herder and Herder, 1972).

47. Fromm, *You Shall Be As Gods*, p. 27.

48. Ibid., p. 62.

49. Amos, 3:6–8, p. 1109; E. W. Heaton, in his work *The Old Testament Prophets*, p. 78, argues that the ethic of Israel was self-interest built around a religion that guaranteed "good fortune for those who participated in its rituals."

50. Johannes Linblom, *Prophecy in Ancient Israel* (Philadelphia: Fortress Press, 1962), p. 353.

51. Massiczek, *Der menschliche Mensch*, pp. 456–66.

52. Isaiah, 2:7–9, p. 825.

53. Gregory Baum, *Religion and Alienation: A Theological Reading of Sociology* (Mahwam, N.J.: Paulist Press, 1975), p. 63. This chapter also appeared in *Theology Today*, January 1977, pp. 344–53.

54. Fromm, *Marx's Concept of Man*, p. 39.

55. Bonino, *Doing Theology in a Revolutionary Situation*, pp. 88–96.

56. Baum, *Religion and Alienation*, p. 64.

57. Isaiah, 44:9–18, p. 877.

58. John McKenzie, *The Anchor Bible: Second Isaiah* (Garden City, N.Y.: Doubleday, 1968), p. 68.

59. Edward Young, *The Book of Isaiah* (Grand Rapids, Mich.: Eerdmans, 1972), p. 172.

60. Karl Marx, "On the Jewish Question," *Marx Engels Collected Works*, vol. 3 (New York: International Publishers, 1975), p. 159, and *Marx Engels Werke*, Band 1 (*MEW 1*) (Berlin: Dietz Verlag, 1961), p. 360.

61. Ibid.

62. Isaiah, 44, p. 877.

63. Karl Marx, "Estranged Labor," in "Economic and Philosophic Manuscripts," *Marx Engels Collected Works*, vol. 3 (New York: International Publishers, 1975), p. 272, and *Marx Engels Werke*, Ergänzungsband, Teil 1 (*MEW EB*) (Berlin: Dietz Verlag, 1968), p. 512. This same idea with its connection to the Hebrew notion of idolatry is reiterated in Marx's *Grundrisse*, trans. Martin Nicolaus (New York: Vintage Books, 1973), p. 453, and *Grundrisse der Kritik der politischen Ökonomie* (Frankfurt/Main: Europäische Verlagsanstalt, n.d.), p. 357.

64. Fromm, *You Shall Be As Gods*, p. 37.

65. Miranda, *Marx against the Marxists*, pp. 197–263.

66. Ibid., p. 197.

67. For an overview of Marx's critique of classical political economy see Bhikhu Parekh, *Marx's Theory of Ideology* (Baltimore, Md.: Johns Hopkins University Press, 1982), chapter 2.

68. Marx, *A Contribution to a Critique of Political Economy*, ed. Maurice Dobb, trans. S. W. Ryazanskaya (New York: International Publishers, 1970), note on p. 125, and *Marx Engels Werke*, Band 13 (*MEW 13*) (Berlin: Dietz Verlag, 1964), p. 103.

69. Marx, *Capital: A Critique of Political Economy*, vol. 1, *A Critical Analysis of Capitalist Production*, trans. Samuel Moore and Edward Aveling (New York: International Publishers, 1967), p. 71, and *Marx Engels Werke*, Band 23 (*MEW 23*) (Berlin: Dietz Verlag, 1962), p. 85. This section on fetishism was not part of the original edition but was included in the second edition to help clarify his methodological purposes in *Capital*.

70. Marx, *Capital*, vol. 1, p. 72.

71. Geoffrey Pilling, *Marx's Capital: Philosophy and Political Economy* (London: Routledge and Kegan Paul, 1980), p. 159.

72. Parekh, *Marx's Theory of Ideology*, p. 65.

73. Marx, *Capital*, vol. 1, p. 621, and *MEW 23*, p. 649.

74. Marx, "Estranged Labor," p. 273, and *MEW EB*, p. 513.

75. Marx, *Poverty of Philosophy* (New York: International Publishers, 1963), p. 107, and *Marx Engels Werke*, Band 4 (*MEW 4*) (Berlin: Dietz Verlag, 1964), p. 128.

76. In a use of the term idolatry with a quite different meaning see Marx's *Grundrisse*, p. 410, and *Grundrisse der Kritik*, p. 313. Here he uses the notion of "nature-idolatry" to refer to the premodern romantic view that nature was alive and dynamic and not an object of pure utility. This approach to idolatry is not pursued because Marx applies the term to the dynamics of modern industrial society.

77. Marx, *Capital*, vol. 1, p. 73, and *MEW 23*, p. 87.
78. Ibid.
79. Marx, *A Contribution to the Critique of Political Economy*, p. 34, and *MEW 13*, p. 23.
80. Marx, *Poverty of Philosophy*, p. 105 and p. 121, and *MEW 4*, pp. 126 and 139–40.
81. Trent Schroyer, *Critique of Domination: The Origins and Development of Critical Theory* (New York: George Braziller, 1973), p. 184.
82. Paul Mattick, *Marx and Keynes: The Limits of the Mixed Economy* (Boston: Porter Sargent Publishers, 1969), chapters 6–9.
83. Marx, *Capital*, vol. 1, p. 86, and *MEW 23*, p. 101.
84. Revelation, 17:13, p. 1508.
85. Ibid., 13:17, p. 1505.
86. Ibid., 17:7, p. 1508.
87. Ibid., 13:15, p. 1505.
88. Van Leeuwen, *Critique of Earth*, pp. 217–33.
89. Marx, *Capital*, vol. 1, pp. 86–87, and *MEW 23*, pp. 101–2.
90. Pachter, "Marx and the Jews," p. 477.
91. Marx, *Capital*, vol. 1, pp. 76–83, and *MEW 23*, pp. 91–98.

Chapter Four: Nietzsche and Classical Antiquity

1. Daniel Breazeale, "Introduction," in *Philosophy and Truth: Selections from Nietzsche's Notebooks of the Early 1870's*, trans. and ed. Daniel Breazeale (Atlantic Highlands, N.J.: Humanities Press, 1979), pp. xx–xxi. For a semester by semester summary see Karl Schlechta and Anni Anders, *Friedrich Nietzsche: Von den verborgenen Anfängen seines Philosophierens* (Stuttgart: Bad Cannstatt, 1962), pp. 20–21.

2. For a brief analysis of the relation between Nietzsche's early lectures at the University of Basel and *The Birth of Tragedy* see M. S. Silk and J. P. Stern, *Nietzsche on Tragedy* (Cambridge, England: University of Cambridge Press, 1981), pp. 35–40. For an analysis of his early school days and reading interests read Otto Manthey-Zorn, *The Tragedy of Nietzsche* (Amherst, Mass.: Amherst College Press, 1956), pp. 12–24.

3. To examine the lectures on pre-Platonic philosophy from the years 1872, 1873, and 1876 see Friedrich Nietzsche, *Friedrich Nietzsche Gesammelte Werke. Musarionausgabe*, Band 4 (München: Musarion Verlag, 1921), pp. 247–364 (lectures from 1869–70 are not available). For a study of the early Plato lectures see *Musarionausgabe 4*, pp. 367–443.

4. As Breazeale discusses in the "Introduction," the unpublished notes or *Nachlass* of the seventies known as *The Philosophers' Book* was made up of the following works on pre-Platonic philosophy, which Nietzsche divided into his historical and theoretical works. The historical analysis of pre-Platonic

philosophy of nature is called *Philosophy in the Tragic Age of the Greeks* (1873), while the theoretical works comprised the following: *The Philosopher: Reflections on the Struggle between Art and Knowledge* (1872), *The Philosopher as Cultural Physician* (1873), *On Truth and Lies in a Nonmoral Sense* (1873), and *The Struggle between Science and Wisdom* (1875).

5. This connection between Nietzsche's early and later critique of knowledge and nihilism has been noticed by Breazeale, "Introduction," pp. vliv–xlix; Arthur Danto, *Nietzsche as Philosopher* (New York: Macmillan, 1965), p. 38; and Schlechta and Anders, *Friedrich Nietzsche*.

6. Breazeale, "Introduction," p. xlviii.

7. There has been a good deal of scholarly discussion about the extent of Nietzsche's knowledge of Kant's philosophy. Some have argued that he really had no training or expertise to understand Kant's philosophical theories. In her essay "The Transfigurations of Intoxication: Nietzsche, Schopenhauer, and Dionysus," *Arion: Journal of Humanities and the Classics*, 1, no. 2 (Spring 1991): 75, Martha Nussbaum has written that Nietzsche's knowledge of German Idealism was "thin and uneven." But throughout the early works, there is constant reference to Kant's writings. Even if the extent and depth of his knowledge of Kant is in question, Nietzsche was certainly influenced by the epistemology and psychology of the Kantian authors such as Friedrich Albert Lange and Arthur Schopenhauer. He breathed the air of the "back to Kant" movement of the late nineteenth century. [See George Stack, "Nietzsche and Lange," *Modern Schoolman*, 57 (1980), and *Lange and Nietzsche* (Berlin and New York: Walter de Gruyter, 1983); Keith Ansell-Pearson, "The Question of F. A. Lange's Influence on Nietzsche: A Critique of Recent Research from the Standpoint of the Dionysian," *Nietzsche Studien*, 17 (1988), and "Nietzsche's Overcoming of Kant and Metaphysics: From Tragedy to Nihilism," *Nietzsche Studien*, 16 (1987): 310; and Thomas Willey, *Back to Kant: The Revival of Kantianism in German Social and Historical Thought, 1860–1914* (Detroit, Mich.: Wayne State University Press, 1978); Herbert Schnädelbach, *Philosophy in German 1831–1933*, trans. Eric Matthews (Cambridge, England; Cambridge University Press, 1984), pp. 102 and 198ff.; and Gilles Deleuze, *Nietzsche and Philosophy*, trans. Hugh Tomlinson (London: Athlone Press, 1983), pp. 89–94.] Silk and Stern in *Nietzsche on Tragedy* report that Nietzsche even considered writing his doctoral dissertation on Kant (p. 50) and that his philology was always, "embraced and defined by a philosophical outlook" (p. 35). In a remarkable incident in 1871, he applied for the chair of philosophy at the University of Basel claiming that "even in my philological studies I have been most attracted by those topics which seemed important for the history of philosophy or for ethical and aesthetic problems" (p. 50). Silk and Stern wrote that, according to Nietzsche, "his dominant inclination had always been towards philosophy." The modern split between philology and philosophy was not present in Nietzsche's work. And it has been the failure to recognize this very point that has caused enormous problems for the interpretation of Nietzsche's ideas about the Greeks.

8. For a more comprehensive overview of the history of classical German theories of tragedy see Silk and Stern, *Nietzsche on Tragedy*, pp. 297–331.

9. Aristotle, *Aristotle's Poetics*, trans. Leon Golden (Englewood Cliffs, N.J.: Prentice-Hall, 1968), p. 22.

10. Ibid., p. 20.

11. Ladislaus Löb, *From Lessing to Hauptmann: Studies in German Drama* (Sussex, England: University Tutorial Press, 1974), pp. 22–23.

12. Robin Harrison, "Lessing's Emancipation from Aristotle: Symmetry of Plot and the Emergence of Character in *Emilia Galotti*," *Patterns of Change: German Drama and the European Tradition* (New York: Peter Lang, 1990), p. 23.

13. Johann Wolfgang von Goethe, *Goethe und die Antike: eine Sammlung*, Hrsg. von Ernst Grumach (Berlin: Walter de Gruyter, 1949); Humphrey Trevelyan, *Goethe and the Greeks* (Cambridge, England: Cambridge University Press, 1981); Georg Lukács, *Goethe and His Age*, trans. Robert Anchor (New York: H. Fertig, 1978); Walther Rehm, *Griechentum und Goethezeit: Geschichte eines Glaubens* (Bern, Switzerland: A. Francke Verlag, 1952); and E. M. Butler, *The Tyranny of Greece over Germany* (Cambridge, England: University of Cambridge Press, 1935).

14. Johann Joachim Winckelmann quoted in Henry Caraway Hatfield, *Winckelmann and His German Critics 1755–1781: A Prelude to the Classical Age* (Morningside Heights, N.Y.: King's Crown Press, 1943), p. 8.

15. Johann Wolfgang von Goethe, "On Interpreting Aristotle's *Poetics*," in *Essays on Art and Literature*, ed. John Gearey, trans. Ellen von Nardroff and Ernest von Nardroff (New York: Suhrkamp Publishers, 1986), p. 198, and *Goethes Werke*, Band 12 (Hamburg: Christian Wegner, 1956), pp. 342–43. Also in this volume read the sublime and beautifully moving essays on Laocoon, Winckelmann and his age, and Greek art and literature.

16. Ibid., p. 198, and *Goethes Werke 12*, p. 343.

17. Ibid., pp. 198–99, and *Goethes Werke 12*, p. 344.

18. E.L. Stahl, *Friedrich Schiller's Drama: Theory and Practice* (Oxford, England: Clarendon Press, 1954), pp. 47–54. Stahl shows how Schiller's early theory of art of the later 1770s and early 1780s was influenced by seventeenth-century rationalism. At this time, he held that the universe, as a work of art, was rational and harmonious. With the later Kantian influence, he began to see that the ideal harmony and rationality lay in the individual artist, for example, Copernicus and Newton and not nature itself. This shift began with *The Artist* (1788–89).

19. Schiller, *On the Tragic Art*, in *The Works of Schiller*, vol. 5, *Aesthetical and Philosophical Essays*, ed. Nathan Haskell Dole (London: Robertson, Ashford, and Bentley, 1902), pp. 73 and 82, and *Gesammelte Werke in fünf Bänden*, Band 5, Hrsg. von Reinhold Netolitzky (n.l.: Sigbert Mohn Verlag, n.d.), p. 218.

20. Schiller, *On the Sublime*, in *Works of Schiller*, vol. 5, p. 122, and *Gesammelte Werke 5*, p. 433.

21. Schiller, *On the Tragic Art*, p. 79, and *Gesammelte Werke 5*, p. 215.
22. Schiller, *On Dignity*, in *Works of Schiller*, vol. 5, p. 217.
23. Schiller, *Of the Cause of the Pleasure We Derive from Tragic Objects*, in *Works of Schiller*, vol. 5, pp. 93 and 94, and *Gesammelte Werke 5*, pp. 187–88. Schiller, as with Nietzsche later, says that "life is the condition of all good" (p. 94).
24. Stahl, *Friedrich Schiller's Drama*, pp. 56–58.
25. Schiller, *On the Sublime*, p. 137, and *Gesammelte Werke 5*, p. 449.
26. Schiller, *The Pathetic*, in *The Works of Schiller*, vol. 5, p. 141, and *Gesammelte Werke 5*, p. 230.
27. Ibid., p. 155, and *Gesammelte Werke 5*, p. 243.
28. Schiller, *On Simple and Sentimental Poetry*, in *The Works of Schiller*, vol. 5, p. 296, and *Gesammelte Werke 5*, pp. 503–4.
29. In his work *The Longing for Total Revolution: Philosophical Sources of Social Discontent from Rousseau to Marx and Nietzsche* (Berkeley: University of California Press, 1992), Bernard Yack contends that Nietzsche's critique of modern culture, his attempt to overcome nihilism, and his goal of saving mankind from dehumanization have their foundations in the writings of Rousseau, the early Hegel, and Schiller (pp. 312, 317, and 332). "For Nietzsche, the tragic sense represents the 'one hope and one guarantee for the future of humanity,' the one influence that may raise man to a 'supra-personal' standpoint and thus save him from the loss of humanity. Dehumanization is clearly the danger that Nietzsche, the 'friend of man,' fears in modern, nontragic culture" (p. 330).
30. Schiller, *Sentimental Poetry*, in *The Works of Schiller*, vol. 5, p. 306, and *Gesammelte Werke 5*, p. 513.
31. Friedrich Schiller, *On the Aesthetic Education of Man*, Eleventh Letter, trans. Reginald Snell (New York: Ungar, 1965), p. 63, and *Gesammelte Werke 5*, p. 356.
32. Schiller, *On the Aesthetic Education of Man*, Sixth Letter, p. 40, and *Gesammelte Werke 5*, p. 336.
33. Löb, *From Lessing to Hauptmann*, p. 72.
34. Schiller, *On the Aesthetic Education of Man*, Thirteenth Letter, p. 69, and *Gesammelte Werke 5*, p. 362.
35. John Prudhoe, *The Theatre of Goethe and Schiller* (Totowa, N.J.: Rowman & Littlefield Publishers, 1973), pp. 120–1.
36. Reginald Snell, "Introduction," in *On the Aesthetic Education of Man*, p. 15. Also see Yack, *The Longing for Total Revolution*, pp. 133–84.
37. Schiller, *On the Aesthetic Education of Man*, Eighteenth Letter, p. 87, and *Gesammelte Werke 5*, p. 380.
38. Schiller, *On the Aesthetic Education of Man*, Twenty-fifth Letter, p. 121, and *Gesammelte Werke 5*, p. 411.
39. Ibid., p. 123, and *Gesammelte Werke 5*, pp. 413–14.
40. Schiller, *On the Aesthetic Education of Man*, Twenty-seventh Letter, p. 138, and *Gesammelte Werke 5*, p. 427.

41. Hugh Lloyd-Jones, *Blood for the Ghosts: Classical Influences in the Nineteenth and Twentieth Centuries* (London: Gerald Duckworth and Company, 1982), pp. 167–68.

42. Friedrich Nietzsche, *The Struggle between Science and Wisdom* in *Philosophy and Truth: Selections from Nietzsche's Notebooks of the Early 1870s*, trans. and ed. Daniel Breazeale (Atlantic Highland, N.J.: Humanities Press, 1979), p. 127, and *Nietzsche Werke. Kritische Gesamtausgabe*, Abteilung IV, Band 1, Hrsg. von Giorgio Colli and Mazzino Montinari (Berlin: Walter de Gruyter & Co., 1967), pp. 173–90.

43. For a comparison of Nietzsche's and Schopenhauer's metaphysics of art and theory of music see Robert Rethy, "The Tragic Affirmation of the *Birth of Tragedy*," *Nietzsche Studien*, 17 (1988): 16ff.

44. Robert McGinn, "Culture as Prophylactic: Nietzsche's *Birth of Tragedy* as Cultural Criticism," *Nietzsche Studien*, 4 (1975): 91.

45. Friedrich Nietzsche, "Notes for We Philologists," trans. William Arrowsmith, *Arion*, new series 1/2 (1973–74), p. 296, and "Notizen zu Wir Philologen," in *Nietzsche Werke. Kritische Gesamtausgabe*, Abteilung IV, Band 1, Hrsg. von Giorgio Colli and Mazzino Montinari (Berlin: Walter de Gruyter & Co., 1967), p. 107. Another question that has fascinated writers for some time is, what was Nietzsche looking for in the Greek view of sensibility and tragedy? As Tracy Strong notices in his essay "Aesthetic Authority and Tradition: Nietzsche and the Greeks," *History of European Ideas*, 11 (1989): 992, Nietzsche rejects the "dialectic of the Enlightenment" and returns to the pre-Platonic Greeks for his model of life and standard for self-development. On the other hand, Bruno Snell in his work *The Discovery of the Mind: The Greek Origins of European Thought* (New York: Harper & Row, 1960) saw the Greeks as the key to self-understanding.

46. See K. Gründer, *Der Streit um Nietzsches 'Geburt der Tragödie': Die Schriften von E. Rohde, R. Wagner, U. von Wilamowitz-Moellendorff* (Hildesheim: Olms Verlag, 1969), which contains Wilamowitz's arguments against Nietzsche in his review essay *Zukunftsphilologie*. Also see William Calder, "The Wilamowitz-Nietzsche Struggle: New Documents and a Reappraisal," *Nietzsche Studien*, 12 (1983): 220. W. Geoffrey Arnott in "Nietzsche's View of Greek Tragedy," *Arethusa*, 17 (1984), outlines the "factual errors" Wilamowitz found in *The Birth of Tragedy* (p. 136). Though he relies on Pickard-Cambridge's 1927 edition of *Dithyramb Tragedy and Comedy* and is quite critical of Nietzsche's philological and historical constructs, especially the latter's theory of the origins of tragedy, Arnott is very appreciative of Nietzsche's philosophical and poetic insights. The issue of "whether Nietzsche got it right" is also discussed by Silk and Stern in their work *Nietzsche on Tragedy*, pp. 166–185. However, in the last instance both William Arrowsmith, "Nietzsche on the Classics and the Classicists," *Arion* (Spring, Summer, Winter, 1963) and Tracy Strong, *Friedrich Nietzsche and the Politics of Transformation* (Berkeley: University of California Press, 1988), p. 35, contend that contemporary scholarship has favored Nietzsche over Wilamowitz.

47. Rethy, "The Tragic Affirmation of the *Birth of Tragedy*," p. 12.

48. Kurt Weinberg makes an important point when he argues that Nietzsche's view of aesthetic experiences has important epistemological and anthropological implications in "Nietzsche's Paradox of Tragedy," *Yale French Studies*, 38 (1967): 256. These themes were developed more in his lectures on pre-Platonic philosophy of nature and in his later revised Kantian epistemology in *The Will to Power*.

49. Friedrich Nietzsche, *The Birth of Tragedy*, in *The Birth of Tragedy and the Genealogy of Morals*, trans. Francis Golffing (Garden City, N.Y.: Doubleday, 1956), pp. 23–24, and *Nietzsche Werke. Kritische Gesamtausgabe*, Abteilung III, Band 1, Hrsg. von Giorgio Colli and Mazzino Montinari (Berlin: Walter de Gruyter & Co., 1972), p. 26.

50. Ibid., p. 21, and *Nietzsche Werke III, 1*, pp. 23–24.

51. Ibid., pp. 10–11, and *Nietzsche Werke III, 1*, p. 12.

52. Suffering is a key concept to understand Nietzsche's view of tragic vision and the heroic individual. [See Leslie Paul Thiele, *Friedrich Nietzsche and the Politics of the Soul: A Study of Heroic Individualism* (Princeton: Princeton University Press, 1990), pp. 24–26.]

53. Schiller, *On the Simple and Sentimental Poetry*, in *The Works of Schiller*, vol. 5, p. 280, and *Gesammelte Werke 5*, p. 488.

54. Ibid., p. 294, and *Gesammelte Werke 5*, p. 502.

55. Ibid., pp. 297–98, and *Gesammelte Werke 5*, pp. 505–6.

56. For an examination of those elements in Schiller's aesthetic theory that Nietzsche expanded upon see Benjamin Bennett, "Nietzsche's Idea of Myth: The Birth of Tragedy from the Spirit of Eighteenth-Century Aesthetics," *Publication of Modern Language Association of America*, 94 (1979): 425: Schiller's ideas about naïve and sentimental poetry, *amor fati*, idea of the "beautiful illusion," creative activity of myth making, self-understanding, theory of aesthetic drives (*Triebe*), and Schiller's distinction between form drive (*Formtrieb*) and substance drive (*Stofftrieb*). See also Udo Gaede, *Schiller und Nietzsche als Verkünder der Tragischen Kultur* (Berlin: H. Walther, 1908); Ernst Behler, "Nietzsche und die Frühromantische Schule," *Nietzsche Studien*, 8 (1978): 59–87; and Yack, *The Longing for Total Revolution*, for further interesting parallels between Schiller and Nietzsche, especially Yack's description of Nietzsche as the modern Orestes who through his knowledge of the ancients returns to the moderns "demanding blood" and purification (p. 328).

57. Nietzsche, "Notes for We Philologists," p. 371, and *Nietzsche Werke IV, 1*, p. 197.

58. Louis Ruprecht, Jr., "Nietzsche's Vision, Nietzsche's Greece," *Soundings*, 71 (1990): 69; and Lloyd-Jones, *Blood for the Ghosts*, pp. 175–81.

59. Nietzsche, *Birth of Tragedy*, pp. 31–32, and *Nietzsche Werke III, 1*, pp. 33–34.

60. Ibid., pp. 32–33, and *Nietzsche Werke III, 1*, pp. 34–35.

61. Ibid., p. 33, and *Nietzsche Werke III, 1*, p. 35.
62. Ibid.
63. Ibid., p. 34, and *Nietzsche Werke III, 1*, p. 36.
64. Ibid., p. 39, and *Nietzsche Werke III, 1*, p. 41.
65. In his essay "Principles of Tragedy," *English Studies in Africa*, 31 (1988), John Coulton makes the connection between the suffering and contradictions of the real world and the philosophical perceptions of Heraclitus. The philosophical foundations of life lie in the pre-Platonic philosophers.
66. Nietzsche, *Birth of Tragedy*, p. 41, and *Nietzsche Werke III, 1*, p. 43.
67. Frederick Copleston, S.J., *Friedrich Nietzsche: Philosopher of Culture* (London: Search Press, 1975), pp. 142–62; Christopher Janaway, "Nietzsche, the Self, and Schopenhauer," in *Nietzsche and Modern German Thought*, ed. Keith Ansell-Pearson (London: Routledge, 1991), pp. 119–142; Nick Land, "Art as Insurrection: The Question of Aesthetics in Kant, Schopenhauer, and Nietzsche," in *Nietzsche and Modern German Thought*, pp. 240–256; F. A. Lea, *The Tragic Philosopher: Friedrich Nietzsche* (London: Methuen & Co., 1977), pp. 15ff.; Georg Simmel, *Schopenhauer und Nietzsche* (Leipzig: Duncker und Humblot, 1907); and Volker Spierling, Hrsg. von, *Materialien zu Schopenhauers "Die Welt als Wille und Vorstellung"* (Frankfurt/Main: Suhrkamp, 1984).
68. Robert Rethy, "The Tragic Affirmation of the *Birth of Tragedy*," p. 3; Martha Nussbaum, "The Transfiguration of Intoxication," p. 93; and Richard White, "Art and the Individual in Nietzsche's *Birth of Tragedy*," *British Journal of Aesthetics*, 28, no. 1 (Winter 1988): 61.
69. Searching for *Objectivity*: Not enough attention has been paid to the development of German Idealism and its theories of consciousness and "objectivity," especially as they apply to the social sciences. In order to appreciate Max Weber's metatheoretical writings and his theory of objectivity, it is crucial to know how the concept has unfolded from Kant, Schiller, Schopenhauer, Nietzsche, and Rickert to Weber himself. The difficulties of appreciating the intricacies and subtleties of Weber's different methodological approaches—his interpretive/hermeneutical sociology with its method of *Verstehen* as expressed in *The Protestant Ethic and the Spirit of Capitalism* and his cultural/historical sociology using a transcendental and structuralist method as found in *The Religion of China, Economy and Society*, and *General Economic History*—rest on an understanding of the evolution of the neo-Kantian view of objectivity. Otherwise, objectivity simply reverts to forms of naïve realism and the potentials of the cultural and historical sciences remains unearthed. Issues of methodological objectivity in the social sciences are ultimately grounded in questions of epistemological, practical, and even ontological objectivity.

The same issues are also found in Marx's metatheory and methodology, since his views of *Wissenschaft* and *Kritik* rest upon the theory of knowledge, subjectivity, and objective experience developed by Kant, Hegel, Schelling, and Feuerbach. For an analysis of the relationships between Weber and

Nietzsche see Bryan Turner, "Nietzsche, Weber, and the Devaluation of Politics," *Sociological Review*, 30 (1982): 367–91; Robert Eden, *Political Leadership and Nihilism: A Study of Weber and Nietzsche* (Tampa, Fla.: University Presses of Florida, 1983); S. A. Kent, "Weber, Goethe, and Nietzschean Allusion: Capturing the Source of the Iron Cage Metaphor," *Sociological Analysis*, 44, no. 4 (Winter 1983): 297–319; Wilhelm Hennis, "Die Spuren Nietzsches im Werk Max Webers," *Nietzsche Studien*, 16 (1987): 382–404 and *Max Webers Fragestellung* (Tübingen: J.C. Mohr, 1987); Georg Stauth and Bryan Turner, *Nietzsche's Dance: Resentment, Reciprocity and Resistance in Social Life* (Oxford, England: Basil Blackwell, 1988), pp. 3–4 and 98–122; Mark Warren, "Max Weber's Liberalism for a Nietzschean World," *American Political Science Review*, 82 (March 1988); Wolfgang Mommsen, *The Political and Social Theory of Max Weber* (Chicago: University of Chicago Press, 1989), pp. 109–10; and Harvey Goldman, *Max Weber and Thomas Mann: Calling and the Shaping of the Self* (Berkeley: University of California Press, 1988) and *Politics, Death, and the Devil: Self and Power in Weber and Thomas Mann* (Berkeley: University of California Press, 1992).

For an analysis of Nietzsche's view of objectivity in the historical sciences see Friedrich Nietzsche, *On the Advantage and Disadvantage of History for Life*, trans. Peter Preuss (Indianapolis, Ind.: Hackett Publishing Company, 1980), pp. 32–38, and *Nietzsche Werke. Kritische Gesamtausgabe*, Abteilung III, Band 1, Hrsg. von Giorgio Colli and Mazzino Montinari (Berlin: Walter de Gruyter & Co., 1972), pp. 281–91.

The reader should be aware that many of Nietzsche's key ideas about life, science, disenchantment, the eclipse and suicide of reason, objectivity and subjectivity, perspectivism and causality, epistemology, and the *Übermensch* found their way into Weber's theories.

70. For a discussion by Schopenhauer of Kant's original and more radical idealism see his comments in the appendix "Criticism of the Kantian Philosophy" in *The World as Will and Representation*, vol. 1, trans. E. F. J. Payne (New York: Dover Publications, 1969), and *Die Welt als Wille und Vorstellung*, Band 1 (Leipzig: F. A. Brockhaus, 1859). Here Schopenhauer discusses a letter written to Professor Rosenkranz in which he mentioned a deleted passage from the first edition of Kant's *Critique of Pure Reason*: "If I take away the thinking subject, the whole material must cease to exist, as it is nothing but the phenomenon in the sensibility of our subject, and a species of its representations" (*The World as Will and Representation*, Appendix: *Criticism of the Kantian Philosophy*, vol. 1, p. 435, and *Die Welt als Wille und Vorstellung*, Anhang: *Kritik der Kantischen Philosophie*, Band 1, p. 515).

71. Arthur Schopenhauer, *The World as Will and Representation*, vol. 1, para. 1, p. 3, and *Die Welt als Wille und Vorstellung*, Band 1, p. 1. Nussbaum in "The Transfigurations of Intoxication" draws the analogy that where Kant's position on knowledge and objectivity is like a world constructed through eyeglasses, which condition the way we perceive the world, Schopenhauer's

metaphor would be "mirrored glasses," which simply reflect ourselves back to ourselves. We only see our own representations (p. 80).

72. Schopenhauer, *World as Will and Representation*, vol. 1, Appendix, p. 419, and *Die Welt als Wille und Vorstellung*, Band 1, p. 496.

73. Schopenhauer delves deeply into a fascinating area in Kantian studies, which is the nature of the objective world in Kant's *Critique of Pure Reason*. The former correctly points out the many inconsistencies in Kant's book that point the reader in different and contradictory directions. Are the objects of experience formed in perception or are they formed through the understanding? Is objectivity the product of experience or thinking (*The World as Will and Representation*, vol. 1, pp. 437–51, and *Die Welt als Wille und Vorstellung*, Band 1, pp. 518–35)?

74. Schopenhauer, *World as Will and Representation*, vol. 1, para. 38, p. 196, and *Die Welt als Wille und Vorstellung*, Band 1, p. 231.

75. Ibid., vol. 1, para. 38, p. 196, and *Die Welt als Wille und Vorstellung*, Band 1, pp. 230–31.

76. Ibid., vol. 1, para. 38, p. 197, and *Die Welt als Wille und Vorstellung*, Band 1, pp. 232–33.

77. Nussbaum, "The Transfigurations of Intoxication," pp. 87 and 90.

78. Schopenhauer, *World as Will and Representation*, vol. 1, para. 48, p. 233, and *Die Welt als Wille und Vorstellung*, Band 1, p. 275.

79. Ibid., vol. 1, para. 51, p. 253, and *Die Welt als Wille und Vorstellung*, Band 1, p. 298.

80. Ibid., vol. 1, para. 55, p. 306, and *Die Welt als Wille und Vorstellung*, Band 1, p. 362.

81. Richard White, "Art and the Individual in Nietzsche's *Birth of Tragedy*," *British Journal of Aesthetics*, 28, no.1 (Winter 1988): 61.

82. Schopenhauer, *World as Will and Representation*, vol. 1, para. 58, p. 322, and *Die Welt als Wille und Vorstellung*, Band 1, p. 380.

83. Ibid., vol. 1, para. 68, p. 379, and *Die Welt als Wille und Vorstellung*, Band 1, p. 448. He quotes a monologue from Hamlet; death or at least a short life are viewed by Schopenhauer as valid alternatives to a grotesque and horrible life of human suffering.

84. Ibid., vol. 1, para. 59, p. 326, and *Die Welt als Wille und Vorstellung*, Band 1, p. 385.

85. Rethy, "The Tragic Affirmation of the *Birth of Tragedy*," p. 4ff. See also Ansell-Pearson, "Nietzsche's Overcoming of Kant and Metaphysics," p. 317.

86. McGinn, "Culture as Prophylactic," p. 89; and White, "Art and the Individual in Nietzsche's *Birth of Tragedy*," pp. 63–66. There may be an overemphasis in the secondary literature on Schopenhauer's influence on Nietzsche. In an interesting work, Erich Heller argues that it is Goethe's vision of the integrity of being, as well as the integration of reason, sensuality, feeling, and will that directs Nietzsche's critique of nihilistic despair and the

call for a tragic reaffirmation of life. With this interpretation, the notion of the reintegration of being in Nietzsche's later writings could be viewed more as a reference to Goethe's realism rather than Schopenhauer's mysticism. Though Heller does not explicitly say so, there is a fascinating integration of mysticism and rationalism in this new realism. [See Erich Heller, *The Disinherited Mind: Essays in Modern German Literature and Thought* (New York: Barnes and Nobel, 1971), pp. 100 and 114–20.]

87. Nietzsche, *Birth of Tragedy*, p. 53, and *Nietzsche Werke III, 1*, pp. 54–55.

88. For a consideration of Nietzsche's general aesthetic method and the philosophical implications of his writing style see Nehamas, *Nietzsche: Life as Literature* (Cambridge, Mass.: Harvard University Press, 1985), pp. 13–41.

89. Nietzsche, *Birth of Tragedy*, p. 52, and *Nietzsche Werke III, 1*, p. 53.

90. A couple of authors have mentioned the connection between Nietzsche's concepts of Dionysus and Apollo and Schopenhauer's notions of will and representation. [See Robert Rethy, "The Tragic Affirmation of the *Birth of Tragedy*," *Nietzsche Studien*, 17 (1988): 3; and Martha Nussbaum, "The Transfigurations of Intoxication," p. 93.]

91. Nietzsche, *Birth of Tragedy*, pp. 63–64, and *Nietzsche Werke III, 1*, pp. 64–65.

92. John Coulton, "Principles of Tragedy," *English Studies in Africa*, 31 (1988): 85–88. Silk and Stern in their *Nietzsche on Tragedy* (p. 85) outlined Nietzsche's rejection of the aesthetic theories that show the purpose of tragedy as being: the portrayal of cosmic harmony and aesthetic beauty in moral education (Schiller), the struggle of tragic heros with fate (Schelling), and the discharge of emotions (Lessing). See also pp. 225–238 for their analysis of the similarities and differences between Nietzsche's *Birth of Tragedy* and Aristotle's *Poetics*.

93. Nietzsche, *Birth of Tragedy*, p. 133, and *Nietzsche Werke III, 1*, pp. 137–38.

94. Ibid., pp. 29 and 30, and *Nietzsche Werke III, 1*, p. 31.

95. In his essay "Nietzsche's View of Greek Tragedy," pp. 139–40, Arnott outlines the philosophical origins of the Apollonian and Dionysian distinction in a work by Schelling (1858).

96. Nietzsche, *Birth of Tragedy*, p. 61, and *Nietzsche Werke III, 1*, p. 63.

97. For a more traditional and purely Apollonian interpretation see Werner Jaeger, *Paideia: The Ideas of Greek Culture*, vol. I, *Archaic Greece: The Mind of Athens*, trans. Gilbert Highet (New York: Oxford University Press, 1965), pp. 251ff. Jaeger argued that the ultimate goal of the tragedies of Aeschylus was psychologically to restore "faith in the ultimate meaning of life."

98. Richard Schacht, *Nietzsche* (London: Routledge & Kegan Paul, 1983), pp. 497–98.

99. Leon Rosenstein, "Metaphysical Foundations of Theories of Tragedy," *Journal of Aesthetics and Art Criticisms*, 28 (1970): 532. Rosenstein quotes an

interesting passage from *Thus Spoke Zarathustra*: "My self-made idea demands this and that virtue of me, that is to say my virtue; this is heroism . . . for being heroic causes one to meet his greatest grief and his highest hope at one and the same time" (p. 530).

100. In his work *Blood for the Ghosts*, Hugh Lloyd-Jones viewed Greek tragedy as providing a "deeper vision of the real nature of ancient religion," since it brings the audience closer to the truths of human existence (p. 174). Lloyd-Jones also held that the ideals of classical Greece—individual excellence, aesthetic creativity, will to power, heroism, and the integration and "sublimation" of the Dionysian (irrational) and Apollonian (rational) forces—made historicism and relativism impossible philosophical positions for Nietzsche (p. 178).

101. Nietzsche, *The Birth of Tragedy*, p. 24, and *Nietzsche Werke III, 1*, p. 26.

102. Silk and Stern, *Nietzsche On Tragedy*, p. 69. A difficulty in interpreting Nietzsche here is that the secondary literature usually does not distinguish these analytic moments clearly and their authors usually chose to emphasize one aspect over the others. Where does the secret to Greek tragedy lie—in the role of the spectator, the tragic hero, or the artist? In recognizing human suffering, achieving reconciliation, or in the process of aesthetic creativity? Where do Dionysian ideals and wisdom lie?

103. Ansell-Pearson, "Nietzsche's Overcoming of Kant and Metaphysics," p. 311.

104. Nietzsche, *Birth of Tragedy*, p. 63, and *Nietzsche Werke III, 1*, p. 64.

105. Weinberg, "Nietzsche's Paradox of Tragedy," pp. 258–59 and 266.

106. Nietzsche, "Notes for We Philologists," p. 359, and *Nietzsche Werke IV, 1*, p. 182.

107. Nietzsche, *Birth of Tragedy*, p. 50, and *Nietzsche Werke III, 1*, p. 52.

108. Ibid., p. 31, and *Nietzsche Werke III, 1*, p. 33.

109. Strong, "Aesthetic Authority and Tradition," p. 993. Stephen Houlgate in *Hegel, Nietzsche and the Criticism of Metaphysics* (Cambridge, England: Cambridge University Press, 1986) in chapter 8, "Hegel and Nietzsche on Tragedy," distinguishes between an early and later theory of tragedy. The main distinction between the two lies in their emphasis. The earlier interpretation steeped in the metaphysics of Schopenhauer stresses Dionysian art and its primordial unity with nature. In the later interpretation, the central focus is on individuality, creativity, destruction, and a critique of metaphysics.

110. Nietzsche, *Birth of Tragedy*, pp. 41–42, and *Nietzsche Werke III, 1*, p. 43.

111. Rethy, "The Tragic Affirmation of the *Birth of Tragedy*," p. 11. See also Rose Pfeffer, "The Problem of Truth in Nietzsche's Philosophy," *Pacific Philosophical Quarterly*, 48 (January 1967): 21–23. Her essay is important because it connects Nietzsche's theory of aesthetics and tragedy to his theory of knowledge and nihilism. There is also a treatment of Nietzsche's

materialism and the relation between creativity and sexuality in Weinberg's essay "Nietzsche's Paradox of Tragedy," p. 253.

112. Nietzsche, *Birth of Tragedy*, pp. 63–64, and *Nietzsche Werke III, 1*, p. 65.

113. Nussbaum, "The Transfigurations of Intoxication," p. 105.

114. Houlgate, *Hegel, Nietzsche and the Criticism of Metaphysics*, p. 191. For a fascinating discussion of Greek tragedy and the different approaches of Hegel and Nietzsche see chapter 8. Houlgate argues that the major difference is that Hegel views tragedy resulting from individual choices and personal action, conflicting rights, and the reconciliation of reason and justice, whereas Nietzsche interprets it as resulting from cosmic forces destroying the individual. For the former, tragedy is the consequence of human action; for the latter, it is the consequence of cosmic contradictions and individual heroism. Also see Leon Rosenstein, "Metaphysical Foundations of the Theories of Tragedy in Hegel and Nietzsche," *Journal of Aesthetics and Art Criticisms*, 28 (1970): 521–33.]

115. Friedrich Nietzsche, *The Antichrist*, in *The Portable Nietzsche*, trans. Walter Kaufmann (New York: Viking Press, 1968), pp. 588–89, and *Friedrich Nietzsche: Sämtliche Werke. Kritische Studienausgabe*, Band 6, Hrsg. von Giorgio Colli and Mazzino Montinari (Berlin: Deutsche Taschenbuch Verlag, de Gruyter, 1988), p. 188.

116. I am indebted to Martha Nussbaum in this section of the book for her analysis of Schopenhauer and Nietzsche in the essay "The Transfigurations of Intoxication."

117. Bennett, "Nietzsche's Idea of Myth," pp. 428 and 429.

118. Ibid., p. 426.

119. Nietzsche, *Birth of Tragedy*, p. 69, and *Nietzsche Werke III, 1*, p. 71. In his work *Dionysus*, Manthey-Zorn refers to the whole history of modern rationalistic thought as the "suicide of reason" (p. 5).

120. Bennett, "Nietzsche's Idea of Myth," p. 427.

121. Ibid., p. 426. See also Houlgate, *Hegel, Nietzsche, and the Criticism of Metaphysics*, p. 57.

122. In his essay "Nietzsche's View of Greek Tragedy," Arnott attributes Nietzsche's criticism of Euripides' tragedies to a broader intellectual tradition whose roots lie in Aristophanes' *Frogs* and A. W. Schlegel's lectures on Greek drama between 1809 and 1811 (*Vorlesungen über dramatische Kunst und Literatur*). In his work *The Discovery of the Mind*, Snell also makes the connection between Nietzsche and Schlegel. It is Schlegel who criticizes Euripides for his realism, rationalism, and immorality (p. 119).

123. Walter Brogan, "Is Platonic Drama the Death of Tragedy?" *International Studies in Philosophy*, 23, no. 2 (1991): 75–82. For a conservative treatment of the relationship between Nietzsche and Socrates see Werner Dannhauser, *Nietzsche's View of Socrates* (Ithaca, N.Y.: Cornell University Press, 1974).

124. McGinn, "Culture as Prophylactic," p. 103.

125. Nietzsche, *Birth of Tragedy*, p. 95, and *Nietzsche Werke III, 1*, p. 97.

126. Rethy, "The Tragic Affirmation of the *Birth of Tragedy*," *Nietzsche Studien*, 17 (1988): 29–30.

127. Max Weber, *The Protestant Ethic and the Spirit of Capitalism*, trans. Talcott Parsons (New York: Charles Scribner's Sons, 1958), pp. 181–83; Rogers Brubaker, *The Limits of Rationality: An Essay on the Social and Moral Thought of Max Weber* (London: George Allen & Unwin, 1984); and Eden, *Political Leadership and Nihilism*.

128. Nietzsche, *Birth of Tragedy*, pp. 111 and 120, and *Nietzsche Werke III, 1*, pp. 114 and 124. Also see McGinn, "Culture as Prophylactic," p. 110, and Ansell-Pearson, "Nietzsche's Overcoming of Kant and Metaphysics," pp. 318 and 323.

129. Heller, *The Disinherited Mind*, pp. 118–19.

130. Friedrich Nietzsche, *Philosophy in the Tragic Age of the Greeks*, trans. Marianne Cowan (Chicago: Henry Regnery Company, 1962), p. 24, and *Nietzsche Werke. Kritische Gesamtausgabe*, Abteilung III, Band 2, Hrsg. von Giorgio Colli and Mazzino Montinari (Berlin: Walter de Gruyter & Co., 1973), p. 295.

131. Ibid., p. 114, and *Nietzsche Werke III, 2*, p. 364.

132. Ibid., p. 41, and *Nietzsche Werke III, 2*, p. 309.

133. Ibid., p. 44, and *Nietzsche Werke III, 2*, p. 311.

134. Strong, *Nietzsche and the Politics of Transformation*, p. 155.

135. Nietzsche, *Philosophy in Tragic Age of Greeks*, p. 52, and *Nietzsche Werke III, 2*, p. 317.

136. Schopenhauer, *The World as Will and Representation*, p. 9, and *Die Welt als Wille und Vorstellung*, Band 1, p. 10.

137. Nietzsche, *Philosophy in Tragic Age of Greeks*, p. 77, and *Nietzsche Werke III, 2*, p. 336.

138. Ibid., p. 104, and *Nietzsche Werke III, 2*, p. 357.

139. Nietzsche, *The Philosopher*, in *Philosophy and Truth*, p. 56 (not in Musarion edition).

140. Nietzsche, *Philosophy in Tragic Age of Greeks*, pp. 44–45, and *Nietzsche Werke III, 2*, p. 311.

141. Ibid., p. 62, and *Nietzsche Werke III, 2*, p. 325.

142. Ibid.

143. Ibid., pp. 112–113, and *Nietzsche Werke III, 2*, p. 363.

144. For a contemporary analysis of the relationship between Greek tragedy and politics see Christian Meier, *The Greek Discovery of Politics*, trans. David McLintock (Cambridge, Mass.: Harvard University Press, 1990).

145. Nietzsche, *Philosophy in Tragic Age of Greeks*, p. 114, and *Nietzsche Werke III, 2*, p. 364.

146. Ibid., pp. 114–15, and *Nietzsche Werke III, 2*, pp. 364–65.

147. Ibid., p. 55, and *Nietzsche Werke III, 2*, p. 319.

148. Ibid., p. 79, and *Nietzsche Werke III, 2*, p. 337.
149. Ibid., p. 82, and *Nietzsche Werke III, 2*, p. 340.
150. Ibid., p. 83, and *Nietzsche Werke III, 2*, p. 340.
151. In his work *Schopenhauer as Educator*, Nietzsche repeats the story of Heinrich von Kleist who after reading Kant's *Critique of Pure Reason* recognized its nihilistic implications, fell into a deep despair, and committed suicide. [See Lea, *The Tragic Philosopher*, p. 86.]
152. Friedrich Nietzsche, *The Will to Power*, trans. Walter Kaufmann and R. J. Hollingdale, ed. Walter Kaufmann (New York: Random House, 1967), note 419, p. 225, and *Nietzsche Werke. Kritische Gesamtausgabe*, Abteilung VII, Band 3, Hrsg. von Giorgio Colli and Mazzino Montinari (Berlin: Walter de Gruyter & Co., 1974), 41[4], p. 412. For a brief analysis of Nietzsche's ideas about humanity's historical consciousness and homelessness see Yack, *The Longing for Total Revolution*, pp. 325–328.

Chapter Five: Decadence of Reason and Objectivity

1. Friedrich Nietzsche, *The Antichrist*, in *The Portable Nietzsche*, trans. Walter Kaufmann (New York: Viking Press, 1968), p. 618, and *Friedrich Nietzsche Werke: Sämtliche Werke. Kritische Studienausgabe*, Band 6, Hrsg. von Giorgio Colli and Mazzino Montinari (Berlin: Deutscher Taschenbuch Verlag, de Gruyter, 1988), p. 217.
2. Bernard Yack, *The Longing for Total Revolution: Philosophic Sources of Social Discontent from Rousseau to Marx and Nietzsche* (Berkeley: University of California Press, 1992), pp. 121–22.
3. See Bernhard Bueb, *Nietzsches Kritik der praktischen Vernunft* (Stuttgart: Ernst Klett Verlag, 1970), pp.1–12; Mark Warren, *Nietzsche and Political Thought* (Cambridge, Mass.: MIT Press, 1991), pp. 116–26: "He [Nietzsche] is deepening and radicalizing the tradition of critical theory that began with Kant" (p. 117); and Richard Schacht, *Nietzsche* (London: Routledge & Kegan Paul, 1983), p. 62. Also see Keith Ansell-Pearson, "Nietzsche's Overcoming of Kant and Metaphysics: From Tragedy to Nihilism," *Nietzsche Studien*, 16 (1987): 317–18; George Stack, "Kant and Nietzsche's Analysis of Knowledge," *Dialogos*, 22 (January 1987): 13ff.; and John Wilson, *Truth and Value in Nietzsche: A Study of His Metaphysics and Epistemology* (Ann Arbor: University of Michigan Press, 1974), pp. 98–126 and 136–54.
4. Nietzsche employs the Kantian concept of the thing-in-itself in his earliest writings such as *The Birth of Tragedy* and *On Truth and Lies in a Nonmoral Sense* in *Philosophy and Truth: Selections from Nietzsche's Notebooks of the Early 1870's*, trans. and ed. Daniel Breazeale (Atlantic Highlands, N.J.: Humanities Press, 1979), and *Nietzsche Werke. Kritische Gesamtausgabe*, Abteilung III, Band 2, Hrsg. von Giorgio Colli and Mazzino Montinari (Berlin: Walter de Gruyter & Co., 1973), pp. 369–84.

356 *Notes*

5. Nietzsche, *The Philosopher: Reflections on the Struggle between Art and Knowledge*, in *Philosophy and Truth: Selections from Nietzsche's Notebooks of the Early 1870's*, trans. and ed. Daniel Breazeale (Atlantic Highlands, N.J.: Humanities Press, 1979), p. 28, and *Friedrich Nietzsche Gesammelte Werke. Musarionausgabe*, Band 6 (München: Musarion Verlag, 1922), p. 30.

6. Nietzsche, *The Philosopher*, p. 58, and not in *Musarionausgabe 6*.

7. Ibid., p. 30, and *Musarionausgabe 6*, pp. 32–33.

8. Alexander Nehamas, *Nietzsche: Life as Literature* (Cambridge, Mass.: Harvard University Press, 1985), pp. 9–10.

9. Friedrich Nietzsche, *The Birth of Tragedy*, trans. Francis Golffing (Garden City, N.Y.: Doubleday and Co., 1956), pp. 102 and 103, and *Nietzsche Werke. Kritische Gesamtausgabe*, Abteilung III, Band 1, Hrsg. von Giorgio Colli and Mazzino Montinari (Berlin: Walter de Gruyter & Co., 1972), p. 105.

10. Nietzsche, *Birth of Tragedy*, trans. Golffing, p. 123, and *Nietzsche Werke III, 1*, p. 127.

11. Friedrich Nietzsche, *Twilight of the Idols, or How One Philosophizes with a Hammer*, in *The Portable Nietzsche*, trans. Walter Kaufmann (New York: The Viking Press, 1968), p. 483, and *Friedrich Nietzsche: Sämtliche Werke. Kritische Studienausgabe*, Band 6, Hrsg. von Giorgio Colli and Mazzino Montinari (Berlin: Deutscher Taschenbuch Verlag, de Gruyter, 1988), pp. 77–78; *Beyond Good and Evil*, trans. Marianne Cowan (Chicago: Henry Regnery Company, 1955), p. 174, and *Nietzsche Werke. Kritische Gesamtausgabe*, Abteilung VI, Band 2, Hrsg. von Giorgio Colli and Mazzino Montinari (Berlin: Walter de Gruyter, 1968), p. 190; and *The Antichrist*, p. 605, and *Nietzsche. Kritische Studienausgabe 6*, p. 204.

12. Maudemarie Clark, *Nietzsche on Truth and Philosophy* (Cambridge, England: Cambridge University Press, 1990), p. 55; and Leslie Paul Thiele, *Friedrich Nietzsche and the Politics of the Soul: A Study of Heroic Individualism* (Princeton: Princeton University Press, 1990), p. 106. For an overview of Nietzsche's theory of science, interpretive objectivity, underlying normative assumptions and values, and metaphysics, which later will have an important impact on Weber's theory science, see Schacht, *Nietzsche*, pp. 82–95; and John Wilson, *Truth and Value in Nietzsche*, pp. 127–54.

13. Nietzsche, *Birth of Tragedy*, trans. Golffing, p. 120, and *Nietzsche Werke III, 1*, p. 124.

14. Ibid., p. 111, and *Nietzsche Werke III, 1*, p. 114; Stack, "Kant and Nietzsche's Analysis of Knowledge," p. 21.

15. Nietzsche relied heavily upon the developments in nineteenth-century philosophy of science. Others have noticed that Nietzsche anticipated the philosophy of science of Vaihinger, Poincaré, and Heisenberg, as well as some contemporary authors, including K. Popper, T. Kuhn, W. Quine, P. Feyerabend, S. Toulmin, and so forth: Gordon Bearn, "Nietzsche, Feyerabend, and the Voices of Relativism," *Metaphilosophy*, 17, nos. 2 and 3 (April/July 1986): 147–51; Stack, "Kant and Nietzsche's Analysis of Knowledge," p.

31, "Nietzsche and Perspectival Interpretation," *Philosophy Today*, 25 (Fall 1981): 237, and "Nietzsche's Critique of Things-In-Themselves," *Dialogos*, 15 (November 1980): 52; John Wilcox, "Nietzsche's Epistemology: Recent American Discussions," *International Studies in Philosophy*, 15 (Summer 1983); and Cornel West, "Nietzsche's Prefiguration of Postmodern American Philosophy," *Boundary* (Spring–Fall 1981): 241–70.

16. Nietzsche, *Birth of Tragedy*, trans. Golffing, p. 112, and *Nietzsche Werke III, 1*, p. 116.

17. As already discussed in Chapter 4, note 7, there is a debate as to how much of Kant Nietzsche had actually read and knew. Some have argued that, because there were no books by Kant in his library at the time of his death, Nietzsche was not knowledgeable about the philosopher. Others have contended that his Kantianism comes from his readings of Schopenhauer and Lange. One must recall the historical and cultural context of Nietzsche's education in the *Gymnasium* at Pforta. Maybe the debate is not as crucial as first thought since his writings show a familiarity with and a creative incorporation of Kantian theory and vocabulary. Most contemporary secondary interpretations have recognized Nietzsche as a radical Kantian philosopher.

Keith Ansell-Pearson, in his essay "Nietzsche's Overcoming Kant and Metaphysics: From Tragedy to Nihilism," *Nietzsche Studien*, 16 (1987): 310, and Karl-Heinz Dickopp in "'Aspekte zum Verhältnis Nietzsche—Kant und ihre Bedeutung für die Interpretation des 'Willen zur Macht,' " *Kant Studien*, 61 (1970): 97–98, briefly outline the history of these critical opinions beginning with the work of Hans Vaihinger, *Die Philosophie des Als-Ob* (Berlin: Reuther und Reichard, 1985), part III:D; Otto Ackermann, *Kant im Urteil Nietzsches* (Tübingen: 1939), pp. 67–68, and *Friedrich Nietzsches Werke des Zusammenbruchs* (Heidelberg: 1939), pp. 420ff.; R. Blunk, *Friedrich Nietzsche. Kindheit und Jugend* (Basel: 1953), pp. 194f.; Bueb, *Nietzsches Kritik der praktischen Vernunft*; W. Etterich, *Die Ethik Friedrich Nietzsches im Verhältnis zur Kantischen Ethik*, dissertation (Bonn: 1914), pp. 33ff.; Martin Heidegger, *Nietzsche*, vol. 1, *Der Wille zur Macht* (Pfullingen: 1961); H. Heimsoeth, *Des jungen Nietzsches Weg zur Philosophie. Studien zur Philosophiegeschichte* (Köln: Kantstudien-Ergänzungshefte 82, 1961), p. 165; and Karl Jaspers, *Nietzsche, Einführung in das Verständnis seines Philosophierens* (Berlin: 1950), p. 36. This theme is again picked up by Martha Nussbaum in "The Transfiguration of Intoxication: Nietzsche, Schopenhauer, and Dionysus," *Arion: Journal of Humanities and the Classics*, 1, no. 2 (Spring 1991): 78.

18. Stack, "Kant and Nietzsche's Analysis of Knowledge," p. 7.

19. There is a very interesting and informative analysis of the importance of Schopenhauer's idealism and theory of representationalism (objects of experience are only representations or products of the mind and life is only a dream) for Nietzsche's early thinking about a theory of knowledge in Maudemarie Clark, "Nietzsche's Perspectivist Rhetoric," *International Studies in Philosophy*, 18 (Summer 1986): 38–39. She argues that Schopenhauer's ideal-

358   *Notes*

ism plagues Nietzsche in *On Truth and Lies in a Nonmoral Sense*, *The Gay Science*, and *Beyond Good and Evil*. Though her essay is helpful, there may be some confusion here between Kant's theory of sensibility and understanding and the very different and more one-sided theory of sensation developed by Schopenhauer. She concludes that the way out of the dilemma for Nietzsche is in the development of his theory of perspectivism.

20. Friedrich Nietzsche, *The Philosopher*, p. 8, and *Musarionausgabe 6*, p. 7.

21. For an examination of the relationships between Nietzsche and Marxism and Critical Theory see Edward Andrew, "The Unity of Theory and Practice: The Science of Marx and Nietzsche," in *Political Theory and Praxis: New Perspectives*, ed. by Terence Ball (Ann Arbor, Michigan: Books on Demand), pp. 117–33; Georges Bataille, "Nietzsche in Light of Marxism," trans. Lee Hildreth, *Semiotext*, 3 (1978): 109–13; Ian Forbes, "Marx and Nietzsche: The Individual in History," in *Nietzsche and Modern German Thought*, ed. Keith Ansell-Pearson (New York: Routledge, 1991); Reinhold Grimm and Jost Hermand, Hrsg. von, *Karl Marx und Friedrich Nietzsche. Acht Beiträge* (Königstein/Ts.: Athenäum, 1978); Nancy Love, *Marx, Nietzsche, and Modernity* (New York: Columbia University Press, 1986), and "Class or Mass: Marx, Nietzsche, and Liberal Democracy," *Studies in Soviet Thought*, 33 (January 1987): 43–64; Reinhart Mauer, "Nietzsche und die Kritische Theorie," *Nietzsche Studien*, 10–11 (1981–82): 34–58; James Miller, "Some Implications of Nietzsche's Thought for Marxism," *Telos*, 37 (Fall 1978): 22–41; Peter Pütz, "Nietzsche im Lichte der Kritischen Theorie," *Nietzsche Studien*, 3 (1974): 175–91, and "Nietzsche and Critical Theory," *Telos*, 50 (Winter 1981–82): 103–14; Richard Schacht, "Hegel, Marx, Nietzsche, and the Future of Self-Alienation," *American Philosophical Quarterly* (April 1991): 125–35; Alfred Schmidt, "Zur Frage der Dialektik in Nietzsches Erkenntnistheorie," in *Zeugnisse—Theodor W. Adorno zum Sechzigsten Geburtstag*, Hrsg. von Max Horkheimer (Frankfurt/Main: Europäische Verlagsanstalt, 1963), pp. 113–32; Georg Stauth and Bryan Turner, *Nietzsche's Dance: Resentment, Reciprocity and Resistance in Social Life* (Oxford, England: Basil Blackwell, 1988), pp. 151–79; Paul Veyne, "Ideology According to Marx and According to Nietzsche," trans. Jeane Ferguson, *Diogenes*, 99 (Fall 1977): 80–102. Also see Martin Jay, *The Dialectical Imagination: A History of the Frankfurt School and the Institute of Social Research, 1923–50* (Boston: Little, Brown and Company, 1973), pp. 48–51; and David Held, *Introduction to Critical Theory: Horkheimer to Habermas* (Berkeley: University of California Press, 1980), pp. 156–57 and 203ff.

22. Nietzsche, *On Truth and Lies in a Nonmoral Sense*, in *Philosophy and Truth*, p. 89, and *Nietzsche Werke III, 2*, p. 381.

23. Jürgen Habermas, *The Philosophical Discourse of Modernity*, trans. Frederick Lawrence (Cambridge, Mass.: MIT Press, 1987), pp. 83–130.

24. Nietzsche, *The Philosopher*, p. 12, and *Musarionausgabe 6*, p. 12.

25. Ibid., p. 12, and *Musarionausgabe 6*, pp. 11–12.
26. Ibid., p. 13, and *Musarionausgabe 6*, p. 13.
27. Ibid., p. 17, and *Musarionausgabe 6*, pp. 17–18.
28. For a discussion of Nietzsche's theory of rhetoric see Alan Schrift, "Language, Metaphor, Rhetoric: Nietzsche's Deconstruction of Epistemology," *Journal of the History of Philosophy*, 23 (July 1985): 371–95.
29. Nietzsche, *The Philosopher*, p. 20, and *Musarionausgabe 6*, p. 21.
30. This early epistemological writing seems to be careless and at times incoherent. Nietzsche is obviously struggling with two different theories of knowledge: a form of subjective idealism and its Kantian constitution theory of truth grounded in appearances [Kant, *Critique of Pure Reason*, trans. Norman Kemp Smith (New York: St. Martin's Press, 1965); and Friedrich Lange, *The History of Materialism*, trans. Ernest Chester Thomas, reprint of the 1879–81 edition (New York: Arno Press, 1974)], and representational idealism and its representational theory of perception grounded in sensory impressions [Arthur Schopenhauer, *The World as Will and Representation*, vol.1, trans. E. F. J. Payne (New York: Dover Publications, 1969)]. In the latter perspective there is no independent, objective world; there is only radical subjective, sensory experience. Knowledge of the world is only self-knowledge. Do we experience appearances or representations? By attempting to incorporate both positions into a systematic epistemology, he is left with a contradictory epistemology. Though both elements are there, the evidence seems to lean towards Kant and Lange, because of the early acceptance of the concept of a thing-in-itself [George Stack, *Lange and Nietzsche* (Berlin: de Gruyter, 1983), pp. 94ff.] and away from Schopenhauer. Schacht contends that Nietzsche "like Kant, stops short of idealism, refusing to equate reality with the world as we experience it" (*Nietzsche*, p. 62). Mark Warren also defends this position in *Nietzsche and Political Thought*, p. 124, as does Arthur Danto, *Nietzsche as Philosopher* (New York: Macmillan, 1965), pp. 40–41. For a defense of the opposing argument see Clark, *Nietzsche on Truth and Philosophy*, pp. 79–83. Nehamas questions in *Nietzsche*, p. 56, whether, like the painter, the knower describes objects or creates them. Nehamas's literary analysis of Nietzsche's perspectivism, objectivity, and self-overcoming emphasizes the creative aspects of life. However, he also argues that Nietzsche is not a relativist (p. 72), especially in his genealogical reconstruction of moral history and his critique of Christianity.

In *Beyond Good and Evil*, Nietzsche does say that "nothing is 'given' as real except our world of desires and passions, that we cannot step down or step up to any kind of 'reality' except the reality of our drives—for thinking is nothing but the interrelation and interaction of our drives" (*Beyond Good and Evil*, p. 42, and *Nietzsche Werke VI, 2*, p. 50). This appears to represent a turn toward Schopenhauer's radical idealism. But this position is not held consistently throughout his writings.

31. Nietzsche, *The Philosopher*, p. 32, and *Musarionausgabe 6*, p. 35.

32. Ibid., p. 31, and *Musarionausgabe 6*, p. 34.

33. Ibid., p. 30, and *Musarionausgabe 6*, p. 32.

34. Marx had the same insight about Greek philosophy in his analysis of Epicurus's physics and theory of atoms and meteors in his doctoral dissertation "Difference between the Democritean and Epicurean Philosophy of Nature," *Marx Engels Collected Works*, vol. 1 (New York: International Publishers, 1975), pp. 66 and 70, and *Marx Engels Werke*, Ergänzungsband, Teil 1 (Berlin: Dietz Verlag, 1968), pp. 298 and 301–2. [See also "Notes for We Philologists," trans. William Arrowsmith, *Arion*, new series 1/2 (1973–74), p. 296, and "Notizen zu Wir Philologen," *Nietzsche Werke. Kritische Gesamtausgabe*, Abteilung IV, Band 1, Hrsg. von Giorgio Colli and Mazzino Montinari (Berlin: Walter de Gruyter & Co., 1967), p. 107.]

35. Stack, "Kant and Nietzsche's Analysis of Knowledge," p. 15. Stack attributes this subjectivism and skepticism to Nietzsche's integration of Kant's theory of knowledge, F. A. Lange's phenomenalism and theory of scientific conventionalism, and Helmholtz's theory of sensations and signs. In another essay entitled "Nietzsche and Perspectival Interpretation," Stack claims that the data ultimately are derived from our "passions and desires," since this is the only reality (p. 237).

36. Nietzsche, *The Philosopher*, p. 43, and *Musarionausgabe 6*, p. 47.

37. Ibid., p. 47, and *Musarionausgabe 6*, pp. 52–53.

38. Ibid., p. 52, and *Musarionausgabe 6*, p. 58.

39. Friedrich Nietzsche, *Philosophy in Hard Times*, in *Philosophy and Truth*, trans. by Daniel Breazeale (Atlantic Highlands, N.J.: Humanities Press, 1979), p. 111, and *Friedrich Nietzsche Gesammelte Werke. Musarionausgabe*, Band 7 (München: Musarion Verlag, 1920), pp. 11–33.

40. Nietzsche, *On Truth and Lies in a Nonmoral Sense*, pp. 87 and 88, and *Nietzsche Werke III, 2*, pp. 379 and 380.

41. Ibid., p. 86, and *Nietzsche Werke III, 2*, pp. 377–78.

42. Ibid., p. 85, and *Nietzsche Werke III, 2*, p. 377.

43. Ibid., p. 86, and *Nietzsche Werke III, 2*, p. 377.

44. Nietzsche, *Twilight of the Idols*, pp. 497ff., and *Nietzsche. Kritische Studienausgabe 6*, pp. 93ff.

45. For a helpful analysis of this point see Stack, "Nietzsche and Perspectival Interpretation," pp. 225–228.

46. Friedrich Nietzsche, *The Will to Power*, ed. Walter Kaufmann and trans. Walter Kaufmann and R. J. Hollingdale (New York: Vintage Books, 1967), note 481, p. 267, and *Nietzsche Werke. Kritische Gesamtausgabe*, Abteilung VIII, Band 1, Hrsg. von Giorgio Colli and Mazzino Montinari (Berlin: Walter de Gruyter & Co., 1974), 7[60], p. 323.

47. The secondary literature is replete with references to Nietzsche's pragmatism and utilitarian theory of knowledge. This position is mentioned in Stack, "Kant and Nietzsche's Analysis of Knowledge," p. 11; Kenneth Westphal, "Was Nietzsche a Cognitivist?" *Journal of the History of Philoso-*

phy, 22, no. 3 (July 1984): 352 and 360; David Freeman, "Nietzsche: Will to Power as a Foundation of a Theory of Knowledge," *International Studies in Philosophy*, 20 (1988): 3; Rose Pfeffer, "The Problem of Truth in Nietzsche's Philosophy," *Pacific Philosophical Quarterly*, 48 (January 1967): 15; Clark, *Nietzsche on Truth and Philosophy*, p. 87, and Wilcox, "Nietzsche's Epistemology," pp. 68 and 74. Wilcox is suspicious of the exact nature of this pragmatism.

For a critique of the relationship between pragmatism and utility as a misunderstanding of the former school of thought see Hans Joas, "Mead's Position in Intellectual History and His Early Philosophical Writings," in *Philosophy, Social Theory, and the Thought of George Herbert Mead*, ed. Mitchell Aboulafia (Albany: State University of New York Press, 1991), pp. 62–63. For a continuation of this view see the German interpretations of American pragmatism in the works of Jürgen Habermas, *Theory of Communicative Action*, vol. 2, *Lifeworld and Systems: A Critique of Functionalist Reason*, trans. Thomas McCarthy (Boston: Beacon Press, 1987), pp. 92–96; and Karl Otto Apel, *Charles Sanders Peirce: From Pragmatism to Pragmaticism*, trans. John Krois (Amherst: University of Massachusetts Press, 1981). Nehamas in his book *Nietzsche* is very critical of the pragmatic and utilitarian interpretations of Nietzsche (pp. 52–55).

What the American secondary literature does not examine when discussing Nietzsche's pragmatism is that he may refer to utility and physical survival as well as the survival of a meaningful life. Aristotle's distinction between being and well-being may be relevant here. That is, practical interests may also refer to ethical concerns about the valuation of life.

48. Nietzsche, *Will to Power*, note 480, p. 266, and *Nietzsche Werke VIII, 3*, 14[122], pp. 93–94.

49. The secondary literature abounds with claims that Nietzsche is a "pragmatist." See the works of Danto, Grimm, Stack, Freedman, and Wilcox.

50. Pfeffer, "The Problem of Truth in Nietzsche's Philosophy," p. 16. She argues that this reliance on instincts and primordial passions (*das Ur-eine*) integrates Nietzsche's interpretations of nineteenth-century philosophy of science, materialism, romanticism of the *Sturm und Drang* period, and Eduard von Hartmann's philosophy of the unconscious into a modern form of the tragic experience.

51. Nehamas writes in *Nietzsche* that perspectivism "seems to be precisely an effort to move away from the idea that the world possesses any features that are in principle prior to and independent of interpretation. In itself, the world has no features, and these can therefore be neither correctly nor wrongly represented. The idea that we are necessarily incapable of representing the world accurately presupposes the view that the world's appearance is radically different from its reality" (p. 45). On page 50, Nehamas has an interesting examination of Nietzsche's use of the term falsification. Nehamas cautions that falsification, which is usually applied with the terms "selection" or

"simplification," is not a falsification of something. This latter would imply a prior existing reality. He states, "The perspective is not the object seen, a self-contained thing which is independent of and incomparable to every other. What is seen is simply the world itself from that perspective."

52. Nietzsche, *Will to Power*, note 507, p. 276, and *Nietzsche Werke VIII*, 2, 9[38], p. 16.

53. Ibid., note 516, p. 279, and *Nietzsche Werke VIII*, 2, 9[97], p. 53.

54. Nietzsche, *Beyond Good and Evil*, pp. 12–13, and *Nietzsche Werke, VI*, 2, p. 19.

55. Nietzsche, *Will to Power*, note 552, p. 297, and *Nietzsche Werke VIII*, 2, 9[91], p. 47.

56. One of the most difficult and frustrating issues in the interpretive literature on Nietzsche deals with whether he is a cognitivist or not. Does Nietzsche have a correspondence theory of truth grounded in essential foundations such as external objects, conceptual forms, or the thing-in-itself? Does he hold to a theory of knowledge that justifies some form of truth about the world? Two secondary interpretations have attempted to outline the debate. The first article was written by John Wilcox, "Nietzsche's Epistemology: Recent American Discussions," and the second by Westphal, "Was Nietzsche a Cognitivist?" Both argued that the cognitivist position has been a minority opinion articulated to some extent by such prominent Nietzschean scholars as Walter Kaufmann, *Nietzsche: Philosopher, Psychologist, Antichrist* (Princeton: Princeton University Press, 1974); Wilson, *Truth and Value in Nietzsche*, pp. 44–66; and Richard Schacht, "Nietzsche and Nihilism," in *Nietzsche*, ed. Robert Solomon (Garden City, N.Y.: Doubleday, 1973), and *Nietzsche* (London: Routledge and Kegan Paul, 1983), pp. 99–117. Schacht in *Nietzsche* states the "the quest for 'foundations' must indeed be abandoned" (p. 85), but does see the possibility for a higher order of knowledge. See also Clark, *Nietzsche on Truth and Philosophy*, pp. 21, 85, and 142.

Westphal lists the noncognitivists, who generally argue that Nietzsche held a systematic antifoundational theory of knowledge: Kantianism, pragmatism, consensus theory, coherence theory, and so forth. The noncognitivist position also involves a discussion about perspectivism and relativism. They represent the prevailing opinion today and include the following: Arthur Danto, *Nietzsche as Philosopher* (New York: Macmillan, 1965); Ruediger Grimm, "Circularity and Self-Reference in Nietzsche," *Metaphilosophy*, 10, nos. 3–4 (July–October 1979): 289–305, and *Nietzsche's Theory of Knowledge* (Berlin: Walter de Gruyter, 1977); Tracy Strong, *Friedrich Nietzsche and the Politics of Transformation* (Berkeley: University of California Press, 1988), and "Reflections on Perspectivism in Nietzsche," *Political Theory*, 13, no. 2 (May 1985): 165–66 and 172; and Mary Warnock, "Nietzsche's Conception of Truth," in *Nietzsche: Imagery and Thought*, ed. Malcolm Pasley (Berkeley: University of California, 1978). See also Freeman, "Nietzsche," pp. 3–4; Pfeffer, "The Problem of Truth in Nietzsche's Philosophy," p. 5; and Robert

Solomon, *From Rationalism to Existentialism: The Existentialists and Their Nineteenth-Century Backgrounds* (New York: University Press of America, 1972), p. 113. One of the main difficulties involved in this debate is that Nietzsche refuses to play by the traditional epistemological rules, which are themselves for him conventional perspectives.

57. Freeman, "Nietzsche," pp. 8–11.

58. Nietzsche, *Will to Power*, note 486, p. 269, and *Nietzsche Werke VIII, 1*, 2[87], p. 102.

59. John Atwell, "Nietzsche's Perspectivism," *Southern Journal of Philosophy*, 19 (Summer 1981): 162. For this insight Atwell draws upon Nietzsche's *Will to Power*, notes 481 and 556. He contends that Nietzsche is not defending an "existential nihilism," but an epistemological contextualism. That is, facts exist only in the context of theories. On this issue see Pfeffer, "The Problem of Truth in Nietzsche's Philosophy," pp. 8–9.

60. Thiele, *Nietzsche and the Politics of the Soul*, pp. 105–6.

61. Nietzsche, *The Genealogy of Morals*, trans. by Francis Golffing (Garden City, N.Y.: Doubleday and Company, 1956), p. 299, and *Nietzsche Werke. Kritische Gesamtausgabe*, Abteilung VI, Band 2, Hrsg. von Giorgio Colli and Mazzino Montinari (Berlin: Walter de Gruyter & Co., 1968), p. 430.

62. Nietzsche, *Will to Power*, note 521, p. 282, and *Nietzsche Werke, VIII, 2*, 9[144], p. 82.

63. Ibid., note 495, p. 272, *Nietzsche Werke VII, 2*, 25[470], p. 134.

64. Ibid., note 533, p. 290, and *Nietzsche Werke VIII, 2*, 9[91], p. 50.

65. Atwell, "Nietzsche's Perspectivism," pp. 164–65.

66. In *A Study of Nietzsche* (Cambridge, England: Cambridge University Press, 1979), J. P. Stern argues that the will to power refers to the desire for "conquest and domination": "If there is anything in the recent 'Nietzschean' era that comes close to an embodiment of the 'will to power,' it is Hitler's life and political career" (p. 120). For an entirely different and more relevant treatment of Nietzsche see Pfeffer, "The Problem of Truth in Nietzsche," p. 17. In a similar vein, Stack states in "Nietzsche and Perspectival Interpretation" (p. 240), "The 'spirit' emerges out of a fecund nature and seeks to master and control its forces for the sake of life, for the sake of an enhanced feeling of potency." This theme is continued in the work of Warren, *Nietzsche and Political Thought*, when he writes, "For Nietzsche, the power motive is not descriptive of classes of external goals of action—such as political domination over others—understood as the aim of all human acts. Instead, he is interested in the meaning that behaviors have for individuals in terms of their experiences of agent-unity. . . . With Marx, one might say that for Nietzsche human agents make history" (pp. 140–41). This argument is also expanded upon in Thiele's analysis of the will to power as noble and heroic self-overcoming in *Nietzsche and the Politics of the Soul*, p. 65.

The centrality of activity has been recognized by Karl Jaspers, *Nietzsche: An Introduction to the Understanding of His Philosophical Activity*, trans.

Charles Wallraff and Frederick Schmitz (Chicago: Henry Regnery Company, 1966), pp. 121 and 176–77; Bearn, "Nietzsche, Feyerabend, and the Voices of Relativism," p. 145; Ansell-Pearson, "Nietzsche's Overcoming of Kant and Metaphysics," p. 332; Marshell Bradley, "Nietzsche's Critique of Pure Reason: With a Nietzschean Critique of Parsifal," *Neophilologus*, 72 (July 1988): 395; and Tracy Strong, "Reflections on Perspectivism in Nietzsche," *Political Theory*, 13, no. 2 (May 1985): 171.

67. Danto, *Nietzsche as Philosopher*, p. 80; Strong, "Reflections on Perspectivism in Nietzsche," p. 177; Bearn, "Nietzsche, Feyerabend, and the Voices of Relativism," pp. 135ff.; Alan Schrift, "Language, Metaphor, Rhetoric," p. 398; and Clark, "Nietzsche's Perspectivist Rhetoric," p. 35, and her analysis of Richard Schacht and Alexander Nehamas in *Nietzsche on Truth and Philosophy*, pp. 150–58.

68. Stack, "Nietzsche and Perspectival Interpretation," pp. 234 and 239–40. Stack refers to Nietzsche perspectivism as a "provisional hypothesis," "a perspectival falsification," "a fictional assumption and posit," and "mythopoetic metaphysics." He also sees the strength and power of the will as necessary to transcend the seductions of traditional metaphysics.

69. Friedrich Nietzsche, *Genealogy of Morals*, p. 255, and *Nietzsche Werke VI, 2*, p. 383. According to Schrift, "Language, Metaphor, Rhetoric," p. 394, this idea is also continued in the *Will to Power* in notes 600, 616, and 655.

70. This idea of truth as a creative act that overcomes epistemological nihilism has been examined by a number of authors including: George Stack, "Nietzsche and the Correspondence Theory of Truth," *Dialogos*, 38 [1981]: 101–102, and Ansell-Pearson, "Nietzsche's Overcoming of Kant and Metaphysics," p. 332.

71. Nietzsche, *Will to Power*, note 585, p. 317, and *Nietzsche Werke VIII, 2*, 9[60], p. 29.

72. Ibid., note 585, p. 318, and *Nietzsche Werke VIII, 2*, 9[60], p. 30.

73. Ibid., p. 85.

74. Ibid., note 617, p. 331, and *Nietzsche Werke VIII, 1*, 7[54], p. 321.

Chapter Six: Morality and Art

1. Friedrich Nietzsche, *The Will to Power*, in *The Portable Nietzsche*, trans. Walter Kaufmann (New York: Viking Press, 1968), note 12b, pp. 13–14, and *Nietzsche Werke. Kritische Gesamtausgabe*, Abteilung VIII, Band 2, Hrsg. von Giorgio Colli and Mazzino Montinari (Berlin: Walter de Gruyter & Co., 1970), 11[99], p. 291.

2. Friedrich Nietzsche, *Twilight of the Idols or, How One Philosophizes with a Hammer*, in *Portable Nietzsche*, trans. Walter Kaufmann (New York: Viking Press, 1968), p. 533, and *Friedrich Nietzsche: Sämtliche Werke. Kritische Studienausgabe*, Band 6, Hrsg. von Giorgio Colli and Mazzino Montinari (Berlin: Deutscher Taschenbuch Verlag, de Gruyter, 1988), p. 131.

3. F. A. Lea, *The Tragic Philosopher: Friedrich Nietzsche* (London: Methuen & Co,, 1977), p. 201. Lea makes the case that the decadence of the "last man" is reflected in the "perfect end-product of utilitarianism."

4. Nietzsche, *Will to Power*, note 75, p. 48, and *Nietzsche Werke VII, 3*, 34[161], p. 195.

5. Ibid., note 55, p. 37, and *Nietzsche Werke VIII, 1*, 5[71], p. 219.

6. With his critique of the idolatry of phenomenology, positivism, idealism, materialism, and transcendent morality, with his critique of self-sufficient objectivity, subjectivity, and values, Nietzsche, according to Leslie Paul Thiele, argues for a higher form of morality and nobility based on the Kantian ideal of morality as autonomy and self-legislation. See *Friedrich Nietzsche and the Politics of the Soul: A Study of Heroic Individualism* (Princeton: Princeton University Press, 1990), pp. 45–46. She says, "True heroism, according to Nietzsche, slakes its agonal thirst within the soul" (p. 47).

7. Nietzsche, *Twilight of the Idols*, p. 536, and *Nietzsche. Kritische Studienausgabe 6*, p. 134.

8. Nietzsche, *Will to Power*, note 59, p. 40, and *Nietzsche Werke VIII, 1*, 2[122], p. 120.

9. Friedrich Nietzsche, *The Antichrist*, in *The Portable Nietzsche*, trans. Walter Kaufmann (New York: Viking Press, 1968), p. 578, and *Nietzsche. Kritische Studienausgabe*, Band 6, Hrsg. von Giorgio Colli and Mazzino Montinari (Berlin: Deutscher Taschenbuch Verlag, de Gruyter, 1988), p. 177.

10. For a comparison of Kant's theory of the categorical imperative, practical reason, individual autonomy, and moral ends and Nietzsche's theory of morality and the sovereign will to power see Alphonso Lingis, "The Imperative to Be Master," *Southwestern Journal of Philosophy* (Summer 1980): 95–107.

11. Nietzsche, *The Antichrist*, p. 577, and *Nietzsche. Kritische Studienausgabe 6*, p. 177.

12. Nietzsche, *Will to Power*, note 326, p. 178.

13. Ibid., note 315, p. 174, and *Nietzsche Werke VIII, 2*, 9[173], p. 101.

14. For an analysis of an extension of Weber's theory of rationalization with its distinctions between formal and substantive rationality see Max Horkheimer, *Eclipse of Reason* (New York: Continuum, 1947); Herbert Marcuse, "Industrialization and Capitalism in the Work of Max Weber," in *Negations: Essays in Critical Theory*, trans. Jeremy Shapiro (Boston: Beacon Press, 1968); and Jürgen Habermas, "Technology and Science as 'Ideology,' " in *Toward a Rational Society*, trans. Jeremy Shapiro (Boston: Beacon Press, 1970); and for an application of these distinctions to an analysis of liberalism and the market economy see George McCarthy and Royal Rhodes, *Eclipse of Justice: Ethics, Economics, and the Lost Traditions of American Catholicism* (Maryknoll, N.Y.: Orbis Books, 1992), pp. 80–87.

15. Immanuel Kant, *Fundamental Principles of the Metaphysics of Morals*, trans. Thomas Abbott (Indianapolis, Ind.: Bobbs-Merrill Co., 1949), p. 50. For

an analysis of Nietzsche's view on freedom see Richard Schacht, *Nietzsche* (London: Routledge & Kegan Paul, 1983), pp. 304–9; Alexander Nehamas, who in *Nietzsche: Life as Literature* (Cambridge, Mass.: Harvard University Press, 1985), pp. 173–74, 186–89, 195, and 205, analyzes the relation between freedom and creativity, self-direction, and self-consciousness; and Robert Solomon, *From Rationalism to Existentialism: The Existentialists and Their Nineteenth-Century Backgrounds* (Lanham, Md.: University Press of America, 1972), p. 126, especially concerning the relation between freedom and Nietzsche's critique of formal rationality.

16. Nietzsche, *Will to Power*, note 269, p. 154, and *Nietzsche Werke VIII, 1*, 7[6], p. 289.

17. Ibid., note 354, pp. 194–95, and *Nietzsche Werke VIII, 3*, 14[158], pp. 134–35.

18. Ibid., note 279, p. 159, and *Nietzsche Werke VIII, 1*, 7[6], p. 289.

19. Tracy Strong, *Friedrich Nietzsche and the Politics of Transformation* (Berkeley: University of California Press, 1988), pp. 73–74. He also connects these ideas with Marx's and Freud's notion of fetishism.

20. Nietzsche, *Will to Power*, note 405, p. 219, and *Nietzsche Werke VIII, 1*, 2[207], p. 166.

21. Hannah Arendt, *The Human Condition* (Chicago: University of Chicago Press, 1958), p. 229.

22. Nietzsche, *Will to Power*, note 200, p. 117 and note 202, p. 118, and *Nietzsche Werke VIII, 2*, 10[191], p. 236, and 10[201], p. 245.

23. Ibid., note 141, p. 91, and *Nietzsche Werke VIII, 3*, 15[42], p. 230.

24. Nietzsche, *Twilight of the Idols*, p. 482, and *Nietzsche. Kritische Studienausgabe 6*, p. 77.

25. Ibid., p. 483, and *Nietzsche. Kritische Studienausgabe 6*, p. 78.

26. Ibid., p. 500, and *Nietzsche. Kritische Studienausgabe 6*, p. 96.

27. Nietzsche, *Will to Power*, note 55, p. 37, and *Nietzsche Werke VIII, 1*, 5[71], p. 219.

28. Nietzsche, *Twilight of the Idols*, p. 502, and *Nietzsche. Studienausgabe 6*, p. 99.

29. Georg Friedrich Hegel, "The Spirit of Christianity and Its Fate," in *On Christianity: Early Theological Writings*, trans. T. M. Knox (New York: Harper and Brothers, 1948), p. 195.

30. Ibid., p. 206.

31. Ibid., p. 209.

32. Steven Smith, "Hegel and the French Revolution: An Epitaph for Republicanism," *Social Research*, 56, no.1 (Spring 1989): 233–61; also see Georg Friedrich Hegel, "Absolute Freedom and Terror," in *Phenomenology of Spirit*, trans. A.V. Miller (Oxford, England: Oxford University Press, 1977), pp. 355–63; Horkheimer, *Eclipse of Reason*, pp. 20–29; and Nietzsche, *The Antichrist*, pp. 577–78, and *Nietzsche. Kritische Studienausgabe 6*, pp. 177–78.

33. Mark Warren, *Nietzsche and Political Thought* (Cambridge, Mass.:

MIT Press, 1991), p. 217. Warren focuses upon Nietzsche's argument that Kantianism and utilitarianism follow from the impulses and values of the Christian tradition.

34. Hannah Arendt, *On Revolution* (Harmondsworth, England: Penguin Books, 1965), p. 149.

35. Ibid., p. 137.

36. Steven Smith, *Hegel's Critique of Liberalism: Rights in Context* (Chicago: University of Chicago Press, 1989), pp. 91–92.

37. Nietzsche, *Will to Power*, note 252, p. 145, and *Nietzsche Werke VIII, 2*, 11[55], p. 269.

38. Nietzsche, *Twilight of the Idols*, pp. 534–35, and *Nietzsche. Kritische Studienausgabe 6*, pp. 132–33.

39. Ibid., p. 516, and *Nietzsche. Kritische Studienausgabe 6*, p. 114.

40. Nietzsche, *Will to Power*, note 304, p. 171, and *Nietzsche Werke VIII, 2*, 11[54], p. 268.

41. For an analysis of this question of freedom and morality see Nehamas, *Nietzsche*, p. 205.

42. Nietzsche, *Beyond Good and Evil*, trans. Marianne Cowan (Chicago: Henry Regnery Company, 1955), p. 175, and *Nietzsche Werke. Kritische Gesamtausgabe*, Abteilung VI, Band 2, Hrsg. von Giorgio Colli and Mazzino Montinari (Berlin: Walter de Gruyter & Co., 1968), p. 191.

43. Friedrich Nietzsche, "Prologue," *Thus Spoke Zarathustra* in *The Portable Nietzsche*, trans. Walter Kaufmann (New York: Viking Press, 1968), pp. 128–31, and *Nietzsche Werke. Kritische Gesamtausgabe*, Abteilung VI, Band 1, Hrsg. von Giorgio Colli and Mazzino Montinari (Berlin: Walter de Gruyter & Co., 1968), pp. 12–15.

44. Nietzsche, *Will to Power*, note 339, p. 186, and *Nietzsche Werke VIII, 2*, 11[226], p. 331.

45. Ibid., note 373, p. 201, and *Nietzsche Werke VIII, 3*, 14[29], pp. 24–25.

46. George E. McCarthy, *Marx and the Ancients: Classical Ethics, Social Justice, and Nineteenth-Century Political Economy* (Lanham, Md.: Rowman & Littlefield Publishers, 1990).

47. Nietzsche, *Will to Power*, note 125, p. 77, and *Nietzsche Werke VII, 3*, 37[11], p. 312.

48. Nietzsche, *Beyond Good and Evil*, p. 110, and *Nietzsche Werke VI, 2*, p. 124.

49. Strong, *Nietzsche and the Politics of Transformation*, p. 28. What is interesting about Strong's analysis is that he interprets the methodology of Nietzsche's critical theory of genealogy in a manner that reflects the approach of Hegelian phenomenology. Since there are no "facts" or pure objects, access to the world is through the constitution of objectivity in history. "Genealogy, does not seek out and describe the 'things' that phenomenology holds to be the world, but rather delineates the *manner* in which the 'things' are 'made' into 'facts.' Nietzsche tries to bring out precisely how a particular

world is put together and made a world; he shows thereby that that world has not natural necessity" (p. 54).

50. Nietzsche, *The Genealogy of Morals*, trans. Francis Golffing (Garden City, N.Y.: Doubleday & Company, 1956), p. 218, and *Nietzsche Werke. Kritische Gesamtausgabe*, Abteilung VI, Band 2 (Berlin: Walter de Gruyter & Co., 1968), p. 339.

51. Ibid., p. 251, and *Nietzsche Werke VI, 2*, p. 378.

52. Ibid., pp. 225–26, and *Nietzsche Werke VI, 2*, pp. 347–48.

53. Ibid., pp. 208 and 211, and *Nietzsche Werke VI, 2*, pp. 329 and 331–32.

54. Nietzsche, *Twilight of the Idols*, p. 505, and *Nietzsche. Kritische Studienausgabe 6*, p. 102.

55. Nietzsche, *The Birth of Tragedy*, pp. 41–42, and *Nietzsche Werke III, 1*, p. 43.

56. Nietzsche, *Twilight of the Idols*, p. 525, and *Nietzsche. Kritische Studienausgabe 6*, p. 123.

57. Ibid., p. 526, and *Nietzsche. Kritische Studienausgabe 6*, p. 124.

58. Ibid., p. 559, and *Nietzsche. Kritische Studienausgabe 6*, p. 157.

59. Georg Friedrich Hegel, *The Philosophy of Right*, trans. T. M. Knox (London: Oxford University Press, 1967), p. 13.

60. For an interesting analysis of Nietzsche's reaction to the German climate of anti-Semitism see Walter Kaufmann, *Nietzsche: Philosopher, Psychologist, Antichrist* (Princeton: Princeton University Press, 1974), pp. 42–46 and p. 22, his introduction to *The Gay Science*; Frederick Copleston, *Friedrich Nietzsche: Philosopher of Culture* (London: Search Press, 1975), pp. 181–95; and Michael Duffy and Willard Mittelman, "Nietzsche's Attitude toward the Jews," *Journal of the History of Ideas* 49, no. 2 (1988): 301–17.

61. Nietzsche, *The Antichrist*, p. 585, and *Nietzsche. Kritische Studienausgabe 6*, p. 185.

62. Ibid., p. 595, and *Nietzsche. Kritische Studienausgabe 6*, p. 194.

63. Ibid., p. 634, and *Nietzsche. Kritische Studienausgabe 6*, p. 232. Strong forcefully argues in *Nietzsche and the Politics of Transformation* that "the pervasiveness and danger of the possibility of being God is Nietzsche's great and true insight into our entire cultural and social condition" (p. 9). This insight is also expressed by Thiele, *Nietzsche and the Politics of the Soul*, p. 146.

64. Nietzsche, *The Antichrist*, p. 605, and *Nietzsche. Kritische Studienausgabe 6*, p. 204. It is interesting to note that in *The Antichrist*, Nietzsche's critique of Christian theology and its misunderstanding of its origins, as well as his outline of a hermeneutical praxis anticipates in the late nineteenth century in many fascinating ways the later development of German political theology and Latin American Liberation Theology in the second half of the twentieth century. A variation of this phrase was employed by Marx in *The Communist Manifesto* (1848): "All that is solid melts into air, all that is holy is profaned, and man is at last compelled to face with sober senses, his real

conditions of life, and his relations with his kind" [*Marx Engels Collected Works*, vol. 6 (New York: International Publishers, 1976), p. 487, and *Marx Engels Werke*, Band 4 (Berlin: Dietz Verlag, 1964), p. 465. See also Warren, *Nietzsche and Political Thought*, p. 45.].

65. Daniel Breazeale, "The Hegel-Nietzsche Problem," *Nietzsche Studien* 4 (1975); Richard Schacht, *Nietzsche* (London: Routledge & Kegan Paul, 1983); and Philip Kain, "Nietzschean Genealogy and Hegelian History in *The Genealogy of Morals*," unpublished essay.

66. Nietzsche, *Genealogy of Morals*, p. 168, and *Nietzsche Werke VI, 2*, p. 282.

67. Ibid., pp. 177–78, and *Nietzsche Werke VI, 2*, p. 292.

68. Nietzsche, *Will to Power*, note 1011, p. 523. (According to Kaufmann, the manuscript source of this passage is uncertain.)

69. Walter Kaufmann, *Nietzsche*, p. 189; and Strong, *Nietzsche and the Politics of Transformation*, pp. 261–63.

70. Arthur Danto, *Nietzsche as Philosopher* (New York: Macmillan, 1965), pp. 210–12. Danto makes the connection between eternal return and the self-overcoming of the *Übermensch*. However, he takes the doctrine of eternal return at face value with its apparent mechanical repetition, eternal monotony, and temporal determinism. Where do the possibilities of the future lie in this understanding of Nietzsche? He does not recognize that this interpretation of time makes an integration of eternal return and self-overcoming impossible. Clark takes a similar position when she accepts a passive and quietist interpretation of the doctrine. The past is given for all eternity. There is no willing backwards and thus we must accept and adjust to that fact of life. There is no will to power in relation to the past. It is this insight that resulted in Zarathustra's nausea and disgust.

71. Friedrich Nietzsche, *Ecce Homo*, in *The Complete Works of Friedrich Nietzsche*, vol. 17, ed. Oscar Levy, trans. Anthony Ludovici (New York: Macmillan Company, 1924), p. 54, and *Friedrich Nietzsche: Sämtliche Werke. Kritische Studienausgabe*, Band 6 (Berlin: Deutscher Taschenbuch Verlag, de Gruyter, 1988), p. 297. In *Nietzsche and the Politics of the Soul*, Thiele looks at this notion of the *amor fati* and concludes that it is not an acknowledgment of fatalism, but an affirmation of life and time, and a liberation *from* hope. "Life must not serve as means to some other end" (p. 201). In *Nietzsche and the Politics of Transformation*, Strong argues that Nietzsche returns to the thought of Heraclitus when he refers to the world as chance and dice playing. This seems not to be an accommodation to necessity, but a recognition of the relationship between time, play (*spielen*), and creativity. Through play, dance, and laughter, the "higher man" can joyously recreate the present. The meaning of the past is altered. All three activities abjure the reified moment and construct new relationships. The rules and connections are changed and the past is no longer idolized (pp. 278–83). In *Nietzsche and Political Thought*, Warren understands *amor fati* as a recognition of our historicity, that we are

fated to be historical beings. Mankind is to be viewed within history and thus having a fate. This recognition is part of the Dionysian tragic wisdom discussed in *The Birth of Tragedy*. It does not mean that we are tied to a deterministic universe, only that we must experience pain and suffering in a temporal world without meaning.

72. Nietzsche, *The Gay Science*, trans. Walter Kaufmann (New York: Vintage Books, 1974), para. 341, p. 273, and *Nietzsche Werke. Kritische Gesamtausgabe*, Abteilung V, Band 2 (Berlin: Walter de Gruyter & Co., 1973), p. 250.

73. Nehamas, *Nietzsche*, p. 77. Nehamas contends that Nietzsche's purpose here is to show that thinking, desiring, wishing, and believing are not independent objects, but part of a single continuum of activity, creativity, and willing. Nehamas's analysis of the thing-in-itself as applied to metaphysics and psychology is very helpful here. He returns to Nietzsche quoting from note 560 of *The Will to Power*: "That things possess a constitution in themselves quite apart from interpretation and subjectivity, is quite an idle hypothesis; it presupposes that interpretation and subjectivity are not essential, that a thing freed from all relationships would still be a thing" (Nehamas, *Nietzsche*, pp. 81–82). And from note 557 he quotes: "The properties of a thing are effects on other 'things' . . . there is no 'thing-in-itself.' "

74. Nehamas, *Nietzsche*, p. 85.

75. Nietzsche, *Genealogy of Morals*, pp. 178–79, and *Nietzsche Werke VI, 2*, p. 293.

76. Friedrich Nietzsche, *On the Advantage and Disadvantage of History for Life*, trans. Peter Preuss (Indianapolis, Ind.: Hackett Publishing Company, 1980), p. 35, and *Nietzsche Werke. Kritische Gesamtausgabe*, Abteilung III, Band 1, Hrsg. von Giorgio Colli and Mazzino Montinari (Berlin: Walter de Gruyter & Co., 1972), p. 286.

77. The theory of eternal return is never clearly stated by Nietzsche and the secondary interpretations have not helped until recently. The perspective is mentioned in four of Nietzsche's books: *The Gay Science* (1882), *Thus Spoke Zarathustra* (1883–85), *Ecce Homo* (1888), and *Twilight of the Idols* (1889). There seem to be two major approaches surrounding the idea of eternal return. The first argues that the past is eternally repeatable and unchanging, and life and the present moment must be continuously reaffirmed and accepted in order for reconciliation to occur. Danto (*Nietzsche as Philosopher*) has articulated this view. The second position contends that the past is a narrative always open to reinterpretation, change, and redemption. This has been most effectively stated by Nehamas (*Nietzsche*) and Gilles Deleuze [*Nietzsche and Philosophy*, trans. Hugh Tomlinson (London: Athlone Press, 1983)].

Looking closely at *The Gay Science*, Debra Bergoffen defends the thesis that the doctrine of eternal return is a response to the death of God and its shadow in nihilism and science. Rejecting the idea of religious salvation and scientific progress, the belief in eternal recurrence reaffirms the necessity of pain and the joy of life in the present. It accepts the totality of existence in all its relationships. Time is redeemed. The death of God and the nothingness of the world are the essential prerequisites to presenting ourselves as the "creators of history." And with this eternal return there is no end or metaphysical goal [Debra Bergoffen, "The Eternal Recurrence, Again," *International Study of Philosophy* (Summer 1983): 36–37]. She also says that by means of the doctrine of eternal return "we storm the gates of heaven in order to create a new vision of time" (p. 43).

Tracy Strong, in his *Nietzsche and the Politics of Transformation*, adds that, according to Nietzsche's genealogical reconstruction, slave morality is always a *ressentiment* and revenge unable to reconcile itself with the present moment (pp. 246–47). The doctrine of eternal return was developed to break free of this deterministic prison of nihilism (p. 288). In *The Tragic Philosopher*, Lea contends that the past can be rewritten because the past, present, and future become the sources for the development of each other (p. 218). The emphasis is placed on mankind's creative side.

In *Nietzsche and the Politics of the Soul*, Thiele sees the eternal return as a form of Dionysian wisdom integrating "stringent determinism with the highest level of moral idealism" in its affirmation of the self in the present moment (p. 205). This perspective contains a certain Hegelian element in the sense that the present is viewed as the historical unfolding of the past. The individual imperative is: Become who you are. [See Herbert Marcuse, *Hegel's Ontology and the Theory of Historicity*, trans. Seyla Benhabib (Cambridge, Mass.: MIT Press, 1987), p. 15.] This approach captures the returning element of time, but not its nihilistic component. For a connection between Nietzsche and Hegel and a critique of Heidegger's metaphysical interpretation of the eternal return see Warren, *Nietzsche and Political Thought*, pp. 198–99.

This also ties into Nehamas's argument of the importance of the eternal return as a critique of the thing-in-itself. With an eternal recurrence, there is an infinite multiplicity of interpretations of experience. There is no thing-in-itself lying behind the world as its foundation. So the theory of eternal return only reinforces the historical and temporal dimension of Nietzsche's theories of perspectivism, will to power, and critique of Kant. Solomon, Deleuze, Magnus, and Clark view eternal return as an ethical doctrine replacing Kant's categorical imperative. [See Solomon, *From Rationalism to Existentialism*, p. 137; Gilles Deleuze, *Nietzsche and Philosophy*, trans. Hugh Tomlinson (London: Athlone Press, 1983), pp. 23–25; Bernd Magnus, *Nietzsche's Existential Imperative* (Bloomington: Indiana University Press, 1978), pp. 111–54; and Maudemarie Clark, *Nietzsche on Truth and Philosophy* (Cambridge, England: Cambridge University Press, 1990), p. 248.] It represents another form of the universalization principle, "What action would you do, if it would be infinitely repeated in time?"

One could take the position that Nietzsche's theory of eternal return is very similar to a Greek tragedy. The interpretive key lies less in the substance of the theory or play than in the creative and formative process itself. By designing this theory, Nietzsche has defined the individual as historical and placed its identity in history. The theory is an example of the practice of the will. (See Warren, *Nietzsche and Political Thought*, pp. 204–6.)

78. Nehamas writes in *Nietzsche*, "The eternal recurrence is not a theory of the world but a view of the self" (p. 150). This represents a rejection of the interpretation that eternal return represents a cosmological theory as developed by Danto and others. Nehamas argues that the secret to Nietzsche's theory of eternal return lies in his view of life as text and narrative, as well as his view of the person as a totality of relationships and activities. He states, "Therefore, Nietzsche's ultimate reason for thinking that if my life were to recur it would have to be in every way identical with the life I have already had is his view of the will to power, of which the rejection of the thing-in-itself is in turn one aspect" (p. 154). There is nothing behind the activity of the will to power—nothing either spatial or temporal.

79. Nietzsche, *Thus Spoke Zarathustra*, p. 251, and *Nietzsche Werke VI, 1*, pp. 175–76.

80. Ibid., p. 251, and *Nietzsche Werke VI, 1*, p. 175.

81. Ibid., p. 253, and *Nietzsche Werke VI, 1*, p. 177.

82. Ibid., p. 227, and *Nietzsche Werke VI, 1*, p. 144.

83. Nietzsche, *Twilight of the Idols*, p. 562, and *Nietzsche. Kritische Studienausgabe 6*, p. 159.

84. Nietzsche, *Beyond Good and Evil*, p. 135, and *Nietzsche Werke VI, 2*, p. 149.

85. Ibid., p. 136, and *Nietzsche Werke VI, 2*, p. 150.

86. Ibid., p. 44, and *Nietzsche Werke VI, 2*, p. 52.

87. Nietzsche, *Thus Spoke Zarathustra*, p. 251, and *Nietzsche Werke VI, 1*, p. 175. Though no direct connection is made between Nietzsche's theory of time and eternal return and the theory of *anamnesis* in the critical theory of the Frankfurt School, there are some interesting relationships between the two. For a discussion of the latter issues, in particular a consideration of *anamnesis*, happy consciousness, and anamnestic solidarity in the moral community see Helmut Peukert's analysis of Max Horkheimer and Walter Benjamin in *Science, Action, and Fundamental Theology: Toward a Theology of Communicative Action* (Cambridge: MIT Press, 1984), pp. 206–210.

88. Nietzsche, *Genealogy of Morals*, p. 298, and *Nietzsche Werke VI, 2*, p. 429.

89. Ibid., p. 299, and *Nietzsche Werke VI, 2*, p. 430.

90. Thiele, *Nietzsche and the Politics of the Soul*, p. 161.

91. For a discussion of Nietzsche's theory of rational will, consciousness, and epiphenomenalism see Schacht, *Nietzsche*, pp. 312–26. There need to be more analyses of the relationships in Nietzsche's thought between materialism and idealism, naturalism and humanism, and biologism and spiritualism, that is, a clarification of the relationships between instincts and reason (especially,

his borrowings from Hume and Kant), causality and freedom, fate and the *Übermensch*. Schacht ends his work on the "higher man": the spirituality, creativity, and new nobility of mankind. Danto in *Nietzsche as Philosopher* also recognized the strong rationalist element in Nietzsche's thought; so did Kaufmann in his *Nietzsche*, pp. 216–27 and 234–35. In examining the relation between passions and reason in Nietzsche, Danto wrote, "Nietzsche hardly deviated from the tradition which goes back at least to Socrates" (p. 149). Otto Manthey-Zorn calls for a broader understanding of the notion of reason that incorporates ideation and sublimation, spirit and matter, reason and instincts, rationalism and mysticism in a "true instinct for intellectual integrity" in *Dionysus: The Tragedy of Nietzsche* (Amherst, Mass.: Amherst College Press, 1956), pp. 5–6.

Robert Solomon also treats Nietzsche as a rationalist in chapter 4, "Friedrich Nietzsche: Nihilism and the Will to Power," of his book *From Rationalism to Existentialism*, pp. 111 and 121. He places the emphasis on reason, morality, and valuation over passions and instincts or at least the latter's incorporation and sublimation by the former. The critique of technical and formal reason (ontology and correspondence theory of truth) is a rejection of idealist and transcendent forms of rationality and morality. The world is irrational, whereas mankind is capable of integrating reason and passions in the experience of the tragic. Solomon finally states that Nietzsche's philosophy, as a spiritual will to truth, is closely related to Aristotle: reason in his moral philosophy compared to Aristotle's rationalism; Nietzsche's theory of the will to power compared to Aristotle's view of life; his theory of power compared to Aristotle's view of potentiality to overcome; his theory of self overcoming compared to Aristotle's view of moral excellence; the primacy of generosity and kindness compared to the centrality of friendship in Aristotle; and Nietzsche's listing of courage, pride, and loyalty as crucial moral values compared to the same values in Aristotle's *Nicomachean Ethics*.

Solomon continues to develop these themes on Nietzsche and Aristotle in his essay "A More Severe Morality: Nietzsche's Affirmative Ethics" in *Nietzsche as Affirmative Thinker*, ed. Yirmiyahu Yovel (Dordrecht, Holland: Martinus Nijhoff Publishers, 1986), pp. 82–86. Here Solomon argues in opposition to Alasdair MacIntyre's *After Virtue* (Notre Dame, Ind.: University of Notre Dame Press, 1984), pp. 109–20, that Nietzsche, as in the case of Aristotle, is a functionalist (valuation in terms of practical interests and survival), naturalist (psychology), and teleologist (will to power and self-realization, *Übermensch* and *megalopsychos*). And both are critics of utilitarian and Kantian moral philosophy: "Nietzsche like Aristotle held onto the vision of an over-riding human *telos*, an enormous sense of human *potential*, a hunger for excellence that is ill-expressed by his monolithic expression, 'will to power' " (p. 86). For a critique of this Aristotelian Nietzsche see Nehamas, *Nietzsche*, p. 175, and Hedwig Wingler, "Aristotle in the Thought of Nietzsche and Thomas Aquinas," in *Studies in Nietzsche and the Classical Tradition*, ed. J. O'Flaherty, T. Sellner, and R. Helm (Chapel Hill: University of North Carolina Press, 1979), pp. 33–54.

92. Nietzsche, *Twilight of the Idols*, p. 563, and *Nietzsche. Kritische Studienausgabe 6*, p. 160.

Chapter Seven: Bridging Madness and Reason

1. See endnote number 21 in Chapter 5 for a general bibliography of works on Marx and Nietzsche. For particular references to both see also Keith Ansell-Pearson, "Nietzsche's Overcoming of Kant and Metaphysics: From Tragedy to Nihilism," *Nietzsche Studien*, 16 (1987): 332; Gordon Bearn, "Nietzsche, Feyerabend, and the Voices of Relativism," *Metaphilosophy*, 17, nos. 2 and 3 (April/July 1986): 145; Karl Jaspers, *Nietzsche: An Introduction to the Understanding of His Philosophical Activity*, trans. Charles Wallraff (Chicago: Henry Regnery Company, 1966), pp. 176–177; Robert McGinn, "Culture as Prophylactic: Nietzsche's *Birth of Tragedy* as Culture Criticism," *Nietzsche Studien*, 4 (1975): 91–96 and 99–101; Robert Solomon, "A More Severe Morality: Nietzsche's Affirmative Ethics," in *Nietzsche as Affirmative Thinker*, ed. Yirmiyahu Yovel (Dordrecht, Holland: Martinus Nijhoff Publishers, 1986), p. 80; Tracy Strong, "Texts and Pretexts: Reflections on Perspectivism in Nietzsche," *Political Theory*, 13, no. 2 (May 1985): 178, *Friedrich Nietzsche and the Politics of Transformation* (Berkeley: University of California Press, 1988), pp. 234, 252, 254, and 293, and "Aesthetic Authority and Tradition: Nietzsche and the Greeks," *History of European Ideas*, 11 (1989): 998; and Mark Warren, *Nietzsche and Political Thought* (Cambridge: MIT Press, 1991), p. 88.

2. Friedrich Nietzsche, *The Will to Power*, trans. Walter Kaufmann and R. J. Hollingdale (New York: Vintage Books, 1967), note 84, p. 52, and *Nietzsche Werke. Kritische Gesamtausgabe*, Abteilung VIII, Band 2, Hrsg. Giorgio Colli and Mazzino Montinari (Berlin: Walter de Gruyter & Co., 1970), 9[168], p. 99.

3. Hugh Lloyd-Jones, *Blood for the Ghosts: Classical Influences in the Nineteenth and Twentieth Centuries* (London: Gerald Duckworth & Co., 1982), p. 174.

4. Friedrich Nietzsche, *The Gay Science*, trans. Walter Kaufmann (New York: Vintage Books, 1974), p. 38, and *Nietzsche Werke. Kritische Gesamtausgabe*, Abteilung V, Band 2, Hrsg. von Giorgio Colli and Mazzino Montinari (Berlin: Walter de Gruyter & Co., 1973), p. 20.

5. The argument is not being made that this is the only possible combination of micro and macro ethics. But it does add another dimension to both their thoughts. The individual and social elements are expanded by the juxtaposition of Marx and Nietzsche.

6. It should be noted that there remain deep problems and contradictions

in the thought of Marx and Nietzsche. Marx uses an immanent critique in *Capital* to undermine the validity and rationality of capital and political liberalism, but he still relies on Aristotle's theory of social justice as the foundation for his *Wirtschaftsethik* (critique of unnatural property acquisition, democracy, *praxis, phronesis*, citizenship, moral economy, modern industry, technology, social relations of production, etc.) and critique of modernity. Nietzsche, in turn, though swiftly moving toward an epistemological nihilism from his earliest writings, still retains a comprehensive *Überwindungsethik* (*Übermensch*, Dionysian celebration of life, self-overcoming, eternal return, etc.) at the very end. Because of his critique of epistemology and metaphysics, and his theory of nihilism, Nietzsche limits his *Überwindungsethik* to formal structures and thereby repeats the same problems found in Kant's formal logic of the categorical imperative. Under these conditions, moral authority can be used for either emancipatory or repressive purposes. These issues have not been dealt with in this work and require their own separate analyses.

Index

abstract labor, 14, 21–25, 28, 44, 59, 60, 101–102, 149, 153–54
abstractionism, xiv, 4, 6, 36, 95, 128, 153, 287, 334
Aeschylus, 5, 65, 157, 170, 171, 172, 185, 187, 188, 194, 203, 223, 224, 245, 250, 351
alienation, xv, 7, 21, 40, 93, 111, 112, 121, 125, 129, 142–46, 144, 148, 171, 301, 302, 309, 310. *See also* fetishism and idolatry
amor fati, 289, 291, 309, 347, 369
Amos, 133, 135, 136, 139
Anaxagoras, 208, 210, 213, 214, 217
Anaximander, 205, 206, 209, 211
anthropomorphism, 205, 211, 216, 233, 234, 239, 241, 242, 244, 250, 304
Antichrist (Nietzsche), 265, 286
anti-Semitism, 126, 139, 310, 337, 368
Apollo (Apollonian), xvi, 163, 169, 170, 172, 176, 177, 187, 188, 189, 192, 193, 194, 196, 198, 199, 224, 237, 252, 270, 272, 283, 284, 301, 314, 351, 352
Arendt, Hannah, 269, 275
Aristotle: epistemology and politics, 86–88; household, 16–21; political democracy, 76–85, 87; moral and political economy, 10ff.; theory of tragedy, 159–62; theory of value, 11–15

Assembly (*Ekklesia*), xiii, 69–74. *See also Boule* (Council of 500) and jury courts (*Dikasteria*)

Bauer, Bruno, vv, 3, 6, 127–31, 143
Baum, Gregory, 141, 340
beauty, 51, 54, 119, 160–62, 167, 168, 172–77, 179, 182, 186, 190, 193, 196, 213, 225, 230, 231, 245, 248, 280–85, 293, 295, 296, 297, 312, 351
Bekker, Immanuel, 9, 33, 58, 326
Bennett, Benjamin, 198, 347
Bentham, Jeremy, 46
Bergoffen, Debra, 290, 370–71
Beyond Good and Evil (Nietzsche), xviii, 249, 293, 297
Birth of Tragedy (Nietzsche), xvi, 158–63, 169, 170, 172, 178, 180, 183, 186, 187, 192, 193, 203, 214, 223, 228, 231, 246, 256, 294, 296, 312, 351, 355, 370
Bloch, Ernst, 138, 335
Böckh, August, 6, 67, 320
Boule (Council of 500), xiii, 70, 71, 72, 73, 74, 311. *See also* Assembly (*Ekklesia*) and jury courts (*Dikasteria*)
Breazeale, Daniel, 158, 341

Capital (Marx), xii, xiii, xiv, 7, 8, 10, 11, 14, 21, 27, 30, 40–41, 48, 53, 57–59, 61–64, 68, 91, 99, 100, 104,

105, 109, 110, 114, 115, 118, 121,
146–52, 302, 307, 325, 336, 341, 375
Castoriadis, Cornelius, 17, 323, 325
catharsis, 159–64, 167, 188, 297
chrematistics (*chrematistike*,
unnatural wealth acquisition), xiii,
7, 9, 11, 20, 21, 29–46, 59, 62–64,
101, 115, 117, 118, 120, 123, 302,
311, 322, 325. *See also* economics
(*oikonomia*, natural wealth
acquisition)
citizenship, 19, 41, 52, 63, 72, 77, 78,
84, 89, 90, 323, 375
commensurability, 13, 15, 18–21, 25,
63, 302, 307, 322
common good, 84, 91, 92, 93, 96, 114
Communist Manifesto (Marx), 95,
115, 327, 333, 334, 368
consciousness, 98, 126, 144, 145, 146,
147, 151, 180, 210, 212, 217, 221,
223, 239, 242, 246, 247, 248, 254,
258, 287, 303, 304, 306, 310, 348,
372
contemplation, 176, 182
contradictions, 42–46, 55, 56, 57, 58,
62, 99, 105, 113, 116, 129, 130, 151,
284, 322, 353
*Contribution to the Critique of
Hegel's Philosophy of Law*
(Marx), 117
*Contribution to the Critique of
Political Economy* (Marx), 8, 9,
117, 146
counteracting influences, 105, 108,
116
covenant, 132, 134
creativity (aesthetic and moral), xv,
xviii, 40, 54, 97, 115, 117, 122, 140,
162, 166, 167, 171, 180, 185, 188,
191–98, 202, 203, 209, 210, 216,
239, 254, 255, 256, 258, 263–67,
270, 272, 276, 277, 282, 283, 284,
289, 292–96, 302, 303, 309, 314,
315, 352, 353, 366, 369, 370, 372

Critique of the Gotha Program
(Marx), 48, 94, 100, 118, 121, 323,
325
Critique of Practical Reason (Kant),
40
Critique of Pure Reason (Kant), 163,
187, 201, 210, 226, 227, 244, 304,
349, 350, 355

Danto, Arthur, 369, 372, 373
de Sainte Croix, G. E. M., 330–31
decadence, xviii, 170–72, 221, 224,
225, 234, 245, 256, 257, 258, 265,
270, 281, 283, 292, 296, 305, 308,
309, 314, 365
democracy, xiv, xix, xx, 7, 8, 14, 17,
21, 30, 41, 64, 65, 68, 278, 288, 302,
311, 315, 316; Aristotle's theory of
democracy, 76–85, 329–30;
Athenian democracy, 69–76;
Marx's theory of democracy, 91–96
Democritus, xi, xii, xv, 4, 97, 301, 309
demos (people), 69, 72, 73, 74
Deuteronomy (Bible), 133
dialectics: (Hegel), 26, 116, 235, 237,
254, 286; (Marx), xvi, 34, 62, 97,
98, 104–11; (Nietzsche), 192, 193,
196, 197, 199, 211, 212, 213, 219,
223–25, 228, 230, 243, 248, 257,
270, 272, 302, 306, 309, 311, 315
*Difference between the Democritean
and Epicurean Philosophy of
Nature* (Marx), xii, 4, 8, 65, 117,
360
Diogenes Laertius, xi, xv, 157
Dionysus (Dionysian), xvi, 163, 169,
170, 172, 177, 187, 188–99, 223,
224, 237, 245, 248, 252, 270, 272,
283, 292, 297, 301, 312, 314, 315,
316, 351, 352; Dionysian wisdom,
196, 199, 200, 227, 291, 313, 370,
371
disenchantment of the world, 202
disproportionality, 105, 114

113, 297, 302, 308, 322, 323, 324,
325, 326, 373
Nietzsche, Friedrich: analysis of
Oedipus and *Prometheus*, 189–200;
Apollo and Dionysus, 185ff.;
cognitivist or noncognitivist,
360–61; epistemology in *The Birth
of Tragedy*, 223–28; epistemology
in early writings, 240–46;
epistemology in later writings,
246–52; epistemology in *The
Philosopher*, 228–31; Greek ideals
169–73; and Greeks, 157–220;
historical critique of morality,
287–88; and Kant, 187, 222–23,
226–27, 231–39, 246ff., 264–66,
343–44, 357; Kantian moral
philosophy, 264–76; liberalism and
socialism, 276–81; and Marx and
Nietzsche, 301–16, 358, 374;
metaphysics of the hangman,
270–76; morality and art, 261ff;
pre-Platonic philosophy and
physics, 200–219; radicalization of
Kant's theory of knowledge, 159,
162, 169, 203, 211, 216, 219, 229,
238, 239, 243, 246, 251, 263, 265,
303, 306, 314, 315; revenge of
reason, 284–86; science, 221–59;
theory of time, 289–97, 372
nihilism, xv, xviii, 100, 170–72, 180,
197, 206, 219, 220, 221, 225, 231,
234, 239, 249, 256–58, 261–64, 288,
305, 306, 308, 311, 345, 350, 352,
355, 363, 364, 370–71, 375
Nous (Mind), 208, 209, 210, 214, 215
Nussbaum, Martha, 89, 196, 332, 337,
343, 349, 353

objectification, 143, 144, 145, 146
objectivity, xviii, 11, 27, 97–99, 111,
112, 142, 147, 148, 153, 154, 171,
175, 179–81, 202, 206, 208, 210,
212, 215, 216, 217, 349, 350, 356,
359, 365; epistemological

objectivity, 221, 226–28, 235–39,
243–50, 254, 256, 258, 265, 278,
348; moral objectivity, 281–84, 286,
288–91, 295, 303, 304, 305, 306,
307, 310, 314, 348; objectivity of
time, 289–297; prison of
objectivity, 221–58
Oedipus (the character), 5, 160, 171,
173, 178, 179, 190–95, 294, 297, 302
Oedipus (tragedies of Sophocles),
187, 189–200; *Oedipus at Colonus*,
162, 191, 194; *Oedipus Rex*, 191
oikos (household), 12–27, 33–44, 78,
323, 324. *See also* household
management
Old Testament, 131–42
oligarchy, 76, 85, 87
On the Aesthetic Education of Man
(Schiller), 166, 167, 168
On the Jewish Question (Marx), 76,
92, 142, 153
On Simple and Sentimental Poetry
(Schiller), 165, 174
On the Sublime (Schiller), 164, 168
On the Tragic Art (Schiller), 163
*On Truth and Lies in a Nonmoral
Sense* (*Nachlass* of Nietzsche),
xvii, 158, 228, 242, 355
Orestes, 161, 173, 190, 347
organic composition of capital, 12, 24,
106, 107, 108
original Oneness, 177, 186, 189, 194,
195, 197
overproduction, 104, 105, 114, 116,
122, 151

Paris Commune of 1871, 68, 70, 91,
92, 93
Parmenides, 206–10, 213, 217, 218,
252
Pericles, 6, 69, 70, 73, 91, 210, 215
perspectivism, xviii, 246, 248, 254,
255, 256, 259, 291, 304, 305, 306,
314, 358, 359, 361, 362, 364, 371.
See also illusions and metaphors

384   *Index*

About the Author

GEORGE E. MCCARTHY teaches social philosophy and theory at Kenyon College, Gambier, Ohio. He holds a Ph.D. in philosophy from Boston College and a Ph.D. in sociology from the Graduate Faculty, New School for Social Research. He has been a Guest Professor at the Geschwister-Scholl-Institut für Politische Wissenschaft at the University of Munich, Germany. He is the author of *Marx and the Ancients: Classical Ethics, Social Justice, and Nineteenth-Century Political Economy* (Rowman & Littlefield Publishers, 1990), editor of *Marx and Aristotle: Nineteenth-Century German Social Theory and Classical Antiquity* (Rowman & Littlefield Publishers, 1992), *Eclipse of Justice: Ethics, Economics, and the Lost Traditions of American Catholicism* with Royal Rhodes (Orbis Books, 1992), and *Justice Beyond Heaven: Ethics and Democracy in U.S., German, and Irish Catholic Social Thought* with Royal Rhodes (Humanities Press, forthcoming).